ALSO BY JULIA MARKUS

NOVELS

Uncle
American Rose
Friends Along the Way
A Change of Luck

EDITION OF
Elizabeth Barrett Browning's
Casa Guidi Windows

DARED AND DONE

DARED
AND
DONE

THE MARRIAGE OF
ELIZABETH BARRETT
AND ROBERT BROWNING

JULIA MARKUS

ALFRED A. KNOPF

NEW YORK   1995

This Is a Borzoi Book Published by
Alfred A. Knopf, Inc.

Copyright © 1995 by Julia Markus

My thanks to Hofstra University for
its constant support of my work and
for a special leave, and to the National
Endowment for the Humanities, which
helped me to complete this book with a
summer research and travel grant and a
Fellowship for College Teachers and
Independent Scholars.

Library of Congress Cataloging-in-
Publication Data
Markus, Julia.
Dared and done : the marriage of
Elizabeth Barrett and Robert Browning
/ by Julia Markus. — 1st ed.
p.   cm.
Includes bibliographical references (p.)
and index.
ISBN 0-679-41602-1
1. Browning, Robert, 1812–1889—
Marriage.   2. Browning, Elizabeth
Barrett, 1806–1861—Marriage.
3. Poets, English—19th century—
Biography.   4. Authors' spouses—
Great Britain—Biography.   I. Title.
PR4232.M27   1995
821'.809—dc20
[B]   94-11573   CIP

Manufactured in the United States
of America

First Edition

FOR MY MOTHER, RUTH SELMAN MARKUS

CONTENTS

A Note on Transcriptions

ELIZABETH BARRETT BROWNING used a particular form of punctuation in her letters, two dots [. .], at times to indicate a pause, a comma, or a dash. I have turned this signature into a comma or a dash very rarely, only when necessary for clarity in the text. With very few exceptions, noted when possible, I retain the poet's usage.

In EBB's time the Moulton was often dropped from her last name; she called herself Elizabeth Barrett Barrett. I do not hyphenate the family name Moulton Barrett when I am referring to her, her father, or her siblings. That came later. In some of the printed texts of the Brownings' letters, there are occasional misspellings as well as occasional spellings and usages that we now consider American. In my transcribing from printed sources, as well as in my transcribing of manuscript material, I have been as faithful as I can to the text as it appears. Because of the signature two dots and the necessity of ellipses in the middle of quoted passages I have avoided ellipses at the beginning and ending of quotations as much as possible. Accuracy and readability have been my goals. All quotations from the Brownings' poetry are taken from the volumes of their work listed in the bibliography.

DARED AND DONE

INTRODUCTION

THE LETTER that began the most famous courtship of the nineteenth century opened, "I love your verses with all my heart, dear Miss Barrett." The writer, Robert Browning, was a young poet and playwright, respected in close literary circles, writing to a woman six years his senior, an invalid, and a poet of national and international fame. It must have delighted him that Elizabeth Barrett had recognized his own genius, that intense poetic heart of his that she had likened to a pomegranate, mentioning it and him by name in a poem of her own. To suggest that Browning's first letter to Elizabeth Barrett was spurred by the slightest notion of self-aggrandizement would be to misunderstand the caliber of the man and to misrepresent the relation these two poets had to each other and to their times. Easy enough to misrepresent. Their courtship, their secret marriage, their fifteen years in Italy, were exceptional—even by the rigorous standards of their own time. Browning, introducing himself to Miss Barrett in that first letter, found his prose soaring ahead of his intentions: "In this addressing myself to you—your own self, and for the first time, my feeling rises altogether," he told her. Then leaving literary allusions and Victorian propriety in his wake, Robert Browning dared to express his feelings: "I do, as I say, love these verses with all my heart—and I love you too."

One might say, at that very moment, as he wrote the words, he fell in love.

"I thank you, dear Mr. Browning, from the bottom of my heart," Elizabeth Barrett answered on the very next day, January 11, 1845, beginning a correspondence that would last for twenty months. The two would write each other 573 letters during that time—574 if we include the one Elizabeth asked him to burn. The last word was Eliza-

beth's, written on a Friday night, September 18, 1846, on the eve of
their journey to Italy.

The letters confirm that the one myth about the Brownings that
was absolutely true was the most romantic one—the drama of their
courtship. Robert Browning fell in love with an invalid poet, wrote to
her, visited. Their love took her from the couch she hardly ever left,
down the stairs of the house on Wimpole Street, to the drawing room,
to a walk in the park, and then to Italy—a climate that would support
their art and her health.

It was a remarkable correspondence and has been the basis of many
an interpretation, among them an enormously successful stage play—
The Barretts of Wimpole Street. Perhaps today, when the drama of family
secrets is in and on the air, this play about what was going on in the
Barrett household in London in the 1840s among a widowed father
and his grown children seems dated, stereotypical, tame. But for an
earlier generation, slowly coming to grips with Sigmund Freud and,
through Eugene O'Neill, beginning to look at the family in a new way,
Rudolph Besier's 1930 work must have been a tantalizing way, a
thrilling way, a less complicated way, of confronting some of the
darker realities of respectable domestic life.

The Barretts of Wimpole Street dealt with the tyrannical aspect of
Elizabeth's father, Edward Barrett Moulton Barrett, who wanted to
keep his children, particularly his favorite daughter, Elizabeth, for
himself and away from suitors. On the stage, when not stern, Moulton
Barrett was overaffectionate toward Elizabeth—the whiff of incest,
like one stick of incense burning through the darkened theater.

Goodness knows what this play stirred up night after night, year
after year, in its devoted audience. I often wonder what my own grandmother felt, with her early experience of a sick mother and a difficult
stepfather, as she, like so many of her generation, picked up the pattern
and knitted her own Barretts-of-Wimpole-Street blanket, modeled
after the one the invalid Elizabeth threw over her lap on stage. What a
beautiful cover it made.

The play was inspired by a fact of Elizabeth Barrett's life evident in
the love letters, a fact again so crazily mythic in its post-Freudian significance that it is difficult to look directly at the implications of its
truth. Her father, a wealthy, landed gentleman, a responsible if stern
father, and a widower, had twelve children, eleven of whom reached
adulthood, nine of whom survived. He simply had one stipulation, as

ironclad as it was unspoken: None of them, male or female, was allowed to marry. The three who did disobey in his lifetime were disinherited, not only from the material things he controlled but from any further contact with their father. To him, they were dead.

Earlier audiences did not have to go far to see psychic roots for the physical maladies, the excruciating condition of the lungs, that wracked Elizabeth Barrett's existence. Nor did they have to linger on the specific pain and guilt that precipitated her isolation on Wimpole Street to empathize with her escape from it. The father was cast as "the villain" and the daughter in her late thirties as the waif rescued by romantic love. Yet in the love letters the daughter does not blame her father for the steps she must take to live her own life. Her cross was heavier to bear. She took full responsibility for her actions, her free will, and the pain she would cause her father. The passion and love between Elizabeth and Robert was not a case of mutual self-absorption, and though it was first love for both, it was not the first love of children.

Who Moulton Barrett really was is more complicated. He was born in Jamaica, the heir of a great fortune as the legitimate grandson of Edward Barrett of Cinnamon Hill. His grandfather was one of the richest landholders, rum and sugar exporters, and slaveholders in the West Indies. The Barrett family had been in Jamaica since it was colonized in the seventeenth century. His daughter Elizabeth was the first Barrett to be born in England in many generations. No wonder when his first son was born less than sixteen months later, drums sounded at Cinnamon Hill and the slaves were given a half-day holiday. Though Moulton Barrett, a deeply religious man, must have had religious scruples against slavery, he was a staunch supporter of the system that supplied his living until its end. His form of devout Christianity led him to a belief that a man's household, wife and children included, were his chattel, and that all were morally obliged to obey his every word. His interpretation of the Bible was underscored by his early years in Jamaica and by his later business concerns. He was born to be the benevolent master.

The miracle of his oldest daughter's story was that, locked as she was into the drama of her own family, into illness, morphine, and dreams, life *did* come to her, *did* seek her out, in her draped and heated room at Wimpole Street. "I do, as I say, love these verses with all my heart—and I love you too." Part of the miracle. A greater part was how she found a way, rooted at the very heart of her father's dictums, to re-spond and find her liberty.

Browning's style of courting, as in his first letter, was much more straightforward than Elizabeth Barrett's. One wonders if the path of indirection she would lead him along was not only frustrating and confusing to him at first, but contributed to those headaches of his that we hear so much about as the letters progress. This is not to sug-gest that Browning was unused to subtlety and indirection—or headaches. Even Elizabeth remarked that in his poetry he seemed to be purposely difficult at times. But in love, Browning was direct.

"I never was without good, kind, generous friends and lovers . . . perhaps they came at the wrong time—I never wanted them." Brown-ing wrote this to Elizabeth Barrett six weeks after his first letter. And two weeks later, "You think . . . that I 'unconsciously exaggerate what you are to me'—now you don't know what *that* is, nor can I very well tell you." What he is allowed to tell her he does: "I never yet mistook my own feelings, one for another—there!"

There! indeed. These letters were all written months before they met.

Elizabeth admonished him to watch his words. She was a middle-aged spinster, an invalid. Romantic love was absolutely out of the question for her. No one would even suspect her being up to it. She had lived her whole life in the bosom of her large family. Her mother had died when Elizabeth was twenty-one. She was doted on by her two sisters and many brothers. Her youngest sister, Arabel, slept on the sofa in her room. After the tragic death of her closest brother, the cen-ter of her life became her father. Her nature was uncomplaining, and she showed no one the depths of her loneliness. She had lived her whole life out of her imagination and through books. She was so other-worldly, and her health so wretched, that she often wondered why she was not totally otherworldly. The woman we meet at the beginning of this correspondence was prepared to die. But she didn't show the ex-tent of this willing preparedness to Browning in her letters, though his intuition of her sadness and failing strength was keen.

That Browning was infatuated was obvious. She was very suspi-cious (Robert's word) of his ardor's duration. Still, this new correspon-dence with a poet who, she believed, cut through to the heart of human nature was giving her pleasure. Her second letter to him was quite playful. "Then you are 'masculine' to the height—and I, as a woman, have studied some of your gestures of language & intonation wistfully, as a thing beyond me far! & the more admirable for being beyond."

Double messages abound throughout the correspondence. The spoken word was that as long as Browning kept his ardor in check, was careful of the words he used in addressing her, stuck to indirect allusions to his love, they could correspond, and it was possible, when spring came and the chill left the air, they might even meet. The unspoken word was that as long as they were writing poet to poet, friend to friend, they could write about anything, could open up mind, soul, and heart.

By March 20, 1845, poet to poet, she communicated to him in the most clear and inspired prose the central paradox of her existence: "And do you also know what a disadvantage this ignorance [of life] is to my art—Why, if I live on & yet do not escape from this seclusion, do you not perceive that I labour under signal disadvantages . . that I am, in a manner, as a *blind* poet? Certainly, there is a compensation to a degree. I have had much of the inner life—& from the habit of selfconsciousness of selfanalysis, I make great guesses at Human Nature in the main. But how willingly I would as a poet exchange some of this lumbering, ponderous, helpless knowledge of books, for some experience of life & man, for some—

"But all grumbling is a vile thing."

It took Browning much longer than usual to answer this letter. He complained of a headache. This was the poet who in his earliest work pictured Andromeda fair, naked, and shackled to the rocks, and professed faith in the necessity of her being rescued. This was the poet who posted a picture of same in his study. But if he wished to stay in correspondence with Elizabeth Barrett, he could not make his solution to her plight plain.

Why? Victorian conventions? Far from it.

In every other area, Elizabeth Barrett wished them to go past the formalities of etiquette between the sexes. She told him to write to her just as if she were a man; that she was an invalid gave her absolute freedom of expression. She might know the world only through books, she might look younger than her age, but she was not girlish in the ways of the world. She discounted Browning's infatuation and reached past it to the man and the poet. At the same time, subconsciously at the beginning, but more consciously as the correspondence progressed, what was left unspoken became her escape route.

The laws of compensation and irony being what they are in human life, it is not startling that a woman who was world-famous in her time should be a shadow in the present, and that a man who was once known only to a few hundred literati would claim posterity for his own. It has often been considered a fair call. But by ignoring the substance of Elizabeth Barrett, we deprive ourselves not only of the best of her work, but of her person, her knowledge, her character. This was an extraordinary woman in her time, and her times knew it. The inner strength, the remarkable scope of mind, the deep understanding of human nature, all of this was part of the love letters. It was Elizabeth who had to search for answers. Robert Browning knew what he wanted. He wanted Elizabeth Barrett. He wanted her at the beginning of the correspondence. He never wavered. He wanted her at the end.

Why shouldn't he know what he wanted, how he felt? No household could be more unlike, his from hers, though they were both strongly Protestant and attended "Independent Dissenting Chapels," and both had West Indian roots. Robert Browning was the center of a middle-class household, the apple of his parents' eye, and the adored brother of one sister, Sarianna. He was encouraged in his artistic leanings by an unworldly, eccentric father who worked as a bank clerk in London but lived for his own scholarly studies and his sketches, and by a Scottish mother who seemed to be the practical heart of the household. Age differences must have been quite normal for Browning; his mother was ten years older than her husband, and his parents' marriage worked. Elizabeth Barrett's mother, Mary, was twenty-four when the nineteen-year-old Moulton Barrett proposed, and their marriage drained her of life.

John Maynard has written compellingly of the young Browning. The picture he painted was of a young man allowed to go his own way, loved unconditionally by his parents, even when he dropped out of university in the first year and returned home to devote himself to study and to art. Browning called himself spoiled as a child because of the loving range and emotional freedom his parents offered. But what other kind of upbringing could make a person so sure of what he felt as an adult, so direct in his love of a woman, when that love did occur?

The sophisticated cynics who debunk the love between Robert and

Elizabeth do it at the expense of two facts: the poets' words, and their lifelong actions. Cynics can spare themselves the effort. There would be shadow enough in the poets' situation beyond the clear light of their love.

At the age of thirty-three, Browning was a fashionable young man in his yellow kid gloves, publishing his early work to the praise of the cognoscenti. He was favored by family and by friends and lovers, yet he had just found something more, something variegated and passionate.

One chilly London day in early spring 1845, he was standing at the corner of Wimpole Street, a good-looking fellow of medium height, five foot eight, dark complexion, brown hair, gray eyes. He seemed to be brooding, or else he was deep in thought. Shelley and Byron were long gone, an age was ending, yet the young Browning was at his most Romantic. What should he do? Well, he did not allow himself to gaze up at Elizabeth Barrett's window. He was too manly for that. He would wait until she gave him permission—not only to see her, when this damned chill was gone, but even to be on her street. He had no idea that Elizabeth Barrett, editing a collection of the new poets of the age along with his friend Henry Fothergill Chorley, had his picture as well as that of Alfred Tennyson on her bedroom wall. That knowledge might have cheered him and allowed him to walk down the block.

He turned the corner at Wimpole Street instead, going to see another woman friend, and later writing to Miss Barrett about it, penning this scene in the letter. His insecurities, the pounding of his heart, the headaches, the impatience—they all just turned the corner. He was as uncomplicated in his motivation as he would ever be again, as he waited to meet the poet.

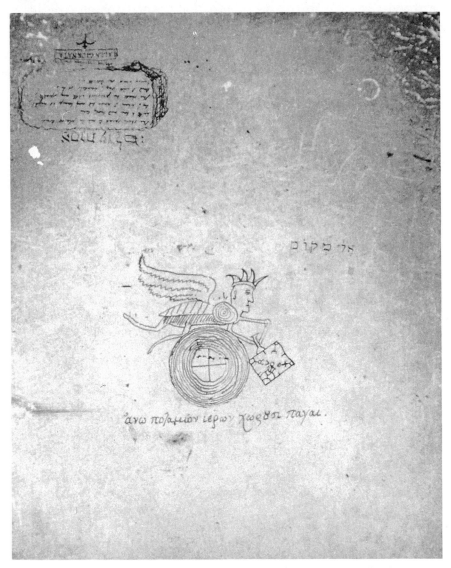

The writing portfolio (1840s) on which Robert Browning wrote his letters to Elizabeth Barrett

PART ONE

DEATH OR LOVE

ELIZABETH BARRETT was admired not only by the literati, including Robert Browning, whom she would marry; she was also idolized by fans. English fans sent her rosebushes; an American admirer wrote a letter to her addressed "Elizabeth Barrett, Poetess, London," and the letter was delivered. Right before she left England she was well enough to visit her old friend the blind Greek scholar Hugh Stewart Boyd. He informed her that several well-born young ladies had asked to be present, dressed as servants, just for the chance to see her as they ushered her in. Some of them swore that, if she would allow, they'd go into service for her.

Yet today, to the world at large, only one line of poetry points its hoary finger back in time to her: "How do I love thee? Let me count the ways"—the opening line of the penultimate sonnet from *Sonnets from the Portuguese.* This slim volume of forty-four love sonnets has had a life of its own. Printed and reprinted—in small format, large format, special editions brought out near the cash registers of bookshops before Valentine's Day. These sonnets have been rendered impotent through popularity, demonstrating that when we take something for granted, we can easily cease knowing it at all. The *Sonnets from the Portuguese* are not an upscale Hallmark card. They are the deepest and at times the darkest thoughts of a woman of genius, in grave health, who finds in middle life not the death she waits for but the love she never expected.

The earliest manuscript of the sequence is at the Pierpont Morgan Library in New York. Each poem is on a single sheet of stationery, written in brown ink in the poet's slender hand. Sonnet I had a title in its manuscript draft, "Death or Love." Surprised, I pointed it out to an acquaintance reading next to me at the Morgan. "Look at this."

"Oh, yes," was the response. "Duet of Love."

An understandable assumption at first glance. For the starkness of the title and the morbidity it reveals clash with the idealized version of an "old-fashioned" Victorian love affair. Yet "Death or Love" succinctly labeled not only the first sonnet of the sequence but the real choice confronting Elizabeth Barrett in London in 1845–46.

When Robert Browning was finally admitted to the sick room of Miss Barrett in 1845, he did not find his picture. Feeling that inappropriate, she had taken it off the wall of her bed-sitting room. She lived her life in that room, protected from the London weather both by fireplace and by complete enclosure. She loved flowers and greenery, but had trouble keeping plants alive in her dark room. The ivy that her cousin John Kenyon had given her a few years back made an attempt to flourish, growing over her window, making patterns in front of the chimney tops beyond it, and giving the cloistered interior a greenish glow. Browning found an invalid whose body could have been the fine lines of her handwriting, whose black hair and soulful brown eyes shone out.

Elizabeth Barrett was always conscious of being dark-complexioned, so one imagines that even in illness she wasn't as pale as she was thin. Shielded from the public's eye, writing inspired poetry, always on the verge of death, her image was mysterious, romantic, otherworldly, aloof. Her public had to see her in their imagination; she didn't publish her picture in her books. She treated another correspondent, the painter Benjamin Robert Haydon, to a verbal picture: "I am 'little & black' like Sappho, en attendant the immortality—five feet one high . . . eyes of various colours as the sun shines . . . & set down by myself (according to my 'private view' in the glass) as dark-green-brown—grounded with brown, & green otherwise; what is called 'invisible green' in invisible garden-fences. I should be particular to you who are a colourist. Not much nose of any kind; certes no superfluity of nose; but to make up for it, a mouth suitable to a larger personality—oh, and a very very little voice." She compared it to Cordelia's voice, which her father, King Lear, described as "Gentle, and low; an excellent thing in a woman." Then short, quick brush strokes to complete her self-portrait: "Dark hair and complexion. Small face & sundries."

Browning saw a woman who looked so ill, so corporally unsubstantial on her couch, that he assumed she suffered from an incurable

"DEATH OR LOVE." *Manuscript of Sonnet I of EBB's* Sonnets from the
Portuguese. *Its original title reflected the choice EBB faced when RB entered
her life in the winter and spring of 1845–46.*

spinal disease and could never walk or lead a normal life. He loved her in spite of this terrible affliction and the limits it placed on physical fulfillment. Finding his prognosis was not the case was so overwhelming to him as a lover that, for months after, he wondered if he could control his emotions if he walked in on one of his visits and found her standing.

What exactly was wrong with Elizabeth Barrett? She had been an extremely lively, precocious child, a tomboy who liked the outdoors, frogs and all. And a traveler—before her illness she'd been to Paris with her parents. Yet when she was fourteen, she and her two younger sisters, Henrietta and Arabel, came down with a similar ailment. Her sisters recovered; Elizabeth never fully did. Living in the elaborate Turkish-inspired mansion that her father had designed for himself on his country estate of almost five hundred acres at Hope End, near the Malvern Hills, she was privy to the best of medical care. By the time she was fifteen her illness was described from doctor to doctor. It had begun as a pain in the head, a pain which, after several weeks, traveled to her right side around the ribs. "The pain commences here, is carried to the corresponding region of the back, up the side to the point of the right shoulder, and down the arm. The suffering is agony. . . . The attack seems gradually to approach its acme, and then suddenly ceases." There were generally three attacks during the day and none at night. Usually she was conscious, but at the end of the attack, there was confusion in her mind. She woke at night in fright and described in her own words that it was as if there were a cord tied around her stomach "which seems to break." She was unable to rest on her right side. Her tongue was clean and her stomach and bowels were kept clean with physic and seemed little affected. Her physician was surprised by her love of spicy food. Since all three sisters had had this illness, it may have begun by eating "something deleterious." "Opium at one time relieved the spasms, but it has ceased to have that effect."

The doctor found nothing wrong with his patient gynecologically, nor did he see any evidence of disease of the spine. What it appeared that Elizabeth Barrett had was the worst illness one could have then or now—an illness not typical enough to be diagnosed. Miss Barrett probably suffered from a "derangement in some highly important organ." The doctor had seen a similar case, a woman who was helped after her vertebral column was treated. Though the doctor stressed that

Mary Moulton Barrett (1781–1828).
*A self-portrait of EBB's mother, who bore twelve children
and was subservient to Moulton Barrett's thunderous
will. When she died, EBB, the oldest, was twenty-one;
Octavius, the youngest, was four and a half.*

Miss Barrett showed no sign of spinal illness, she would be treated for disease of the spine.

Her health continued to be precarious. Her lungs were weak. She could hemorrhage. "Congestion," it has been called. But if it were tuberculosis, that would have been diagnosable.

It may have been abscesses on the lungs. Her lifelong symptoms, attacks of racking coughs, pain, struggle for breath, phlegm, and complete loss of appetite, are similar to those of bronchiectasis, now treatable with antibiotics. Though both doctors and patient could see an emotional component to her physical decline, it was too early for the

SEPTIMUS (1822–70) AND OCTAVIUS (1824–1910)
MOULTON BARRETT.
*This watercolor by their mother, Mary, was done in 1825, three
years before her death, when her next-to-youngest, Sette, was three
and her youngest, Occy, was a year old. The grounds are
those of the Moulton Barrett estate at Hope End.*

standard diagnosis offered in a later century for illnesses with atypical symptoms.

No doubt her deep sensibility, startling brilliance, and uncanny intuitiveness alerted her too deeply to the tears of things in her household. She spoke of never having been happy after childhood; she spoke of unspecified trials and sufferings that marked her life before Browning entered it. The specific event that turned her into a recluse she would find difficult to allude to throughout her entire life. It was the power of love that allowed her to broach the subject in a letter to Browning.

She had been born on March 6, 1806, and on June 26, 1807, less than sixteen months later, her brother Edward Barrett Moulton Barrett was born—the first son for whom the drums beat in Jamaica. He would become her beloved "Bro," the sibling and the human being closest to her in affection, spirit, and temperament. She loved him more than anyone in the world, though her two sisters, Henrietta and Arabel, were close to her and so was George, the barrister, who would, after her marriage, come back most directly into her life. "Stormie" (Charles John), the stutterer, carried her up and down the stairs at

GEORGE GOODIN (1816–95), ARABEL (1813–68), SAMUEL (1812–40), AND CHARLES JOHN "STORMIE" (1814–1905) MOULTON BARRETT, *in a painting by William Artaud.*

Wimpole Street, and Alfred and Henry bungled the ransoming of her dog, Flush, while Sette helped get him back. These young brothers, along with the youngest, Occy, would play less of a role—not in her love but in her life.

Nicknames were rampant among the Barretts, who tended to keep from generation to generation the same Christian names. No one who knew of the poet ever called her Elizabeth. Outside her circle she was Miss Barrett; inside it she was known as "Ba." Ba and Bro were as close as two siblings could be.

In a revealing passage about her mother, the month before she married Browning, she wrote, "Scarcely was I woman when I lost *my* mother—dearest as she was & very tender . . . but of a nature harrowed up into some furrows by the pressure of circumstances: for we lost more in Her than She lost in life, my dear dearest mother. A sweet, gentle nature, which the thunder a little turned from its sweetness— as when it turns milk—One of those women who never can resist,— but, in submitting and bowing on themselves, make a mark, a plait, within, . . a sign of suffering."

The thunder that soured the milk was the temper of Moulton Bar-

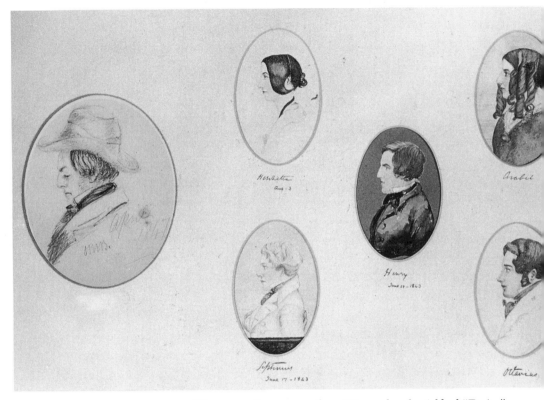

THE BARRETTS AT WIMPOLE STREET, 1843. *Watercolors by Alfred "Daisy"*
Moulton Barrett (1820–1904) of his siblings Henrietta (1809–60), Arabel,
Henry (1818–96), Septimus, Octavius, and the last-known image of his father,
Edward Barrett Moulton Barrett (1785–1857), which was done in 1847.

rett. The mother, like the poet herself and all her siblings, quaked before it. Certainly Moulton Barrett was a concerned father and an up-
right man of high if narrow values, but as every contemporary account
verifies, he was also a domestic tyrant. Since he believed he had a God-
given right to be obeyed, it would seem he did not have to temper his
cruelty ("unkindness" is Elizabeth's word); any disobedience against
him called down the wrath of God—and after the thunder subsided,
the calm of disdain. Sometimes, however, she or he who disobeyed was
punished so severely by the thunder of the Father in Heaven that the
father on earth could show compassion. So it was at the time of Elizabeth Barrett's greatest tragedy, a tragedy that stemmed from the turmoil inside the Barrett household.

After his wife died, Moulton Barrett found himself the father of
both young and adult children. At the same time, his loss of a long,
bitter lawsuit limited his great wealth and sent him from his castle at
Hope End into the city of London. All of his children would live under
his roof there except on the occasions when his sons went away to university or traveled, mainly to Jamaica to aid his brother Samuel, the
one sent there after the lawsuit to manage the problemsome estates.

The father's system of denying marriage did not seem to affect
Elizabeth as much as her siblings. She could echo Robert Browning's
words to her: "Do you suppose I ever dreamed of marrying?—what
would it mean for me." Conventional Victorian marriage, with its patriarchal rights, domestic squabbles, and materialistic concerns, was
against her nature. She did have her admirers all through her life—
apparently to correspond with her by letter or in person was to fall in
love. But she seemed to have been a shrewd judge of men, wary of their
words, attentive to their actions.

As the oldest child, and as a child of incredibly precocious talents
in languages, philosophy, and the writing of poetry, she had early seen
the expense of her mother's marriage and her father's iron rule. Why
would she even think of trading the known burdens she carried as a
daughter for the unknown burdens of being a stranger's wife? Her poor
health helped her avoid the main area of her father's strict prohibition.
And since she alone of her siblings had an independent income from
her grandmother's and her uncle's estates, she could see her role as
dutiful daughter as an act of free will, not as an act of financial
necessity.

She was a person of high moral caliber, and she was conscious of being free under a slack yoke. Since she believed the yoke was wrong, she opposed it on behalf of others. In her poetry she spoke out eloquently against all forms of political tyranny, all systems of slavery. Within the bosom of her family, she helped her siblings snatch their enjoyment secretly, away from their father's eyes. Even a strawberry pick at the kindly invitation of the older writer of the English countryside Mary Russell Mitford was not told to the father. Of course, Elizabeth was too ill to go. But she supported her siblings' secret fun.

"I have loved him better than the rest of his children," she wrote to Robert. "I have heard the fountain within the rock, & my heart has struggled in towards him through the stones of the rock." She knew what was excellent in him and had loved and been proud of his "high qualities." She pointed particularly to "the courage & fortitude" she had witnessed when he lost the lawsuit and with it Hope End. She had loved him "as my only parent left, & for himself dearly, notwithstanding that hardness & the miserable 'system' which made him appear harder still."

Still, after his financial misfortunes came "trials of love," and she was repulsed often and "made to suffer in the suffering of those by my side . . depressed by petty daily sadnesses & terrors." She, too, was depressed to a point that "my friends used to say 'You look broken-spirited'—& it was true. In the midst, came my illness,—and when I was ill he grew gentler & let me draw nearer than ever I had done." During these years after her mother's death, Bro had the deepest claim on her heart. In 1839, when Ba was thirty-three and Bro thirty-one, the father wanted to send Bro back to Jamaica on another business trip. There was a lot of trouble and confusion on the estates in the aftermath of emancipation. Bro felt the horror of the system and way of life in Jamaica, as did his sister, and did not want to go. He may have wanted to get married. Elizabeth wanted to help him out, perhaps financially. Something of that nature caused "a storm of emotion & sympathy on my part, which drove clearly against" their father.

This storm further undermined her health, and she was sent to her aunt's by the sea in Torquay in 1840. Dr. William Frederick Chambers had said she could not survive a London winter. Bro was sent along to take Elizabeth and her sister and then to return. But when the time came for him to leave, Elizabeth could not "master my spirits or drive back my tears—& my aunt kissed them away instead of reproving me as she should have done; & said that *she* would take care that I should not be grieved . . *she!* . . and so she sate down & wrote a letter to Papa to tell him that he would. 'break my heart' if he persisted in calling away my brother—As if hearts were broken *so!*"

Her father answered in words "burnt into me, as with fire." He didn't exactly consent, he "did not refuse to suspend his purpose," but at the same time "he considered it to be *very wrong in me to exact such a thing.*" Month after month passed and she was sometimes better and sometimes worse, and the doctors said they could not answer for her life if she were agitated, so there was no more talk of Bro's leaving. "And once *he* held my hand, how I remember! & said that he 'loved me better than them all & that he *would not* leave me—till I was well,' he said! how I remember *that!* And ten days from that day the boat left the shore which never returned; never—& he *had* left me! gone! For three days we waited—& I hoped while I could—oh—that awful agony of three days! And the sun shone as it shines to-day, & there was no more wind than now; and the sea under the windows was like this paper for smoothness—& my sisters drew the curtains back that I might see for myself how smooth the sea was, & how it could hurt no-body—& other boats came back one by one."

Bro's body was not washed ashore for a month, and was identified in part by his long hair. He and two friends, all first-rate sailors, were inexplicably lost on a downed boat on a calm and windless sea.

The shock of it brought father and daughter together. "And I was grateful to him for not saying aloud what I said to myself in my agony, *If it had not been for you!*" Comparing her father's self-reproach with her own, she imagined he suffered more: "(for if I had loved selfishly, *he* had not been kind)." She also felt she "could love & forgive him for two . . (I knowing that serene generous departed spirit, & seeming left to represent it)."

With her own generous, if hardly serene, spirit she could have compassion for her father, but she was unable to forgive herself. Even her father wondered that she did not die of the blow. She was too sick to be taken away from Torquay—at night she would hear the wind and the sea and the thunder. She relived the tragedy and lived in hell. Finally the next year she returned to London, where she became a recluse. Her room had a connecting door to her father's. He would come to her at night, take her hand, and they would pray.

Her health slowly improved. There was no more hemorrhaging, but there was bleeding from the lungs. For her occasional visits to the

EDWARD BARRETT MOULTON BARRETT
(1807–1840). *EBB's favorite brother, "Bro."*
Before he left Hope End at the age of thirteen to
attend Charterhouse, the prestigious boarding
school, he and his sister shared tutors
in Greek, Latin, art, and poetry.

street in front of her house, there was a wheelchair. Still, her room was her world, crowded with sofa, bed, washstand, and the crimson bookcases bursting with books and lined with busts of the poets. She threw herself into poetry and literary work—was in fact saved by the very imagination that her doctors attempted to curb. Aided by her belief in God, by her family, and by the morphine she had taken since the age of fourteen, that "red hood of poppies" that calmed her and allowed her sleep, she waited for death. A letter arrived instead.

Beyond the trappings of romance, which in the Brownings' days included the exchange of lockets (not of gold but of hair), and which in Robert Browning's case included jotting down on the envelope of Elizabeth's most recent letter, the number of the letter, the date of the last visit, the length of the visit, and before it all the "+" sign of addition and of the cross—there was the strength of mature, passionate love. It was a love based on the unshakable belief that the other must have absolute freedom to choose or to reject it. It made no claims beyond love itself. "The selfishness I depreciate," Robert Browning wrote, "is one which a good many women, & men too, call 'real passion'—under the influence of which, I ought to say 'be mine, what ever happens to *you*'—but I know better and you know best."

The fact that this rich correspondence comes down to us is a story in itself. There was no more private a person than Robert Browning. Only one long poem out of his life's work is expressly autobiographical—*La Saisiaz*. Almost every other work at least attempted to disguise the living impetus. And toward the end of his life he went through his correspondence and burned anything he thought not meant for the public eye.

Now the love letters, with their many references to the Barrett household and the peculiarities of Moulton Barrett, or to Henrietta's romantic situation, similar to Elizabeth's, the thoughts about dear friends, John Kenyon and Mary Russell Mitford and Anna Jameson, are quite revealing. Matters were alluded to that the poets at times found difficult to broach out loud, even to one another—such as Robert's need always for a separate dressing room. Love letters. What could be more personal? Yet Browning did not burn them after his wife's death, nor did he give his son specific instructions as to what he should do with them after his own demise.

"I, for my part, value letters . . . as the most vital part of biography," Elizabeth once wrote to him, objecting to his view that personal letters should be destroyed. For without them "Death would be deader from henceforth."

About to leave London, Elizabeth, who must pack the minimum, wrote: "Your letters to me I take with me, let the 'ounces' cry out aloud, ever so. I *tried* to leave them, & I could not. That is, they would not be left: it was not my fault."

Just as their marriage day became their holy day—excluding other anniversaries and reverberating politically, artistically, and personally right on through their lives—their letters became a holy text, scripture of sorts. Robert Browning considered his wife the superior artist. She certainly was one of the greatest letter writers in the English language.

The letter that began "I love your verses with all my heart, dear Miss Barrett" might not have been written at all. Ten months later, Robert told Elizabeth that he had prided himself on not writing to her, because he never wished "to reach you out of the foolish crowd of rushers-in upon genius." He hadn't wanted to be one of those fools who are "never quiet till they cut their initials on the cheek of the Medicean Venus to prove they worship her." It was only when he returned from Italy in December and read of her reference to his *Bells and Pomegranates* in her collected *Poems* of 1844 that he wondered if he should write "on *account of my purely personal obligation.*" He did so "on the whole, UNWILLINGLY," once more prompted by John Kenyon, who had earlier said he thought she would be happy to hear from him. "I shall only say I was scheming how to get done . . . and go to my heart in Italy. . . . And now, my love—I am round you . . my whole life is wound up and down and over you." That heart of Browning's was the one Elizabeth Barrett referred to in "Lady Geraldine's Courtship":

> *or from Browning some "Pomegranate," which, if cut deep*
> *down the middle,*
> *Shows a heart within blood-tinctured of a*
> *veined humanity.*

That heart occasioned his first letter.

In his letter of January 10, 1845, Browning mentioned having come with John Kenyon to visit her in 1842, but not being received because of her illness. It was "as if I had been close, so close, to some world's-wonder in chapel or crypt." What brutal words for any woman to hear (particularly if they were true). They just may have opened a crack in the crypt. She answered the next day. "BUT . . you know . . if you had entered the 'crypt,' you might have caught cold, or been tired to death, & *wished* yourself 'a thousand miles off.' " Not that she wanted to make him think that their not meeting was for the best. "I would rather hope (as I do) that what I lost by one chance I may recover by some future one. Winters shut me up as they do dormouse's eyes: in the spring *we shall see*: & I am so much better that I seem turning round to the outward world again." So much for crypts. She ended the letter, "I will say that while I live to follow this divine art of poetry . . in proportion to my love for it and my devotion to it, I must be a devout admirer & student of your works. This is in my heart to say to you—& I say it."

Two days later, still filled with the images of the Italy he had re-

RB's FIRST LETTER TO EBB,
*January 10, 1845, pages 1 and 4.
Note how the constricted handwriting
of page 1 loosens by page 4. Receiving
the letter, EBB wrote to a friend,
"And I had a letter from Browning
the poet last night, which threw me
into ecstasies—Browning . . . king
of the mystics."*

turned from, and realizing his gaucherie, he turned the crypt image as jeweled and graceful as Pre-Raphaelite stained glass. "I will joyfully wait for the delight of your friendship, and the spring, and my Chapelsight after all!"

Within the first four days of their correspondence, the spring brought forth new meaning for each. Within sixteen days Browning told her, "this does me real good, gives real relief, to write. After all, you know nothing, next to nothing of me, and that stops me. Spring is to come however!" A month later: "For reasons I know, for other reasons I don't exactly know . . . I had rather hear from you than see anybody else." By the end of February: "I never was without good, kind, generous friends and lovers, so they say—so they were and are— perhaps they came at the wrong time—I never wanted them." On February 27 she wrote to tell him that her spring came later than his, but that "that spring will really come some day I hope & believe, & the warm settled weather with it, and that then I shall be probably fitter for certain pleasures than I can appear even to myself, now."

By March 11, Robert Browning was discernibly in love: "I never yet mistook my own feelings, one for another—there! Of what use is talking?"

She didn't answer for nine days. It was more difficult than she realized to admit springtime. She wondered if perhaps he could "penetrate my morbidity & guess how when the moment comes to see a living human face to which I am not accustomed, I shrink & grow pale in the spirit." Did he understand, this man who had lived such a different life than she?

"You seem to have drunken of the cup of life full. . . . I have lived only inwardly,—or with *sorrow,* for a strong emotion." Even when she was healthy, before her illness, a child at Hope End, she lived in isolation. Her spirits drooped to the ground "like an untrained honeysuckle" except for one person in her house, her brother, but she did not name Bro to Browning because "of this I cannot speak." Still, "It was a lonely life. . . . Books and dreams were what I lived in. . . . And so time passed, and passed." After her illness, and after Bro's death, when she believed there was no prospect "of ever passing the threshold of one room again," she began to think bitterly that she was leaving a world she had never experienced. "I had stood blind in this temple I was about to leave." She had seen "no great mountain or river—nothing in fact." Could Robert Browning understand?

By 1845 she understood that she was gaining some semblance of health. Suppose her collected *Poems* of 1844 were not her last? Would she live on "as a *blind* poet"? Robert had written to her that he was tired of society. She, however, wanted to see more of the world. If she were to live, she wanted to write works that explored new forms. As artists, "Let us all aspire rather to *Life*—& let the dead bury their dead."

Browning couldn't answer for eleven days. On March 31, when he did, it was a short, convoluted letter. How much should he say? Waiting for her springtime was affecting his own. "I would give you all you want out of my own life and gladness." Then he alluded to the fact that he would not travel, not to his beloved Italy, if it meant leaving Miss Barrett.

When Elizabeth answered on April 17, almost a month had passed since her last letter, and she was still concerned about the limitations of her existence: "Every life requires a full experience, a various experience—& I have a profound conviction that where a poet has been shut from most . . . aspects of life, he is at a lamentable disadvantage." It was two more weeks into spring before Browning responded, telling her he had been suffering from headaches. By May 3 he sounded quite unstable. "I have had a constant pain in the head for these two months"—since the time Elizabeth told him her spring fell quite late in the season.

"Shall I have courage to see you soon, I wonder! If you ask me, I must ask myself," she deliberated during the first week in May.

Robert shot back, " 'If you ask me, I must ask myself'—that is, when I am to see you—I will *never* ask you! You do *not* know what I shall estimate that permission at,—nor do I, quite—but you do—do you not? know so much of me as to make my 'asking' worse than a form—I do not 'ask' you to write to me—not *directly* ask, at least."

Then he pulled back. "No, no, that is being too grand! Do see me when you can, and let me not be only writing myself,

"Yours."

Mistrustful? She was not mistrustful, she was shy, she answered, and she could not "admit visitors in a general way . . . it would be unbecoming to lie here on the sofa & make a company-show of an infirmity, & hold a beggar's hat for sympathy." Then telling him he was extravagant in wishing this permission that would mean "nothing to you afterwards," and after assuring him that she would in the future understand his disappointment, she wrote simply, "Come then." Exactly two months after Elizabeth admitted to the bitterness of living apart from human experience, Browning recorded on the back of her last letter:

+ Thursday, May 20, 1845

3–4 $^1\!/_2$ p.m.

The first visit.

Elizabeth had opened her door to the stranger. The great and reclusive poet, stretched on her sofa, had admitted the young suitor. Browning entered the Chapel, flowers from his mother's garden in hand, and found not saints' bones but the living and vulnerable woman, frail and delicate, with her big dark eyes and long black hair. She found him much better-looking than the picture that she had once hung in her room. Much more masculine than that image, he looked, she would later tell him, like her early fantasy of the ideal man. The subtext of the five months of correspondence had been devotion, kindled and kindred feelings, great sympathies, warm friendship. Now spirit met flesh. "You can't kiss mind," they would agree in later letters. The visit so affected Elizabeth that she remarked on it to her father. Robert Browning had unsettled her. She couldn't sleep. She couldn't get him out of her mind. She felt strange. The poet could not identify her emotion. Unparalleled blunder, she'd worry later, having mentioned her turmoil to her father.

Robert as always knew exactly what he felt. Right after their first meeting he wrote her the one letter of the correspondence that does not survive. Most definitely he declared his love. An intemperate wild letter, Elizabeth labeled it. "You do not know what pain you give me in speaking so wildly." How could he?

"You remember," she wrote, "surely you do—that I am in the most exceptional of positions: & that, just *because of it,* I am able to receive you as I did on Tuesday." If he wrote about or alluded to what he had in his last letter, "*I must not . . I WILL not see you again*—& you will justify me later in your heart." Browning interpreted this as well as he could without knowing anything of her father's "system." He assumed Elizabeth Barrett did indeed suffer from an incurable spinal condition as had been rumored. Why else would a declaration of love be so out of the question? It was not as if she didn't want to see him again. "So for my sake you will not say it—I think you will not—& spare me the sadness of having to break through an intercourse just as it is promising pleasure to me,—to me who have so many sadnesses & so few pleasures."

"Wise man, was I not, to clench my first favorable impression so adroitly," he answered in a long letter, the tone of which shifted from aloof sophistication to fear, to literary allusion, to biblical anecdote. He wrote, in panic, what he imagined Elizabeth wanted to hear. Much later in their relationship he'd admit: "And do you think you *could* have refused to see me after that visit? I mean, do you think I did not resolve so to conduct myself; so to 'humble myself and go still and softly all my days'—that your suspicion should . . . clear up." It did clear up; she returned his wild letter as he asked and also requested that he destroy her letter that misunderstood his intentions. One day she'd want his letter back, to find he had obeyed her and destroyed it, although he had kept her alarmed response.

The friendship wobbled, but within a few weeks amid much talk of Prometheus, interspersed with Greek quotations—as if to prove literary companionship—the relationship continued. Little could Browning understand, at the time, the magnitude of his mistake.

That Elizabeth had had the courage to admit him to her room was, in fact, a first step in her return to life. Her sisters, knowing her as they did, were quite surprised she had allowed the visit. She had not climbed mountains or seen rivers, but by the late spring of 1845 she had gained the courage to admit a friend.

Elizabeth Barrett had opened the crypt to see. And all the life she had not lived in thirty-nine years rushed in upon her. The light did not blind her; it made her face that it was not her bad health, not the tragedy of Bro's death, not God's will, not her luck, that would deny her life. It was the system, her father's system. Browning's words, and the possibilities they opened to her, were a sin against her father. Her knowledge of how to sustain the relationship with Browning went deeper than thought. It came from being the child of such a father. She had shown Browning the role he must play. He seized upon it immediately. No more wild letters. As a result, he could visit again.

"On tuesday week you can bring a tomahawk & do the criticism [of her work], & I shall try to have my courage ready for it.—Oh, you

EBB AS AN INVALID WITH
HER DOG, FLUSH. *Pencil
sketch by her brother Alfred
dated "12 December 1843." The
window opening onto a summer
garden is a pleasant fantasy.
Her enclosed upstairs room on
Wimpole Street got little sunlight,
and its window overlooked
chimneytops.*

will do me so much good!" The visits continued, always in the late afternoon, after lunch and before her father returned for dinner. Moulton
Barrett knew she corresponded with the "pomegranate poet," and on
the rare occasion that he was alerted to Browning's having been at the
house, he was either benign or vaguely annoyed.

Her sisters, Henrietta and Arabel, witnessed all the comings and
goings, as did her maid, Elizabeth Wilson. The Barrett brothers were
less involved. George, the barrister, met Robert Browning socially on
occasion and spoke highly of him as man and poet. Alfred (nicknamed
"Daisy") once amused his sisters by pretending to faint and swoon onto
a couch so that he, like Elizabeth, could receive romantic visitors. But
that was all in fun.

Elizabeth's was not the only secret courtship in the household. Her
sister Henrietta, three years younger, in her mid-thirties, healthy,
lively, and pretty, was seeing her cousin William Surtees Cook. Accepted into the house because he was a relative (on the maternal side),
he, too, was in love—constant and persistent and regular as the furni-

ROBERT BROWNING. *From an*
engraving by J. C. Armytage in
Richard H. Horne's Spirit of
the New Age *(London, 1844).*
This portrait hung in EBB's
room before she met Browning.
After meeting him, she found it
quite inferior—effeminate—
compared to the real man.

ture—but this couple had longer to wait: until Surtees Cook got his
military commission and they could afford to marry against the will of
the father. It was simply an established function of the household that
the less the brothers knew the better, and that all life existed away
from the father's eyes.

How necessary was the secrecy? Later in the relationship she would
tell Browning what had happened to Henrietta as a young woman:
"But now I must remember—& throughout our intercourse *I have remembered.* It is necessary to remember so much as to avoid such evils as
are evitable." She looked back "shuddering to the dreadful scenes in
which poor Henrietta was involved who never offended as I have offended." Henrietta had asked her father for consent to some outing or
occasion that involved, evidently, a young man. "In fact she had no
true attachment, as I observed to Arabel at the time: a child never submitted more meekly to a revoked holiday. Yet how she was made to
suffer—Oh, the dreadful scenes!—and only because she had seemed to
feel a little. I told you, I think, that there was an obliquity . . an eccen-

EDWARD BARRETT MOULTON BARRETT. *Detail of an oil of EBB's father
by Henry William Pickersgill. EBB's father did not allow any of his adult
children to have suitors. Although he knew "the pomegranate poet" visited his
invalid daughter, he had no idea how often. The poets met while he was at work.*

tricity—or something beyond . . on one class of subjects. I hear how her knees were made to ring upon the floor, now!—she was carried out of the room in strong hysterics." Elizabeth had tried to follow her out. "Though I was quite well at that time & suffered only by sympathy, [I] fell flat down upon my face in a fainting-fit. Arabel thought I was dead."

How much power did Edward's "eccentricity—or something beyond . . on one class of subjects" have over Elizabeth? One incident seemed to turn the tide of the courtship, admitting Browning as lover as well as friend. There was a lot of talk in the summer of 1845 about Elizabeth's traveling for her health. Her father might decide to send her to Alexandria or Malta without consulting her. Then her physician, Dr. Chambers, the physician of Queen Victoria as well, prescribed that she must go abroad, that she would not survive another winter in London. Pisa was considered. Had Moulton Barrett approved, she would have been accompanied on the trip by her pious youngest sister, Arabel, and by Stormie. Browning, who canceled all thoughts of travel within a month of his first letter to the poet, would have shown up wherever she wintered. Everyone close to the Barrett household believed that it was of the utmost urgency that Elizabeth leave London in order to stay alive. Her father weighed the idea, but by September 17, 1845, "it is all over with Pisa." Still, *do not blame me,* for I have kept my ground to the last, & only yield when Mr. Kenyon & all the world see that there is no standing. . . . I spoke face to face & quite firmly [to her father]—so as to pass with my sisters for the 'bravest person in the house.' "

But her father was not the insurmountable difficulty. She wrote again that evening: "The 'insurmountable' difficulty is for you & everybody to see,—& for me to feel, who have been a very byword among the talkers, for a confirmed invalid through months & years, & who, even if I were to go to Pisa & had the best prospects possible to me, should yet remain liable to relapses & stand on precarious ground to the end of my life. . . . A plain fact, which neither thinking nor speaking can make less a fact." As clear as it was to her that bad health was her real obstacle, in her first disappointment she wondered, "I had done *living*, I thought, when you came & sought me out! and why? & to what end? *That*, I cannot help thinking now."

Still, she was obedient to her father's wishes. She would stay home. But Moulton Barrett's reaction to her obedience was to complain of the "undutifulness & rebellion (!!!) of everyone in the house." She asked her father if he meant her, and he answered that he meant every one of them. This seemed to be the straw that broke the camel's back. "He would not even grant me the consolation of thinking that I sacrificed what I supposed to be good, to HIM. I told him that my prospects of health seemed to me to depend on taking this step, but that through my affection for him, I was ready to sacrifice those to his pleasure if he exacted it—only it was necessary to my self-satisfaction in future years, to understand definitely that the sacrifice *was* exacted by him & *was* made to him, . . & not thrown away blindly & by a misapprehension. And he would not answer *that.* I might do my own way, he said—*he* would not speak—*he* would not say that he was not displeased with me, nor the contrary:—I had better do what I liked:—for his part, he washed his hands of me altogether—"

Should she give up the idea? She certainly didn't want to involve Arabel and Stormie in displeasing their father for her own gain. But George had counseled that whether she stayed or went "there will be displeasure just the same." She asked Browning, "Think for me."

He thought. "All our life is some form of religion, and all our action some belief. . . . In your case I do think you are called upon to do your duty to yourself; that is, to God in the end. . . . Will it *not* be infinitely harder to act so than to blindly adopt his pleasure, and die under it? Who can *not* do that?"

The wisdom of that advice was then balanced by Browning's rashness in going beyond his vow of silence. "You are in what I should wonder at as the veriest slavery—and I who *could* free you from it, I am here—scarcely daring to write." He took the plunge. "I would marry you now." Her physical condition was no impediment. "I would be no more than one of your brothers—'*no more*'—that is, instead of getting to-morrow for Saturday, I should get Saturday as well—two hours for one—when your head ached I should be *here.*"

This time she blessed him for his words, those he had written and those of the visit that had just transpired on September 26—a visit that seemed to have settled her heart. "Henceforward I am yours for everything but to do you harm. . . . A promise goes to you in it that none, except God & your will, shall interpose between you & me, . . I mean that if He should free me within a moderate time from the trailing chain of this weakness, I will then be to you whatever at that hour you shall choose . . whether friend or more than friend . . a friend to the last in any case. So it rests with God & with you—Only in the meanwhile you are most absolutely free . . 'unentangled.' "

And at the end of this letter, which changed both of their fates, she almost asked a "boon." No, she could not. Another day. She was not *that* brave. Many days would pass in fact before she gained the courage to ask Browning for a lock of his hair.

Once Elizabeth Barrett chose love over death, she did everything in her power to live. Some contemporary critics fault her for not having the courage to tell her father of Robert Browning's love. Browning at first wondered if he shouldn't meet the father face-to-face and declare his intentions. But the oldest child of Edward Barrett Moulton Barrett had one iron rule herself: Her father must not know of her attachment to Browning; the scenes, such as the one in which Henrietta's knees were made to ring upon the floor, must be avoided if at all possible. After hearing of these incidents, Robert understood her caution and wrote: "The one trial I *know* I should not be able to bear,—the repetition of those 'scenes'—intolerable—not to be written of, even—my mind *refuses* to form a clear conception of them."

Perhaps if she had been twenty-one rather than thirty-nine she might have believed the power of love would cause her father to change. Perhaps if she had known herself less, if she had thought the power of her love could keep her from a dead faint should her knees be made to ring upon the floor or if the thunder of the father's voice rang through the house, she might have told her father. Perhaps if she loved Browning less, were less committed to living and to writing poetry that concerned the new day, she would have. Or perhaps if she were less certain of herself, if deep down she wasn't sure of her intentions. Browning had said it. It is harder to act than to submit to someone else's pleasure and die. "Who can *not* do that?"

And then the biggest perhaps. What if she hadn't been able to accept the limitations implicit in her father's love? "The bitterest 'fact' of all is, that I had believed Papa to have loved me more than he obviously does—: but I never regret knowledge . . I mean I never would *un*know anything . . . & this must be accepted like the rest." How many a child has grown old refusing that knowledge and staying put? In any of the cases above, Elizabeth might have somehow declared, or let slip, her secret love. But instead she faced reality, faced her choices, and lived to effect them.

The real circumstances of the courtship decry the myth of the *help-*

less damsel in distress being saved despite herself. What was in Elizabeth Barrett's power was her deep and intimate knowledge of her father and of herself. It was important that her siblings be kept in the dark as much as possible. Friends must not be told. John Kenyon could not be trusted with the burden of the knowledge, nor Anna Jameson, nor her correspondent Mary Russell Mitford. The only way to keep a secret was to keep a secret. Suppose Robert told someone and someone told someone and someone . . . leaked their relationship to the press! Wouldn't that be nice for her father to read while relaxing at the Jamaican Coffee House.

The day that Browning came to visit her on Wimpole Street she would come to call "my great Compensation Day." Life, in fact, had had to invade her sick room and physically yank her by the hair, the image she used in the first of the *Sonnets from the Portuguese.* If she were to marry Browning she would have to get well. And from that first sonnet, through all forty-four, there was hardly a hint of the father. These deeply personal poems, filled with a profound sadness and morbidity, shared with no one, not even Browning, prove that the long reclusive period and the tragic losses of the first forty years of her life had taken their toll on her spirit and her self-confidence. In making the choice between death and love, it was not her father whom she battled but her pain, her memories, herself. Her father or Browning? She had already chosen.

LOVERS' LUCK

THE LONDON WINTER became their ally. "What weather it is! & how the year seems to have forgotten itself into April," Elizabeth Barrett wrote in November. In January it was like summer. "The weather is as 'miraculous' as the rest." Without going to Pisa, her health was improving steadily. The couple was also given a period of unrushed time. Letters were exchanged daily; visits occurred now twice a week with regularity. There were no false starts, unannounced visitors, or unforeseen complications. Instead, warm days, time to get to know each other, time for Elizabeth to heal. There was no doubt that in the winter and spring of 1846, the poets were having lovers' luck—that uncanny suspension of the outside forces that can upset the most heartfelt and most careful plans.

One January day, the temperature reading sixty-eight degrees, Elizabeth felt a burst of well-being, put on her cloak, and walked out of her room where she had spent the last six years. Even in the days before Bro's death when she did go downstairs, she was carried by one of her brothers. She stood at the head of the stairs in the dark hallway, paused a moment, took a look around, and then, holding on to the railing, she walked two flights down. Her siblings were in the drawing room; she could hear them. In her cloak, but hatless, she walked in. Her sisters and brother were speechless. It was her brother Stormie, the one with a stutter, who broke the silence, addressing her in poignant understatement as the guest she was: "That kind dear Stormie who with all his shyness & awkwardness has the most loving of hearts in him, said that he was '*so* glad to see me'!"

From that day in 1846, though she would never dine with the family, she was up and down the stairs. In the context of this physical recovery in winter turned spring, the love between the poets grew. Like lovers before and after, they felt they knew each other so well that they could intuit each other's deepest thoughts. They actually shared an uncanny sympathy; still, like lovers before and after, their assumptions could lead them down some dark roads.

Robert thought he knew why Elizabeth took opium. She had had a prescription since the first illness at fourteen. By early February she must have told him during a visit that she was using less, because he was delighted enough to write: "I never dared, nor shall dare inquire into your use of that—for knowing you utterly as I do, I know you only bend to the most absolute necessity in taking more or less of it."

She was quite honest in her reply. That "you should care so much about the opium—! Then *I* must care, & get to do with less . . at least." She wrote as if *he* had just given her the idea to use less. However, his utter knowledge was mistaken, and she built a graceful path in pointing it out. It might seem strange that she should need "opium in any shape," since she did not need it to keep down pain. "But I have had restlessness till it made me almost mad—at one time I lost the power of sleeping quite." Even in the daytime, her weakness, her palpitations, were so severe "as if one's life, instead of giving movement to the body, were imprisoned undiminished within it, & beating & fluttering impotently to get out, at all the doors & windows." For this feeling of impotent revolt against imprisonment, the medical men prescribed opium, "a preparation of it, called morphine, & ether—& ever since I have been calling it . . . my elixir . . the tranquillizing power has been so wonderful."

Her nervous system, "irritable naturally, & so shattered by various causes," made her need it "until now." And she had been told it was dangerous to leave off except slowly and gradually. Browning was "to understand that I never *increased* upon the prescribed quantity . . prescribed in the first instance—no!—Now think of my writing all this to you!"

Elizabeth had perhaps forgotten the physical pain of her childhood illness, which her father recorded at the time. Or was the pain of the fourteen-year-old in fact the result of a restlessness so severe that it was maddening? Whatever the answer, for twenty-five years a mixture of morphine and ether had been calming her down—*physically.* Three months earlier, rather defensively, she told Robert, "My opium comes in to keep the pulse from fluttering & fainting," to balance the nervous system. "I don't take it for 'my spirits' in the usual sense,—you must not think such a thing."

By the end of February, Robert was thanking her for "the good news of the increasing strength and less need for the opium." But it would remain her elixir, this drug that seemed to have the property of indefinitely prolonging her life. For her shattered nerves and by extension her damaged lungs, she had her medicine.

Elizabeth also had her own concerns about Robert's health. He was given to bad headaches. The remedy she suggested for them was one she used herself—good, strong coffee. And that paleness of his—perhaps it was related to his abstemious nature. She suggested a cure. Wine. "Perhaps it would be better for your health to take it habitually—It *might,* you know—not that I pretend to advise."

The only disagreement that touched live nerve during the courtship started innocently enough. While visiting Elizabeth, the art historian and feminist Anna Jameson had said, "Artistical natures never learn wisdom from experience." She considered artists "like children, all of them,—essentially immature." Elizabeth told Robert "she did not persuade me." Anna Jameson could have had no idea that two of her favorite children were five months from matrimony, nor that she would precipitate their one big spat.

Browning, in answering the older woman's charge, was stoical concerning the world's mistrust of genius: "we will *live* the real answer" of "all the stupidity against 'genius' 'poets' and the like." Not that he was immature enough to have the boyish expectation that at their marriage "our happiness will blaze out apparent to the whole world lying in darkness, like a wondrous 'Catherine-wheel,' now all blue, now red, and so die at the best amid an universal clapping of hands." He looked forward instead to "a long life of real work 'begun, carried on and ended,' as it never otherwise could have been (certainly by *me* . . .)."

After that blazing image he lost his thread, and associated the word *genius* with an issue in the day's news. Both poets had vowed not to cross out or rethink their words in their letters, but to share emotions and thoughts as they arose. The daily news, often in his new life to be a source of his poetry, in this case became a thorn in his relationship. That day's *Athenaeum* (April 4, 1846) was full of the "French Duel." The manager of a colorful Parisian newspaper had been murdered in a duel that developed during a party in a Paris restaurant. The trial was causing a sensation, involving such witnesses as Alexandre

Dumas and Lola Montez. Browning's mention of the scandal led Elizabeth to believe he looked down on dueling, but that misreading was
apparently cleared up on Browning's next visit, which he noted as on
"+ Monday, Apr. 6/ 3–5³/₄ p.m." and which he counted as visit "(57)."
During it he upheld that a man's honor might demand a duel.

If Robert thought his future wife overpraised his poetry, he should
realize she told him only the truth. "For instance, did I flatter you &
say that you were right yesterday? Indeed I thought you as wrong as
possible" on the subject of dueling. "You would abolish the punishment of death too . . & put away wars, I am sure! But honourable men
are bound to keep their honours clean at the expense of so much gun-
powder & so much risk of life . . *that* must be, ought to be." Why, even
setting Christian principle aside, there's no rational basis to justify or
excuse such behavior. Dueling was so terribly wrong that Robert's defense of it was disturbing in a universal way. "If you are wrong, how are
we to get right, we all who look to you for teaching?" How could a
great poet believe in dueling? Should Robert even be involved in a
duel, "instead of opening the door for you & keeping your secret, as
that miserable woman did last year, for the man shot by her sister's
husband, I would just *call in the police,* though you were to throw me
out of the window afterwards. So, with that beautiful vision of domestic felicity (which Mrs. Jameson would leap up to see!), I shall end my
letter."

By that evening she punned on her *"disagree* . . able letter this
morning." But she was quite worried by the end of the letter: "Tell me
if you are angry, dearest! I *ask* you to tell me if you felt (for the time
even) vexed with me . . I want to know . . I NEED to know." If
Browning believed a man was right to defend his honor through a
duel, then should such a situation arise, nothing would stop him from
dueling and either killing or being killed. "So I spoke my mind—&
you are vexed with me which I feel in the air. . . . Forgive, as you can,
best, Your Ba."

"First of all kiss me, dearest," Robert responded, "and again—and
now, with the left arm round you, I will write what I think in as few
words as possible." It took him many, many words to say that dueling
was a man's duty. "Mr Ba, what is Evil, in its unmistakable shape, but
a thing to suppress at any price." *Mr* Ba? Strong words for this lover.

Not only that: "I *do* approve of judicial punishment to death under
some circumstances—I think we may, *must* say . . . '*it* shall not be en-

dured or *we* shall not be endured!' " She is "Dear Ba" again when he implored, "is Life to become a child's game?"

She kissed the envelope of this letter before opening it, telling by his handwriting that he was not angry with her. Her joy was intensified by the magic of his putting his arm around her, kissing her by mail.

But that her poet of the *Bells and Pomegranates* could believe in dueling, "it is very ill, wonderfully ill . . so ill, that I shut my eyes, & have the heartache (for the headache!) only to think of it." For, "If anyone had asked me, I could have answered for you that you saw it quite otherwise. And you would hang men even—you!"

She wouldn't argue anymore. "If I went on to write disagreeing disagreeable letters, you might not help to leave off loving me at the end." That wouldn't surprise her. "Good Heavens!—how dreadfully natural it would be to me, seem to me, if you DID leave off loving me!" Natural as the sun setting. "Only, more darkness, more pain."

What was he doing while she brooded? On the morning of April 9 he was busy counting anniversaries, just as he counted visits. Next Saturday, the one following Good Friday, would be four years to the day of Mr. Kenyon's first asking " 'if *I would like to see Miss B.*' " (That was the visit her illness precluded.)

As luck would have it, this letter did not arrive until late that evening. She had finally asked her maid, Wilson, to go down to look for it and then waited to hear "the footsteps of my letter. If I had not heard them directly, what should I have thought?"

But her relief did not preclude the realization of an insurmountable breach in their opinions on the matter of dueling and that neither of them should or could "submit" to the other. Best not to talk about it. "I have had some pain from it, of course . . but I am satisfied to have had the pain, for the knowledge . . which was as necessary as possible . . . for more reasons than one." Depression was setting in. Before Anna Jameson visited that day, "I went down to the drawing-room, I & Flush [her dog], & found no one there . . & walked drearily up and down the rooms, &, so, came back to mine. May you have spent your day better."

Robert obviously had. After a perfectly civil debate on the function of dueling and how it related to society, along with an expressed belief in the necessity of capital punishment, he had counted out the first possibility of having met Elizabeth years before. This same woman had just ended her letter, "I think of you, bless you, love you—but it would have been better for you never to have seen my face perhaps, though Mr. Kenyon gave the first leave. *Perhaps!!*"

That he would stop loving her! That he would be angry at her. It was "hitherto undreamed of, a new faculty—altogether an inexplicable, impossible feeling." But what he could imagine was "your being angry with me, very angry." Perceptive, very perceptive. Didn't she realize: "My own Ba!—My election is made, or God made it for me,—and is irrevocable. I am wholly yours. I see you have yet to understand what that implies."

It implied that he wanted to learn from her. "Oh, Ba, did I not pray you at the beginning to *tell* me the instant you detected anything to be altered by *human* effort? to give me that chance of becoming more like you and worthier of you?" Why, she had done just what he had asked, and "I am growing conscious of being in the wrong." Such was the result of her " 'disagreeable letters.' " The warrior was still in armor, but now he pledged to his lady: "YOU ARE RIGHT and I am wrong and will lay it to heart, and now kiss, not your feet this time, because I am the prouder . . . by this admission and retraction."

Robert Browning gave in to "Mr Ba" on the dueling issue, and he was proud of it. The last thing he wanted to occasion was Elizabeth's suffering. His knightly duty was toward his lady, who had the God-given female power to teach him values higher than his own. She was his Laura, his Beatrice, and he was luckier than Petrarch and Dante. He was going to marry the woman of his dreams and have a lifetime of such guidance. He wanted her to "persist in hoping better things" of him, and to hold fast to her opinions. In doing so, "you begin setting me right, and so I am set far on towards right—is not all well, love? And now go on, when I give next occasion, and tell me more, and let me alter more, and thank you,—if I can, *more*,—but not, not love you more, you, Ba, whom I love wholly."

She responded to Browning's letter, saying that she had never loved him so entirely. "It went to my heart, & stayed there, & seemed to mix with the blood of it." Still she joked of his "submissiveness." After all, their relationship was not built on letters alone. He visited her two times a week. He knew his power over her and certainly must "understand, in the midst of the obeissances, that you can do very much what you please, with your High priest."

Then, in making light of her depression, she revealed its roots: "It was just natural that when we differed for the first time I should fall into low spirits." For "whenever I am not *glad,* the old fears & misgivings come back—no you *do not understand* . . you CANNOT, perhaps!" She became "sad even to tears." The drowned brother reemerged as she argued with her lover over an issue that might lead to death.

Three years before she met Browning, Elizabeth Barrett defended him to Mary Russell Mitford, who had accused him of effeminacy, for living at home and fearing that his mother and sister might take "his horse away from him." "I call it affectionateness," Elizabeth answered, "that he should not bear to do what wd. occasion them anxiety. If he had been afraid himself, he wd. himself have abjured the horse—and that WE might have called effeminacy—but love, love, . . who dares say a word against the influence of love? It is strongest, be sure, with the strongest."

"I feel I *must* live with you," Browning wrote in his next letter, "if but for a year, a month—to express the love which words cannot express, nor these letters, nor aught else." And this first, and most dangerous, disagreement passed, leading them to greater intimacy. They had become lovers who knew how to make their love work. Call it adjustment on both their parts, call it compromise on Robert Browning's, they were now much closer to marriage. It was time for Elizabeth to allude to another dangerous subject. This time it was not morphine or dueling—the subject was money. The agent that precipitated the discussion was John Kenyon.

John Kenyon (1784–1856) was born in Jamaica, came to school in England, and never returned. For a brief time he was a classmate of Elizabeth's father, who was a cousin. At the time of the courtship, Kenyon, just over sixty, was twice a widower. His relationships with women who might lead to "bridescake" were a constant source of lively gossip in the letters between Mary Russell Mitford and Elizabeth Barrett in the 1840s. Kenyon had introduced the two women. He was independently wealthy, wrote some verse himself, and was well known in literary circles for his generosity, his grace, and his wit, among other things. He knew everyone. When Elizabeth's family moved to London in 1836 he introduced himself to her, and though Moulton Barrett was not hospitable to him, he became Elizabeth's devoted friend. He even succeeded once in getting his shy cousin Miss Barrett in the same room with William Wordsworth.

In 1839 he introduced himself to the son of another old school friend, Robert Browning, and was a champion of his work as well. John Kenyon, the distinguished minor poet and lover of literature, became the cupid of the courtship. It was Kenyon who suggested (on that Holy Saturday in 1842) that Robert meet Elizabeth. Elizabeth had actually documented this in a letter to Miss Mitford on March 27–28, 1842. "Dear Mr. Kenyon came here again yesterday (Sunday) I am writing now on monday. . . . Mr. Browning, the poet, passed saturday & a part of sunday with him, & pleased & interested him very much! He has bad health—swimmings in the head—& a desire (if any loosening of family ties should give him to himself) to go to a Greek island & live & die in the sunshine. Mr. Kenyon says he is 'a little discouraged' by his reception with the public, which I am very sorry to hear . . but 'a strong sense of power' which is equally obvious may obviate the effect of the depression."

It was the persistent Kenyon who sent Robert's sister, Sarianna, a copy of Elizabeth's *Poems* of 1844 with its reference to Robert Browning's pomegranate heart. Robert read this copy on his return from Italy. Then Kenyon suggested that Elizabeth would be happy to receive a letter from Robert about the poems, and it was he who once more urged his young friend to write before Robert actually sent his fateful letter.

This patron of the arts, this kind and tactful man, turned, unknown to himself, into a bespectacled nemesis as the courtship developed. Every time he visited Elizabeth, mentioned Robert, looked her in the eye, she felt his eyes, behind his glasses, prying into her and she was fearful. Had she forgotten—or was she guiltily remembering—the many times she had subtly pried into his love life, relishing every tidbit she could discern and sending it on to Mary Russell Mitford?

On John Kenyon the poets differed. Robert was certain he must know of their relationship. Left to his own, he would have confided in Kenyon. Elizabeth was totally opposed to this. Kenyon could not bear the responsibility of direct knowledge. He would try to talk them both out of the relationship and might even let on to her father. She was certain he'd be all for the union, after it occurred, for then he'd have borne no responsibility. He'd be able to think of himself as someone who would have supported the relationship had he known. But she was adamant in her belief that he'd be temperamentally unequal to advance notice. This resolved itself into her constant and growing fears concerning what lay beyond those damned spectacles that seemed to magnify his eyes into a piercing question mark.

This scene spurred Elizabeth Barrett to speak to Robert Browning about money.

Enter John Kenyon, culprit cupid, his eyes burning into Elizabeth: "I suppose now that Mr. Browning's book is done & there are no more excuses for coming, he will come *without* excuses."

She changed the subject. But Kenyon returned to it. What were Mr. Browning's objects in life? Mrs. Procter, the wife of the poet Bryan Waller Procter, "had been saying it was a pity he had not seven or eight hours a day of occupation."

How could she say that! Why, Mr. Kenyon, Mr. Browning "did not *require* an occupation as a means of living, having simple habits & desires." Nor did he need one "as an end of living" as he had one in the exercise of his genius. In fact, had Mrs. Procter's husband "looked as simply at his art as an end, he would have done better things."

"Ah now! You are spiteful," Kenyon returned, "and you need not be, for there was nothing unkind in what she said."

"But *absurd!*" Absolutely absurd, "seeing that to put race horses into drag carts, was not usually done nor advised!"

There was no need to be angry.

"But what business have worldly women to talk their dusts & ashes over high altars in that way?"

Still trying to appease his cousin, and at the same time considering the possibility of Browning's getting a job, he told her, "Wordsworth had given himself to the service of the temple from the beginning," but "he did not escape *so* from worldliness."

She answered, "But William Wordsworth is not Robert Browning!"

It was time for the peace-loving man Elizabeth had portrayed to back off. Thus, Elizabeth concluded, "Mr. Kenyon spoke of your family & of yourself with the best & most reverent words."

Still, Kenyon had brought up the subject his cousin had ripped up letters about, "torn the paper now & then." It was a subject Robert had attempted to broach the previous Saturday while they were still dueling. Hardly the time. Even now the time was not right, but when it did come "let this be a point agreed upon by both of us. The peculiarity of our circumstances will enable us to be free of the world . . of our friends even." She wanted them to "use the advantage which falls to us from our misfortune,—&, since we must act for ourselves at last, let us

resist the curiosity of the whole race of third persons . . even the affectionate interest of such friends as dear Mr Kenyon." Nobody should
have the power to count "whether the sixpence, we live by, came most
from you or from me . . & as it will be as much mine as yours, & yours
as mine, when we are together . . why let us join in throwing a little
dust in all the winking eyes round—oh, it is nonsense & weakness,
I know—but I would rather, rather, see winking eyes than staring
eyes." Why should anyone, friends or family, know anything about
their affairs when it came to "mere money"?

For the fact was, Elizabeth Barrett had money. Up until then,
Robert Browning had devoted himself entirely to his poetry and his
studies. He lived at home, socialized in London, traveled, and wrote—
subsidized by his father. Marriage and its greater financial responsibilities were the furthest things from Browning's mind. As was the gossip
about his living arrangements. He was a single man, living frugally. A
few months before he wrote to Elizabeth, he confided in Anna Jameson
that he did not believe in romantic love.

Now, a person who up until a few days before agreed with the conventional wisdom about the relationship between a man's honor and
dueling certainly would feel it was a man's duty to support his wife.
The creative artist needed time, a husband needed money. Money
would never be as "mere" to Robert Browning as it always would be to
Elizabeth Barrett.

For Elizabeth, her being of independent means was simply a part
of their good luck. Mere money would fulfill the "condition" of their
union, which she had discussed with him long ago—"leaving England
within the fewest possible half hours afterwards." For "I should not
dare breathe in this England—Think!—There is my father—& there
is yours!—Do you imagine that I am *not afraid of your family?*—&
should be still more, if it were not for the great agony of fear on the
side of my own house. Ah—I must love you unspeakably . . even to
dare think of the possibility of such things." They would leave conventions behind.

Elizabeth Barrett had the heart of a Romantic poet in the body of
an ailing woman living in one of the most repressed households of the
Victorian period. A convergence of luck and love backed by money was
about to set her free. It would bring this poet who lived in books to
the land that inspired Keats and Shelley and Byron—and the young
Browning. Browning's older friend and admirer Walter Savage Landor

had put it in the words to Robert that would reverberate through the lovers' letters:

> *But warmer climes*
> *Bring brighter plumage, stronger wing:*
>   •   •   •
> *Beyond Sorrento and Amalfi, where*
> *The Siren waits thee, singing song for song.*

What awaited Elizabeth Barrett was the land that would one day claim her as its own. She would become the poet of its fight for unification. "I would not see Italy without your eyes," she told Browning when yet another friend offered to accompany her there for her health. To go with anyone else would be to go "as a dead Ba clasped up between the leaves" of a book. The Italy she did travel to with her husband was not yet a sovereign state; it was, as Metternich disdainfully declared it, a geographical expression. Right now, on the brink of the revolutionary year of 1848, it awaited her, singing song for song.

By mid-April the lovers had resolved their one true altercation and were beginning to discuss the financing of their new life. Elizabeth had bought a bonnet, one that looked a bit like a Quaker's, only to learn that by "blind instinct" she had hit the style that was the height of fashion for that season. This bonnet buying proved "a serious purpose of going out, walking out, driving out, now doesn't it?"

"I expect everything from your going out of doors . . . what a joy to write it, think of it, expect it!" Browning replied. On May 5, 1846, she'd "like to carry this letter to the post myself—but no, I shall not be able." That evening: "We talk of the mild weather doing me good . . of the sun doing me good . . of going into the air as a means of good!— Have you done me no good?" she asked, and answered, "I have been drawn back into life by your means & for you."

And then on the eleventh of May—nine days short of Robert Browning's first visit a year before—he received a flower. "Look what is inside of this letter—look! I gathered it for you to-day when I was walking in the Regent's Park. Are you surprised?"

She and Arabel and Flush went in a carriage. The sun was shining through the trees, casting "that green light" which so attracted her that "I wished so much to walk through a half open gate along a shaded path." They stopped the carriage and got out: "I put both my feet on

the grass . . which was the strangest feeling! . . & gathered this labur-
num for you. It hung quite high up on the tree, the little blossom did,
and Arabel said that certainly I could not reach it—but you see!" What
did it feel like to be standing under trees and in the grass? "It
was like a bit of that Dreamland which is your special dominion,—& I
felt joyful enough for the moment to look round for you, as for the
cause. . . . Dearest, we shall walk together under the trees some day!"

On May 29, at the Botanical Gardens, Elizabeth committed a
crime: "Is it felony, or burglary?" Outwitting the Queen's gardeners,
she picked Robert Browning another flower. The act did not cast a
dark shadow. On the contrary, sitting in the Summer House, where the
band sat on high days, she experienced what she enjoyed most in nature, "the green under the green . . where the grass stretches under
trees. *That* is something unspeakable to me, in the beauty of it. And to
stand under a tree & feel the green shadow of the tree! I never knew before the difference of the *sensation* of a green shadow & a brown one. I
seemed to feel that green shadow through & through me, till it went
out at the soles of my feet and mixed with the other green below."
Quite a trip.

From defacing property to going in a carriage with John Kenyon
to see the new train pull in, to mailing her own letters at the post office behind which she would meet Browning on their wedding day, to
visiting her old friend the blind and reclusive Mr. Boyd, to Mrs. Jameson's taking her to Samuel Rogers's private art collection at his home
at St. James's Place . . . lovers' luck had prevailed.

On June 18, after a day of contemplating Robert, by eight, when
the rest of the family was at dinner, "I remembered that I had not been
out." She did not want to upset the family's dinner, and Wilson
was off. "Therefore I put on my bonnet, as a knight of old took his
sword, . . aspiring to the pure heroic . . & called Flush, & walked down
stairs & into the street, all alone—*that* was something great!—And,
with just Flush, I walked there, up & down in glorious independence.
Belgium might have felt so in casting off the yoke." This first casual
joining of personal liberation with political liberation was to have
untold reverberations in her later work.

By summer Elizabeth Barrett had returned to health and to a more
active life: "Did I ever think I should live to thank God that I did not
die five years ago?—Not that I quite, quite dare to do it yet."

By August 21, at the beginning of her evening letter, she exulted,

"Can I be as good for you as morphine is for me, I wonder," and then expanded on the metaphor: "even at the cost of being as bad also?—Can't you leave me off without risking your life,—nor go on with me without running the hazards of all poison—?" She stopped. The image was becoming convoluted. "The figure exceeds me, let *it* be ever so fatal. I may not be your morphine, even if I shall be your Ba!—you *see!*—"

Well, not exactly. What one does see is that as she regained her health, their lovers' luck shifted. Browning had precipitated Elizabeth's rambling metaphor by alluding to the curtailed visits with her. On August 20, the previous day, he had seen her for the first time in a week! Without meaning to complain selfishly, he asked her how she supposed he felt "without my proper quantity of 'morphine'?" Then, perfect gentleman that he was, he inquired, "May I call you my morphine?" which led to her image.

The world could no longer be kept at bay. The circumstances of their courtship were becoming more dangerous that summer.

When Robert walked into Elizabeth's room on his June 20 visit, he found it filled with art—with the sketches and portraits and paints, palettes, and brushes of the historical painter and lecturer Benjamin Robert Haydon. The painter had been a correspondent of Elizabeth's since 1842—not that she had ever admitted him to her room. Mary Russell Mitford had first introduced her old friend to Arabel Barrett, who had artistic inclinations. Arabel had not been at all impressed by his frescoes. His reckless life would not impress her either. She certainly wouldn't listen to his accounts of his romantic adventures or of his faithful wife, who followed after him to prison.

Haydon was one of those artists who lived extravagantly, ran up debts, landed in jail, battled his critics, and always insisted on his own way. He kept a journal of his exploits which Elizabeth did read and which he meant to publish. The largeness of his historical paintings limited their market. The largeness of his ego led to public ridicule. He was capable of writing to Elizabeth that, at an exhibition, Queen Victoria gave him the glad eye.

He had previously stored his effects with Elizabeth in 1843 when he lost out in the competition for decorating the new House of Parliament, for which he had submitted grand cartoons. He discussed the historical details and checked facts by letter with the helpful poet as he created *Adam and Eve* and *The Black Prince Entering London in Triumph*.

After his failure to win the commission, "he set out to 'educate' the British public and his presumption and uncritical self-esteem became a regular butt of laughter in *Punch*" and elsewhere. Now, three years later, he repeated the gesture of storing his effects on Wimpole Street after what he considered the crowning disappointment of his artistic career.

In 1846, at the age of sixty, he mounted an exhibition of his work in London at the Egyptian Hall. As many times before, he put great enthusiasm into this endeavor, and though it was commonplace to deride his extravagance and his ego, at his age, after a lifetime devoted to art, it was quite understandable that he'd hope that this showing would be appreciated, and that he'd make the money he desperately needed.

For poor Haydon (to adopt an adjective much in use in the correspondence), there was bad news and there was worse news. Few visitors came to his exhibit, and he was losing money on it. Yet in the same hall there was an exhibition that was drawing thousands of visitors weekly. In his diary for the week of April 21 he noted twelve thousand people came to the other exhibit, and "113½" came to his.

One wonders if the "half" was his nemesis. For all of London was buying tickets to P. T. Barnum's exhibition of Tom Thumb. Every day, the grandiose Haydon, in the grand hall, watched as the philistines of the world flocked past his large-scale paintings to gawk at an American dwarf.

Haydon attempted to stem the tide with Barnum-type advertisements for himself at the expense of Tom Thumb. This held the painter up to public ridicule yet again. Ten days after he sent his effects to Elizabeth, and after writing in his diary as usual, he shot himself and slashed his throat.

Robert read of the death in the newspaper. He worried that Ba might be startled and grieved, particularly since Haydon's death was accompanied by a lightning storm. "How glad I am you told me you had never seen him. And perhaps he may be after all a mere acquaintance . . anything I will fancy that is likely to relieve you of pain! Dearest dearest!"

"Oh yes—it has shocked me this dreadful news," Elizabeth replied. Could she have done something to prevent his suicide? She'd been told time and again that to offer him money "was to drop it into a hole of the ground." Even so, she "cannot turn the thought away— *that I did not offer.*" Imagine, just yesterday she and Anna Jameson had been looking at his *Napoleon at St. Helena* at Mr. Rogers's collection. The death of an artist whose effects were crowding her room, a lightning storm in the background, which stirred thoughts of Bro, a conscience disturbed thinking that she might in some way have been able to help . . . would it cause a return of morbidity? Robert didn't have to worry.

"Oh—we are so selfish on this earth, that nothing grieves us very long, let it be ever so grievous, unless we are touched in *ourselves* . . in the apple of our eye . . in the quick of our heart . . in *what* you are, & WHERE you are . . my own dearest beloved! So you need not be afraid for *me!* We all look to our own, as I to *you;* & the thunderbolts may strike the tops of the cedars, & except in the first start, none of us be moved."

Her analysis of Haydon's psychological state was as accurate as her analysis of her own reaction. "The world did not recognize his genius, & he punished the world by withdrawing the light. If he had not that thought in him, I am wrong. The cartoon business, & his being refused employment in the houses of parliament . . *that* was bitter: & then came his opposition with Tom Thumb & the dwarf's triumph . . he talked bitterly of *that* in a letter to me of last week. . . . Poor Haydon! . . . with all of his weaknesses, he was not certainly *far* from being a great man." In July she wrote again of his "elements of greatness" despite his vanity. Yet "His conscience was not a sufficient witness, . . nor was God. He must also have the Royal Academy & the appreciators of Tom Thumb." And then she made an observation which Robert found quite profound. "Often it has struck me as a curious thing (yet it is not perhaps curious) that suicides are occasioned nearly always by a mortified self love."

Her correspondence with Haydon and her involvement in his unfortunate end was life knocking on Elizabeth Barrett's door once more. Haydon had wanted her to edit and publish his voluminous diaries. In July, Robert wrote: "to lay the business of editing the 'twenty-six' (I think) volumes, with the responsibility, on *you*—most insane! Unless, which one would avoid supposing, the author trusted precisely to your ignorance of facts and isolation from the people able to instruct you." The posthumous revelations would be dreadful, and Robert acted the man of the world on her behalf in this matter. He defended Elizabeth Barrett at a dinner party, saying he knew for a fact that she had had no personal meetings with the man.

Haydon's choice of editor (albeit she was second choice) was not "most insane." Elizabeth had earlier read manuscript versions of his "Memoirs," advising him against publishing parts. On the whole, however, she was for their publication. Through the mail he spoke to her of the necessity of the nude in art and confided in her of his passion for the poet Caroline Norton, including its effect on his wife and children. His letters at times seemed big and bawdy, although filled with paranoia against the public and an unbalanced sense of his own importance. In them he sketched his work as well as the treachery of the world. Elizabeth was by her own admission the greatest novel reader in the world. The installments of Haydon's life read as melodrama, told from the point of view of a self-obsessed and licentious artist. By 1846, she was no longer encouraging his correspondence, for by then she was entering into her own life.

Earlier, his letters had brought her hulking slices of life. His outrageousness did not daunt her, but as she wrote to him in November 1842: "Alas, no! I do not indeed go out. You must not fancy me a hypochondriac, nor even *saddened* into all my solitude. Some three or four years since, I broke a blood vessel on my chest, & altho, I have rallied at different times & very much for the last year, it is only within these two months that there is evidence of its healing. And even now, I am so weak as to stagger like a drunken man when I attempt to walk without assistance. . . . But I believe I am gradually reviving. . . . And with care & *heat* during the winter, I have hope for next summer." But that hope, three years before her first letter to Browning, had included no mention of any possibility of spring bringing a visit from him.

She told Browning she wanted her letters back from Haydon's estate. "I threw away my thoughts without looking where they fell. Often my sisters have blamed me for writing in that wild way to strangers—& I should like to have the letters back before they have served to amuse two or three executors. . . ."

Still, on the matter of the publication of the diaries, she had a definite opinion. "Your argument does appear to me to sweep out too far on one side, so that if you do not draw it back, Robert, you will efface all autobiography & confession—tear out a page bent over by many learners—I mean when you say because he is above (now) the passions & frailties he has recorded, we should put from us the record." However, "this record is not for the angels, but for *us*, who are a little lower at the highest." And she suggested that three volumes could be taken from the twenty-six, "full of character & interest, & not without melancholy teaching." She stuck to her guns, but she did not undertake the task.

Haydon's death marked one of many breaks from her former life. Another figure from the past was an older tie, the blind Greek scholar and her former neighbor at Hope End, Mr. Boyd. She visited him in London when her health improved in the spring and summer of 1846. In her typical way, she made a preliminary trip to his house with Arabel, who went "to his room to tell him of my being there." Nine days later, on June 30, she left a card for Mr. Kenyon, who was not home, "Then Arabel & Flush & I proceeded on our way to Mr. Boyd's in St. John Wood, & I was so nervous, so anxious for an excuse for turning back," that Arabel said, " 'Oh, Ba . . . such a coward as *you* are, never will be married, while the world lasts' which made me laugh." But finally, there she was, "at the door of poor Mr Boyd's dark little room, & saw him sitting as if he had not moved these seven years—these seven heavy, changeful years. Seeing him, my heart was too full to speak at

BENJAMIN ROBERT HAYDON (1786–1846). *This self-portrait was done in 1846, just before the disappointed painter committed suicide. Three years before, he had sent another portrait to EBB, with whom he corresponded but who would not meet him in person. "A merry Xmas to you, my sweet invisible,"* he wrote on December 19, 1843. *"I have sent you my Portrait—Can't you let me see yours? I think that's fair & like* Royal Persons. *Are we not royal?"*

first, but I stooped & kissed his poor bent-down forehead, which he never lifts up, his chin being quite buried in his breast." She had earlier described him to Robert: "Quite blind he is—& though scarcely older than Mr Kenyon . . . so nervous, that he has really made himself infirm, & now he refuses to walk out or even to go down stairs. A very peculiar life he has led ever since he lost his sight, which he did when he was quite a young man."

The first visit went well, although he forced her to drink some of that wine of Cyprus that she would rather write about than imbibe: "If old Bacchus were the speaker, / He would tell you with a sigh, / Of the Cyprus in the beaker / I am sipping like a fly."

On another visit, Mr. Boyd asked her "if I were going to be a nun." The blind man had actually intuited what she was up to. He pressed her the following time she arrived, and "I allowed him to see the truth—& he lives such an isolated life, that it is perfectly safe with him, setting the oath aside. Also, he was very good & kind, & approved highly of the whole, & exhorted me . . . to keep to my purpose, & to allow no consideration in the world or out of the world, to make any difference."

Not that she had an idealized view of her earliest friend, as she wrote to Robert: "Poor Mr Boyd. He cares for me perhaps more than he cares for anyone else . . far more than for his own only daughter,—but he is not a man of deep sensibility, &, if he heard of my death, would merely sleep a little sounder the next night. Once he said to me that whenever he felt sorry about anything, he was inclined to go to sleep."

The world came knocking at Wimpole Street again in July with the arrival of the Hedleys from Paris. Jane Hedley was Elizabeth's aunt (her mother's sister) and Robert Hedley was her favorite living uncle, even though he was not related by blood. They had been with her in Torquay and were privy to the tragedy of Bro. When Uncle Hedley came from France to England three years later, Elizabeth confided in Mary Russell Mitford of the overwhelming reluctance she had to seeing him again after that tragedy. She didn't want him to see how she had fared, nor did she want to relive the memory. When he arrived at her room, she cried, unable to help herself, and he comforted her with the great loving kindness he felt for her. That first meeting was also part of the past. The Hedleys had returned from the continent with their daughter Arabella. She was about to be married in England to a

ROBERT HEDLEY. *EBB's favorite uncle by marriage.*

MARY RUSSELL MITFORD (1787–1855). *One of the only people outside
the Barrett family who knew of EBB's devastation after the death of her brother.
Mitford published an account of Bro's death in her* Recollections *of 1851. "I
have been miserably upset by your book," EBB wrote in January 1852. Though
she did not "mistake" Mitford's kind intentions, her voluminous correspondence
with her older friend dwindled to twenty-four letters in its last three years.*

wealthy man. Aunt Hedley was planning one of those lavish traditional weddings that demand such attention to detail and cost so much
money. It was the type of society wedding that neither Elizabeth nor
Robert would consider, even if it were possible. The ongoing prepara-
tions were an ironic counterbalance to Elizabeth and Robert's secret,
and modest, plans.

What the arrival of the Hedleys in London did was upset the couple's schedule. Their long tête-à-tête was interrupted. Accidents were
more likely to occur. Visits had to be delayed (depriving Robert of his
morphine). The Hedleys had eyes to see, and they were clearly upset by
Moulton Barrett's treatment of his grown children. Visiting a household where middle-aged children were not allowed to marry? What
would Jane Hedley's sister have thought had she lived? What was
wrong with their brother-in-law? They saw the attachment between
Henrietta and Surtees Cook, one which Moulton Barrett seemed as
blind to as he did to more than a year and a half of fresh flowers arriv-

ing from Robert to Elizabeth. The Hedleys were advocates for Henrietta, and some of their two-edged remarks hit Elizabeth in a way they could not possibly have imagined at the time.

On July 13, Elizabeth had to sign a paper moving some of her money to the Eastern Railroad. She would later list that along with the assets she described to Robert: "Stormie told me the other day that I had eight thousand pounds in the funds: of which the interest comes to me quarterly . . . & from forty to forty-five pounds Papa gives me every three months, the income tax being first deducted. . . . Then there is the ship money, a little under two hundred a year . . . which I have not used at all." (Her only expense, she told Robert, was her morphine.) It was that annual ship money that she transferred to the Eastern Railroad. "That investment is to yield a large percentage, I heard." Lest one considered her in too good a position, "there are the ten shares in Drury Lane Theatre—out of which, comes nothing."

Well, on July 13, as she signed that paper, her aunt "by way of saying a lively thing, exclaimed, 'Is that your marriage-settlement, my dear?' . . which made me so nervous that I wrote my name wrong & vexed Papa into being almost cross with me."

Two days later the Hedleys were at 50 Wimpole Street having dinner with Papa Barrett and his children. The oldest daughter as always ate in her room. Aunt Hedley told her brother-in-law, "I have not seen Ba all day—and when I went to her room, to my astonishment a gentleman was sitting there."

Moulton Barrett turned immediately to Arabel, his eyes speaking the family's language. "Who was *that?*" they implored.

"Mr. Browning called here today," Arabel answered.

Aunt Hedley broke into the silent dialogue, "And Ba bowed her head as if she meant to signify to me that I was not to come in—"

It was Henrietta's turn to save the situation. She, the sister next in age to Ba, had her own lover, and unlike her younger sister, the pious Arabel, was not unused to playing lawyer with the truth. "Oh! *that* must have been a mistake of yours. Perhaps she meant just the contrary."

Moulton Barrett appeared to have recovered his equilibrium. "You should have gone in and seen the *poet.*"

Earlier that very same day, the kindhearted Stormie told his aunt, "Oh Mr Browning is a *great* friend of Ba's! He comes here twice a week—is it twice a week or once, Arabel?"

And if these two scenes weren't enough, as Elizabeth wrote them down for Robert, who interrupted her letter but Aunt Hedley, leading in Papa and her future son-in-law, James Johnston Bevan: "I was nervous . . oh, so nervous! & the six feet, & something more, of Mr Bevan seemed to me as if they never would end, so tall the man is."

Aunt Hedley, being charming once more, informed her future son-in-law, "You are to understand this to be a great honour—for she never lets anybody come here except Mr Kenyon, . . & a few other gentlemen." And then she laughed.

To which Papa replied, "Only ONE other gentleman, indeed. Only Mr Browning, the poet—the man of the pomegranates."

The well-meaning Hedleys were also concerned about Elizabeth's spending another winter in London. No one, it would appear, expected spring to strike two winters in a row. Her aunt and uncle would have her go back to France with them. Anna Jameson, who would be traveling with her niece Gerardine, earnestly desired to take her to Italy. The mild-mannered Mr. Kenyon spoke with Elizabeth's sisters about how he had answered Mrs. Jameson's offer. He had told the art historian, Elizabeth wrote, that "only a relative would be a fit companion for me, & that no person out of my family could be justified in accepting such a responsibility." And he informed Jameson of what had happened between father and children the previous year when Pisa was discussed for Elizabeth's health, adding "that if I offended by an act of disobedience, I might be 'cast off' as for a crime. Oh—poor Papa was not spared at all—not to Mrs. Jameson, not to my sisters."

Mr. Kenyon was not the cautious bystander Elizabeth had considered him when it came to saving her life. "It is painful to you perhaps to hear me talk so, but it is a sore subject with me, & I cannot restrain my opinions," he told Henrietta and Arabel. He had "told Mrs. Jameson everything—it was due her to have a full knowledge, he thought . . & had tried to set before her the impossibility" of her doing any good. He asked the sisters if Ba ever spoke of Italy since her father had disallowed it. Did she dwell on the idea?

Both sisters answered in unison here, "Yes." In their opinion she had made up her mind to go.

"But *how*?" John Kenyon asked. "What is the practical side of the question? She can't go alone—& which of you will go with her? You know, last year, she properly rejected the means which involved you in danger."

To this the daring Henrietta answered, "Ba must do everything for herself—Her friends cannot help her. She must help herself."

Again, Kenyon was perplexed, "But she must not go to Italy by herself. Then *how?*"

"She has determination of character," Henrietta told him. "She will surprise everybody some day."

"*But* HOW?" Kenyon repeated, looking quite uneasy.

Silence.

Elizabeth was angry—at Henrietta. She believed her sister had let the cat out of the bag. How could she have told Mr. Kenyon that she would do everything for herself! Henrietta had given it away.

Browning tried to lead her from the details to the picture itself. What she should be facing was "how the ground is crumbling from beneath our feet." They had to act quickly. He assumed Kenyon must know the truth now. If this intrigue kept up, Robert wouldn't be surprised if Kenyon himself next applied to Browning to take Elizabeth to Italy! And what if her father had walked into the middle of Kenyon's conversation with the sisters? "I dare say we should have been married to-day."

In her next letter Elizabeth's nerves were frayed. Her lover had once again asked her to decide on the time of their marriage. Hadn't she asked him to decide? All right, if she must: "Let it be September, if *you* do not decide otherwise." This on July 29. She seemed annoyed a month later as well: "I told you in so many words in July that, if you really wished to go in August rather than in September, I would make no difficulty—to which you answered, remember, that *October or November would do as well.*" At the end of July they wondered if they should both travel with Mrs. Jameson and her niece, and decided against it.

On the first of August, Browning visited Elizabeth in the midst of the greatest storm to hit London since 1809. So much for the luck of good weather. And good timing! Moulton Barrett had returned home during a lull in the storm and was fully aware of Browning's being in his daughter's room—hour after hour. She was so aware of her father's being downstairs that during the visit "I was looking at Papa's face as I saw it through the floor." Her fear of his displeasure was such that she allowed her lover out into the raging storm.

Not an hour had passed before her father came up to her room. She had changed into a white dressing gown. "Has this been your costume since the morning, pray?" he asked his daughter.

"Oh no, only just now, because of the heat."

"Well, it appears, Ba, that *that man* has spent the whole day with you." His daughter had a fear of lightning and might have become ill of it. Ill with "only Mr. Browning in the room!!"

This indiscretion "was not to be permitted."

It was "a terrible day, when the lightning of it made the least terror." Enter Mr. Kenyon as she wrote this. Those awful spectacles that magnified his questioning eyes were broken, and he carried them in his hand. "On which I caught at the opportunity & told him that they were the most unbecoming things in the world, & that fervently (& sincerely) I hoped never to see them mended."

"Did you see Browning yesterday?"

"Yes."

"I thought so, I intended to come myself, but I thought it probable that he would be here, and so I stayed away."

For the first time she wondered if Robert were right and John Kenyon did know. Then he shocked her further.

"Is there an attachment between your sister Henrietta & Capt. Cook?"

The poet's heart leapt up as "Wordsworth's to the rainbow in the sky." "Why Mr. Kenyon!" she answered, "what extraordinary questions, opening into unspeakable secrets, you do ask."

"But I did not know that it was a secret. How was I to know?—I have seen him here very often, & it is a natural enquiry which I might have put to anybody in the house. . . . I thought the affair might be an arranged one by anybody's consent."

"But you ought to know that such things are never permitted in this house. So much for the consent. As for the matter itself you are right in your supposition—but it is a great secret,—& I entreat you not to put questions about it to anybody in or out of the house."

Robert took this scene as final proof of Kenyon's knowledge. Yet Elizabeth's uncanny intuition, her novelistic sense of human character, carried the day. For in late August the Hedleys spoke to her in similar terms: "Ah Ba, you have arranged your plans more than you would have us believe. But you are right not to tell us—Indeed I would rather not hear. Only *don't be rash—That* is my only advice to you." Had they guessed? No. She realized that the Hedleys thought Henrietta and Surtees Cook were going to get married and then were going to take Elizabeth with them to Italy. That was what Kenyon pieced together as well. The obvious pair of lovers in the Barrett household was Henrietta and Surtees Cook. They were the storm that was brewing, the rebellion in this household of middle-aged celibacy.

Elizabeth Barrett's marriage to Robert Browning actually would take everyone by surprise. As the Hedleys discussed their version of the secret plans with Elizabeth, supporting her and advising her against rashness, something that Browning had predicted happened. Papa walked in.

Aunt Hedley applied a pressure point. "How well she is looking."

"Do you think so?" her brother-in-law replied.

"Why, . . do not *you* think so? Do you pretend to say that you see no surprising difference in her?"

"Oh, I dont know. She is mumpish I think."

Mumpish?

"She doesn't talk."

"Perhaps she is nervous."

"I said not one word," Elizabeth wrote. "When birds have their eyes out, they are apt to be mumpish." These words were crossed over in nervous agitation. "Mumpish!—The expression proved a displeasure—Yet I am sure that I have shown as little sullenness as was possible—To be very talkative & vivacious under such circumstances as these of mine, would argue insensibility, & was certainly beyond my power."

Elizabeth seemed to be destined to a life of extremes. She had a father and was to have a husband who were diametrically opposed. Her sister Henrietta, too, had found a man who did not want to dominate her life. If no Robert Browning, Captain Surtees Cook was a devoted and steadfast lover who had the patience to wait . . . and wait. Arabel found a nurturing man as well, not in a lover but in a clergyman. In an age of paternal domination it is good to remember that there was a Robert Browning, a William Surtees Cook, and also a Reverend James Stratten of Paddington Chapel.

Elizabeth attempted to attend chapel once she was able to walk about. At first the music from the service was too much for her to overcome. It stirred up deep memories of Bro. But on August 30, less than three weeks before her marriage, she went to Paddington Chapel with Arabel. When the singing started the sisters left and stood outside the door—"& the next time I shall care less." If it had been possible, Elizabeth would have liked to be both advised and married by Mr. Stratten. He might mumble his sermons and not appreciate Shakespeare, but he had a "heart of miraculous breadth & depth,—loving further than he can see."

Stratten's children had "reverence" in their love for him, "yet no fear." He had encouraged them all to speak out in front of him on religion and other subjects, freely and from their own individual consciences. The eldest daughter of Moulton Barrett described how Mr. Stratten turned "to his little daughter seriously 'to hear what she thinks.' "

And the other day Mr. Stratten's eldest son, who he had hoped would succeed him at the dissenter's chapel in Paddington, decided to enter the Church of England. His wife became ill with grief, and for him, too, it must have been an enormous trial. How did the preacher react? "With the utmost gentleness & tenderness however, he desired him [the son] to take time for thought & act according to his conscience,—I believe for my part that there never was a holier man."

But if Elizabeth turned to this man for the wedding, it would mean, after the fact, that her sister Arabel would never be allowed to attend Paddington Chapel again. So such a choice would be wrong.

By the end of August Robert saw clearly that "a new leaf is turned over in our journal, an old part of our adventure done with, and a new one entered upon, altogether distinct from the other." The end of September was the latest they could wait, before the weather changed. These were days of plans and anxiety. They might have escaped the formal trappings of the Arabella Hedley wedding, but leaving England without anyone's knowing and getting safely to Italy, particularly with a woman who for years had never left her room—well, the arrangements were staggering. Neither poet, to pay some homage to Anna Jameson's point of view, had had much experience in such practical matters. Finally, circumstances pushed them toward immediate action; but in the middle of all their planning, as if to underline a shift in luck and timing, Flush was stolen!

Flush, the golden spaniel, has not yet taken center stage, though he was central to the life of Ba after Bro's drowning. He truly was venerable and has had his own kind of Alice B. Toklas fame. Virginia Woolf wrote *Flush: A Biography,* the Brownings seen through the eyes of the dog. The Bloomsbury circle, with their own lives too close to Victorian roots for comfort, had a fascination with the period that was best expressed ironically, if not outright satirically. Still, it took a lot of

interest to write a book about a spaniel who traveled to Italy. And
under wit, there were similarities: threatening men—Woolf's step-
brother terrorized her—and loss—a beloved brother—though it was
Woolf herself who would drown. Also, Woolf learned from Barrett
Browning. In her novel-length poem *Aurora Leigh,* Elizabeth would
tell the world for the first time that what a woman artist needed was
enough money for a room of her own.

Flush had been a gift to Elizabeth from Mary Russell Mitford. It
had been Mr. Kenyon—who else?—who convinced his cousin when
she was thirty to go for a carriage ride with him and Miss Mitford, assuring her of the older writer's kindness and admiration. Why would
the author of the acclaimed drama *Rienzi* and the wonderful scenes
from country life want to meet Elizabeth? As shy as she was, Elizabeth
acquiesced, a fortunate decision that made her a friend for life. When
she stepped into the carriage the rapport between the women began.
They corresponded voluminously thereafter.

Mary Russell Mitford's father was an invalid, by the 1840s an octogenarian, who was as demanding on the author's time as Moulton Barrett was on Elizabeth's obedience. Both wrote about their fathers to
each other in the highest terms. It would be hard to discern from the
letters that Dr. Mitford's extravagances had led to his daughter's becoming his financial support. According to Meredith Raymond and
Mary Rose Sullivan, he was "a spendthrift doctor." He preferred playing cards and raising greyhounds to practicing medicine. He ran
through his wife's fortune quickly. Gambling must have seemed natural to the young Mary Mitford, because the doctor also ran through
her own early lottery winnings of twenty thousand pounds. After her
mother's death, Mitford became her father's sole support in every way,
and he often cautioned his daughter against walking in the woods that
she loved so. He assumed that was what tired her out.

Mary Mitford, as we've already seen, was not an admirer of Browning, yet it was she who might have opened up the possibility of entertaining him, long before the meeting. On October 21, 1842, Elizabeth
referred to Mr. Kenyon's asking "once, not long before" if he could
bring Mr. Browning to see her. At the same time she was in correspondence with Richard Henry Horne, whom Miss Mitford considered an
eccentric literary man. Imagine how astonished her father would be "if
I had Mr. Horne & Mr. Browning upstairs in my bedroom!! He wd.
certainly open his eyes & set me down among the *inclined*-to-be-'good-

for-nothing poetesses.' " She herself, however, agreed with Miss Mitford's opinion "that it wd. be not only innocent, but what is quite another thing, *proper.*" Still, even if she were fifty her father would demur, though Miss Mitford thought her "old enough to have twenty gentlemen in my bedroom if I please, according to the order of the garter! Agreed! but then, but then . . this Papa of mine . . ."

After Bro drowned Elizabeth didn't write to anyone for months, but finally to Mary Mitford she was able to express some of her grief. She was so beside herself, had become so reclusive, that Mary Mitford sent her Flush, the offspring of her own champion spaniel, also named Flush, to give her new companionship and an outlet for her affections. Flush seized on his new mistress greedily, and just as hungrily Elizabeth seized on her Flush. Taking care of Flush was very good for Elizabeth, the bathing him, the spoiling him, not to mention the fact that Flush sprang into her life, offering her, just as so many humans would, a rather exclusive adoration. Flush, along with poetry and letters, helped to keep her alive. "His ears which you were inclined to criticise are improved—grown thicker & longer, and fall beautifully in golden light over the darker brown of his head & body. He is much admired for beauty—particularly for that white breastplate which marks him even among dogs of his colour—Flush, the silvershielded!" She wrote about Flush with all the verve she would later bring to writing about her son. It made sense. As she told Mary Mitford early on, she loved dogs and children.

And on the first of September, even before Elizabeth and Robert knew they would marry within two weeks, Flush was kidnapped by the London dog-stealers, an organized band of banditti of whom the infamous Taylor was captain. Robert had in fact warned Elizabeth of the possibility. He was a prophet! She and Arabel and Flush had gone in a cab to Vere Street, and Flush followed them as usual into a shop and out again—was in fact at Elizabeth's heels when she stepped up to the carriage. "Flush!"

Flush? He was gone. "He had been caught up in that moment, from *under* the wheels, do you understand?" Well, "When we shall be at Pisa, dearest, we shall be away from the London dog-stealers." Then she turned her attention to wedding plans and travel routes.

She would rather marry after she left Wimpole Street forever. Robert insisted they marry before. "If I accede to your 'idée fixe' about the marriage," well then "let us go away as soon as possible afterwards, at least." She was afraid "of breaking down under quite a different set of causes, in nervous excitement & exhaustion. I belong to that pitiful order of weak women who cannot command their bodies with their souls at every moment, & who sink down in hysterical disorder when they ought to act & resist."

She planned to ransom Flush back—as she had done twice before. Browning, perhaps picking up on her light tone, could joke. Flush had bitten him when he first came to visit Elizabeth. He had responded by offering the dog biscuits, but it took many visits to get Flush to stop growling and attacking his competition. "Poor fellow—was he no better than the rest of us, and did all that barking and fanciful valour spend itself on such enemies as Mr. Kenyon and myself, leaving only blandness and waggings of the tail for the man with the bag?" He then used Flush's predicament as an analogy, telling her not to allow their happiness "to be caught up from us, after poor Flush's fashion—there may be no redemption from *that* peril." With a slip of the pen (or the psyche) he talked of Flush in the past tense.

" 'Our friend & follower, that *was* to be'—is *that,* then, your opinion of my poor darling Flush's destiny," she teased him that same evening. "There is a dreadful tradition in this neighbourhood," of a lady who did not pay and in holding out had "her dog's head sent to her in a parcel." So "Get Flush back, whatever you do," she told her brother Henry. Where did Henry find the captain of the dog bandits? Why, "smoking a cigar in a room with pictures!—They make some three or four thousand a year by their honorable employment." And forget Flush's submitting without a fight; why he was caught and gagged, Browning could depend on that. "If he could have bitten, he would have bitten—if he could have yelled, he would have yelled."

And on another issue: She wanted *him* to tell *her* when and how they'd leave England. She would do as he said. "Have I refused one proposition of yours when there were not strong obstacles? . . . For instance, I agreed . . . to your plan about the marrying—and I agreed to go with you to Italy in the latter part of September —did I not?" Her only suggestion was that there should be as little excitement as possible because of her nervous temperament. "But I shall not fail, I believe—I should despise myself too much for failing."

On September 3, mistakenly thinking Flush had been found,

FLUSH, 1843. EBB's drawing of her golden-haired spaniel given to her by Mary Russell Mitford after the tragic death of EBB's favorite brother. In "To Flush, My Dog," published in the Athenaeum, July 22, 1843, EBB wrote:

> This dog watched beside a bed
> Day and night unweary,
> Watched within a curtained room
> Where no sunbeam broke the gloom
> Round the sick and dreary.

Robert told Elizabeth he would not have given in to the kidnappers, arguing the morality of "religion, right and justice" in resisting wickedness, and sounding much as he did when he had advocated the honor of dueling. He was so sick with a headache that his sister had to mail the morning letter for him.

Elizabeth replied the same evening, first intent on his health, then on to the saga of the "archfiend Taylor" and to domestic politics. Taylor had come the previous night and told Henry that the bandits would accept six pounds with an extra half guinea for his own trouble in the negotiations. Papa interposed exactly as he had three years before: Henry should not pay that amount, and he should not tell a word of it to Elizabeth. But Henry told his sister that he hadn't paid what Taylor asked. She was annoyed, since she had expected the ransom to be higher. She told Henry that he must go at once and finish the business.

The next day still no Flush, but a very long and very earnest letter from Browning on good and evil and social responsibility. What would he do if she, not Flush, were kidnapped? The inner knight in Browning came galloping forth. "I would pay every farthing I had in the world, and shoot with my own hand the receiver of it after a chase of fifty years—esteeming *that* to be a very worthy recompense for the trouble." Not that he meant to be domineering in approach. "My own Ba, if I thought you could *fear* me, I think *I* should have the courage to give you up to-morrow!" His headache was chronic that week.

By September 5, Flush was still not home. Henry had been far too lukewarm. If he didn't get Flush back, she would go to the bandits to-morrow despite her brother's telling her she'd be robbed and murdered. Three years ago after Flush was dognapped, the accursed Taylor had told her brother Daisy that they had been watching for Flush for two years and "that they had hoped to get hold of him the other day when he was out with the lady in the chair, as he had been several times lately." "Conceive the audacity!" she wrote to Mary Mitford, "and the hardheartedness!! They must have guessed at my state of health by the very movement of the chair,—drawn for a few steps & then resting!—and to calculate coolly on such an opportunity of taking away the little dog of which I was obviously so fond!—I said so to my brothers; & they laughed. 'Hardheartedness! Why they wd. have cut your own throat for five pounds'!—And that is true."

No longer "the lady in the chair," she took Wilson and the two of them went by cab, asking at a public house where Taylor could be found. Everyone there knew who she was looking for before she mentioned Taylor's name. "An unsolicited philanthropist ran before us to the house & out again to tell me that the great man 'wasn't at home!—but wouldn't I get out?' " By then a group of men and boys had gathered around, and Wilson was in terror. Elizabeth decided not to get out of the cab, declining to go in to meet Mrs. Taylor. The philanthropist ran back with this message and then brought out to them "An immense feminine bandit . . fat enough to have had an easy conscience all her life," who asked if she'd care to leave the cab and wait for Taylor to get home. She left a message instead: "That Mr. Taylor should keep his promise about the restoration of a dog which he had agreed to restore—& I begged her to induce him to go to Wimpole Street in the course of the day, & not defer it any longer."

Taylor actually did come to Wimpole Street. Elizabeth sent down the money even though he hadn't brought the dog, as she knew it was the only way. But Alfred (Daisy) arrived and swore at Taylor calling him a thief, and the art-collecting, cigar-chomping bandit rushed out swearing they'd never see Flush again. "Angry I was with Alfred, & terrified for Flush,—seeing at a glance the probability of his head being cut off as the proper vengeance!" Now she came downstairs and was ready to go to Taylor wherever he was and save Flush at any price. "Everybody was crying out against me for being 'quite mad' & obstinate, & willful—I was called as many names as Mr. Taylor." Finally Sette (brother number seven) said he'd go, and he took the money and was civil with Taylor and at eight o'clock Flush returned—dirty, thinner, and frightened. Counting in the six guineas for this ransom, she had by then paid twenty to the dog-stealers in all.

On September 6, Elizabeth wrote to tell Browning that "Flush is found, & lying on the sofa." Browning was so ill, the dizziness in his head was so bad, that not only would he miss a visit the next day, but when he received a letter about her trip to the banditti and the return of Flush, he had only one sentence of happiness for Flush's return and only one to remark on her extraordinary trip into the underworld of the dog-snatchers.

Three days later came the final crumbling of their old order. On September 9, on the spur of the moment, asking no one's opinion and after the heat of summer which would have made it pleasurable, Moulton Barrett informed his family that they would leave the house on Wimpole Street for a month so that it could be properly aired and cleaned. Browning had predicted the possibility. "This night, an edict has gone out, and George is tomorrow to be on his way to take a house for a month either at Dover, Reigate, Tunbridge." It happened "too soon & too sudden for us to set out on our Italian adventure now." However, "you must think for both of us."

Browning did. "We must be *married directly* and go to Italy—I will go for a licence today and we can be married on Saturday. I will call tomorrow at 3 and arrange everything with you." Browning accepted the authority she asked him to take. More firmness and insistence on his part would have been welcomed earlier. But it was obvious that the last thing he wanted to be, or to have her imagine him to be, was a dominating and threatening figure. Besides finding her father's act "quite characteristic," Browning felt "the departure with its bustle is not unfavourable."

They met in her room at Wimpole Street for the last time on September 11, and on September 12 in St. Marylebone Church they married. His signature was strong, hers looked as if it were written with a fish bone. The witnesses were his cousin James Silverthorne and her maid, Elizabeth Wilson.

On the next day, a Sunday afternoon, he wrote to her that her proof of love to him had been made and that his whole life would be spent in attempting to furnish proof of his affection for her. "Do you feel what I mean, dearest? How you have dared and done all this, under my very eyes, for my only sake? I believed you would be capable of it— What then? What is a belief? My own eyes have seen—my heart will remember!"

On the morning after their marriage, Robert Browning "woke . . . *quite well*—quite free from the sensation in the head—I have not woken *so,* for two years perhaps—what have you been doing to me?"

"Dearest, I am so glad!—I had feared that excitement's telling on you quite in another way." The excitement had told on her in quite another way. She had woken up that Sunday after the marriage with all her brothers in the house and coming into the room "laughing & talking & discussing this matter of leaving town" and also at the same time "two or three female friends of ours, from Herefordshire— and I did not *dare* to cry out against the noise, though my head seemed splitting in two (one half for each shoulder), I had such a morbid fear of exciting a suspicion." Not only that, Mary Trepsack, with whom she was to dine the next day, came in. All this commotion—"It was like having a sort of fever." In the middle of it, the church bells rang. " 'What bells are those?' asked one of the provincials. 'Marylebone Church bells' said Henrietta, standing behind my chair." And as she wrote this to Browning, having escaped the din of her household, who walked in, "Who do you think?—Mr. Kenyon." And in his repaired specs, "looking as if his eyes reached to their rim all the way round; & one of the first words was '*When did you see Browning?*' "

Among all the "emotion and confusion" of their wedding day, only one thought had come that was not a feeling. Of all the many women who had stood where she had stood marrying at Marylebone Church, perhaps not one of them "has had reasons strong as mine, for an absolute trust & devotion towards the man she married,—not one!" But

50 WIMPOLE STREET.
*The London home of the
widowed Edward Barrett
Moulton Barrett and his
adult children. It has
since been torn down.*

perhaps they had less need of such a husband as Robert Browning. They "have that affectionate sympathy & support & presence of their nearest relations." That "which failed to *me.*"

Elizabeth had to spend six more days at Wimpole Street after her marriage and without seeing her husband. The thought of visiting together under Moulton Barrett's roof as man and wife was out of the question. The anxious week echoed the months she was forced to stay at Torquay after the death of Bro. Where Browning's headache ended, Elizabeth's began. His choice was made against no obstacle. His parents were informed, and whatever disappointment they might have felt about not being able to meet their daughter-in-law, not being able to have a public wedding for their gifted son, it was their son's welfare that was most important to them, and his decision was theirs. Still, it was no wonder that his mother's headaches increased as her son's disappeared. The worry the family had at the time they seemed to have spared their son, or perhaps he spared his wife. Robert was taking responsibility for the life of a famous British poet and the great-grand-daughter of Edward of Cinnamon Hill. What would happen to him in the eyes of the world if this former invalid were to die on their wedding voyage?

Elizabeth's anxieties centered on the consequences of the choice she had made on September 12, 1846. She began to experience them fully the next day. By September 14 she wrote that no one, not even John Kenyon, must be given an intimation of their marriage till after they were gone. "Remember that I shall be *killed*—it will be so infinitely worse than you can have an idea." Was she exaggerating? Or did she know her father? She certainly knew John Kenyon, the blind Boyd, the painter Haydon, Anna Jameson. . . . Was her repeated image about being thrown out of windows should knowledge come to light excessive, or was it a metaphor for the physical violence that disobedience to her father could produce on Wimpole Street? "I told you once," she had written to Robert eight months before, "that we held hands faster in this house for the weight over our heads."

As much as she feared her father's finding out while she was still within reach, she felt the guilt of what her leaving was going to mean to him. On Monday evening, for the first time in a long while, her father walked into her room and spoke kindly to her, asked how she felt. Gone were the days in which he would emerge from his adjoining room every night and, holding her hand, lead her in spontaneous evening prayers. How did she feel?

"Once I heard of his saying of me that I was 'the purest woman he ever knew.'" Her response to this news had been to smile, or, she believed, she actually laughed out loud. "Because I understood perfectly what he meant by *that*—viz—that I had not troubled him with the iniquity of love-affairs, or any impropriety of seeming to think about being married. But now the whole sex will go down with me to the perdition of faith in any of us. See the effect of my wickedness!—'Those women!'"

What preoccupied her was the letter she was going to write to him. She had many letters to write, but to him, what was she going to say? Papa, I am married—I hope you will not be too displeased? She composed part of the letter to Browning: "With the exception of this act, I have submitted to the least of your wishes all my life long—Set the life against the act, & forgive me, for the sake of the daughter you once loved." Surely she can say that and "then remind him of the long suffering I have suffered.—and entreat him to pardon the happiness which has come at last—."

She knew his reaction. "*He* will wish in return, that I had died years ago!—For the storm will come & endure—And at last, perhaps, he will forgive us—it is my hope."

She had also to compose a wedding advertisement to be published after they left, and she wanted to do it without a date. Should it include the fact that Browning was the author of *Paracelsus,* the fact that she was the eldest daughter of Moulton Barrett of *Jamaica* or Cinnamon Hill, Jamaica, as well as Wimpole Street? Should Wimpole Street include the number 50?

This announcement was very important to the couple. For finally there is a myth to debunk. Elizabeth Barrett, forty-year-old spinster, and Robert Browning, thirty-four-year-old bachelor, both of age and certifiably in their right minds, did not elope!

On August 22, Mrs. Jameson had made a joke. Well, if no one could convince her to go to the continent with a companion, why then "there is only an *elopement* for you."

"I was obliged to laugh," Elizabeth wrote to Robert. But surely no one was going to use the word *elopement* to describe the event. "We shall be in such an obvious exercise of Right by Daylight."

Browning's response the next day: " 'Elopement'! Let them call it 'felony' or 'burglary'—so long as they don't go to church with us, and propose my health after breakfast!"

But they weren't running away in order to marry. They were exercising their Christian rights as adults. They married secretly. Henrietta, having once had her knees brought to the floor, carried on a love affair under her father's nose. But if he found out, she had the ability and the nerve to run. It had taken the courtship for Elizabeth to develop the strength to walk. She was a consenting adult. "When I hear people say that *circumstances are against them,* I always retort, . . you mean *that your will is not with you!* I believe in the will—I have faith in it."

On Wednesday she reported that the family was to leave for the house at Little Bookham, which was six miles from the railway, on Monday. She seemed to consider going on to Bookham with them as she hadn't written half her letters. She "began to write a letter to Papa this morning, & could do nothing but cry, & looked so pale thereupon, that everybody wondered what could be the matter." She assured Robert she was better now, but should she go with the family or was it possible she could write her letters from the road? She and Wilson had packed lightly. But the bags that had to be sent later, to what post office should they go? His mother was ill; would it be better to wait on her account?

"The way will be to leave at once," Browning wrote back. His mother would feel worse if they stayed and got into trouble. "Take *no* desk . . I will take a large one."

On Thursday, Elizabeth's handwriting showed her fatigue and weakness. She told Robert that she was "so tired" that the earliest she could go would be Saturday. On Friday, her handwriting was again strained as she wrote a few sentences, asking for the time of the express train. For she realized his hour was wrong, even in the midst of what she called her confusion.

Friday night, September 18, was the last night Elizabeth would spend at Wimpole Street. The letters she could write were written, including the one to her father. Tomorrow she and Wilson and Flush would leave. It would have to be at an hour late enough not to compromise Arabel, who slept on the couch in her room. There could be no goodbyes, not even to her sisters. "Your letters to me I take with me, let the 'ounces' cry out aloud, ever so. I *tried* to leave them, & I could not. That is, they would not be left: it was not my fault—I will not be scolded."

And she ended this extraordinary correspondence, "Is this my last letter to you, ever dearest?—Oh,—if I loved you less . . a little, little less."

In the postscript she added how perfect Wilson had been to her through this hectic time, Wilson, whom she had once called timid. "I begin to think that none are so bold as the timid, when they are fairly roused."

Something crucial had happened to Elizabeth Barrett Browning in the week since her marriage, and her time at Wimpole Street as a married woman had allowed her to dwell on it. She became fully aware of the repercussions of her choice. The ultimate knowledge of the last letter was that, in taking responsibility for her life, she took responsibility as well for the pain she was going to cause. "It is dreadful . . dreadful . . to have to give pain here by a voluntary act—for the first time in my life." Before she left her father's house to live her own life, to see the mountains and rivers for herself—and before her marriage was consummated—she had already entered the world.

Riding an
Enchanted Horse

"I REALLY BELIEVE I have saved her life by persuading her to rest." Anna Jameson was sitting in her hotel room in Paris on September 24, 1846, writing to her dear friend Lady Noel Byron, widow of the Romantic poet. On Monday, while Anna Jameson and her young niece Gerardine were out in the City of Light, most probably at a picture gallery, a British gentleman had come looking for her at her hotel and had left a cryptic note: "Come to see your friend & my wife EBB . . . RB."

She had stood in a daze trying to comprehend. What logic she could make out of the initials, out of the handwriting itself, made no sense. How could she piece together the incredible possibility?

Anna Brownell Murphy Jameson had gained entrance to Elizabeth Barrett's room through her own insistence and through an introduction from Mary Russell Mitford. It was Anna's close friendship with Robert Browning that subsequently opened Elizabeth's affections toward her. She was now on her way past Pisa to Rome to write her most renowned work, the voluminous *Sacred and Legendary Art*, with her seventeen-year-old niece Gerardine Bate as her assistant.

Anna Jameson's father had been an artist, a portrait painter of miniatures. An Irishman married to an Englishwoman, he emigrated from Dublin to England when Anna was four. With a well-to-do British wife and five daughters to support, Denis Brownell Murphy had trouble making ends meet. Precocious Anna, with her love of Italian art and literature, helped him by going to work. Perhaps it was from her lively and witty father that she developed the idea of the impractical, childlike nature of all artists, which made them unfit to handle the daily responsibilities of life. From the earliest age she was accustomed to managing these ethereal creatures' daily affairs.

Denis Murphy was poor because of his calling. Dr. Mitford was strapped because of his gaming. Two daughters, Anna Brownell, born in 1794, and Mary Russell Mitford, born seven years earlier, found themselves as young women with fathers to support.

Anna Brownell hadn't her older friend's proclivity for the wonders of nature that drew her to the English countryside. The sophisticated, cultivated city life, the art centers of the world, were for Anna. She was an intelligent woman who prided herself on her practicality, yet certainly she was high-spirited as well, and had the imagination to make the most of what life brought her. For fifteen years off and on she was employed as a governess by some of England's finest families. She was frugal and spent her money on helping her siblings (a lifelong endeavor) as well as her parents. Traveling through Europe with a wealthy family on the grand tour, she kept two journals of the trip—almost as one might keep two sets of books. One was a factual record, the other a fictionalized travel journal—that paid off. It was published anonymously as *A Lady's Diary.* In 1826, titled *Diary of an Ennuyée,* the book had popular success in England. Its heroine died of the heartbreak of having to leave her love behind her, not the practical Anna. She resumed the relationship she had severed before leaving England and indeed married the man she had left behind, Robert Sympson Jameson, who later became Upper Canada's first Vice-Chancellor. Unlike her heroine, she lived to experience the heartbreak of a failed marriage. It was a rocky marriage from the beginning, and her husband, in Canada finally, and a terminal drunk, seemed to have disappeared from her life. "Why should we urge these young people to marry and get into want and perplexities and ill humour?" asked Denis Murphy before his daughter's wedding. Where are the good marriages? Elizabeth Barrett once asked Robert Browning.

Anna Jameson had to support herself, which she did, as a writer on art and women's rights. She was fifty-two years old at the time Robert Browning appeared at her hotel in Paris and left her the enigmatic note. She was no longer the fiery-haired young woman who had begun to make her mark on the world, but rather a more maternal figure—an aunt. Nathaniel Hawthorne, in Italy, described her ten years later as old and dumpy. In her fifties, she appeared in Elizabeth's letters generous of figure as well as heart. Hawthorne and Barrett Browning agreed that in matters of art she was an eager teacher who assumed her pupil's

ANNA JAMESON (1794–1860) *at age sixteen, from an engraving of the miniature by her father, the artist Denis Brownell Murphy. When her friend Lady Byron saw it in 1841—Jameson was then forty-seven—she wrote a poem to the once fiery-haired young woman that began:*

> *In those young eyes, so keenly bravely bent*
> *To search the mysteries of the Future hour,*
> *There shines the will to conquer, and the power*
> *Which makes the conquest sure.*

total ignorance and at picture galleries attempted to wash it away in a flood of talk. Both writers assessed it was breadth of knowledge, rather than originality of mind, that characterized her intellectually—a charge that might have pleased her. "Genius," as we've seen in the love letters, did not impress her. Lady Byron's husband had been a genius!

Anna Jameson's views about women (such as their being equal in intelligence to men) were more radical than Elizabeth's; at times, for example, when Elizabeth spoke of the masculine mind being at its best stronger than the feminine, Elizabeth knew Mrs. Jameson wouldn't agree or approve. Anna Jameson was an early feminist. She had to work hard to make a life for herself, and she wished to help other women (as well as all art lovers). Visiting Elizabeth Barrett at Wimpole Street, she had a vivid example of how one child prodigy had fared, a genius who also happened to be a woman. She had sincerely wanted to accompany her away from that closed life, that cramped and deathly room. Her nature attracted her to the messes in other people's lives.

She hadn't the genius of Elizabeth or of the heroine of Elizabeth's last long work, her novel in verse, *Aurora Leigh*—Aurora shared that with her creator as well as with her namesake, George Sand. But Anna Jameson did share with Aurora Leigh her independence of spirit.

She was one of that band of English-speaking travelers, both women and men, who found on the continent a way of life that was less constrained by Puritan values and much more economical than in England or the United States. With taste one could travel very well on very little—as the Brownings planned to do. By happy coincidence that worldly woman was now in Paris, pondering over "Come to see your friend & my wife EBB . . . RB" and "wondering what the two things could mean." While she pondered, night fell, and Elizabeth insisted that Robert go into a separate room of their hotel where he could not be disturbed and get some sleep. He was thoroughly worn out and had scarcely eaten anything for three weeks. In those weeks he planned the secret marriage, and then, in his own way, executed the travel arrangement. That he listened to his wife, left her to wait for Anna Jameson alone, revealed the depth of his exhaustion.

The Brownings had had a rough channel crossing at Southampton. The Havre passage had been "a miserable thing in all ways." She and Robert and Wilson arrived exhausted "either by the sea or the sorrow." They hired a diligence to get them to Rouen, and Elizabeth's description of the ride painted a morphine-tinged picture. "It was as comfortable & easy as any carriage I have been in for years—now five horses, now seven . . all looking wild & lovely— . . some of them white, some brown, some black with the manes leaping as they galloped & the white reins drifting down over their heads . . such a fantastic scene it was in the moonlight—& I who was a little feverish with fatigue & the violence done to myself, in the self control of the last few days, began to see it all as in a vision & to doubt whether I was in or out of the body—they made me lie down with feet up—Robert was dreadfully anxious about me."

After that haunting, feverish, and vision-ridden journey, they arrived at Rouen to find they had been confused by the customs of the country. Although they could stay overnight, their luggage must leave directly. "What was to be done? So I prevailed over all the fuss,—we should continue on route, after a rest of twenty minutes at the Rouen Hotel," and of course after some coffee. What a spectacular sight they made, she wrote to Arabel: "You would have been startled, if in a dream you had seen me, carried in & out, as Robert in his infinite kindness would insist on between the lines of strange foreign faces of the travellers room back again to the coupe of the diligence which we placed on the railway . . & so we rolled on towards Paris." One wonders what went on behind those foreign faces as they stared at the feverish British lady carried in to coffee and out by her husband, and followed by her maid and her dog. Did they know they were poets? From those strange British on tour, one could expect just about anything.

The Brownings arrived in Paris on Monday at ten in the morning, lacking their visas, which the mayor of Rouen promised they'd have in two days, and also lacking two nights of sleep. They settled into small rooms in the first hotel they could find. Elizabeth didn't mind the hotel at all, she wrote to her sister. The coffee was good and everything was clean. Robert went out to speak to Mrs. Jameson. From Elizabeth's view they had agreed to this because "her goodness to me deserved some passing look & sign." From Robert's point of view it might have been also the case of genius seeking guidance. He must have been quite alarmed by his wife's state and her persistent desire to make this trip from Wimpole Street to Italy as fast as she could. She had, in Anna Jameson's words, "a feverish desire to go *on on*—as if there was to be neither peace nor health till she was beyond the alps."

"I promised to receive Mrs. Jameson myself . . imagine with what terrors." She would come face-to-face for the first time with a response to her act of voluntary will. Anna Jameson "came in with her hands stretched out & eyes opened as wide as Flush's—'Can it be possible? is it possible? You wild, dear creature.'" Never a woman of few words, she went on, "all this in intensified interjections." Why, they were poets: each should have married a good provider " 'to keep you reasonable.' " But no matter, " 'he is a wise man in doing so—& you are a wise woman, let the world say as it pleases. I shall dance for joy both on earth & in heaven my dear friends.' " She was "the kindest, the most cordial, the most astonished, the most out of breath with *wonder*—& I could scarcely speak."

Anna Jameson looked at silent, anxious Elizabeth and realized, as

she'd tell her later, that the poet appeared to be " 'frightfully ill.' "
She "would not stay . . I was to rest . . . nor to think for the second
of travelling all night in that wild way any more." The older woman
took over. Good sense prevailed. She arranged rooms for the couple at
her Hôtel de la Ville de Paris. Wilson had a separate room above them,
she and Gerardine the apartment below them; the Brownings had privacy and Anna Jameson had letters to write to Lady Byron.

The art historian who spent much of her life caring for others (an
occupation fraught with disappointment) had quite a healthy sense of
her own importance as well. "I really believe I have saved her life by
persuading her to rest" has been interpreted as an example of this. But
more miraculous than Elizabeth Barrett's marrying was that a woman
who had hardly left her room as an adult survived the trip to Pisa.
Anna Jameson really may have saved the poet by getting her to abandon her frantic race from Wimpole Street.

During the courtship Elizabeth and Robert had wondered if they
should tell their friend of their relationship and then travel with her
and her niece—she had already asked to accompany Elizabeth to Italy,
but the offer had been declined. After one day of rest in Paris, it was
the Brownings' turn to request Anna's company on the trip. Now the
hesitation was the older woman's. Would such travel arrangements be
a proper environment for her niece Gerardine? Her good heart came to
her rescue, and she agreed quickly. Luckily, Elizabeth did not know of
her doubts. As Anna observed, Elizabeth appeared "nervous, frightened, ashamed, agitated, happy, vulnerable." Not to be considered
proper company to the "serious" Gerardine, whom Elizabeth had met a
few times and liked, would have been a blow to a nature that was extremely vulnerable at this time.

"You may think how grateful we are, I am—& *he* is still more, perhaps . . . for it lifts from him a good half of the anxiety about moving
me from one place to another, which well as I bear it all," he feels is too
much.

If Anna Jameson was "out of breath with *wonder*" at the marriage,
what a shock it must have been to the public. In England, John Forster,
editor of the London *Daily News,* did not want to print the wedding announcement the couple had labored over, thinking it some cruel joke.
He stopped it angrily, before finding out that the couple had indeed
married and the announcement should run. The secret of their love, as
Elizabeth had insisted, had been well kept.

In Paris their marriage was consummated. "Now he is well . . I thank god . . & I am well . . living as in a dream . . loving & being loved better everyday—seeing near in him, all *that* I seemed to see afar. Thinking with one thought, pulsing with one heart."

They kept to a leisurely schedule. "We see Mrs Jameson at certain hours, but keep to ourselves at others." They breakfasted alone and then had "bread & butter at one (& coffee)" and in the evening they dined with their friend at the restaurants, as the Parisians do, walking to meet her, and walking home afterward. "He *will* carry me upstairs." Then alone again, they watched "the stars rise over the high Paris houses" or told each other "childish happy things," or made "schemes for work" that they would achieve once they reached Pisa. Everybody told her, she reassured her sister Arabel, that she looked well. "The first fatigue has passed & the change & the sense of the Thing Done (assuming the place of a painful recollection) & the constant love . . . have done me good."

Why, "He loves me better he says than he ever did—& we live such a quiet yet new life, it is like riding an enchanted horse."

EVEN ON her honeymoon, one thing kept Elizabeth from being "the happiest of human beings": the "dreadful, dreadful" thought of the letters from home that would catch up with her at Orléans. To both her sisters she confided that the letters with their responses to her act were her " 'death warrant' . . . I was so anxious and terrified."

Three years before, she had written to Mary Mitford, "I like letters *per se* . . & as letters! I like the abstract idea of a letter—I like the postman's rap at the door—I like the queen's head upon the paper—and with a negation of queen's heads (which does'nt mean treason), I like the sealing wax under the seal and the postmark on the envelope. Very seldom have I a letter which I would rather *not* read. . . . Even people's stupidities emit a flash of liveliness to my eyes, between the breaking of the seal & the closing of the letter—and people's vivacities grow of course more vivacious in proportion. Perhaps this is almost natural considering my solitude. . . ." Now, at the opposite extreme, letters still loomed larger than life. She heard the postman's rap, saw the Queen's head, felt the sealing wax . . . and mounted the scaffold.

As early as Rouen, as tired as she was, she wrote to her sister about the Thing Done. "That miserable Saturday . . when I had to *act out a*

part to you—how I suffered!" At least her sisters knew that she was involved with Browning and would find her own way of leaving. Her
brothers and her father were completely unaware. The friends she
didn't have the time to write to . . . the friends she did write to . . .
what would their reaction be? Anna Jameson described her state quite
·well; it bears repeating. She began her marriage "nervous, frightened,
ashamed, agitated, happy, vulnerable."

Her state was balanced by Robert Browning's sheer joy. "As to
him—his joy & delight & his poetical fancies and antics—with every
now & then the profoundest seriousness & tenderness intercepting the
brilliance of his imagination make him altogether the most charming
companion." This report to Lady Byron was verified by Elizabeth's letter to her sister. Mrs. Jameson "repeats of Robert that she never knew
anyone of so affluent a mind and imagination combined with a nature
and manners so sunshiny and captivating, which she well may say . .
for he encases us from morning till night—thinks of everybody's feelings . . is witty and wise . . (and foolish too in the right place), charms
cross old women who cry out in the diligence 'mais, madame, mes
jambes!' talks Latin to the priests who enquire at three in the morning
whether Newman and Pusey are likely 'lapsare in erroribus' (you will
make out *that*) and forgets nothing and nobody . . except himself . . it
is the only omission." Here was the portrait of a happy man. A man
who at one moment of time had gotten from life exactly what he had
wanted—and was able to appreciate it.

Happiness is not the stuff of biography, and to the intellectual
and scholar its proximity to simplemindedness often makes it particularly repugnant. Many fine minds have worked out suitable
responses to show that this great man of letters wasn't really happy, or
better yet that he knew (or didn't know) that he wasn't really happy.
Robert Browning just another foolish bridegroom who, on
the trip from London to Pisa, shared the overflowing of a full heart
with everyone he met? This was not the enigmatic older Browning
Henry James would observe in society years later. Where was the
ambiguity?

What Robert Browning's happiness revealed was his character. His
abundant, energetic, and supportive love on the wedding trip to Italy
was the perfect balance to Elizabeth's anxiety, and a clear mirror for her
of the rightness of her decision. All the world is supposed to love a
lover, but this lover appeared to love all the world.

The day before his wife left Wimpole Street, on what she would call "That miserable Saturday," she wrote to Mary Russell Mitford in the most agitated handwriting. "*I* who loved Flush for not hating to be near me . . I, who by a long sorrowfulness & solitude, had sunk into the very ashes of selfhumiliation—Think how I must have felt to have listened to [words of love] from such a man. A man of genius & miraculous attainments . . but of a heart & spirit beyond them all!"

In calmer spirits, in Pisa, in late October, she wrote to her friend Julia Martin, her old neighbor from her childhood days at Hope End, an extraordinary account of her earlier inner landscape. She didn't have to convince her of Robert's worth, the way she did Mary Russell Mitford, so she could concentrate on her own earlier morbidity:

"We all get used to the thought of the tomb; and I was buried, that was the whole. It was a little thing even for myself a short time ago, and really it would be a pneumatological curiosity if I could describe and let you see how perfectly for years together, after what broke my heart at Torquay, I lived on the outside of my own life, blindly and darkly from day to day, as completely dead to hope. . . . Nobody quite understood this of me, because I am not morally a coward and have a hatred of all the forms of audible groaning. But God knows what is within. . . . Even my poetry . . was a thing on the outside of me, a thing to be done, and then done! What people said of it did not touch *me.* A thoroughly morbid and desolate state it was, which I look back now to with the sort of horror with which one would look to one's graveclothes, if one had been clothed in them by mistake during a trance."

She had chosen love over death. Yet far from Torquay's cruel sea, in Orléans, there was a warrant out on her still. In the two days before she left Wimpole Street she wrote a letter to her brother George. It began, "I throw myself on your affection for me & beseech of God that it may hold under the weight—dearest George, Go to your room & read this letter." After reading it, "George, dear George, read the enclosed letter for my dearest Papa, & then—breaking gently the news of it—give it to him to read." It ended, "If you have any affection for me, George, dearest George, let me hear a word—at Orleans—let me hear. I will write—I bless you, I love you—" And she signed it

"I am

Your Ba—"

In Orléans, the mail arrived. When Robert brought "a great packet of letters," she took them, "growing paler and colder every moment." He wanted to sit by her, be with her as she read. "I had resolved never to let him do *that,* before the moment came—so, after some be-seeching, I got him to go away for ten minutes, to meet the agony alone, and with more courage *so,* according to my old habit."

The letters from her brothers, represented by George, were worse than she could have imagined. Whatever her intentions, to spare them trouble with Moulton Barrett, to spare herself a milder form of nega-tive reaction, they on their part had had the wool pulled over their eyes and they were furious. An understandable human reaction to being tricked by one's sister, though one imagines that for the sons of such a father, it was particularly painful to look foolish as a result. George, who had actually stood up for Elizabeth's Italian plans in the face of their father's objection, wrote to her "with a sword." She told her sis-ters: "To write to me as if I did not love you at all. . . . Only he wrote in excitement and in ignorance." Still, "They were very hard letters, those from dearest Papa and dearest George—To the first I had to bow my head—I do not seem to myself to have deserved that full cup." Dearest Papa believed she had "sold my soul—for *genius* . . mere ge-nius. Which I might have done when I was younger, if I had had the opportunity . . but am in no danger of doing now."

One can imagine Robert's consternation at this sword thrust of the brothers. Thank God for the sisters. "Now I will tell you—Robert who had been waiting at the door, I believe, in great anxiety about me, came in and found me just able to cry from the balm of your tender words—I put your two letters into his hands, and *he,* when he read them, said with tears in his eyes, and kissing them between the words—'I love your sisters with a deep affection—I am inexpressibly grateful to them,—It shall be the object of my life to justify this trust, as they express it here.' He said it with tears in his eyes. May God bless you—bless you!"

If they could have "seen him that day at Orleans. He laid me down on the bed and sate by me for hours, pouring out floods of tenderness and goodness, and promising to win back for me, with God's help, the affection of such of you as were angry. . . . It is strange that anyone so brilliant should love *me,*—but true and strange it is . . and it is impos-sible for me to doubt it any more. Perfectly happy therefore we should be, if I could look back on you all without this pang."

And then for some good news that had its own edge: "His family have been very kind," she told her sisters. "His father considered him

of age to judge, and never thought of interfering otherwise than of saying at the last moment, 'Give your wife a kiss for me,' this when they
parted. His sister sent me a little travelling writing desk, with a word
written, 'E.B.B. from her sister Sarianna.' Nobody was displeased at
the reserve used towards them, understanding that there were reasons
for it which did not detract from his affection for them and my respect." One can only imagine with what concern the Browning family
now waited for their own mail. Still, the kind letters from her sisters,
her in-laws, her friends, and the love of Robert Browning constituted a
stay of execution.

A letter from John Kenyon came in the same mail. It was addressed to Elizabeth, and it acknowledged receipt of "your husband's
letter yesterday." He reassured her that "the very peculiar circumstances of your case have transmuted what might have otherwise been
called 'Imprudence' into 'Prudence,' and apparent wilfulness into real
necessity." He called her "my dearest cousin," and he delighted in the
union. "If the thing had been asked of me, I should have advised it, albeit glad that I was not asked for the reason which I have given."
Whatever "reason" Kenyon gave for being glad he had not been asked
did not appear in the transcription she sent her sisters.

Other helpful and soothing notes came, too, not the least being
from Charles Trelawny Jago, the medical man who supplied her prescription for morphine, "with ever so many good wishes."

Orléans was a turning point, as Mrs. Jameson told Lady Byron.
"In short she is much comforted & certainly gaining strength in
spite of the exertion & fatigue—as yet there is not a trace of
animal spirits, tho evidently a sense of deep happiness, gratitude &
love. . . ."

But Anna Jameson was not privy to the whole story. She and Elizabeth were quite close by now: In Paris, "Robert told Mrs. Jameson to
call me Ba . . & I am to call her *Aunt Nina* which is her favorite name
for relation or friend." Though Mrs. Jameson would never agree to
"Ba," which she deplored even on Robert's lips, she was, by Orléans,
Aunt Nina. Before the letters arrived, she had assumed (as Elizabeth
hoped) that the sympathy of her friend's whole family was secure "except that of her father—& with him, the disapprobation—without de-
signing to give a reason—seems like a madness." At Orléans, Mrs.
Jameson reported that *all* letters from her family offered comfort and
that "there is no letter from her father—but she *hopes* he will relent."

Part of what Mrs. Jameson was told was accurate. Elizabeth would always hope that her father would forgive her. She could be angry at every form of political and moral tyranny she found in the world, but anger for the position her father had put her in, anger at his letter? The fantasy in her evasion was that Papa's letter actually hadn't arrived. There was still hope. That eternally hopeless hope about dearest Papa, Elizabeth Barrett Browning carried with her to her new life.

But the highlight of this honeymoon was a poet's (two poets'?) Victorian version of Niagara Falls. It occurred at Avignon, the birthplace of Petrarch's lifelong love and obsession, Laura. The trip had been difficult physically. If it were not for Aunt Nina, we would not know how difficult: "We have brought our poor invalid so far in safety," she wrote to Lady Byron on October 7. Because of Elizabeth's condition, it had been a much slower trip than Anna had originally planned. There had not been any *"increase* of indisposition—or any return of her disorder—but the suffering has been very great—not only we have had to carry her fainting from the carriage but from her extreme thinness & weakness every few hours journey has bruised her all over—till movement became almost unbearable." As always she bore bodily agony with patience: "The unselfish sweetness of the temper—the unfailing consideration for others, I did not quite expect."

Elizabeth spared Arabel her bruised body. She informed her, briefly and simply, that the journey had been trying. At Avignon, however, there was consolation. They stayed a few days and made a pilgrimage to "Vaucluse as becomes poets" to commemorate the love of Petrarch and Laura. "My spirits rose & the enjoyment of the hour spent at the sacred fountain was complete. It stands deep & still & grand against a majestic wall of rock & then falls, boils, breaks, foams over the stones, down into the channel of the . . . river winding away greenly, greenly. . . . A few little cypresses & olive trees—no other tree in sight . . . Robert said, 'Ba, are you losing your senses?' because without a word I made my way over the boiling water to a still rock in the middle of it . . but he followed me & helped me & we both sate in the spring, till Mrs Jameson was provoked to make a sketch of us."

Of course Petrarch and Laura hadn't a spaniel. "Also Flush proved his love of me by leaping (at the cost of wetting his feet & my gown) after me to the slippery stone and was repulsed three times by Robert . . . till he moaned on the dry ground to see me in such . . . danger."

And so the lovers sat on the rocks under the spray of the fountain at Vaucluse, where the Italian poet Petrarch immortalized his Laura in his love sonnets. Dante had his Beatrice, Petrarch had his Laura in poetry and in heaven. The Brownings, through extraordinary circumstances, were to have each other in their lifetimes—they would add "as well."

Aunt Nina told Elizabeth, "Well, it is the most charming thing to see you and Mr. Browning together. If two persons were to be chosen from the ends of the earth for perfect union and fitness, there could not be a greater congruity than between you two." To Lady Byron she wrote, "he is on all the common things of this life the most impractical of men—the most uncalculating—rather,—in short the worst *manager* I ever met with—*she*—in her present state—& from her long seclusion almost helpless—now only conceive the menage that is likely to ensue & WITHOUT FAULT on either side!—" From Pisa on October 15, after their long, arduous trip, the poor woman sounded like an overburdened mother-in-law.

But almost immediately, the magic of Italy, the needed distance it provided between her old and new lives, between her father and her husband, granted the poet what she had predicted she would need to feel safe. Anna Jameson scarcely finished lamenting the utter greenness of the newlyweds when she found fit to crosswrite her postscript, squeezing it into the last letter of the series of five she wrote to Lady Byron on the subject. "I have just seen EB—looking wonderfully well—considering all the fatigue undergone—under her husband's influence and mine she is leaving off those medicines on which she existed, ether, morphine, & I am full of hope for her."

"The Runaway Slave"

Settled in Pisa finally, Browning wrote to his new sisters, Arabel and Henrietta: "every day and hour reveals more and more to me the divine goodness and infinite tenderness of her heart;—while that wonderful mind of hers, with its inexhaustible affluence and power, continues unceasingly to impress me. . . . It is nothing to me that my whole life shall be devoted to such a woman,—its only happiness will consist in such a devotion." If their brothers could see her now, "so changed as to be hardly recognizable, and with a fair prospect of life and enjoyment for many years to come . . they could *not* be very angry I am sure!"

Elizabeth wrote Julia Martin: "Every day I am out walking while the golden oranges look at me over the walls, and when I am tired Robert and I sit down on a stone to watch the lizards. We have been to your seashore too. . . . Also we have driven up to the foot of the mountains, . . . and we have seen the pine woods and met the camels laden with faggots all in a line. So now ask me again if I enjoy my liberty as you expect. My head goes round sometimes, that is all. I never was happy before in my life."

Except for visits from Anna Jameson and Gerardine, who left Pisa for Rome in early November, and for an occasional talk with the Italian Professor Ferucci, who Jameson had introduced them to, they saw nobody. Elizabeth told her sisters she had many more visitors in her room on Wimpole Street. The two lovers had a daily, uninterrupted tête-à-tête. They ate like poets: "We have our dinner from the Trattoria at two, and can dine our favorite way on thrushes and chianti with miraculous cheapness, and no trouble, no cook, no kitchen. . . . It is a continental fashion which we never cease commending. Then at six we have coffee, and rolls of milk, made of milk, I mean, and at nine our supper . . . of roast chestnuts and grapes."

Robert spoke of their uninterrupted time together as a test of true love, and Elizabeth remarked as well on their ability to get on so well together. Robert, who had seen much of the world, now wanted only to be by her side. She had to convince him to take his own vigorous daily walk by himself. And he had vowed never to go where she could not. Elizabeth was the one more willing to meet the world, and she convinced him finally to take a subscription to "a better library than the purely Italian one," even though economy was a keynote to their plans. The access to more continental literature was worth the price, not to mention the bonus—a daily French newspaper, Le Siècle. Now, when they sat down to their daily coffee, which Elizabeth poured "(I pour out the coffee now . . it is my only 'active duty' I think—that and to keep Flush in sight, to prevent his barking)," they read. "We never see a creature, and to talk for four and twenty hours together, would be rather exhausting—and one is not always in a humour for writing prose or rhyme."

Pisa was—for all its literary associations, and its tower and duomo —dull. In one sense the couple lauded the dullness, as they were living on their love. In another sense, the contemporary Italy they were viewing was one that had no vitality. They were in the land of what-had-been. There seemed to be no modern thinking: The modern writers were hackneyed. Professor Ferucci visited and praised a work by Alessandro Manzoni's son-in-law. Robert, who had been reading the novel out loud to Elizabeth, among mutual yawns and sighs, tried to be polite. Elizabeth came right out against its banality: "I not being so humane."

They had taken a six-month lease on what Robert called a pile of rooms—he counted some forty-seven doors and windows—at the front of a palazzo, Collegio di Ferdinando. "We sit there alone in mornings and evenings, seeing nobody in this strange silent old city." What might sound like a lament was actually an exultation. Still, Elizabeth wished they had taken a shorter lease so that they could travel sooner.

At first everything in Pisa seemed inexpensive by British standards. They had no idea that their way of taking a lease and Wilson's way of shopping was causing an avalanche of rumor. All the landlords and greengrocers in Pisa assumed the Brownings were wealthy. What else would explain why they accepted whatever price they were quoted and did not bargain? Landlords were so jealous of the padrone of Collegio di Ferdinando that they bragged they, too, could have rented to the English couple if their own integrity hadn't demanded they honor previous commitments. No wonder their landlord sent the poets presents. How innocent Elizabeth still was in December in a letter to Mary Mitford: "The 'padrone' in this house, sent us in as a gift (in gracious recognition, perhaps of our lawful paying of bills) an immense dish of oranges." So much for absorbing the customs of the country and not being seen as typical British travelers.

Elizabeth had said she needed distance from London to flourish—and flourish she did. Robert wrote that she had filled out remarkably. Mrs. Jameson told her, "You are not *improved*, you are *transformed*." She was taking less morphine than she had on her difficult voyage from Wimpole Street—and the Italian druggist, seeing Mr. Jago's prescription, cut it down. It seemed he at least was not cheating the British: "He really believes *his* morphine to be so superior to what we could get in England that he felt himself bound to diminish the quantity." By early February, "Ba sleeps admirably—and is steadily diminishing the doses of morphine, quite as much as is prudent." By the first week of March, "I gradually diminish to seventeen days for twenty-two doses which I used to take in eight days."

Home thoughts continued to bring bittersweet memories, and during the early part of the honeymoon, Elizabeth and Robert were still explaining their actions by mail. "Am I bitter? The feeling . . . passes while I write it out." And write it out Elizabeth did to many of her correspondents. In this letter to Julia Martin she confided, "Assuredly, . . . however, my case is not to be classed with other cases—what happened to me could not have happened, perhaps, with any other family in England." Were there many other families in England (in the world?) in which the father would not allow the marriage of any of his adult children?

Both Robert and Elizabeth attempted to bridge the rift with the brothers. The sisters acted as intermediaries. Robert wrote to them of how he believed Elizabeth's life was at risk at Wimpole Street. If, after the brothers had had the time to think things through, they "can honestly come to the opinion that, by any of the ordinary methods applicable to any other case, I could have effected the same result," he would "express all the sorrow they can desire." The current winter in England was as brutal as the last winter had been mild, a fact both the Brownings repeated. Was it lost on the brothers that this might have been the London winter she would not have survived? Elizabeth wondered if it mattered as little to them as to her father that she was alive and happy.

At the beginning of the new year, 1847, Elizabeth dared not hope her brothers would accept "the peace offering I sent them.—I suppose they mean to salute me with the point of the sword for the rest of my life." What they were attempting to do was reconcile with her while snubbing Browning. She told Henrietta that they must "have better taste than to dream of such an impossible thing." She asked about all of them: "Does Alfred get on in the railroad? Has Occy made any good drawings lately? Did George go to Cambridge? How is the Law, too, with . . . Sette? And tell me of Henry. As to dear Stormie, I do trust that he has other plans than for that dreadful Jamaica." She loved them all dearly, better than they loved her, or this rupture would not be continuing. Just that morning she and Robert were talking over breakfast "of O'Connell and the Irish," and she described Stormie's enthusiasm for both:

"He is so generous and tenderhearted, that he naturally takes the part of every party or person attacked by others—He defends everyone who is *accused*."

Robert looked at her, and said, "Everyone, except *you*."

At the end of February, Elizabeth took her stand. The brothers "must choose," she wrote to Arabel, "& if they do not love me enough to accept *mine* with *me*, why they may cast me off at their pleasure. I cannot help it. I say it in sorrow more than in any anger." But anger showed. "I should not have acted to them as they have acted to me."

She would never admit to what she called a formula for kindness "which insultingly excludes the one who has given up his life to me with the very perfection of tenderness! He who from first to last never for a moment failed to me." They wanted her "to stand aside from *him* as if he *had* failed: No!—As my *husband* he has claims on the respect of those who also love me—but as *Robert Browning* [double underline], he has stronger claims on *me* than even the word 'husband' suggests. . . . If I sinned against him *so,* I should scorn myself— . . . Tell dear George that I dearly love him . . better than he ever loved me, . . but that I do not answer his letter for these reasons."

Robert tried to convince her to accept her brothers' terms. He told her, "It is enough for me, darling, that *you* understand me . . that *you* know my heart & my motives." She answered by asking him what he would do if his family tried to blot her "out of the world after that fashion." Could he bear it?

His answer was simply astonishment. "*He! his* family! to *me!*"

In this letter to Arabel she concluded quite strongly, "So then he was able to observe that it was my affair & concerned my own feelings & that he had no right to interfer. And in fact it is simply my affair. My brothers confer no honour on my husband by their notice, nor inflict any injury by their neglect—the injury is *mine* . . to my feelings . . my affections—the blow falls *there.* This is all, I think, that is necessary to say."

There was only one person with whom she would reconcile singularly, her father. "If he said 'I will write you . . I will see you . . your husband's name never being named between us' . . I should think it my duty to accept under any condition . . any alms of kindness from him—He is my father. I would kiss his hands & feet at any moment. Also he has peculiarities, which I deeply pity the tendencies of, & which, where it is possible, should be dealt with tenderly." Her father's tendencies may underlie the one poem she wrote in Pisa.

"THE RUNAWAY SLAVE AT PILGRIM'S POINT" was a peculiar poem to write on one's honeymoon. Elizabeth recorded that the Americans had asked her for an abolitionist poem. But why write it then? There was a great passion in this poem, an undercurrent of psychological penetration of the nature of racism that was so sharp and clear that one wonders, in the happy honeymoon in that dull town of Pisa, what made it so relevant, so near? The impetus of *Sonnets from the Portuguese* was the love of Robert Browning, which made the poet confront life, not death. What was the impetus of her only other poem of this period?

"I'm not mad: I am black," cried the female slave who narrated "The Runaway Slave at Pilgrim's Point." That explanation of her condition and her action could echo a reggae or rap lyric or suit the psychology of the disenfranchised today. "Mad and Black at Pilgrim's Point" was the original title. It has been customary to dismiss this powerful antislavery poem, just as it has been customary to assume Elizabeth Barrett Browning was herself sort of a runaway slave finding her own freedom. Although Robert Browning spoke of Moulton Barrett's treating his children as chattel, and the ever-present Surtees Cook once had the gumption to ask his future father-in-law if he considered his children his slaves, Elizabeth, who called herself a "prisoner" in terms of her former life, would never consider herself a "slave." For her that would be as immoral as it was cowardly. She was a Christian woman, in the broadest sense, a Protestant who had absolute belief in the freedom of will. Elizabeth Barrett Browning, away from Wimpole Street and with a new last name, was writing about slavery—the psychological state of the real thing.

The locale of "The Runaway Slave" seemed as much British Jamaica as the American South. The slave remembered:

> *In the sunny ground between the canes,*
>   *He said "I love you" as he passed;*
> *When the shingle-roof rang sharp with the rains,*
>   *I heard how he vowed it fast:*
> *While others shook he smiled in the hut,*
> *As he carved me a bowl of the cocoa-nut*
>   *Through the roar of the hurricanes.*

This Caribbean echoing was not surprising in a poem by the great-granddaughter of Edward of Cinnamon Hill. In fact, the poem has been seen as based on a true story first told to Elizabeth as a child by a prominent relative who lived both in England and in Jamaica, her illegitimate cousin Richard Barrett. But Richard Barrett, whom she disliked, was a staunch supporter of slavery, and the tale he wrote down for her was about a "bad" runaway African slave in Jamaica who was killed by the "good" Creole slave who defended his master's plantain. This was a far cry from the poem she wrote on her honeymoon.

Everything the Barretts owned, and what they had to give up, came from sugarcane and was based on the slave trade, the same West African slave trading on which the system in the United States was based. It was only Elizabeth, not her father, who was pleased when slavery was abolished in 1833, and he was no longer a slaveholder in absentia. The importation of slaves into Jamaica was illegal after 1809, which meant slaves were systematically bred on the plantations up until 1833. The morality of the law was perverted by its loophole. The four thousand pounds left her by her adoring Uncle Samuel came from the estates that he had returned to Jamaica to manage, and which were owned by him and her father. The four thousand pounds Elizabeth's namesake and grandmother left her favorite grandchild came from the profits of the enormous holdings of *her* father, Edward of Cinnamon Hill.

Jamaican roots were part of the everyday life of this British poet who drank not tea but good strong coffee. At the time of the poem she was worried that the oldest remaining brother, Stormie, might be going off to that dreadful place to oversee the family interests. Slavery was by then illegal, but the system it bred was not overcome in a decade. How close the family was to Jamaica was seen as the poet decided what to put into the newspaper announcement of her secret marriage. In describing her father, "You might put in the newspaper . . of Wimpole Street & Jamaica, or, . . & Cinnamon Hill, Jamaica." For so many years the myth of the family has been based on *The Barretts of Wimpole Street,* but Edward, as well as all of his sons, had two addresses.

"The Runaway Slave" had to be written by someone who had a true feeling for the darkest underside of the system, by someone like Elizabeth, who from the earliest age was exposed to it not only through tales and letters but through members of her household. There were intimate accounts from dear Bro, who would have been sent there against his will once more if he hadn't stayed with her at Torquay. She was saving him from that fate when the brother sent to Jamaica, Sam, died. Sam was the hard-drinking son who, on an earlier trip to the family's estates, had upset the missionary Reverend Hope Waddell and had corrupted at least one Christian black woman with trinkets, to the disgust of the woman's father and the pastor. Sam repented of his sins, which seemingly were many, before his death, witnessed by Reverend Waddell. And Sam requested that the news of this deathbed repentance be sent by the pastor to his father and his dear sister. All of this occurred a short time before Bro drowned.

There was Elizabeth's grandmother's companion—not her servant, her lifelong companion, Mary Trepsack—Treppy or Trippy, as she was called. Treppy, the daughter of a British planter and a Negro slave, was the ward of Edward of Cinnamon Hill's brother Samuel, who died in 1782. In his will, Samuel bought the freedom of his African concubine, Magekan, and her issue. His ward, Treppy, the main concern of his will, went on to Cinnamon Hill, where she was adopted by Edward himself. Treppy accompanied Edward's daughter, the first Elizabeth

EDWARD BARRETT
(1734–98). *Miniature of
EBB's great-grandfather by
John Barry, 1791. Edward of
Cinnamon Hill was one of the
wealthiest land and slave
owners in Jamaica in the
eighteenth century. EBB's
grandmother and namesake; her
father, Edward Barrett Moulton
Barrett; and her uncle Samuel
were his legitimate heirs.*

SAMUEL BARRETT MOULTON BARRETT (1787–1837). *EBB described him
after his death as "My beloved uncle . . . for many years a member of the English
House of Commons . . . & at one time himself a man of large fortune. . . . Oh
to look back & think! What he might have been. . . . A bright, gifted being!"
Samuel died in Jamaica, where he was sent to supervise the family estates
while his brother, Edward, conducted business from London.*

MARY TREPSACK, "TRIPPY" or "TREPPY" (1768?–1857). *The daughter of a
planter and a female slave, she became the ward of Edward of Cinnamon Hill.
She came to England with her lifelong companion, EBB's grandmother, and
was treated as family by four generations of Barretts. Late in life Mary
Trepsack suffered from dementia.*

Barrett Moulton Barrett, to England and survived her by twenty-seven years. She was an intimate of the Barrett household until she died in 1857. After her marriage, Elizabeth Barrett Browning wrote to her sisters in letters sent in care of Miss Trepsack. Treppy, who the poet said was as proud of being a Creole as if she were a Roman, knew and was treated as family by four generations of Barretts. She was a lively woman, full of the gossip and tales of that benevolent slavemaster Edward and of the old Barrett and Moulton involvement in the slave trade.

In the poem, the runaway slave's love was dragged away from her by white men.

> *We had no claim to love and bliss,*
> *What marvel if each went to wrack?*
> *They wrung my cold hands out of his,*
> *They dragged him—where?*

Well, "wrong, followed by a deeper wrong!" The white men raped her. And she gave birth to a child with very white skin. It is the treatment of this mulatto child that haunts the imagination, and reflects back on the impetus of the poem.

> *My own, own child! I could not bear*
> *To look in his face, it was so white.*

The black slave could not help herself. Every time she looked at the white face of her own dear child, she looked into the hated face of the master's race. Placing a kerchief over his face, she suffocated him. He moaned and struggled:

> *For the white child wanted his liberty—*
> *Ha, ha! he wanted the master-right.*

She was crazed by her action, kept her dead child by her breast, and was unable to look at his fair skin without seeing the white man. The awful irony:

> *For hark! I will tell you low, low,*
> *I am black, you see,—*
> *And the babe who lay on my bosom so,*
> *Was far too white, too white for me.*

Quite an abolitionist poem, this one that dealt with the rape of black women and the birth of mulatto children. After the runaway slave finally buried the child under a grove of mango trees, she went through forests until she got to Pilgrim's Point in New England, which might as well have been Montego Bay in Jamaica.

John Kenyon once said that all Jamaican planters were cousins. The brothers who opposed their sister's marriage on account of Browning's lack of funds must have known through their own circle, and from Kenyon directly, why Robert's father wasn't wealthy. Robert's father, another heir to colonial wealth, was sent to his mother's St. Kitts plantation by his father. The system was deplorable to Robert Browning, Senior, and he got in trouble when he was caught teaching a black to read. When he returned to England, he renounced his inheritance, to the eternal displeasure of his father. He might not have been a bank clerk had he been able to abide slavery. Of course, he wouldn't have been as rich as the Barretts either, but his money would have come from colonial sources.

IT HAS BEEN relatively easy to place Moulton Barrett, the poet's father, on the furthest side of the Victorian view of the patriarch as the voice of God in the family. Yet a man who had sired twelve children of a desirable wife, and then refused permission for these adult children, male or female, to pursue romantic attachment and marriage was obviously an enigma in his own time.

Since the opening of *The Barretts of Wimpole Street, A Comedy,* critics have been content to shadowbox the image of the despotic father as he appeared in the hit Broadway play. After the stage character was debunked, contemporary critics even assumed what Elizabeth Barrett and her siblings discounted as a family joke: that had the right gentleman or lady, of the right class and connection, come along, the father might have, perhaps, permitted a courtship. Moulton Barrett has been seen as a wealthy country gentleman, a man rich enough to build a gingerbread palace on almost five hundred acres near the Malvern Hills but who, after his grandfather's will was contested, lost considerable money and eventually had to sell Hope End; a man who never really got over that turn of fortune, though, as Elizabeth said, he faced adversity with stoicism and strength. Certainly this was part of the story: the human seen structured and controlled through the prism of time; a man of means, a country gentleman, a believing Christian, the father of

EDWARD BARRETT MOULTON BARRETT AS A YOUNG MAN AND MARY
GRAHAM-CLARKE. *Miniatures of EBB's parents before their marriage.
They had known each other since childhood.*

MAP OF JAMAICA. *St. James Parish, which included Montego Bay and
Falmouth, was the seat of Edward Barrett's estates, slaves, and fortune.*

twelve; his peculiarity aside, a Victorian gentleman, reflecting an age heralded in by Queen Victoria, when family values and domestic life reigned supreme. At the backdrop, Western civilization as clear-cut as our literary tastes, as free from world history as our imaginations.

Yet Moulton Barrett's grandfather, Edward of Cinnamon Hill, was one of the greatest plantation owners of Jamaica. As late as the year in which the slaves ended a period of apprenticeship and in reality gained freedom, 1838, the Barretts still owned 31,000 acres. The legend that in the past Robert Browning's great-grandparents had made boots for the Barretts in Jamaica has truth to it, but only if we compare the means of the wealthy house of the Tittles, who became wainwrights and landowners in the colonies, to the extraordinary wealth of Edward Barrett, who veritably owned the Northside of Jamaica—including Barrett Town—and whose fortune from the exportation of sugar and rum was made on the backs of close to ten thousand slaves.

Life in Jamaica among the colonists had since the eighteenth century more affinity to America's wild, wild West than to the stately drawing rooms of England. Making money was the name of the game, and the pretensions of respectability and sexual restraint were left at home. The "gold rush" was slavery. Slaves were bought in West Africa for four pounds a head and sold in Jamaica at eighteen pounds. The "gilt-edged" security you left your child in Jamaica was a nubile female slave. Rum became demon for colonial women as well as men, and opium was widely used in the eighteenth century among the wives of the planters, who often lived in proximity or in the same house as their husbands' African mistresses. Many of these wives were involved in the running of the plantation and/or business, and became rich in their own right after their husbands' deaths. "Marry and bury" was the way it was phrased, and often "marry and bury" again.

Jeannette Marks traced this colonial culture in her tome *The Family of the Barretts* in a style as circuitous as the subject matter was explosive. She went to Jamaica in the 1930s, stayed with members of the Moulton-Barrett family, and examined state records and wills, deactivating land mines inherent in the information by the vagueness and open-endedness of her prose style. Her information was exact, but often she seemed to be mulling it over under her breath. It was clear to her that beyond the sinister aspects of the white male's sexual dominion over the African slave woman, these beautiful black women who came from a culture that was not sexually repressed often won the hearts of the colonial men. The colonists preferred them to their English wives. The study is yet to be made of the contribution these women still in chains made to the lives and destinies of these British families and to British culture. Marks, seeing through the eyes of her time, emphasized the cleanliness of the women, their gleaming white teeth, the way they bathed daily and then rolled in the sand before rinsing off. Their diet was mainly vegetarian, their habits close to nature. And many of them saw a way for a better future for their children sired by their masters rather than their slave men. Certainly Elissa Peters's children were given freedom because of her union with Colonel George Goodin Barrett, a son of Edward of Cinnamon Hill.

It was not unusual for the colonial men to send their mulatto and quadroon children back to England to be educated along with their legitimate sons and daughters. But George Goodin Barrett went further. He provided for his children's education in England and stipulated that after that education he hoped they would not return to Jamaica but settle in a country where racism would not hinder their development. (Many settled in France.) On October 7, 1795, close to his early death, he freed—manumitted—Elissa Peters and her issue:

"I George Goodin Barrett Esquire . . . in consideration of the long and faithfull Services of my Housekeeper Eliza alias Elissa Peters . . . manumit herself, her Issue and Offspring and make the same free from all servitude, whatever to me, my Heirs and Exors for ever from the date hereof." That his father, Edward of Cinnamon Hill, accepted the relationship between George Goodin and Elissa Peters was inherent in his earlier having released his claim on his slave Elissa Peters to his son.

George Goodin's brother Samuel Barrett had four illegitimate white children with his cousin Elizabeth Barrett Waite Williams. She was and always would be held in respect by the Barretts, perhaps because she was a woman of wealth in Jamaica. She had previously married and buried Martyn Williams. During his marriage, Martyn Williams had eight mulatto children by Eleanor Williams, "a free negro woman," and he petitioned the House of Assembly for their rights and privileges. What a complicated web of interracial family affairs existed in Jamaica.

An integral part of the poet Elizabeth Barrett Browning's early life was the fact that her own father suffered emotionally and financially when the will of his grandfather Edward of Cinnamon Hill was contested during the first quarter of the nineteenth century. What has never been emphasized is that all of the contesters were illegitimate, and what has never been mentioned is that six of them early on were quadroon. From the illegitimate Caucasian branch of the family, Richard Barrett led the legal battles; Thomas Peters represented the quadroon.

Edward of Cinnamon Hill had done his best to avoid this eventuality. He had spent more than four years creating his will after the last of his sons, George Goodin and Samuel, had died. He was generous to Samuel's illegitimate sons, though he never referred to them as his grandchildren. He left his fortune to his surviving child, his daughter Elizabeth Barrett Moulton, and to his legitimate grandchildren Edward (the poet's father), Samuel (her uncle), and Sarah (who died young).

Edward of Cinnamon Hill had a stipulation in his legacy. It was that his daughter Elizabeth Barrett Moulton and her children add another Barrett to their last name. In generation after generation of Elizabeth Barretts, his daughter became the first Elizabeth Barrett Moulton Barrett. Her husband, the poet's grandfather Charles Moulton, would have to agree to this change, and he did. By 1789, seven years after she married Charles, her marriage had failed. Charles Moulton became a lieutenant of the Trelawny Militia around that time. Sixteen years later he was probably a slave merchant in New York. The will of Edward of Cinnamon Hill alluded time and time again that his daughter's inheritance was hers, not her husband's, and that she and her children were living and could continue to live on her father's estates "at all times whilst she lives separate and apart from her husband or at any time during widowhood."

Edward Barrett Moulton Barrett, the poet's father, seemed never to have had more than a biological father. One wonders how he would have felt with Moulton as his last name, particularly since his father continued to procreate and to give his children familiar Barrett Christian names. In England, in the county of Cambridge, Frances Petite bore Charles Moulton two children, named Henrietta and Charles Washington. They were granted use of the Moulton name before Charles left England and returned to Jamaica. In Middlesex, he had another mistress, Louisa Cohen of Portland Road, who bore him two sons, William and Samuel. This family lived eight miles north of Richmond, Yorkshire, where Edward's mother, the first Elizabeth Barrett Moulton Barrett, lived with Mary Trepsack, "Treppy."

By the 1810s, Charles settled down, purchased Wakefield Jamaica, and lived with Jane Clark of St. Ann, "a free woman of color who bore him a son, James Moulton." As Jeannette Marks succinctly phrased it in her study of the Jamaican Barretts, "The vital records for the living Charles Moulton continue, many years after the Barretts were content to have it understood he was dead." He did die in Jamaica in July 1819, and Charles John, "Stormie," because he bore the same Christian name as his grandfather Charles, was awarded a thousand pounds when he reached maturity on December 21, 1835.

Edward Barrett Moulton Barrett, the poet's father, was born in 1785, the second child and first son of Elizabeth Barrett and Charles Moulton. He enjoyed a privileged early childhood as the grandson of a man of great wealth in the Caribbean. In her book on Elizabeth Barrett Browning, Margaret Forster described the beauty of Cinnamon Hill. Later owned by Johnny Cash, "It stood, and still stands, halfway up a hillside rising above the coastal plain stretching from Montego Bay to Saltmarsh Bay. Surrounded by trees, it has even thicker woods and higher hills behind, and in front, far off, the long rollers of the Caribbean break in a thin white line on the coral reefs. . . . In Edward's day there was an English lawn lovingly maintained in front of the house and a garden in which English lilacs mixed with the spice trees. . . ." Still, she concluded, "No child, however privileged or protected, could escape knowing about the savageries of slavery. The sugar cane, its green swathes forever rustling in the trade wind breezes, was harvested at the cost of floggings and brutal suppression. Thirty-nine lashes of a thick cattle whip was the standard punishment for any misdemeanour and spiked dog collars could be forced onto slaves who had tried to escape. More haunting than any of the bird songs was the long, mournful, eerie blast on the conch shell that signified the hunt for an escaped negro. Edward, leaving this life at the age of seven, had memories which were impressionistic, fragmented, heavily influenced by his own immature perceptions."

As was normal for a child of colonial wealth, Moulton Barrett was separated from his mother and sent to England for his education, enduring the two-month boat trip at the age of seven along with his siblings, Sam and Sarah. (Sarah was the subject of Thomas Lawrence's famous portrait of the child, *Pinkie*.) Edward sent his mother a souvenir of that trip—his tear-stained glove, a story that would one day impress his daughter Elizabeth. (The small glove of good linen is today in the Berg Collection in the New York Public Library.) Her own mother, Mary Moulton Barrett, gave it to the future poet because she "expressed a wish to possess this glove." And Mary went on to explain: "Papa when on board the ship *Elizabeth* sailing for England in the year 1792 gave this glove, with his tears, to Doctor Archer, with strict charges to deliver it unto Betsey's [his mother's] own hands."

Arriving in England the children must have felt as dismal as the weather, as well as confused by a society so completely antithetical to the West Indies they had known. Moulton Barrett, the future country gentleman, did not adapt readily to this life. Sent to Harrow, he soon withdrew. According to Robert Browning, the reason was that he fagged for a boy who beat him for burning toast. This was a traumatic experience for him. What must it have been like for one raised in utmost luxury at Cinnamon Hill, the young master of his own slaves, the heir to incredible wealth, to face the cold halls of Harrow, and to find himself a slave, a fag, whipped if he disobeyed an upperclassman. His mother had arrived in England by then and, according to Jeannette Marks, had withdrawn him to be educated at home. Edward went on to Trinity College in Cambridge in 1801 but didn't take a degree.

During all this time in England he spent holidays at the home of wealthy business associates of his grandfather, the Graham-Clarkes. John Graham-Clarke was at the time the guardian of Thomas Peters and the other quadroon children of George Goodin Barrett. This dead uncle of Moulton Barrett's was the first in any known will to leave property to such children. Others bought their children's freedom and stopped there. George Goodin had made his quadroon son Thomas, as well as his father, Edward of Cinnamon Hill, executor of his will. Moulton Barrett could not have frequented the Graham-Clarkes' as much as he did without being constantly reminded of the mixed blood of his first cousins.

By the time he was nineteen, he wished to marry the Graham-Clarkes' oldest daughter, Mary, who was twenty-four. They had known each other for years. He was so close to the Graham-Clarke household that he seemed in spirit if not in blood to be continuing a Barrett propensity to mate within the family. His guardian, James Scarlett, at first thought him too young, but when he met Mary he was charmed and considered Edward quite lucky. In marriage and within the circle of his own wife and children, Moulton Barrett came into his own, de-

JOHN GRAHAM-CLARKE
(1736–1818) CA. 1795.
EBB's maternal grand-
father, who was a business-
man and merchant, had
industrial interests, plant-
ations in Jamaica, and
trading ships in the West
Indies. From his first wife
he inherited a brewery. He
had nine children by his
second wife, the oldest of
whom, Mary, married
EBB's father.

ARABELLA GRAHAM-
CLARKE (1760?–1827)
CA. 1785. *EBB's maternal*
grandmother and John
Graham-Clarke's younger
second wife.

veloping into the country gentleman and patriarch that has come down to us.

Why didn't Edward Barrett Moulton Barrett want his children to marry? One reason given has been that he desired to keep his children at home and under his control. This was certainly true. Another has been that he had an unease about his children's sexuality. A father who insists on his daughters' purity is not an unfamiliar type. One who insists that his sons not marry is a unique type. If it were abstinence the father required of the sons, Jamaica was hardly the place to send them on business for months or years at a time. Beautiful and compliant women were for the asking, not to mention the curse of generations of proper planters, men and women, demon rum—and opium. The shift from Wimpole Street to Cinnamon Hill, from the harsh Atlantic to the soft trade winds of the Caribbean, was sybaritic. His hard-drinking son Sam had not escaped the temptations open to him in a transplanted African culture just loosened from the bonds of slavery. He died there. Edward knew well what Jamaica implied to the white men of his class. So did his eldest daughter. At the time of her honeymoon she feared Stormie's departure. Wasn't there another career he could undertake? If it was his sons' virginity the father demanded, if that was what constituted what Elizabeth called his one area of peculiarity, he certainly insisted they travel to the wrong place.

The absolute consequence of not allowing your children to marry is having no legitimate grandchildren, no legal heirs. Eleven children reached adulthood. Had each had half the number of children his or her parents bore, there'd be the possibility of sixty-six grandchildren. It seems that what Edward did not want to do was to carry on the Moulton Barrett line. When Bro, the first son, was born, the Negroes in Jamaica were given a holiday; when Henrietta was born, Treppy reported back to Elizabeth Barrett Waite Williams that the family was grieved at the birth of another girl. The male line, as Jeannette Marks pointed out, was important enough to be counted: Septimus (Sette), Octavius (Occy)—eight Barrett sons. This was not, early on, a line bent on extinction. What we have by the time the children were adults is the singularly peculiar fact that a Victorian father and the surviving heir of Edward of Cinnamon Hill not only wished his daughters to be spinsters, but wished all of his sons to remain bachelors. He did not want them to have, in terms of his grandfather's will, legitimate heirs "out of their own bodies."

Why? Moulton Barrett might very well have either learned after his children were born or become increasingly concerned with the possibility that he had mixed blood. After his wife died in 1828, and his beloved mother soon after, did Treppy have more tales to tell? Certainly, during the long years of the contested will, Edward was brought in daily reminders of the mixed blood in the Barrett line, the underside of the system that brought him wealth. Yet it was the lineage of his father, Charles Moulton, that affected his own.

Jeannette Marks concluded that although there was some possibility of African blood in Robert Browning's line, there was no official documentation that Charles Moulton, Edward's father, Elizabeth's grandfather, had black blood. She tells us that Elizabeth's inclusion among the writers who have such blood, in *What the Negro Thinks* (1929) by Robert Russa Moton, for example, was erroneous. Then she quotes a section from the love letters, one that has been there to read since the end of the nineteenth century. Where is the scholar or historian or biographer who has not read these words—including this writer. Jeannette Marks quotes them in order to overlook them once more, but what they say is quite clear. In the passage, Elizabeth Barrett tells her future husband what he must know. He must know what's in a name. She called herself Elizabeth Barrett Barrett, often signed her letters EBB. The oldest legitimate grandchild of Charles Moulton did not use "Moulton."

"My true initials are E.B.M.B.—my long name, as opposed to my short one, being: . . Elizabeth Barrett Moulton Barrett!—there's a full length to take away one's breath!—Christian name . . Elizabeth Barrett:—surname, Moulton Barrett. So long it is, that to make it portable, I fell into the habit of doubling it up & packing it closely, . . & of forgetting that I was a *Moulton,* altogether. One might well write the alphabet as all four initials. Yet our family-name is *Moulton Barrett,* & my brothers reproach me sometimes for sacrificing the governorship of an old town in Norfolk with a little honorable verdigris from the Heralds' Office—As if I cared for the *Retrospective Review!* Nevertheless it is true that I would give ten towns in Norfolk (if I had them) to own some purer lineage than that of the blood of the slave!—Cursed we are from generation to generation!"

The poet herself believed she had African blood through her grandfather Charles Moulton. And she linked that fact to being "cursed from generation to generation," a sentiment of her father's.

Rather than being her grandfather's theoretical heir, she would prefer "to own some purer lineage than that of the blood of the slave!"

Jeannette Marks described the Creoles of mixed blood as often particularly attractive, unusually intelligent, and of a high nervous susceptibility. The irregularity of Elizabeth Barrett's features, seen clearly in verbal and photographic pictures, is notable—what she herself called her lack of nose, her overgenerous mouth. One can consider the effect of the face, dominated by those deep, searching eyes, as quite exotic. There was nothing in her features to mitigate her own belief in her African blood. One doesn't see in portraits the dark complexion she and others often described, a complexion she had in common with her father. "I am 'little and black,' " she told Haydon. Anne Thackeray wrote, "She is very small, she is brown . . ." Thomas Chase described her "dark complexioned face" compared to Robert's "rather dark complexion." She was not proud of this lineage "of the blood of the slave." She was much too close to its ramifications, both in moral and in family matters. Yet in the high pitch of her creative intelligence and her nervous susceptibilities, she may have left the world a body of poetry that to some extent merged disparate cultures into a unique and increasingly radical voice.

The impetus for "The Runaway Slave," the passion behind it, was a particular evil of slavery. The poem exposed the rapes and mixed blood that resulted, and the psychotic disorientation this could engender. Had Elizabeth, with the eerie closeness of an oldest daughter to a once-devoted father, "written out" her father's deepest, most unspoken fear? Was there, in her poor father's peculiar imagination and in his Christian conscience, the possibility that among his grandchildren he might someday be faced with one who was *not* of the slave master's race? Was he suffocating that dark-skinned grandchild by not allowing his children the slightest romantic interest?

He had married at nineteen, surrounded by his Creole connections, and begun his family in a mansion of his own imagination at a time when his wealth made his world impenetrable. This was before he understood the dangers of the ongoing lawsuit and while his mother, the Graham-Clarkes, James Scarlett, and perhaps Treppy had some influence over him. As he reached middle age, did he then try, in his accustomed secretive way, to control what he would consider the sins of his own father from working themselves out on another generation?

RICHARD BARRETT
(1789–1839). *Edward
Barrett Moulton Barrett's
illegitimate first cousin,
upholder of slavery, and
three-time Speaker of the
House of Assembly in
Jamaica. He died suddenly,
perhaps murdered, in the
newly emancipated Jamaica
of 1839.* "A man of talent
& violence & some malice,
who did what he could, at
one time, to trample poor
Papa down," EBB *wrote of
him on January 12, 1842.*
"He was *a handsome man
. . after a fashion. . . . Still
it was a face that I, as a
child, did not care to look
upon.*"

By the 1830s, Moulton Barrett's world was crumbling. The out-
lawing of slavery was the death knell to his way of life. In 1833 his
cousin Richard Barrett, the prominent Jamaican assemblyman, once
the nemesis of the lawsuits, was sent to England to speak against
emancipation at *A general Meeting of Planters, Merchants, and others Interested in the West-India Colonies,* assembled at the Thatched-House Tav-
ern on May 18, 1833. Jeannette Marks considered his speech "one of
phenomenal ability." But toward what end? He told his audience, "I
was under the galley at the House of Commons when Mr Stanley made
his speech which introduced his resolution for Emancipation." That
was four days before, on May 14. Stanley's speech "proceeded from one
topic or reproach to another; holding up the Colonists to universal
odium." It was "as if the act of spoilation he contemplated was not sufficiently dreadful, at the instant that he proposed his project to plun-
der us of our property, he consigned our name to everlasting infamy.
Hundreds of thousands of petitioners, and the multitude of election-
eering pledges, had not done enough to predicate our cause; but the

Right Honourable Secretary must crown our injuries by borrowing the errors, the prejudices, and the abuse of the petitioners." The evil of slavery was being blamed not on England itself but on the Creole planters.

There was little sympathy for Richard Barrett's view that "There is not a peasant in the world that walks abroad with a more contented countenance and a more confident bearing than the Colonial Slave." But even this prominent Jamaican politician had moments of doubt:

"It must be confessed that the requisition of the Colonial Minister to discontinue the flogging of women has not been obeyed. . . . This part of Mr Stanley's speech was received with loud applause. . . . I own that for a moment I felt ashamed that I was a Colonist. I was restored to my self-esteem by recalling that these Gentlemen of the House of Commons probably thought only of the delicate and accomplished wives and daughters of the higher ranks, or the retiring modest of the middle orders, and the virtuous and chaste female of the lower; for I remember that within a very few years whipping was the common punishment of women confined [to prison]. . . . I do not (God forbid that I should!) vindicate the corporal punishment of women; but of this I am convinced, that the women of Jamaica, and I do not mean to deny them a sense of shame, would rather suffer the really light switching which is now the usual punishment of their faults than to have it replaced by the fieldstocks, by the tread mill, by the solitary confinement, or any other ingenious mode of protracted torment, which the lovers of the negro race have discovered."

To use Richard Barrett's own words, it gives the contemporary reader "a sense of shame" to see sharp logic used throughout to validate slavery as a form of beneficence to the African. Still, the speech by Edward's illegitimate first cousin offers a glimpse into the colonial mind and temperament. Moulton Barrett was a Creole, never really at home in England outside the confines of his Creole relatives and concerns. How much more alienated must he have felt as he declined not only in wealth but in prestige as the majority of British people came to despise slavery and blame it on the Creole planters. He may have found out about the possibility of his mixed blood during the later years of his marriage, or it might have been that the issue of mixed blood was not a concern to the powerful heir to Cinnamon Hill during the years of prosperity. After all, such things were common in Creole families. But as his private fortunes declined, and the source of his wealth became

ROBERT BROWNING, SR.
(1782–1866). *An unworldly man of
scholarly interests, the poet's father
was a caricaturist of notable talent.
He encouraged his son's artistic and
philosophic interests, while his own
father had thwarted his.*

anathema to the British people, he grew to believe he and his family were cursed, and he tried to control his children and to extinguish the possibility of a next generation. Who knows the mental sufferings of Edward Barrett Moulton Barrett in this area of legitimate procreation? Racist fears based on family secrets would certainly explain why the news of grandchildren did nothing to mollify his extreme position. A married child was a dead child. His grandchildren didn't exist for him.

The founder of the London Browning Society and Browning's friend, Frederick James Furnivall, wrote in a footnote to a paper he had delivered to the society after Robert's death, "It is possible that this colour business may have had something to do with Mr. Barrett's un-justified aversion to his daughter's marriage to the poet." He wasn't referring to Elizabeth Barrett's "Moulton" grandfather, he was refer-ring to Robert Browning's "Tittle" grandmother. A few months after Browning died in 1889, Furnivall investigated family records and tombstones to find out if Browning had Jewish blood as rumored. (After all, he had an uncle named Reuben.) He found instead much circumstantial evidence that Margaret Tittle, Browning's grandfather's first wife, had black blood. "In colour, the poet's father was so dark that when, as a youth, he went out to his Creole mother's sugar-planta-tion in St. Kitts, the beadle of the Church ordered him to come away from the white folk among whom he was sitting, and take his place among the coloured people." Robert's grandfather favored the children

MARGARET TITTLE (1754–1789). *Oil by Wright of Derby. The poet's paternal grandmother, a Creole, according to Frederick J. Furnivall, of mixed blood, with claims to plantations on St. Kitts. Her surviving son, the poet's father, outraged by slavery, rejected his claim on them and on a comfortable colonial livelihood. She died at the age of thirty-five, and this portrait, taken down when her husband remarried, went to her son.*

ROBERT BROWNING (1749–1833). *The poet's paternal grandfather, an ambitious man who worked for the Bank of England for more than fifty years and rose to Principal of the Bank Stock Office. On October 13, 1778, he married Margaret Tittle, a Creole, and had three children, Robert (the poet's father), Margaret Morris, and William, who died in infancy. After Mary Tittle died he married a well-connected Englishwoman, Jane Smith, and had nine children by her.*

of his second, highborn wife, and left his children by Tittle out of his will. Some of his children by the second wife, as well as certain unnamed old friends of the family, concurred on this issue of blood, according to Furnivall. This report infuriated Browning's sister, Sarianna, and his son, Pen. They both denied vehemently that the Brownings descended from a butler, another Furnivall assertion. Yet neither said one word on the issue of mixed blood on their Creole side.

Instead, they allowed Mrs. Sutherland Orr to write a *Life and Letters of Robert Browning.* Furnivall's assertion "was, on the face of it, not impossible, and would be absolutely unimportant to my mind, and I think I may add, to that of Mr. Browning's sister and son. The poet and his father were what we know them, and if negro blood had any part in their composition, it was no worse for them, and so much better for the negro." She disputed, through family friends, assertions of Browning's father's dark skin, and in the Wright of Derby's portrait of his grandmother "any indication of possible dark blood is imperceptible to the general observer, and must be of too slight and fugitive a nature to enter into the discussion." This, too, must have been told to her, for Mrs. Orr was nearly blind. Her evidence was as circumstantial as Furnivall's, but she did verify the "systematic unkindness under which" Browning's father grew up under his stepmother and his father. His father wouldn't look at his son's first completed picture when he wanted to be an artist, and even when Browning's father pleaded to go to "a university . . . at his own cost," his father forbade it.

Jeannette Marks wrote that Robert Browning's father, when in the West Indies, "came to know something about his grandmother's family: the St. Kitts Strachans, father and son, surgeons, through whom may have been inherited, quite as well as through the Tittles, 'the dash' of the tar brush of which Dr. Furnivall wrote." Mrs. Orr never discounted the possibility of some black blood. What Creole family who had come to prosper from generations of slave trade could? Up until now it has been a possibility confined to footnotes, though such an issue must have reflected a concern in many a Victorian household. Four days after the Brownings' marriage, on September 16, Elizabeth wrote to her husband: "You might put in the newspaper . . of Wimpole Street & Jamaica, or . . & Cinnamon Hill, Jamaica. That is right & I thought of it at first—only stopped . . seeming to wish to have as little about poor Papa as possible. Do as you think best now."

The next day, two days before they left England, Browning did what he (and others) have thought best since: "As you leave it to me,—the name, & 'Wimpole St.' will do—Jamaica,—sounds in the wrong direction, does it not? and the other place is distinctive enough."

If Robert Browning's grandmother, as well as Elizabeth Barrett's grandfather, had had African blood, one person who would have known it would be their Jamaican cousin John Kenyon (who himself had a "half-sister of color Hannah Kennion")—that dear friend who Elizabeth passionately insisted would not want any responsibility for her union with Robert before the fact.

One can disregard these accounts—"His peculiarities and defects

JOHN KENYON (1784–1856). *One of the Barretts' Jamaican cousins, Kenyon was a wealthy and cultivated patron of the arts and a minor poet. He encouraged RB to write to EBB and was a benevolent friend to both.*

are obvious," Browning said of Furnivall, a respected scholar. One can keep all mention of Jeannette Marks's careful genealogical research in footnotes forever. But Elizabeth Barrett Browning might have had, not only on her Moulton side but on her husband's side, powerful motivation for writing a poem on her honeymoon about a black mother who suffocated her mulatto child because of his white skin. She might have even had secret reasons for fearing John Kenyon's magnified eyes discerning courtship between the children of his two Creole classmates. Certainly she would not be the only child of planters in England who might have had secret preoccupations about the color of their skin.

While she wrote her poem on her honeymoon, she herself was pregnant. She wouldn't believe it, even after she had been pregnant for five months.

"I have been *stupid* beyond any stupidity of which I ever, that I know of, was thought capable, by me or others—and the consequence has been a premature illness, a *miscarriage,* at four o'clock last Sunday morning, and *of five months date,* says Dr. Cook, or nearly so." This she wrote to Henrietta from Pisa in late March 1847. She had been perfectly well until about six or seven weeks before, when she became sub-

ject to violent night pains. She'd have a bit of brandy, Robert would rub
her stomach, and the pains would disappear as suddenly as they arrived.

Wilson finally told her that she suspected Elizabeth might be
pregnant, and that if this were so, the pains were not a good sign, that
they might signal miscarriage. Wilson also "had great fears about the
influence of the *morphine* etc." At this juncture Robert pleaded with
her to call Dr. Cook. Why didn't she?

"I was frightened out of my wits by the suggestion about the morphine, and out of my *wit* by the entreaty about Dr. Cook." Being implored on both sides by Robert and Wilson, she decided on a way to
pacify Robert and her own apprehensions. She was sick in Pisa, well,
she'd write to Mr. Jago, that should clarify matters.—Dear Mr. Jago,
should she be pregnant, *would* the morphine have a negative effect?—
The minute the letter was mailed, she realized it was ridiculous to send
him a hypothetical case.

But never mind; she wasn't pregnant. Wilson had been sick at the
end of January, and Elizabeth had rushed to her in the middle of the
night. Hadn't Robert scolded her for going to her maid "without any
stockings. 'I wanted to kill him . . I played with his life.' " Now she
was willing to concede the point to Robert. Perhaps she had caught
cold on that occasion. That must be it. "I unconsciously caught cold by
going out into the passage, I might be affected so and so and so."

By then Robert was beseeching her to see Dr. Cook, but she would
not do it. In the second letter she ever wrote to Robert, a little over two
years before, she told him that ever since she was a child she had been
stubborn; *testa lunga* was her Italian master's word for it. She did not
misrepresent herself. No one could convince her that she was pregnant.

The night pains went away, but about three weeks into March she
felt sick enough to submit to seeing Dr. Cook. On Friday he looked
around, saw the fire was too high, her pulse too irritable, saw she was
doing everything wrong for a pregnant woman. He told her to lie
down, prescribed cold tea; he'd be back on Sunday. "Though his opinion went with the majority, the minority of one remained obstinate."
Elizabeth still did not believe, but she did what she was told and felt
better on Saturday. On the day of the miscarriage itself, "I was perfectly convinced, would have died for it at the stake, that I had just
caught cold! Most stupid, stupid!"

That evening, in the third week of March, she began to have pains,
and they "came on, every five minutes" for more than twenty-four

hours. "Oh, not so very violent, I have had worse pain I assure you." Worse pain than a labor of more than twenty-four hours and a miscarriage of a five-month fetus. Only during this labor did Elizabeth come to her senses: "When my eyes were open to the truth, I was as little frightened or agitated as at this moment, and bore it all so well (I mean with so much bodily vigour) as to surprise Wilson . . and Dr. Cook too indeed."

Robert took her suffering worse than she. As soon as he was allowed back in her room after it was over, "he threw himself down on the bed in a passion of tears, sobbing like a child . . he who has not the eyes of a ready-weeper. He had better scolded me well, I say, for bringing all this agitation on him—for Dr. Cook pronounces that if he had been called in six weeks ago, everything would have gone as right as possible." So her willfulness had led to this punishment, the termination of a *five-month* pregnancy. But she was getting well, and waited a week to inform her sisters, so that she could write the letter in her own hand, in order to reassure them as to the state of her health. It was a long letter, but she would have written even more if Robert hadn't insisted that she not overtax herself. "And just at present my mood inclines to be a more obedient wife than I have been."

Her postscript, however, indicated the return of the *testa lunga.* "The morphine did *no* harm at all." And the fetus, one assumes, was white.

At the time of this unacknowledged pregnancy she wrote to Mary Mitford, "In the way of writing I have not done much yet . . just finished my rough sketch of an antislavery ballad & sent it off to America, where nobody will print it, I am certain, because I could not help making it bitter." Racial concerns, patriarchal rejection, family secrets, may have played a part in what she called her "stupidity," and what she described as an incredible, headlong denial of a pregnancy that ran five months. Her whole life, her whole world, had been turned upside down in the last six months. Now not only had she married against her father's wishes, but she was immediately pregnant with the legitimate grandchild that was never meant to be. For that first pregnancy, that concrete flesh-and-blood betrayal of her father's wishes, for that child who might be born with skin as dark as, or darker than, her own and Robert's, she was not prepared.

PISA POSTSCRIPT

IF ON THEIR honeymoon the Brownings lived as if the world did not exist, it was Elizabeth who saw that the circle must be widened. If Robert had vowed never to be where she could not go, they must live in places where there would be plenty for him to do in her vicinity. She, too, and perhaps more than he, needed a wider circle. She loved her husband dearly, there was no doubt about that. But her circumstances were different. He chose her out of a world of women, and out of a world he had experienced. He was ready to "settle down."

In choosing him, she also chose not to live as a "*blind* poet," but to see rivers and mountains, experience the world. Given her peculiar situation, this man was her great love and her escape route. It was now time for both of them to move on. The months in Pisa, the inexhaustible relying on their love alone, the honeymoon, was over.

"He loves me too much . . so much that I feel humiliated, as someone crushed with gifts," she wrote to her sister Arabel from Pisa. Less than four weeks after the miscarriage, "Robert's goodness and tenderness are past speaking of, even if you could answer me. He reads to me, talks and jests to make me laugh, tells me stories, improvises verses in all sorts of languages . . . sings songs, explains the difference between Mendelssohn and Spohr by playing on the table, and when he has thoroughly amused me accepts it as a triumph. Of course I am spoilt to the utmost—who could escape?"

Before the miscarriage, Elizabeth thought Robert had written to her sisters of an erroneous travel plan, and she scolded him for it. When she found out it had been she who had erred, she told him, "Whenever I blame you, I find myself in fault afterward."

To this humble apology she expected a pretty reply, something to the effect of "My darling, when you find fault with yourself, you are most in fault of all."

Instead, Robert paused for a moment, and then answered very quietly, "It is a satisfaction, at any rate, that you should admit it."

Robert Browning was not looking for wifely obedience. He couldn't tolerate that any more than he could tolerate Victorian papas with ironclad rules and thunderclaps to enforce them.

One day, over some small point relating to Flush, he said, " 'I do wish, Ba, you wouldn't do so and so.' To which I answered:

" 'Well, I won't do it any more,' was ever a more unexceptionable answer? Yes, and it was meekly delivered too. But *he* didn't like it at all, nevertheless, and cried out quite quickly:—

" 'Don't say such words to me, Ba.'

" 'Why what ought I say then?'

" 'Say that you will do as you please as long as you please to do it.' "

*The earliest known
photograph
of Robert Browning,
Paris, 1856.*

*Portrait of Elizabeth
Barrett Browning
by Michele
Gordigiani,
in 1858.*

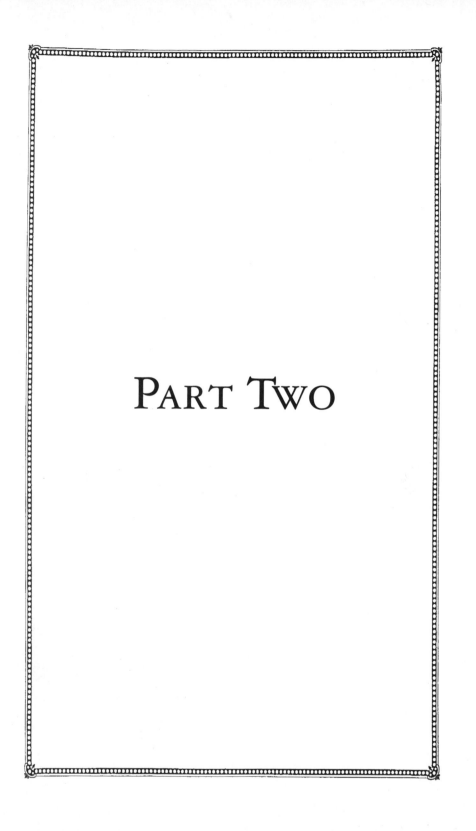

PART TWO

THE MARRIAGE OF
TRUE MINDS

HERS

AUNT NINA might have been a seasoned traveler, but when it came to Florence, Browning advised Elizabeth's sisters not to take her advice. For she had described the city as British to the teeth and bursting at the seams with balls and hoopla, and this had contributed to the Brownings' overlong stay in Pisa. Fulfilling their half-year lease, they now planned only a short stop at Florence on their way to Rome. One might say Anna Jameson had given them the gift of discovering their home for themselves. And providence led them to where Tuscany itself, after a three-hundred-year slumber, was going to ignite.

Though the couple excelled at local color, their initiation into foreign life was not complete. In Pisa, if it had not been for a friendly English woman, they would not have realized how they were being cheated day by day. They had the blessing of the devoted and gentle Elizabeth Wilson, who was more than a lady's maid; Robert wrote home that she was their friend. A friend of the Brownings would not be adept at haggling. So timid was she that her mistress marveled at her strength in leaving Wimpole Street with them and heading on, valiantly, to help them in their (and her) new life. She was certainly not one to rush to the marketplace and scream out in shocked horror at the price of chestnuts and grapes, especially if one were able to buy a store of them for a penny. One Mrs. Taylor, who opened Elizabeth and Robert's eyes to their millionaire status among the Pisans, went with Wilson to the market to show her how to shop. There were three customs of the country: bargain, bargain, bargain.

The treat of Florence was double. For not only were the poets immediately attracted, but they could compare it to Pisa. It was cheaper, it was far more beautiful, and it was full of life. If Robert had vowed to go nowhere without Elizabeth, here was a place of interest to roam within walking-miles of her chair. Not that Elizabeth didn't go outside and walk. Her general health, which she noted as always good, had not been undermined by her lungs, and she made many trips, walking, riding mules, and climbing stairs.

The couple had first stayed at rooms in the Casa Guidi. This four-story palazzo was across the way from the Pitti Palace. It was on the "other side" of the Arno. One could reach it by going over the Ponte Vecchio, the venerable bridge on which Dante first saw his Beatrice. After another miscarriage, this time in the pregnancy's second month, which made traveling to Rome for the winter too dangerous, they had to look for a new apartment. They tried to bargain for another lease on their apartment in the Casa Guidi. Unfortunately, they took the padrone's poker face seriously and moved on; their straight-line British integrity once more made them deficient in the nuances of Italian life.

Short-term rentals were as short-term rentals still are . . . some were too shoddy, some in the wrong part of town, some too expensive. Finally, the couple decided on some nice rooms on Via Maggio. They must have considered them much better than their comfortable pile of rooms at Pisa, because they were willing to pay the same price. The one deficiency was lack of sun, but they felt that the beauty of the rooms and the use of the fireplace would compensate.

Within ten days, abstract logic did what it usually does in the face of life—it backed off. The rooms were too cold. They had left London for the sun, yet now they were in an apartment that could be on Wimpole Street. Elizabeth's lungs started to react, and Robert was in a great rush to move her out of there. They made an agreement with the padrone to pay the rent until he found another tenant. Now here was a situation in a foreign country that could dent the happiest marriage. What a botch. How hard is a landlord going to look for tenants for sunless rooms when he's still collecting rent? Many a marriage has been undone in picturesque climes, with "I told you so!" ringing in the air. Why did we rush into rooms with no sun? It was your idea. My idea? You mean you didn't bargain with the landlord? Pay him until he finds a new tenant? We'll go broke!

No such scenario for the Brownings. Robert accused himself for the compromise; Elizabeth believed she had convinced him to make it.

CASA GUIDI (*bottom*) AND THE BROWNINGS' DRAWING ROOM, *an engraving after the painting by George Mignaty (top). The Brownings celebrated their first anniversary here. They moved out in October 1847 and returned seven months later to the apartment on the* piano nobile *that became their home.*

Each offered praise of the other; this time they didn't even argue over who was more forbearing.

To add to the annoying situation, after they signed their lease, they heard that the padrone of Casa Guidi had been ready to accept their terms and they really could have kept their old apartment. For the time, it was too late.

While they were still at the Casa Guidi, that early lovers' luck, what Robert called "providence" in his love letters, came rolling back to them again. For they were at the right place at the right time. History itself knocked on their door—in actuality, it came to their window.

On September 12, 1847, the Brownings celebrated their first wedding anniversary as witnesses to a massive and joyous political demonstration. From the front windows of the Casa Guidi, they watched people from all over Italy march to the courtyard of the Pitti Palace across the way. There the masses gathered to thank the Austrian Grand Duke, of Italian blood, Leopold II of Tuscany, for granting the Florentines the right to form a militia, a civic guard, an act which promised the type of liberality that would lead to a constitution and to the unification of Italy into a nation. For the first time, the Florentines could bear arms to protect themselves.

"So wasn't our day kept well for us?" Elizabeth wrote to her sister Henrietta. The poets who had left England to find personal freedom and fulfillment found in Florence a public correlative to their new lives. The streets were so crowded on the Monday after their anniversary that it would have been impossible to get to the post office. Luckily, Henrietta's and Arabel's letters of congratulation had come before the Brownings' sacred day. "The fact was, that our Italians had resolved to keep our day for us on a most magnificent scale."

There were forty thousand strangers in Florence that Sunday, from every part of Italy, and from every class, including the priesthood. There were also expatriates from every nation, and they all paraded past the Brownings' windows into the Piazza Pitti, where the Duke and his family stood in tears, at a window themselves, greeting the populace. All along the way, "The windows . . . seemed to grow larger with the multitude of pretty heads, & of hands which threw out flowers & waved white handkerchiefs—There was not an inch of wall not alive. . . . Clouds of flowers & laurel leaves came fluttering down on the advancing procession—and the clapping of hands, & the fre-

FRANCIS V, *Modena*

LEOPOLD II, *Tuscany*

FRANCIS JOSEPH
Austria

FRANCIS II, *Naples*

FERDINAND II, *Naples*

ITALIAN DESPOTS. *EBB embraced the cause of Italian unity at a time when the city-states were ruled by retrogressive forces.*

DEMONSTRATIONS IN FLORENCE FOR THE RIGHT TO FORM A CIVIC
GUARD. *EBB and RB watched the procession from the windows of Casa Guidi
on their first wedding anniversary, Sunday, September 12, 1847.*

netic shouting, and the music which came in gushes, & then seemed to
go out with too much joy, and the exulting faces, and the kisses given
for very exultation between man & man, and the mixing of elegantly
dressed women in all that crowd & turbulence with the sort of smile
which proved how little cause there was for fear."

What a sight! The Brownings "went to a window in our palazzo
which had a full view, and I had a throne of cushions piled up on a
chair." Then they waved their own handkerchiefs until their wrists
ached. At night there were fireworks, and the couple walked over to
the Arno to see them. They were struck by the civility of the crowd as
well as by the unleashing of joy. People were embracing. "It was a state
of phrensy or rapture, extending to the children of two years old, several of them whom I heard lisping *'Vivas,'* with their little fat arms
clasping their mothers necks. So wasn't our day kept well for us?"

Flush, not to be upstaged, sneaked out into the crowd, and celebrated freedom in his own way. He came back the next day looking
very guilty and very tired. "Quite disgraceful for a respectable dog,"

Robert said. Elizabeth made excuses for him, calling his prowling a case of confusion.

The crowds, the demonstrations. The Brownings were standing on the brink of that revolutionary year throughout Europe, 1848.

Italy. "If only you were less beautiful," lamented the seventeenth-century Italian poet Vincenzo da Filicaia. Lord Byron echoed this refrain, as did Elizabeth Barrett Browning in her book-length poem about the Italian struggle for liberty, *Casa Guidi Windows.* The art and architecture and poetry that impelled the civilized world to Italy were, as the Brownings witnessed in Pisa, all of the past. And while the past was passionately admired, the present was in shambles. Italy was a group of politically repressed city-states, with no unified culture and no contemporary power or life. The Austrians ruled Tuscany; the Vatican had authority over the Papal States. Naples and the Two Sicilies had a tyrant. The people were ruled by foreign leaders and by the Church. But the Age of Metternich was nearing its end, and one of the oldest civilizations was poised on the threshold of becoming, in less than three decades, its youngest country.

For three hundred years Florence had slept. In the sixteenth century, between 1524 and 1534, Michelangelo sculpted his great marble statues *Night, Day, Dawn,* and *Twilight* for the New Sacristy of the Church of San Lorenzo. The political situation in Florence had then deteriorated under the rule of the descendants of the father of his people, Lorenzo de' Medici. The sculptor saw the political situation represented by his statue *Night,* and wrote of it:

> *Happy am I to sleep, and still more blest*
> *To be of stone, while grief and shame endure;*
> *To see, nor feel, is now my utmost hope,*
> *Wherefore speak softly, and awake me not.*

From their windows, more than three hundred years after Michelangelo's disillusionment, the Brownings witnessed the wake-up call.

Theirs were not lone voices of isolated *stranieri* in the politics of a foreign land. In the procession they had watched, "there was a place for them [foreigners]—& there were so many foreign residents here that it was by no means unimportant to admit their sympathy—French, English, Swiss, Greek (such a noble band of Greeks!) all with their national flags."

POPE PIUS IX, CA. 1855.
*Giovanni Maria Mastai-
Ferretti, "Pio Nono," was
elevated in June 1846,
three months before the
Brownings married. His
early liberal views pro-
pelled the forces of Italian
unity that EBB cham-
pioned in all of her late
poetry.*

These foreign residents were in a special sense patriots. The "tourists" among them had fled Florence at the first signs of life. Their *Night* was the one on view in the Church of San Lorenzo. The last thing they wished was for it to awake. Their parade was the one that took place daily at the Cascine, where residents greeted each other from their graceful, and at times eccentric, carriages. Their Florentines did not bear arms but existed to supply local color. And their exit gladdened the stouter hearts of liberals such as the Brownings.

Change had been in the air even before the Austrian Duke Leopold II allowed the Florentines to form a militia. That decision itself was based on an extraordinary happening in Rome—an oxymoron: the election of a liberal Pope. This new Pope—Pius IX, "Pio Nono"—was, by papal standards, young, handsome, and graced with a beautiful singing voice. On his elevation, Pio Nono granted political amnesty in the prisons and freedom of the press in Italy for the first time in two hundred years. His reign began in a burst of popularity and cheering among young and old, among conservative Catholics and liberals, and among Protestant foreigners. His spirit generated a sense of amelioration.

Giuseppe Mazzini, a leading proponent of Italian unity, advised his followers to keep up the applause and, with it, to keep demanding more. To the Young Italy party he gave these instructions: "Take advantage of the smallest concession to make an opportunity for bringing together masses of the people, if only in attestation of gratitude. Festi-

vals, songs, agglomerations of people, numerous relationships established between men of every shade of opinion, suffice to cause the generation of ideas, to give the people the sentiment of its strength, and to
render it exigent." Reforms meant by Pio Nono to be gestures on his
ascent, equivalent to commissioning a beautiful fountain for a town
square, turned into a floodgate. He had not understood the thirst of
parched hearts.

Into this rush of events Elizabeth Barrett Browning plunged with
a long poem. It opened with the poet and her husband watching the
procession that occurred on their first anniversary. It was Robert who
"concluded" that the little child they heard from the window, singing
a song for liberty, was the voice of Italy, the voice of a new day. By the
time she sent the hopeful poem to *Blackwood's Magazine* the following
year as a "Meditation in Tuscany," the new voices had broken off, the
children were once more asleep "upon their mothers' knees."

By November 15, 1848, the Pope's minister, Count Pellegrino
Rossi, had been assassinated on the steps of the Roman Senate—Caesar
fashion. All had raised their knives and testified " *'I killed him!—I am
Brutus.—I avow.'* " Pio Nono sneaked out of Rome in disguise, and
the former liberal accepted in Naples the hospitality of the retrogressive Ferdinand II, King of the Two Sicilies. The Florentine Grand
Duke had agreed to a Constituent Assembly in Rome before he realized that such an assembly would most certainly turn his Tuscany into
a republic and wash him away. In February 1849 he fled from Florence
and joined the repentant Pope at Gaeta.

At the end of March 1849 the Italian troops had suffered defeat by
the Austrians at the battle of Novara. At that point, many moderate
Florentines championed the return of their Grand Duke. Leopold became a "traitor" when he came back not at the calling of the Florentines but under the auspices of the hated oppressors—the Austrians.
The Brownings, once again settled in an apartment in the Casa Guidi,
witnessed the somber reentry of Austrian troops in advance of the dis-
credited Duke—Robert, hearing gunshots, went down to the street,
Elizabeth to her second-floor terrace. When Leopold returned he emphasized his Italian blood by wearing the uniform of the Tuscan Civic
Guard, creating an ambiguity of intention. A few nights later, however, he wore an Austrian uniform to an opera ball, bowing to either
Austrian pressure or the dictates of fashion. From then on he was
clearly no longer "Leopoldo Secondo" but "Leopold d'Austria," as the

Florentine newspaper the *Alba* would henceforth call him. All of Florence remembered that the *gran duca* (Grand Duke) had a nickname before September 12, 1847, *gran ciuco* (Grand Ass).

The poets who watched this somber parade after the defeat of Novara had a personal reason for joy that was not reflected by the political gloom. On March 9, 1849, after suffering two miscarriages, Elizabeth Barrett Browning had given birth to a healthy, fair-skinned baby boy. "I shall get Wilson to help my inexperience and tell you all the wonderful points," Robert wrote to his sisters-in-law four days later. Wilson confined herself to one point. She "*never* did see such a delicate & beautiful skin." What is "peculiarly beautiful in him, is & has always been his complexion, never a taint upon it, as clear as a flower," Ba informed her sisters a month later.

Elizabeth's new friend and upstairs neighbor at the Casa Guidi, Eliza Dick Ogilvy, recollected, "Mrs. Browning was by no means an ordinary patient. The old Italian nurse said to me after the birth, 'E un miraculo quello bambino e venuto da quel corpo.' " (It's a miracle that baby came from that body.) The previous months had been spent in concern over her confinement and in fear of another miscarriage. She confided her anxieties to Eliza, who had just had her third child. Issues of childbearing, not issues of poetry, united them. She had given up morphine during her pregnancy, exhibiting, as Robert boasted to her sisters, an extraordinary strength equal to that of a thousand men.

Her labor had lasted twenty-one hours, yet "when I heard the first cry, the unspeakable rapture of it!" she wrote to Arabel a month later. "I who had been a good deal tired & exhausted by the prolongation of the pain . . . rose up suddenly in my spirits to a sort of ecstasy . . not only forgot the pain but . . . slapped my hands & clasped them & exclaimed aloud. . . ."

It was as a new mother that Elizabeth Barrett Browning watched the Austrians and the Grand Duke reenter Florence. She remembered:

> *I wrote a meditation and a dream,*
> *   Hearing a little child sing in the street.*
> *I leant upon his music as a theme,*
> *   Till it gave way beneath my heart's full beat,*
> *Which tried at an exultant prophecy*
> *   But dropped before the measure was complete—*
> *Alas, for songs, and hearts! O Tuscany, . . .*

And she then wrote a second part to her meditation, bringing the two parts together under a very appropriate title, *Casa Guidi Windows.*

She also wrote a foreword, an "Advertisement," to the completed work: "This poem contains the impressions of the writer upon events in Tuscany of which she was a witness. 'From a window,' the critic may demur. She bows to the objection in the very title of her work. No continuous narrative nor exposition of political philosophy is attempted by her. It is a simple story of personal impressions, whose only value is in the intensity with which they were received, as proving her warm affection for a beautiful and unfortunate country, and the sincerity with which they are related, as indicating her own good faith and freedom from partisanship."

Critics have "demurred" ever since. They didn't have to understand the Florence or the history of Elizabeth Barrett Browning's day. This was a "simple story," it was about "personal impressions." They undervalued the poetic "intensity" with which the impressions were received. Why? "Because I am a woman." That was the image she chose to express her earlier mistaken faith in the Grand Duke:

> I saw the man among his little sons,
> > His lips were warm with kisses while he swore,—
> And I, because I am a woman, I,
> > Who felt my own child's coming life before
> The prescience of my soul, and held faith high,—
> > I could not bear to think, whoever bore,
> That lips, so warmed, could shape so cold a lie.

Her foreword and this image would later harm her critical reputation.

No woman poet in the last two centuries has been as misconstrued by American and British critics as Elizabeth Barrett Browning. Lauded by the Italians to this day as the poet of the Risorgimento, considered for the poet laureateship in the England of her own day, she, in her late work, has been considered everything from "misguided" up through "hysterical." And the complaints mounted as time passed and the critics understood even less of the historical backdrop against which she had her vision. As "Mrs. Browning," not as a wife and mother, but as a *poet,* she suffered an unjust fate. The feminist critics have begun a resurrection of her art centered around her own feminist manifesto, her novel in verse, *Aurora Leigh.* They have shifted that chameleon name of hers once more. The poetry of her married years has become the work of "Barrett Browning." If Barrett Browning still sounds strangely new, unexpectedly powerful, perhaps slightly strident, so was the poetry of her maturity.

In *Casa Guidi Windows* the married poet who had experienced the mountains and the rivers could finally become what she had always wished to be, the poet of the new day. "And I, a singer also, from my youth, / Prefer to sing with these who are awake." To sing "With birds, with babes, with men who will not fear / The baptism of the holy morning dew." Many of those "wakers now are here," and she would rather sing liberty with them than join the "old thin voices" and mourn the past. "We do not serve the dead—the past is past!" Viva Barrett Browning.

" 'Casa Guidi Windows' is the poetic cry which rises from Tuscany to the world in praise of the desire for liberty," wrote the twentieth-century Florentine critic Giuliana Artom Treves. The poem in which Barrett Browning "describes the upheavals in Tuscany deserves the perennial gratitude of Italians for the way she frankly assumes the role of poet of the Italian Risorgimento."

English and American critics have not seriously considered Barrett Browning in this role. On the contrary, because of its political concerns, the poem has often been dismissed. Henry James understood the perceptivity of the poet's political point of view; he was closer to her time, but he felt that politics as a subject diminished her poetry. "The cause of Italy was, obviously, for Mrs. Browning as high aloft as any object of interest could be; but that was only because she had let down, as it were, her inspiration and her poetic pitch." Certainly this formalistic stance merged well with the ensuing New Criticism, and one can understand why a poem such as *Casa Guidi Windows* would be overlooked through the 1950s.

As the critics of the 1960s began to discover that a poem can both "mean" and "be," and as political commitment began to be viewed as no anathema to artistic expression, one could have hoped for a reevaluation of Barrett Browning's Italian period. None was forthcoming. Worse, as the historical issues of 1848 faded into obscurity, critics began to misinterpret the political basis of her works in a way Henry James never would have.

When the poet looked back at her early optimistic view of Leopold II, she repented that she had believed in his oaths "like a woman."

Well, this was not an individual blunder. The enthusiasm for the Grand Duke in 1847 and the disillusionment with him in 1849 accurately reflected the attitude of all of liberal Europe before and after the revolutions of 1848.

When the poet's relation to the attitudes of the day is completely forgotten, and her similes based on womanhood and motherhood are taken as felonies, critical stereotypes abound: "The fullest expression of her own feeling at this time—it can hardly be called thought—is *Casa Guidi Windows*. . . . The poem is a single instance of the way in which the use of verse pumps Elizabeth up beyond any possibility of coherent and rational discussion. Metaphoric violets, swords, crowns, and croziers accumulate until there is no room for realities. Politics founder in rhapsody and anecdote about dead Florentine poets and artists." The authors of this, William Irvine and Park Honan, were writing in the early 1970s a biography of her husband, a man they respected, and showing absolute condescension to a woman they did not understand. How could they account for the fact that the Brownings shared the same political ideas? "Yet one suspects, making allowances for its childlike vision and its frantic idiom, that this poem sets forth the essential elements of thought and feeling for both Elizabeth and Robert. His 'Why I am a Liberal,' for example, is not inconsistent with the sentiments of *Casa Guidi*." Presumably, had Elizabeth Barrett Browning believed "like a man," she would have written not a book-length poem but "Why I am a Liberal," a minor sonnet.

In actuality, Elizabeth Barrett Browning was on the forefront of liberal European thinking. Since childhood she had felt she was to write about issues that could change society. When she turned fifteen, she wrote in her "Autobiographical Essay": "I always imagine that I was sent on the earth for some purpose! To suffer! to die! to defend! To save by my death my country or some very very dear friends! To suffer in the cause of freedom!! I know, I understand not how this is but I feel it to my heart core & so strong is this feeling that it amounts almost to presentiment!"

More than twenty-five years later, living her own life in Italy, she found her cause. Though she had trusted Grand Duke Leopold, seeing the events of her first anniversary as prelude to even greater reform, she herself escaped what she called the epidemic "falling sickness" of enthusiasm for the Pope. At the time, Vincenzo Gioberti's idea in "Il Primato" (1843) that the various states of Italy could become federated under a Pope was taken up very seriously by the popular neo-Guelph movement, which thought it had found in Pio Nono 'an ideal leader. That Barrett Browning disagreed with this position is a tribute to her political astuteness and to her nonconformist point of view. Many of her countrymen living in Florence had a different outlook.

After the abolishment of press censorship, not only did two liberal Italian papers arise in Florence, the *Alba* and the *Patria,* but an English-language paper as well, the *Tuscan Athenaeum,* edited by Thomas A. Trollope, brother of the novelist. Articles and poetry praising the Pope and the new regime appeared. The politics of the English-language paper, its tongue-in-cheek irony, so Florentine in character, made its fifteen months of publication part of the history of its time. The *Tuscan Athenaeum* brought to the forefront a new type of foreign resident. These *stranieri* were so intimately involved with the progress of their adopted land that they formed a community that could be called Anglo-Florentine.

In its pages, from October 30, 1847, through January 22, 1848, we can see that for the intellectuals and artists in Florence in the Brownings' time, the "falling sickness" for Pio Nono *was* epidemic. "We are rather overwhelmed with poetry," Trollope wrote in November. The poem of his future wife, Theodosia Garrow, was entitled "The English Heart to the Roman Pontiff" and began:

> *Sovereign Pontiff! Gracious Ruler!*
> *When we view thee from afar,*
> *Waving back the mists of error,*
> *Strengthening faith, dispelling terror,*
> *Patient as the angels are . . .*

Why, when we view him, we have "eager kindred feeling" for this "Promethean soul!"

Walter Savage Landor, the man who would three years later write bitterly against the Pope and Cardinal Nicholas Wiseman, sent this to the *Tuscan Athenaeum*: "Never until now, most holy father! did I hope or desire to offer my homage to any potentate on earth; and now I offer it only to the highest of them all."

Barrett Browning knew better. Her dissent stood out dramatically. "We want thee, O unfound / and sovran teacher!" But where can the teacher be found? A Pope? She understood that the politics of an individual is a result of the individual's circumstances. "Distrust / The rich man reasoning in a poor man's hut." Distrust "The poet who neglects pure truth to prove / Statistic fact." Distrust the child who will pick the easier rather than the harder road. Distrust "The woman who has sworn she will not love." And distrust that a Pope, sitting on the papal throne, will become an Andrea Doria, a liberator of his people.

At his best, a Pope is a Pope; we want a teacher, a man who is not "enchanted to the waist," one who is "complete and all alive." Half travertine (the Roman material used to build the Vatican), "Half suits our need and ill subserves our plan." Her estimation proved correct. She wrote half-jestingly to Mary Russell Mitford on October 2, 1849: "The Pope is just a pope; and since you give George Sand credit for having known it, I am more vexed that Blackwood . . . did not publish the poem I wrote two years ago, in the full glare & burning of the pope-enthusiasm which Robert & I never caught for a moment. Then, *I* might have passed a little for a prophetess, as well as George Sand! Only, to confess a truth, the same poem wd. have proved how fairly I was taken in by our Tuscan Grand Duke. Oh!—the traitor!!"

Another disappointment she wrote about in part two of the poem was the laxity of the Florentines:

> *Bitter things I write,*
> *Because my soul is bitter for your sakes,*
> *O freedom! O my Florence!*

The *Alba* published an address "To the Tuscans," which the *Tuscan Athenaeum* translated: "We see splendid banners, flowers, illuminated processions, and civic parades. But we do not see, by God, soldiers with packs on their backs ready to depart! We hear the happy songs of children and women, choruses of grown-ups, the same old proclamations, schemes, protests, ponderous discussions;—but we do not hear war cries and goodbyes from those ready to leave for the battlefield." Ultimately, Barrett Browning, like so many other Italian patriots who saw defeat and ruin all around them, turned her eyes to the constitutional monarch of the House of Savoy in Turin, to the intentions and acts of Victor Emmanuel II and, by extension, to the King's reforming minister, Camillo Benso di Cavour. Cavour would become the teacher, the complete man. The poem ended on a note of hope and prophecy: "Life throbs in noble Piedmont." Which, it turned out, was true.

Although in her disastrous "Advertisement to the First Edition" Barrett Browning presented herself with her usual diffidence, she was a very famous poet. She could have no idea that in the next century the "value" of her intense personal impressions would be at such a low ebb that readers could mistake her words for a straightforward apology for what they could then assume to be a long, random, impressionistic poem of no evident artistic centrality. What unified the poem was the radical use of the "I" narration. She was the individual woman, and at the same time the poet, who saw with intensity and conviction the true and the beautiful and attempted to translate this vision for mankind. As a woman, as a wife and mother, she felt herself for the first time in her life to be a vital part of humanity. She was no longer a "*blind* poet."

There is hardly an image in the poem that does not testify to the poet's lived life after her marriage. When she spoke of Petrarch at Avignon and Vaucluse she and Robert had sat on the rocks underneath the spray of the fountain. When she spoke of Savonarola, she had just read his poetry in a new edition. Her reference to Lorenzo the Magnificent's deathbed at Careggi? She mentioned in her letters the present occupants of the villa. Cellini's *Perseus* in the Loggia, Michelangelo's New Sacristy, Dante's Stone, Santa Maria Novella, the beauties of the Arno, of Vallombrosa, of Tuscan Bellosguardo, were as much a part of her daily experiences as the demonstration that marked her first anniversary and the return of the Grand Duke after the birth of her child. She captured it all, from the chalking of slogans on the walls of the churches, the song to liberty the child sang that inspired her poem, and the smile of her own child that led to the end of her work: "This world has no perdition, if some loss. / Such cheer I gather from thy smiling, Sweet!" Centrality is achieved in *Casa Guidi Windows* by the poet's linking of all her immediate personal experience and newfound freedom to her intense poetic voice which sang out for the birth of an Italian nation.

Barrett Browning was aware of the problem all Victorian poets faced (and all poets face). Can poetry ultimately have an effect on life? Does poetry matter? To her, poetry was a form of action. Like Shelley, she saw the poet as the unacknowledged legislator of mankind. Unlike many more pessimistic nineteenth-century British poets, she did not emphasize the negative connotations of "unacknowledged." She did not look back to the defeat of the principles of the French Revolution, but forward to the live France of 1848. And there she found that the artist's words still had effect, whether they expressed the intense perceptions of her heroine, George Sand, of Victor Hugo, or of the poet who would become part of the provisional government after the "February" revolution, Alphonse de Lamartine.

Who spoke for Italy other than to bemoan the beauty that kept her powerless, as had Filicaia, Lord Byron, and Auguste Barbier? Her intention was to speak for Italy *in the present*. What was daring about her narrative point of view was that she consciously presented herself as the poet, the singer of the new day. There was splendid confidence in her voice when she assumed the role of the poet of the Italian Risorgimento. It was a confidence that many of the Victorian poets less sure of the effect of their poetry, such as Robert Browning at the time and Matthew Arnold, might envy. Even in her disillusionment she found herself not in Arnold's words, "here as on a darkling plain /Swept with confused alarms of struggle and flight, /Where ignorant armies clash by night." In her disillusionment she still wrote of *We* thinkers, *We* hopers, *We* poets who have had dreams of what Italy could become. As a poet she was still vitally connected to the world and to history.

The Paris of Ernest Hemingway and F. Scott Fitzgerald and Gertrude Stein is one with which we are quite familiar, and the art that emerged from Americans free to be themselves among the inexpensive delights of the Parisian cafes in the 1920s resonates to this day. The Italy that formed the background for all of Barrett Browning's late works, and for the masterpiece of Robert Browning's middle years, was in a sense, and more politically, their Paris. Not only is it less known today, it wasn't well known in its own day.

Blackwood's Magazine rejected the first part of the poem, calling "Meditation in Tuscany" a " 'grand poem' but past all human understanding." Elizabeth wrote to her sister that she was perplexed that Mr. Kenyon "seems to do more than *agree* with Blackwood's complaints," especially since "the best is that poor Robert had congratulated me on being so 'perfectly clear this time.' "

The cry of this poem, however, reaches beyond the locale. The final exultation of Barrett Browning's voice in *Casa Guidi Windows* is that what the poet experiences matters. She had not a social theorist's program for amelioration. She was a poet with a fierce and final confidence in poetry, and a great belief in freedom. To that vision of a better world she contributed what she could—her voice.

In 1852 she would look out of yet another window, this one in Paris, to see the coup d'état that would make Louis Napoleon emperor. She would write of it on February 15, 1852, to John Kenyon: "As it was in the beginning, from 'Casa Guidi Windows,' so it is now from the Avenue des Champs-Elysées. I am most humanly liable, of course, to make mistakes, and am by temperament perhaps over hopeful and sanguine. But I do see with my own eyes and feel with my own spirit, and not with other people's eyes and spirits, though they should happen to be the dearest—and that's the very best of me, be certain, so don't quarrel with it too much."

THE MARRIAGE OF
TRUE MINDS

HIS

TWO AND A HALF YEARS after their marriage, Robert Browning became a father. Before then, he had watched the passion he shared with
his wife lead to two miscarriages. He told Elizabeth that he could
never love a child the way he loved her, and had repeatedly denied that
he had parental instinct. When Elizabeth caught cold in late winter
1849, in the ninth month of yet another pregnancy, Robert wished the
unborn child would disappear in some magical way without harming
his wife. During her twenty-one-hour labor, Robert had been with her
as often as he was allowed, witnessing her incredible forbearance; she
never cried out. "I sate by her as much as I was allowed, and shall never
forget what I saw, tho' I cannot speak about it," he wrote to her sisters.
When, on March 9, 1849, she gave birth to a healthy baby boy, the joy
and relief Robert experienced were witnessed by the nurses, who portrayed him as dancing rather than walking as he spread the news.

The letters he wrote immediately after the birth were very happy
ones. To Mary Mitford: "Ba desires me to tell you that she gave birth,
at $2^{1}/_{4}$ this morning, to a fine, strong boy, like Harry Gill with the voice
of three,—a fact we learned when he was about half born." Still, he
didn't go to see his son immediately. It was Eliza Ogilvy, the upstairs
neighbor whose maternal experience had supported Elizabeth during
the anxieties of this pregnancy, who was the first to hold the baby.
Browning had to be told by the nurses of his infant's good health. The
child's head was so big that the caps Eliza knitted before the birth, to
cheer the doubting Elizabeth into the belief in a happy outcome to the
confinement, did not fit. To his sisters-in-law Browning wrote: "Was it
not dear of Ba to refuse to look at the Babe till I could show it her? as I
did." He brought his son to his wife in his arms and placed the infant

in hers. It was then that he found that the caps, being too small, only meant " 'as they were tied!' " The couple clipped three strands of the infant's hair—one to send directly to Browning's mother.

Here joy ended. His mother did not live to receive her strand, nor did her doctors allow her to know the child—her only grandchild— was born and survived. Supposedly, it would overexcite the woman who was now dying from a sudden ossification of the heart. Robert received three notices from his sister, Sarianna. The first congratulated him on the birth of their child; the second said, "I grieve to say our dearest mother is very ill." Then the third, "that dreadful letter" that told him of her death. Sarianna had been attempting to lessen the shock, for the second note was "written when all was over—Sarianna had great courage."

Two and a half years since he had last seen her. It had been Elizabeth, hadn't it, who'd wondered if they should postpone their voyage until his mother's health improved. They left on Browning's insistence, never imagining they'd be away so long. Browning's memory of the week after their marriage, as he busily prepared for their departure, would now be as well his last memories of his mother. "He goes back to his first memories when he was a little child & she knelt every night by his bedside. . . . Through childhood, through youth . . . to the last night of his leaving home for Italy."

No consolation to Robert that "Her death in its suddenness was very beautiful." Her last words, "God bless my dear . . dear . . dear," and then, "Come, come quickly . . quickly . . quickly . ." and, finally, "even so."

Robert Browning had been devoted to Sarah Anna Wiedemann Browning. In the love letters she was felt as an aromatic presence, the flowers from her garden always in Elizabeth's room. They, unlike the hothouse flowers Elizabeth's father brought her, seemed never to die. Sarah's husband, ten years her junior, had the temperament of a scholar; a bank clerk by day, at home he delighted in exploring subjects in his wonderful library and drawing his political, social, and lighthearted caricatures. Practical sense was no more his forte than travel arrangements or choosing apartments was his son's. It was Browning's mother who kept the household in order, and her gifts were shared by his energetic sister, Sarianna.

The mother was remembered affectionately by Browning's mentor Thomas Carlyle as a "true type of a Scottish gentlewoman." Browning's

SARAH ANNA BROWNING (1772–1849). *Caricature by her husband, Robert Browning, Sr., ca. 1826. The only known likeness of the poet's mother. She was an accomplished gardener. Her deep interest in the natural world and in music, as well as her great fondness for animals, was passed on to her son.*

friend Alfred Domett remembered her as a woman with the squarest head he had ever seen. It put him in mind "absurdly enough no doubt of a tea-chest or tea-caddy," but he also remembered the great affection Robert had for her, and his gentleness toward her as well.

Sarah Anna Browning had married in midlife, and she died a few months short of completing her seventy-seventh year. In his late thirties, Robert experienced for the first time crushing human grief. It was the type of pain none of us escapes, as Elizabeth noted. The birth of the child and simultaneous death of the mother unhinged him. Just as he was beginning to draw close to his child, he could not help drawing away. The joy he had felt at the birth seemed a devilish irony. Whatever guilt he felt for leaving a mother in her mid-seventies, for her never having met his wife, never knowing of the birth of her only grandchild, never having the normal compensations from a son's marriage, came crashing in. In his grief, he could not accept his new happiness. It was now Elizabeth who had to take care of her husband, through a long stretch of despondency. She, who was well acquainted with grief, said she never experienced one as deep as Browning's over his mother.

During these early years of the marriage, there had been other times when Robert's health had suffered—incidents perhaps leading to this crisis in 1849. The previous summer, before the birth of his son, he had had a serious bout of influenza. Florence lies in a picturesque valley surrounded by rolling hills, immortalized in Renaissance painting. In the dog days of summer, aesthetics can't save it; it can smolder. The Arno quivers not as the arrow in Elizabeth's poetry but in simulation of a low boil. Elizabeth herself had just recuperated from the miscarriage she had in late February or early March 1848. Arabel copied her sister's letter out for Henrietta. "It appears that I am not strong enough for some blessings—but others are lavished on me." As Robert recovered from influenza, the couple decided on a trip to the Adriatic in the middle of a blistering July.

The first stop was Fano, outside Ancona. They had come toward the Adriatic for cool breezes, but once more their travel plans were overly optimistic. They had relied on the Murray guidebook, which said Fano was a good summer residence—but it, too, was baking. They found "vegetation scorched into paleness, the very air swooning in the sun, and the gloomy looks of the inhabitants sufficiently corroborative of their words, that no drop of rain or dew ever falls there during the summer." After three days they "fled" to Ancona, a "sea-city" beautiful to look at but so hot that they stayed a week "living upon fish & cold water. Water, water, was the cry all day long." Elizabeth spent her time stripped down to her petticoat in her hotel, hardly caring if the waiter saw her, "demoralized out of all sense of female vanity, not to say decency." But it had been in the terrible heat of Fano a week before that Robert became inspired to write the first poem since his marriage.

There, in the blessedly cool, dark interior of the Church of St. Augustine, Robert became transfixed by an altarpiece by Guercino, the *Guardian Angel.* This angel, a rather monumental, androgynous central figure with glorious outstretched wings, had its long, graceful hands around a small kneeling child, whom it was teaching how to pray. For it, not just for cool sanctuary, the couple reappeared three times in three days.

Part of Robert's restlessness in those days, an unease he could not explain, might have been because of his unproductivity. His dream had been to marry his love and for both of them to escape the world and to write. Elizabeth had written and sent off to America "The Runaway Slave"; she had completed the first part of *Casa Guidi Windows.* She was readying the next edition of her works; he, too, was busily preparing his old poems for publication. Both were editing more than writing. Neither of them, at this period, could be called prolific. But Robert Browning had written nothing new at all.

Another part of his unease was his anxiety about money. That her brothers were now accusing him of living off his wife must have brought to the fore his worst fears. The only vulnerability to the world the couple acknowledged was this defensiveness about their combined income. And by Fano, Elizabeth might have either suspected or known she was once more pregnant. He had saved his wife from death by British winter, and had exposed her to death by hemorrhaging. Was any child worth the risk?

Robert Browning now had the love he wanted. Did he need anything else? Where would this third pregnancy lead? He did not pursue a career in order to be free to write, yet he wasn't writing. Was he another one of those gifted men, like his friends in England, who wrote and published verse in their youth, then drifted to other things and never really found themselves? Men who suffered from religious doubts? Had he lost the promise of his youth? Was he homesick for what had been? He brought anxiety into church with him.

In the cool interior of St. Augustine, detached from the heat of the day, Browning looked up at Guercino's *Guardian Angel* with its flowing robes, its outstretched wings, and its eyes pointing the child toward heaven. And he asked the angel to leave that child it was teaching to pray, "when thou has done with him, for me!" He wanted those hands that clasped the small hands of the child to cure his malaise. He wished them to close his eyes and draw him near, and then the "healing hands" would act much like human hands ministering to a migraine:

> *Pressing the brain, which too much thought expands,*
> *Back to its proper size again, and smoothing*
> *Distortion down till every nerve had soothing,*
> *And all lay quiet, happy and suppressed.*

In this wish to "lay quiet, happy and suppressed," his biographer Betty Miller saw "something which corresponded closely with an omnipresent need of his own nature," that of "childhood's surrender to the ministering presence of a supreme being." Today we are less uncomfortable when an adult asks the "bird of God" to suspend his flight and "see another child for tending, / Another still, to quiet and retrieve."

We are less uncomfortable when an adult comes in contact with his own need for succoring and nurturing, which Browning so clearly captured in the poem.

The poet prayed for healing, the repair of "all worldly wrong" so that he could view the world once more as God had made it. With these newly opened eyes, he could see that

> *All is beauty:*
> *And knowing this, is love, and love is duty.*
> *What further may be sought for or declared?*

These strong lines seem to complete the five-stanza poem.

One wonders if these stanzas were all composed at Fano and the three additional stanzas added in Ancona the next week. The poet was no longer in church. The voice of the three ending stanzas used an "I" much more personal and subjective than the one his wife had employed in the first part of *Casa Guidi Windows.* The poet spoke directly to a friend:

> *Guercino drew this angel I saw teach*
> *(Alfred, dear friend!)—that little child to pray.*

In an awkward parenthesis, Alfred Domett, whom Browning hadn't seen since Domett abruptly left for New Zealand in 1842, popped right into his poetry.

WHEN ONE THINKS of Alfred Domett, one thinks first of the George Lance watercolor of him, the poet in his youth. A sensuous, dark-haired, handsome young man with a cleft chin, clothed in a romantic cape, and wearing a wide-brimmed and floppy hat. This was the image Browning would keep for thirty years, till Domett, the ex–prime minister of New Zealand, returned one day, as abruptly as he had left, and called on the poet in London. Browning captured the earlier romantic wandering poet in a poem published in 1842, "What's Become of Waring?" In it Waring was glimpsed on a pirate ship.

The real Waring, Alfred Domett, wrote to say goodbye to his friend Browning, dating the note simply "Saturday." Browning recorded in his own hand: "April 30, 1842—the day he set sail aboard the S.S. Sir Charles Forbes."

Dear Browning—

I return your books with many thanks—I need not assure you of my love nor that my wishes for all good for you will be as lasting as life. God bless you for ever—*Write* (to *the world*)—& to me at New Zealand. Say goodbye for me to your family—I have no time to call—

Yrs ever
Alfred Domett

Domett quietly sent along a book of his own, his *Poems* of 1833. Possibly too rushed or too proud to autograph it, he left it for Browning to record carefully: "From A.D. May 2, 1842 RB."

Twenty days and two attempts later, Browning wrote his first letter to his friend. "I have a sort of notion you will come back some bright morning a dozen years hence and find me just gone—to Heaven, or Timbuctoo; and I give way a little to this fancy while I write, because it lets me write freely . . . my real love for you—better love than I had supposed I was fit for."

When he was a boy, he told his friend, as he would later tell his wife-to-be, "I had fancy in plenty and no kind of judgment," but as a man, he grew. "However I am so sure now, of my feelings, when I do feel—trust to them so much, and am deceived about them so little—(I mean, that I so rarely believe I like where I loathe, and the reverse, as the people round me do)—that I can speak about myself and my sentiments with full confidence. There!"

Once again—"There!" Browning did not confuse his emotions one for the other. He knew his own feelings. "I shall never read over what I send you,—reflect on it, care about it, or fear that you will not burn it when I ask you," he told dear Alfred. "So do with me. And tell me all about yourself, straight, without courteously speculating about my being . . . and by my taking the same course . . . we shall get more done in a letter than when half is wasted."

Three years later, in her third letter to Robert, Elizabeth wrote the exact same thing. She asked him for a straightforward, honest, "masculine" correspondence: "*Don't* let us have any constraint, any ceremony!

ALFRED DOMETT
(1811–87) AS A YOUNG
MAN. *A pencil sketch by
Robert Browning, Sr., the
poet's father. Previously
identified as a possible early
portrait of the poet. Domett
was a constant visitor to the
Brownings' home in what RB
called "the suburban shade of
Camberwell" in the late
1820s through the early
1840s.*

ALFRED DOMETT. *Engraving
of the sketch by George Lance.
Domett, a close friend of the
young Browning, left England
in 1842, three years before RB's
courtship of EBB, and did not
return for thirty years. He
emigrated to New Zealand,
where he was a journalist and
later became prime minister
(1862–63).*

Don't be civil to me when you feel rude. . . . & let us rest from the bowing and the curtseying. . . . You will find me an honest man on the whole, if rather hasty & prejudging, . . which is a different thing from prejudice at the worst. And we have great sympathies in common. . . ." Talk about the marriage of true minds.

Two months before his marriage Browning hinted of the possibility to Domett. "I have some important objects in view with respect to my future life—which I will acquaint you with next time I write, when they will be proved attainable or no." The poet did not write to him again for twenty-six years.

After the marriage, their mutual friend Joseph Arnould, a lawyer who was also managing Browning's part of the marriage settlement, kept Domett up-to-date. He heard from Browning "a week back, in which he mentions you most kindly, and begged me to tell you all about him." Arnould didn't need much prompting. In his letter of November 30, 1846, he had already written, "I think the last piece of news I told you of was Browning's marriage to Miss Barrett—which I had then just heard of. She is, you know, or else I told you or ought to have told you, our present greatest living English 'poetess.' "

He then told Domett: "She had been for some years an invalid, leading a very secluded life in a sick room in the household of one of those tyrannical, arbitrary, puritanical rascals who go sleekly about the world, canting Calvinism abroad, and acting despotism at home. Under the iron rigour of this man's domestic rule she, feeble and invalided, had grown up to eight and thirty years of age in the most absolute and enforced seclusion from society: cultivating her mind to a wonderful amount of accomplishment, instructing herself in all languages, reading . . . original Greek, and publishing the best metrical translation that has yet appeared of the 'Prometheus Bound'—having also found time to write three volumes of poetry, the last of which raised her name to a place second only to that of Browning and Tennyson."

The love story was told from the groom's side of the aisle: "Well, this lady so gifted, so secluded, so tyrannised over, fell in love with Browning in spirit, before ever she saw him in the flesh—in plain English loved the writer before she knew the man. Imagine, you know him, the effect which his graceful bearing, high demeanour, and noble speech must have had on such a mind when she first saw the man of her visions in the twilight of her darkened room. She was at once in love as a poet-soul only can be, and Browning, as by contagion or electricity, was no less from the first interview wholly in love with her. . . . He of course wished to ask the father openly. 'If you do,' was her terrified answer, 'he would immediately throw me out of [a] window, or lock me up for life in a darkened room.' There was one thing only to be done, and that Browning did: married her without the father's knowledge, and immediately left England with her for Italy, where they are now living in Pisa in as supreme a state of happiness as you can fancy two such people in such a place. The old rascal father of course tore his beard, foamed at the mouth and performed all other feats of impotent rage: luckily his wrath is absolutely idle, for she has a small independence of some £350 per ann., on which they will of course live prosperously."

He almost forgot to mention that the "invalid of seven years, once emancipated from the paternal despotism, has had a wondrous revival, or rather, a complete metamorphosis; walks, rides, eats and drinks like a young and healthy woman." He referred to her as in her thirties, not forty, but still "a little old—too old for Browning—but then one word covers all: they are in Love, who lends his own youth to everything."

The next letter Robert Browning wrote to Domett was in 1872. "How very happy I am that I shall see you again! I never could bear to answer the letter you wrote to me years ago, though I carried it always about with me abroad in order to muster up courage some day which never came: it was too hard to begin and end with all that happened during the last thirty years."

The last three stanzas of "The Guardian Angel" were an attempt to answer "Alfred, dear friend!"—or at least send a picture postcard of the *Guardian Angel*:

> *We were at Fano, and three times we went*
> *To sit and see him in his chapel there,*
> *And drink his beauty to our soul's content*
> *—My angel with me too.*

As Browning viewed Guercino's angel, with his wife by his side, Domett on his mind, he realized he cared that Guercino's fame should be recognized. Guercino did not work "earnestly" at all times, and he had "endured some wrong." So what Browning attempted, he told his friend, was to help spread the fame of an artist who had problems similar to his own—and to Domett's—being misunderstood, and not always being hard at work. He took the magnificent pathos of the picture "And spread it out, translating it to song." There was nostalgia and longing as he ended in a poet's postscript.

> *My love is here. Where are you, dear old friend?*
> *How rolls the Wairoa at your world's far end?*
> *This is Ancona, yonder is the sea.*

The longing was deeper, the vision less flippant and more personal than it had been six years before when Browning wrote

> *What's become of Waring*
> *Since he gave us all the slip,*
> *Chose land-travel or seafaring,*
> *Boots and chest or staff and scrip,*
> *Rather than pace up and down*
> *Any longer London town?*

Recuperating from influenza, traveling with his angel, who was once more pregnant, the poet had the need of healing hands. The sea did not bring relief from the intense summer heat; its beauty pointed yonder, to all that went before and was now so far away.

Returning to Florence in the fall of 1848, the Brownings settled in at the home that would be theirs throughout their marriage, the apartment in the Casa Guidi, the building a "stone's throw from the Grand Duke's," the Pitti Palace. Explaining why they had taken the rooms unfurnished this time, Elizabeth had written to Arabel in May that such a choice would expedite their ability to spend summers in England: "Now, Florence is the cheapest place in Italy, which brings it to being the cheapest place in the world. Also this is the cheapest moment in Florence, through . . . really a silly panic. After a good deal of thinking then, we resolved on taking advantage of the cheapest moment in this cheapest place, to adopt the infinitely cheapest means of life." By furnishing the rooms themselves, they would later be able to "sell furnishings or let the apartment using the proceeds to travel to England." No doubt this was the logic she applied to her frugal husband. No doubt she also fell in love with the empty apartment. She was willing to sacrifice a carriage for it. After all, she was well enough to walk. In May she sketched for Arabel "our seven rooms, three of which are magnificent & the others are excellent . . to say nothing of our terraces." The rather narrow terrace that opened out to the courtyard was the one the Brownings would go out on after coffee and walk back and forth for hours, till night fell. "The church of San Felice is opposite, so we haven't a neighbour to look through the sunlight or moonlight and take observations. Isn't that pleasant altogether?"

Yet a badly ulcerated throat followed Browning's summer influenza, and he was laid up at the Casa Guidi in September and October, refusing to see a physician. Nothing seemed to make him improve. Unlike the *Guardian Angel,* Browning's angel was unable to heal her husband, and as a result fell into what she described to her sisters as an un-Christian funk. Politically, more conservative forces were mounting in Italy. Physically, Elizabeth was past her first trimester. A letter

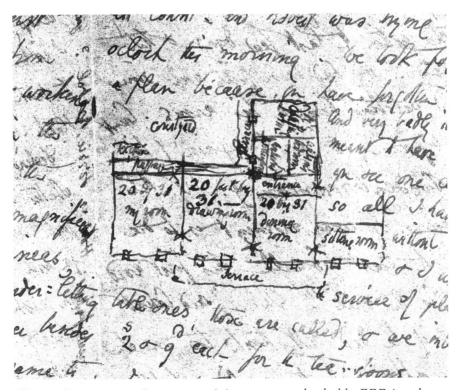

FLOOR PLAN OF THE BROWNINGS' APARTMENT, *sketched by EBB in a letter to her sister Arabel, May 1848. It was EBB's idea that the couple rent the apartment in the Casa Guidi unfurnished, furnish it themselves, and sublet it during their long stays in Paris and England.*

to Mary Mitford was full of her usual concern for the older woman's health. "Were you never tempted to see into the meaning of that advertisement about 'constipation'?—and a little book has appeared, I think, on the same subject." She then told her friend that on October 8, two days ago, she had fallen forward out of her "lolling chair." She hit her forehead with violence, but this protected her stomach. "Here's the end of keeping in the house for months together, to avoid shakings & strainings! One falls out of an easy chair into the arms of destiny." She hoped that all she'd get from it was "a week's disfigurement & an hour's headache—but the shock stunned me & couldn't have happened *at a more unfortunate time.* Nobody was ever born to be happier & unhappier than I—the 'mingled yarn' is black & white."

Robert Browning with his sore throat was no longer the lover in yellow gloves who would not walk on the street where she lived, no longer the deliciously foolish wise man on his wedding trip. He was a husband about to become a father. He had written one new poem since his marriage and was unable to support his wife on the proceeds from his poetry. Since the time of the love letters he thought of seeking employment. Elizabeth vehemently urged him to stay constant to his art. But his unease about his finances continued. In Pisa, on the election of Pio Nono, it was thought there might be a British Legation to the Holy See. Browning wrote to inquire about filling that post. He had experience. Before he met his wife, he had been part of a delegation to Russia. Though in his letter he stated he would do this for patriotic reasons alone, and did not want a stipend, he probably envisioned one. The project, however, did not materialize.

Many of Browning's friends and acquaintances were writers who made a living as journalists. Among them were William Makepeace Thackeray, Charles Dickens, and the Reverend Francis Sylvester Mahony, known in his day as "Father Prout." The novelist Thackeray was often the voice of Mr. Punch. Dickens, along with John Forster, was the founder of the *Daily News* during a time when events often brought him to Rome. In Rome, his paper had a brilliant, if erratic, Vatican correspondent—that flamboyant literary man, poet, and Jesuit, "Frank" Mahony. Through Mahony, Browning was going to have a ringside view of the papacy, without being in a delegation.

As a young man, Mahony had had great theological potential. He was educated by the Jesuits in Ireland and abroad and became prefect of studies at Clongowes Woods, his own as well as James Joyce's alma mater. Mahony was forced to resign from this position after returning late and drunk from an expedition with students. Hardly the prefect of studies James Joyce would one day immortalize. Apparently the Jesuits still held hopes for Mahony, as they sent him to Rome on a period of probation. Of this period he told his friends that "he might have had a Cardinal's hat, but for that which is imputed to him as his one great fault—conviviality."

By 1834, in London, the priest Mahony found a second profession, one more suited to his bohemian way of life and his love of drink—he became a journalist. He started to write for *Fraser's Magazine,* taking as his persona the deceased Father Prout, whom Mahony had known as a child. He wrote lively articles interspersed with poetry in the manner of a witty, learned, but essentially frolicking and gentle-hearted priest. He lived addicted to club life, as one of the hard-drinking Fraserians. In the Daniel Maclise caricature of that famous group, we pick out, among the splendid array of wineglasses, Thackeray and Mahony.

Browning met Father Prout in London in the 1830s. "I never knew where he lived; he used to disappear, and return as unexpectedly. . . . One day I began 'I go to Italy—'

" 'We shall probably meet there,' he said.

"I started a few days after, spent a month on the road and reached Leghorn; as I was being rowed past the Lazaretto to land, I looked up at the knot of passengers just deposited there by a steamer of longer passage than mine. Mahony was leaning over the rail."

Mahony had an uncanny way of popping up at significant moments in Browning's life. However, when Browning remembered this unexpected meeting at port thirty years after it occurred, he tailored his impressions away from the personal. For it had occurred during Browning's wedding trip just as the couple finally disembarked in Italy. It had been prepared for by a meeting at another significant occasion—on the day Browning picked up the fateful passport which would get him and his wife out of England. As he crossed Poland Street with the passport in his hand, "just at the crisis, he met—Father Prout."

"Oh, of course, I met him just then," Robert told Elizabeth. "It was a moment worthy of being so signalized!"

"Curious," Elizabeth responded.

She didn't think more of it. Then, at the end of their arduous wedding trip, finally arriving in Italy, "landing at Leghorn, at nine o'clock in the morning, our boat which was rowed from the steamer to the shore, passed close to a bare jutting piece of rock on which stood a man wrapt in a cloak, he also having just landed from an English vessel bound from Southampton—*Father Prout!!* Wasn't it an extraordinary 'dramatic effect?'. . ."

"Robert cried out, 'Good Heavens, there he is again!—there's Father Prout!'

"We went to the inn and breakfasted, and after breakfast the reverend Lion came into the room, and I had the honour of introduction—not of examination though, for as he told Mrs. Jameson afterwards, when he met her in Rome, he couldn't see my face through my black veil." She had drawn it down when he approached.

Seeing Father Prout from their boat, standing on a rock, wrapped in a cloak, as Elizabeth reported at the time, or seeing him bending over the rail of a ship, as Browning remembered it years later, was quite reminiscent of how Browning envisioned a glimpse of Waring on the pirate ship:

> *And one, half-hidden . . .*
> *Under the furled sail soon I spied,*
> *With great grass hat and kerchief black,*
> *Who looked up with his kingly throat*

and "then the boat, /I know not how, turned sharply round." A case of life imitating art. But Father Prout turned up in more than poetry.

Two months after their first anniversary, Robert came home from his walk one evening in Florence and said to Elizabeth, "Ah, ha! I have been kissed by somebody since I saw you last."

Rather than teasing her to jealousy, he jolted her. For she was suddenly seized with the idea that her two sisters had arrived in Florence, "Arabel at any rate! Yes I thought it was Arabel!"

Seeing her gasp for breath Robert quickly explained "it was only his haunting friend, Father Prout," who was just there for an hour or two on his way to Rome.

Father Prout's greeting—he "*kissed* him in the street, mouth to mouth, a good deal to his surprise." During their few hours together Prout inquired about Elizabeth, "reiterated his regret at my veil being down at Leghorn," promised to send them "from Rome a letter of introduction to our Grand Duke's librarian of the Pitti," went to a cof-

feehouse with Robert, and then, with Robert helping him, got into the
diligence to Rome. He hadn't time "to go home with Robert and see
his unveiled prophetess."

But he would. In the fall of 1848, the period of the assassination of
the Pope's minister and the Pope's disguised retreat to Naples, Father
Prout came to Florence. He walked in on the couple. "If you could see
us in these great rooms (they are so immensely high that they look still
larger) you would think it all rather desolate still. No carpets down,
no curtains bought yet," Elizabeth had written to Arabel in May. By
fall she had decided to do the bedroom in whites, and they were still
waiting for fresh curtains that were taking forever to be delivered.
Mahony certainly arrived at another significant moment. Among the
scant new furnishings and the newly laid carpet, he found his friend
Browning burning with fever, pale, sleepless, his eyes languid, his
pulse racing. The unveiled prophetess had a nasty bruise on her
forehead. Only two days before she had fallen from her chair and
toward her destiny. She was bruised, pregnant, staying away from
morphine, and worried about a possible miscarriage and her husband's
health. There stood Father Prout, in the middle of what could be
called a low point of loving domesticity. The couple's situation seemed
as dire as his friend Anna Jameson's predictions.

The Jesuit was chameleon in dress, witty in speech, and perceptive
enough to see at a glance that things were in disarray. He had that combination of charm and audaciousness that often accompanies a dissolute
nature—that sense of being kinder than his comments. His friend
Browning needed strength and his friend's wife needed humor. Elizabeth credited his perceptivity as part of "knowing everything as those
Jesuits are apt to do." He saw that Robert's fever was advancing because
his general condition was too weak to fight it. And that the unveiled
Elizabeth was frightened to death. He worked his magic, preparing a
cure "with his own kind hand," Elizabeth reported. It was a mixture of
eggs and wine. Their new Italian servant, watching this, rolled his eyes
to the heavens, crying "O Inglesi, Inglesi!"—which one can translate,
What will these foreigners think of next? But the cure worked.

In 1864, sixteen years later, Robert remembered the scene in almost the same words as Elizabeth, but he added that even after the
spiced wine, "I could not get sleep for the pain, and my wife took my
head in her two little hands, in broad daylight, and I went to sleep at
once, and woke better." Browning's guardian angel, prayed to a few

months before in Fano, arrived in Florence as a renegade Jesuit aided by his own wife's healing hands. "My husband is perfectly well, thank God, better than he has been for years, he says, in certain respects . . as in the power of eating and absence of headache. As for me, I am quite well too, . . &, so *far* have not appeared to suffer from my fall. If really no harm has been done . . . it is all but miraculous, considering the circumstances."

Robert remembered that after his cure "to assist convalescence" Prout "came six weeks together, without the interval of a day, spending evenings hilariously." Or as Elizabeth exclaimed to her sisters, "Father Prout has spent *every evening here except one,* since I wrote last!" Her eternal gratitude gave way to impatience. "As a matter of course the wine is rung for instantly, with an apparatus for spitting!"

Prout told the couple that "Florence agreed with him better than Rome did, that he liked the place, liked the beef, liked the bread and especially liked his Attic evenings with Browning and Ba!"

From her couch, where she spent her pregnancy, Ba observed she had never seen two brilliant men with such diametrically opposed ideas. But this was the type of dueling Browning loved; it brought him out of himself. Browning and Mahony could argue about religion, politics, literature; they could gossip about friends. Two minds brimming to the full in learning and perception, one an atheistic priest, the other a believing and at the same time brooding poet.

A Haydon in the living room? Even one who cured sore throats? A little more difficult than outrageous behavior by letter, though not impossible. "I lie on the sofa, and listen, and let myself be called 'Ba!' (for I assure you it comes to that,) without much minding: and when he goes away, there's a general burst of indignation and throwing open of doors to get rid of smoke and malice. After all there are things in the man which one can't help liking."

The "malice" that had to be aired out was Mahony's staggering cynicism. The more he drank, the more sardonic he became, seeing anew how unfair was life.

Robert must have spoken of their scorching summer trip, and of the days in Ancona, in which the only reprieve from the heat was the interesting meetings they had with the mother of the British Roman Catholic Bishop, soon to be Cardinal, Nicholas Wiseman. The mother, like the son, was cultivated and aristocratic, combining wealth, good taste, and intelligence.

Mahony knew Wiseman from earlier days. Why, if Mahony were a hypocrite, he could have been a Bishop, too. Others had said he could have been. Why, if he could leave off or hide his bottles, if he could flatter and cajole, and suppress his doubts, why, his early promise would have borne its fruit, and he'd be way up there in the Church as was Wiseman. Mahony was too honest to pursue a Cardinal's hat. In vino veritas. He was a poor literary man assigned by Dickens, at the moment, to cover the Vatican—his ecclesiastical duties, he called them. His newspaper work, in which he often satirized the Pope and Nicholas Wiseman, was anonymous, but as early as these meetings with Browning, he had been found out.

Father Prout's doubt echoed Domett's. Dear Alfred had already been in the news defending the colonial interests against a Maori uprising—the Wairau affair—but at the same time trying to be "fair" to the "native rights" of "savages." They should be treated with "the kindness and patience, but with the firmness and authority, requisite in the management of children." He defended the New Zealand Company's rights against the natives using the words of Carlyle. His remarks were published and copies taken to Australia—"Mr. Domett and the Press." Browning tried unsuccessfully to get Domett's remarks published in England. One is not surprised his correspondence with Domett ended after his marriage to Elizabeth Barrett. Soon Domett would propose subsidizing public education, and keeping mention of Christianity out of these schools. Again, the logic here was complicated, but it filtered to the press and to the people as a manifesto of anticlericalism and secular education. At its best, Domett's view of Christianity was not Christ-centered; he saw religion as a moral code. Father Prout, with his blade of logic, saw religion as the vehicle for the advancement of hypocritical men.

For Browning, these six weeks of wine and conversation would be the seeds of inspiration for one of the great poems of his married years. Perhaps Mahony was already telling him of the rumors that in a few years would ignite into fact.

Since Henry VIII broke from Rome and established the Church of England, Roman Catholics in England had practiced their religion as quietly as possible. They were "low church," sacrificing anything flamboyant in ritual or costume. In the nineteenth century there were movements within Anglicanism itself to reestablish some of the old ceremonies of the mass, a return to flowing robes and to incense, a

sense of "high church." While the Anglican Church pondered reintro-
ducing earlier Catholic doctrines and practices, the Roman Catholic
Church in England remained as hushed as possible, not to draw down
upon itself and its Pope the wrath of John Bull.

For example, a British Roman Catholic Bishop did not become a
Bishop of a specific geographical location. He was given a spiritual, not
a temporal, realm. As Cardinal, Wiseman would assume the title of St.
Pudentiana, a church name. What Pio Nono did when he elevated
Nicholas Wiseman was daring and startling—and urged by Wiseman
himself. He reestablished the Roman Catholic hierarchy in England
and gave Nicholas Wiseman a real place name, the name such a Bishop
might have had in England before Henry VIII. Cardinal Nicholas
Wiseman came back from Rome the Archbishop of Westminster.

"We ought to have our Abbey back" were the words Bishop
Blougram used at the beginning of Browning's poem "Bishop
Blougram's Apology." The line evoked the mood in England in
1850–51, when it was widely suspected that Pio Nono might actually
attempt to reclaim Westminster Abbey. In the *Punch* cartoon of November 23, 1850, Wiseman acts as the shifty-eyed lookout as Pio
Nono attempts to break into Westminster Abbey. The tool the Pope
used to wedge open the door was embossed the "Roman Archbishopric
of Westminster," and the cartoon read, "The Thin End of the Wedge.
Daring attempt to break into a church."

The unmitigated outrage against the reestablishment of the Roman
Catholic hierarchy was exacerbated by an ill-timed "Pastoral Letter"
written from Rome in which Wiseman seemed to ignore both the
Anglican crown and clergy and seemed to suggest a direct relationship
between papal authority and the sovereign state of Great Britain.
When Wiseman realized the extent of commotion caused by his "Pastoral Letter"—he was burned in effigy on Guy Fawkes Day—he returned immediately to London, took the bull by the horns, and
published his own apology, called "An Appeal to the Reason and Good
Feeling of the English People on the Subject of the Catholic Hierarchy," which was reprinted in full in five London newspapers. Thirty
thousand copies of the pamphlet were sold in a few days. Of course, he
didn't assuage such fears much by the way he returned. He came off the
ship in full cardinal's regalia, wearing his red cardinal hat and carrying
the bones of a saint. This inspired *Punch*'s New Year's Day cartoon for
1851. *Punch*'s "Proposal for a Happy New Year" was to ship the newly

CARDINAL NICHOLAS WISEMAN (1802–65). *Engraving after a watercolor by F. Rochard, 1836. The prototype for RB's Bishop Blougram. He was born in Spain of Anglo-Irish parents. His cultivated Roman Catholic mother, Xaviera Strange Wiseman, was an acquaintance of the Brownings, whom they met in Fano, where Wiseman's sister the Countess Gabrelli lived. It was Nicholas Wiseman who convinced Pio Nono to reestablish the Roman Catholic hierarchy in England and to send him back to London as the first Archbishop of Westminster. This caused a furor in England that RB satirizes in "Bishop Blougram's Apology."*

"I LIKE TO BE DESPISED." Punch, *December 7, 1850. A caricature of Nicholas Wiseman in his satirized big cardinal's hat; he had returned to England in November 1850 to a barrage of press criticism. "So, you despise me, Mr. Gigadibs," Bishop Blougram tells his adversary, the newspaperman, at the beginning of RB's "Bishop Blougram's Apology."*

THE FRASERIANS. *Contributors in 1835 to* Fraser's Magazine *by Daniel Maclise. The Jesuit Frank Mahony, who wrote under the name of Father Prout, was one of the many literary men in London RB knew, though RB himself never wrote for the newspapers and magazines. Clockwise from the standing Maginn, one picks out Irving, Mahony, Carlyle, D'Orsay, Lockhart, Fraser with his back toward the viewer, Coleridge with a cane, Thackeray, and Southey, among others.*

appointed Cardinal, "from Westminster to Melipotamus," back to a legendary see.

The newspaper battle that ensued was scurrilous and unmitigated enough to equal a later "media frenzy." Thackeray led the Protestant attack, in the voice of John Bull in *Punch* editorials. The Catholic attack was anonymous as well, but Wiseman knew immediately who was leading it. It was Father Prout, writing now for the *Globe.* Cardinal Wiseman responded in the Catholic *Rambler.* "We have read, occasionally, articles of the *Globe* upon the late agitation, the brilliancy of illustration, the richness of apt quotation, the wit of reckless satire, and the inaccuracy of detail, confirmed what we had heard, that they are the productions of a pen, once more innocently employed on the literary forgeries of Father Prout. It strikes us with a melancholy regret, to witness the prostitution of talents apparently destined for a nobler cause, to think of the heart in which the convictions of early education and a sacred vocation, are day-by-day made objects of derision, and what has been taught as holy, is scoffed at, as absurd. One so engaged we must leave to grace, acting perhaps through present remorse; we can only say, that though generally these have been the most *telling* articles against us, we have felt them the least. In other writers we say there was often the conviction of a hearty bigotry; in these there was the hollowness of the mere vanity to dazzle."

Elizabeth saw this vanity in Father Prout. "I firmly believe that he is kind-hearted, in spite of his cynicism brought up on every occasion. . . . What is the unpleasant part of it, is the defect in delicacy, conventional or otherwise—and of course it is this which prevents him from perceiving at a glance that the constancy of his evening visits is an excess—to say the least of it. Still, one likes the human nature of the man."

"Hilarious" was the way Robert Browning would, decades later, recall those evenings of his early marriage. That was his impression of his friend of the wine and the spittoon: The Rome correspondent of a Vatican in crisis was another friend from earlier days.

One day Robert had the surprise of seeing this squib in the Paris paper, extracted from the *Daily News.* "Rome is less happy than Florence in possessing *only* Mrs. Trollope and Lady Charlotte Bury, whereas Florence has Mr. Grattan, Mr. Lever, and Robert Browning and his gifted wife." He showed the French notice to Elizabeth, and they laughed over it "a little at coffee-time. . . . We suspect Father Prout of being the expounder of the supreme happiness of Florence."

Their own supreme happiness and relief after the birth of their healthy son four months later was badly shaken by the death of Browning's mother. "He has loved his mother as such passionate natures only can love, and I never saw a man so bowed down in an extremity of sorrow—never."

A love relationship exists on balances, as well as shared sympathies. And Browning at his weakest moment had a wife who had never been as strong. Her strength in labor led her doctor to tell a nurse, "In all his practice he has never seen the functions of nature more healthfully performed." Elizabeth realized she had suffered labor of less duration and given birth to a child more robust than those "active, blooming women" whom she knew in Florence. Wasn't it curious, she wrote, that "MY child should be remarkable for strength & fatness?"

She wanted to nurse herself: She certainly had the milk for it. Though her medical adviser Mr. Jago agreed with her, she had abdicated "by force of public opinion." The child went through many strong wet nurses instead in the year and a half before he was weaned. Elizabeth joined the majority opinion, thought the decision wise. "After the rapture of hearing my child's first cry, I thought of nothing but of what was best for him—and the farther from me the better surely!—It was enough that I had not injured him so far!"

Three days after her forty-third birthday, a woman who had been an invalid all of her adult life, whose slight body, like her handwriting, could be described as a whisper, against all probabilities, and against her father's wishes, had given birth to a healthy child.

In the summer of 1849, her husband in mourning, she had come into her own as a woman. "I can do as much, or more, now, than at any point of my life since I arrived at woman's estate." It was also the first time since the age of fourteen that she had been off morphine for a considerable length of time. Robert boasted of this and of her concentration on good nutrition. "That resolution of leaving off the morphine," had "one among a thousand 'strong men' " that determination? "Then in her food, habits . . she was perfect and faultless from first to last . . the nurse says of the babe 'how well nourished he has been.' " In the love letters he referred to her as his Ba, who preferred morphine to pork chops, but the truth is that both the Brownings had terrible eating habits.

Perhaps one didn't have to be as learned as a defrocked Jesuit to take one look at Robert Browning ill and realize he needed some eggs in his wine. Elizabeth and he ate very little. They favored a poet's food group and seemed to exist on coffee, a bit of bread, chestnuts, and grapes. The two of them were once seen sharing a squab! Pomegranates, we are told straight out, are only to be admired visually and written about. One of the joys of Italy, the glorious fruits and vegetables, is occasionally mentioned—Robert loved watermelon—but sun seemed to supply vitamin C. Though we know neither could abide garlic or olive oil, one wonders if either ever ordered a salad. And when Elizabeth was overexcited or depressed, or when her lungs acted up and the coughing and phlegm reappeared, she took more morphine and ate even less. And drank more good strong coffee for those shattered nerves. Pregnancy changed this for its duration, and it along with her new motherhood contributed to a burst of well-being.

After her mother-in-law's death, Elizabeth was greatly disappointed about canceling the plans to travel to England, but she didn't let Robert know. They never read each other's letters in order to give each other absolute latitude, so she was able to confide to Mary Mitford: "He says it would break his heart to see his mother's roses over the wall & the place where she used to lay her scissors & gloves. Which I understand so thoroughly that I can't say 'Let us go to England.' We must wait & see what his father & sister will choose to do or choose us to do—for of course a duty plainly seen, would draw us anywhere. My own dearest sisters will be painfully disappointed by any change of plans," but they were too understanding not to understand the motive.

Browning didn't want to go anywhere. His wife convinced him to look for a summer place by swearing that she and baby would not be able to bear the summer heat. It might have also helped that the two of them went on their exploratory trip alone, leaving the baby with his nurse and with Wilson. They traveled along the coast to La Spezia, saw the white marble mountains of Carrara, and had a glimpse of Shelley's house at Lerici. To go to where Shelley had drowned was not particularly foresighted of the couple. It brought back Elizabeth's memories of her beloved Bro.

Retracing their steps and going high into a mountain village, they found out once again that "just in proportion to the want of civilization the prices rise in Italy. If you haven't cups & saucers you are made to pay for plate." Elizabeth then persuaded Robert to take just a look at the Baths of Lucca. He had a particular aversion to them, hearing they were a "wasp's nest of scandal & gaming." Once more, rather than finding a place "trodden flat by the continental English," they were charmed by the cool mountains, the exquisite scenery, and the lack of their countrymen. It was cheap and away from it all, and they took an apartment for four months, till the end of October, for a reasonable rate. "We have taken a sort of eagle's nest in this place, . . the highest house of the highest of the three villages which are called the Bagni di Lucca." Here they would not hear the Austrians drumming from their windows. Returning to Florence, Elizabeth had a momentary dread that something would be wrong with the baby, but they opened the door of the Casa Guidi to find him happy, healthy, and content.

The child was baptized Robert Wiedemann Barrett Browning.

They meant to call him Wiedemann, Browning's mother's maiden name. "It was all Ba's doing—strange to say—tho' I have been thinking over nothing else, these last three months, than Mama and all about her, and catching at any little fancy of finding something which it would have pleased her I should do,—yet I never was struck by the obvious opportunity I had of doing the honour in my power, little as it was, by keeping up the memory of that dearest of names." When they decided to christen the child before leaving for the summer vacation, "Ba told me I should greatly oblige *her* by not only giving our child that name but by always calling him by it, when he is old enough." She told Robert she found the name "very pretty in itself, and sees many advantages in distinguishing between the two Roberts, avoiding nicknames for either of us." No greater love hath woman. She proudly called her son "Wiedeman" (with one "n"), until Wiedeman, being a Barrett as well, found himself a nickname. To Robert, such a christening "is, of course, a very insignificant instance of Ba's sympathy with me,—still I mention it, because it gratified me more as coming from her, than from anybody else."

By early July they had arrived at Bagni di Lucca. Robert was thin, haggard. Any effects of the prescription of "wine and good things" had long since worn off. At the Baths less than a week, he brought his grief to the mountaintop. "This evening I climbed to the top of a mountain, over loose stones in the dry bed of a torrent, and under vines and chestnuts, till I reached an old deserted village, with perhaps a half dozen inhabitants—one of whom, an old woman, told me I was 'too curious' by far, and should lose myself up there." The old mountain woman was talking to a lost, middle-aged man. He wrote to his sister, realizing that Sarianna hadn't such a place as the mountains of Bagni di Lucca to exercise in, "but this place, or any other, would do me no good of itself, any more than Florence—for, apart from the folly and wickedness of the feeling, I am wholly tired of opening my eyes on the world now." It was almost as if the one poem he had written, in which he closed his eyes and prayed for healing, was prophetic.

Browning was tired of the world. His remote eagle's perch became him; he climbed from it to an even more isolated place. The "baby"—he didn't call him "Wiedeman" in this letter to his sister—appeared to be as healthy as Ba insisted. Robert told his sister, "Sophia Cottrell came up here with her child yesterday,—12 months old,—with nothing like the size of our baby." Everyone talked about how remarkably the baby was flourishing. "All which ought to be unmixed pleasure to me, but is very far from it." This letter, which alternated between attempting to comfort his sister and his own despondency, ended on a peculiar note. "I had a bilious fit, these two days, but it is over this morning."

By the middle of July Elizabeth was delighting in the fact that "Ever since my confinement I have been growing stronger & stronger." For her "it seems like a dream when I find myself able to climb the hills with Robert & help him to lose himself in the forests."

Another gesture of Elizabeth's to help him had profound reverberations for the world. She had a risky card to play. One morning she told him that she had written some poems during their courtship that she had never shown him, because he had once said "something against putting one's love into verse." But the night before she heard him say the opposite. That gave her courage. " 'Do you know I once wrote some poems about *you?* . . . There they are, if you care to see them.' " And Browning learned, for the first time, of *Sonnets from the Portuguese.*

He read them; she gave them to him at the perfect time. The old morbidity of a humiliated and dying woman, choosing between death and life, seemed as far away from her in her present condition as it would ever be. If the age difference had never been an obstacle between them, the extent of her pull toward the crypt might have been. If one were wise, as Elizabeth was, they were not the type of poetry to show a younger (or perhaps not even an older) lover.

> *I lift my heavy heart up solemnly,*
> *As once Electra her sepulchral urn,*
> *And, looking in thine eyes, I overturn*
> *The ashes at thy feet—Behold and see*
> *What a great heap of grief lay hid in me,*
> *And how the red wild sparkles dimly burn*
> *Through the ashen grayness.*

That was from Sonnet V. Pick them at random. In Sonnet XVIII, after giving her lock of hair to Browning, she wrote that it was virginal. Her days of youth went yesterday, her hair was no longer girlish, her cheeks were pale from tears. Here was how in her heart she gave the traditional lock to her lover:

I thought the funeral-shears
Would take this first, but Love is justified,—
Take it, thou,—finding pure, from all those years,
The kiss my mother left here when she died.

It is simply an irony of literary fashion that these poems have landed on the cute shelf.

Elizabeth shared what Robert called that "strange, heavy crown, that wreathe of sonnets" at the very moment when her husband himself was experiencing for the first time, as a middle-aged man, the ashes of grief. He was ready to read them now. His love for her had taken her past death. Look at her. Look at the robust Wiedeman. Could her love for him now help him to accept grief and comfort him in this prolonged period of mourning? The sonnets, the last one dated two days before their marriage, were strong medicine.

Browning was greatly moved. "How I see the gesture, and hear the tones," he would remember years later. "And, for the matter of that, see the window at which I was standing, with the tall mimosa in front, and little church-court to the right."

Beyond the personal, he considered the poems the greatest sonnet sequence in the language since Shakespeare. "When Robert saw them he was much touched & pleased—& thinking highly of the poetry he did not let . . could not consent, he said, that they should be lost to my volumes [1850] & so we agreed to slip them in under some sort of veil, & after much consideration chose the 'Portuguese.' " Elizabeth herself was "the Portuguese." She noted: "Observe—the poem which precedes them [the sonnets], is 'Catarina to Camoens.' In a loving fancy, he had always associated me with Catarina, and the poem had affected him to tears he said, again & again. So Catarina being a Portuguese, we put 'Sonnets from the Portuguese'—which did *not mean*, as we understood the double meaning, *'From the Portuguese Language'* . . . though the public (who are very little versed in Portuguese literature) might take it as they pleased." "Purposely an ambiguous title," Robert remembered. And uncharacteristically, when people pulled down the mask, "I never cared."

The trials of life did not disappear that summer, but the couple arrived at a further level of intimacy.

And when they returned from Bagni di Lucca, Wiedeman, whom Robert bathed daily, had a new tooth, and both poets got back to work.

Elizabeth completed the second part of *Casa Guidi Windows.* Robert wrote *Christmas-Eve and Easter-Day*, two long poems published as a small book. But it took him another year for the questionings and experiences of his own life to meet history head-on. Then some of the religious speculation of the earlier poems became part of a drama that was greater than the sum of its parts—the drama for which his nights with Father Prout had prepared him, "Bishop Blougram's Apology."

"Bishop Blougram's Apology" paralleled and parodied a major news event of 1850–51: Pio Nono elevated the Anglo-Irish Nicholas Wiseman to Cardinal, and bestowed on him a bishopric with a real British place name. This daring move of the Pope and the Cardinal caused an uproar at the time. If history came up to Elizabeth's windows, it came to Robert in the newspapers and journals and pamphlets of the day. And through his friends.

"Bishop Blougram's Apology" seemed ripe for the stage. Two men, one the wealthy Bishop of keen intellect and sophisticated tastes and the other the doubting, indigent literary man who holds the Bishop in contempt, had been sitting at the Bishop's full table at his chapel in London. During a long night's journey into day, complemented by wine and more wine, they revealed levels of themselves and their souls. Their clash of values and passions had been on "the dangerous edge of things." The reader joins them as the Bishop, having heard the cynical journalist Gigadibs out, offers his defense. Had the Roman Catholic Bishop been born three hundred years ago, before the Reformation, he tells Gigadibs, the British public would have said of him, " 'What's strange? Blougram of course believes.' " Had he been born seventy years ago, educated by the Enlightenment, " 'disbelieves of course.' " But in the contemporary England of deep-rooted skepticism and doubt, " 'He may believe; and yet, and yet / How can he?'—All eyes turn with interest."

The difference between the two ship passengers, a simile Blougram used, perhaps referring to the *Punch* cartoons satirizing Wiseman's return to London, was one not of taste but of temperament. Bishop Blougram took what he rationally could from life and therefore had a "snug and well-appointed berth." Gigadibs, if he could not have all that he wanted, got in "a pique" and came on board bare, "While sympathetic landsmen see you off." Both Gigadibs's bare appearance and pique remind one of Mahony. In London, he had been "a remarkable figure. . . . A short, spare man, stooping as he went, with the right arm clasped in the left hand behind him; a sharp face with piercing gray eyes that looked vacantly upwards, a mocking lip, a close-shaven face, and an ecclesiastical garb of slovenly appearance." His slovenly appearance at times made people think him a beggar.

In the poem, the Bishop asks the literary man, "What's wrong? Why won't you be a Bishop too?" In life, Mahony told his friends he could have been a Bishop, too, could have worn Wiseman's cardinal's hat, which he later satirized in the *Globe* in such pithy statements as "his shocking bad hat has set us all by the ears." Like Wiseman and Mahony, Blougram and Gigadibs "have minds and bodies much alike." Whereas Wiseman, " 'The Outward-bound,' " became "the great Bishop," Mahony, the bohemian priest, became a hard-drinking literary man. One was a success in life, one a failure. "Why won't you be a Bishop too?" The echo of the central conflict of the Reverend Frank Mahony's life is heard in the poem.

Mahony's friend John Sheehan (who wrote poetry under the name of "The Irish Whiskey Drinker") summarized Mahony's plight. His genius "would have ensured him a place in the first rank of any profession but the one to which he unfortunately had committed himself." Dissatisfied with any other profession, he would have been able to "break new ground, and try his fortune in a more congenial calling." But not as a priest. For "a bad wife or a bad husband can be got rid of," but an ordained priest is bound to celibacy and committed forever. Bishop Blougram touched on this predicament when he told Gigadibs:

> *In every man's career are certain points*
> *Whereon he dares not be indifferent.*

A man can choose what he wants from life, but

> *he should wed the woman he loves most*
> *Or needs most, whatsoe'er the love or need—*
> *For he can't wed twice.*

According to the Irish Whiskey Drinker, a person like Mahony, in a profession "for which God never intended nor nature constituted him," is condemned "to a life of secret sorrow, self-reproach, and inevitable hypocrisy."

At the end of the poem, Blougram, comparing his success, his "daily bread," "influence," and "state" to Gigadibs's obscurity, asked again, "In truth's name, don't you want my bishopric?" What has Gigadibs's truthful doubting brought him? If he were one of the "privileged great natures" of his time, his self-abnegation would be valid: "But you,—you're just as little those as I." Once more we have the inevitable comparison between the similar range of talents of both men and the contrast between the success of the Bishop and the failure of the literary man.

Browning interpreted the outcry against Cardinal Wiseman in 1850–51 as a strong indication of the deterioration of faith among the British people. He might well have agreed with the *Chronicle* that what John Bull really objected to was the audacity with which Wiseman, the brilliant churchman, upheld and insisted upon his beliefs and practices. For, surely central to the theme of the poem are the Bishop's arguments against succumbing to doubt, his apology for belief as an active agent for the good in this world. What beliefs did the English public offer in place of Wiseman's? Thackeray's "Mr. Punch's Appeal" that satirized Wiseman unmercifully and that Thackeray himself later regretted, implied that to be British was religion enough! British religion seemed to be proudly equated with antispiritualism and the sneering habit.

What about Frank Mahony? Brilliant, clever as he was, ripe with talent and wit, astute about the retrogressive and tyrannical elements of the papacy and its attempt at European influence—how was this renegade priest's life a better model to follow than Wiseman's? An alcoholic, Mahony lived a life full of bohemian negligence. As Father Prout, he was famous in his time. An amusing writer and a light poet, he was not a great artist. His loss of a religious career had meant the loss of spiritual and psychological focus.

There was much to object to in the "great Bishop," and Browning, in his portrait of Blougram, pointed out his political conservatism, his excessive worldliness, his casuistry. But he was a man who had made faith work in his life. Once he was "back on Christian ground," the sophistic Bishop's words became as healing as the *Guardian Angel's* hands.

> *You call for faith:*
> *I show you doubt, to prove that faith exists.*

The more of doubt, the stronger faith, I say.
If faith o'ercomes doubt. How I know it does?
By life and man's free will, God gave for that!
To mould life as we choose it, shows our choice:
That's our one act, the previous work's His own.

Free will. That tenet of Christianity that allowed Elizabeth to marry the man she loved allowed Robert to understand his own doubts, and allowed both of them their marriage of true minds.

Browning seemed to feel that the danger to England was not from the Pope breaking into Westminster Abbey, but from the stultification of the spiritual life from within. "Bishop Blougram's Apology," like Wiseman's "Appeal to the English People," which sold so many copies, was directed against the spiritual malaise of the times.

In the context of the abusive treatment Wiseman received in the British press, Browning's words about the character reported by Charles Gavan Duffy should be taken seriously. "Yes, he said, Bishop Blougram was certainly intended for the English Cardinal, but he was not treated ungenerously."

In fact, he was treated dramatically and wittily enough to have appealed to a wider audience than Browning had up till then. In 1850 the poet published *Christmas-Eve and Easter-Day,* poems related to "Bishop Blougram's Apology" in terms of religion and doubt. The book sold around two hundred copies. Had "Bishop Blougram's Apology" been published separately after it was completed, this long poem, based on a contemporary outrage, would have had a chance to sell briskly. But Browning never published the poem separately, never called attention to all of its contemporary and political references. It appeared in *Men and Women* in 1855.

Clearly, Browning had purposely separated himself from the literary men and the topical event. He who followed the newspapers and journals so avidly and knew so many journalists in Italy, France, and England was never a journalist himself. He bemoaned his lack of sales and worried about not being the main support of his family, yet he held back a work on a contemporary theme by which he would have profited. Artist and gentleman, he dissociated himself from Fleet Street and searched for that which was meaningful in his time and durable for all time.

Today, after the pamphlets and the newspapers and the journals are forgotten, and Nicholas Wiseman, the great mover of the Victorian Roman Catholic Church, is hardly more remembered than his adversary, the Reverend Francis S. Mahony (Father Prout), "Bishop Blougram's Apology" remains. That work of art is the significant document of its times.

THE ROADS THAT
LED TO ROME

THE BROWNINGS' married years have become intrinsically connected to their lives in Florence. But their long lease on the Casa Guidi evolved circumstantially. They spoke of giving it up when they traveled to Paris in 1851. Instead, on Elizabeth's advice, they sublet. After five years of marriage and the birth of a son, they didn't consider themselves tied down. They were still travelers on slender means, artists with worlds to discover. Jerusalem, Egypt . . . When Elizabeth once suggested California as a place of opportunity for her future brother-in-law, one wonders if her thoughts led her there as well.

In terms of a permanent home, Elizabeth championed Paris as the Brownings' final destination; events within Browning's family made that choice, finally, acceptable to him. Right up to the very end of their fifteen years together, on her deathbed in Florence, she and Robert spoke of where they planned to settle down.

Their many travels were more confined than their imaginations—to the continent and to England. Money was a small part of it; the major, of course, was Elizabeth's health.

Cold weather still had a pronounced effect on her lungs. She began to cough strenuously, lost her voice, her breath, her weight, and was confined to her rooms. She was not long off her morphine. To catch a cold meant the danger of renewed and dangerous bouts of pulmonary congestion. In an age in which infectious diseases were rampant, when influenza and malaria abounded, and child mortality was very high—even in the best circles—the Brownings were dauntless and daring travelers. They seemed to catch revolutions the way other people caught colds, but without the slightest fear for themselves or their child. Amid the political upheaval in Paris, it was a stranger who, on the street, had to advise Wilson to turn around and go home with Wiedeman, as stray cannon fire could be a problem on such flat terrain.

Elizabeth once more watched history unfold. Just settling in Paris at 138 avenue des Champs Élysées in December 1851, she witnessed the celebration of the coup d'état bringing Louis Napoleon to power, the beginning of the Second Regime. And by now she was back in correspondence with her brother George. She had "scarcely left the window these two days, watching the pouring in of the troops, to music, trumpets & shouting, with splendid military maneuvres of every kind. The president himself rode immediately past our windows through the great thunder of a shout . . . 'vive Napoleon'—People tell us it was 'Vive l'empereur,' but I tell *you* what I heard myself." Her sympathy for the "president," Louis Napoleon, is "with his audacity & dexterity," and "is rather artistical sympathy than anything else." It would be after he crowned himself emperor that artistic sympathy turned more militant. Napoleon III would take a prominent role in Italy's struggle for unity.

Though her sister Arabel would frown on her behavior, she and Robert went to see Dumas's *Camille*, "which you moral English are crying out against," and the acting was so exquisite that it "almost killed me out of my propriety—I sobbed so, I could scarcely keep my place." Robert sobbed, too. "When people want their hearts broken, they have only go to & see—There is a caricature representing the whole pit with umbrellas up to defend themselves from the tears raining out of the boxes."

As an advanced "citizeness of the world," she was also on the side of humanity, not the side of narrow national interests. For the British, another Napoleon was as ominous as Pio Nono making claims on Westminster Abbey by the change of titles—and just about as dangerous, according to Barrett Browning.

She could excuse Louis Napoleon's coup d'état, "no revolution ever took place in France with so little bloodshed & suffering." Indeed, he had suppressed his opponents, but by "the exiling of the head of parties," not by the cutting off of heads. And then with a logic that would have done any statesperson proud: "The president seems to choose to have all the reins in his hand, but to pull them only when the necessity occurs. A bad system of government, you will say, & I agree with you entirely." Still, "*a* democracy with a responsible man at its head, is no *despotism* whatever ugly despotic signs may be shown by the actual executive." It vexed her that the "great fact" of Louis Napoleon's being freely elected was overlooked by the English journals. "Truth, truth— do let us have truth—'C'est la vérité—' said George Sand—."

George Sand. If Arabel would object to *Camille,* imagine her disapproval of her sister's vast admiration of this woman, this novelist, who lived in utter freedom, among and with different men. In a sense, Paris was, to Elizabeth, synonymous with meeting George Sand. Sand was said to be not often there but at home writing plays and employing "a house-full of men, her son's friends & her own, in acting privately with her what she writes—trying it on a home stage before she tries it at Paris." Elizabeth heard her son was "a very ordinary young man of three & twenty, but she is fond of him. As for 'les amours' she has lived purely enough for the last year, they tell me . . she talks of herself as being less tormented by 'ces passions d'enfer,' & seems to resign herself, after some lingering struggles, to passing into a sort of elderly womanhood of George Sandism." Robert might contribute to the rain of tears falling on the coughing, dying Camille, but, just as he had trouble with his wife's views of Napoleon, he had trouble with making the first social move to see the one woman Elizabeth admired as much as she did a strong and liberal man. "No," she told him, "you *shant* be proud . . and I *wont* be proud—and we *will* see her—I won't die, if I can help it, without seeing George Sand."

In February 1852, Sand was in Paris, under an alias, attempting to escape "the plague of her notoriety." People told Elizabeth, " 'She will never see you—you have no chance, I am afraid.' " They couldn't have sent a better letter of introduction—one of Mazzini's, along with a note from both of them, written by Elizabeth. Sand sent an invitation by return post to Elizabeth—or was it to the poet of the Italian cause—the poet of the now-published two-part *Casa Guidi Windows?* In the second paragraph she also invited "Monsieur Browning."

In the middle of February, wrapped from head to foot, carried out by Robert into a closed carriage, Elizabeth went to meet her heroine, "rather at the risk of my life." Her reward: "I have seen George Sand."

The Brownings were received in a room with a bed in it, "the only room she has to occupy, I suppose, during her short stay in Paris." George Sand came toward them. The giant of Elizabeth's imagination was actually not much taller than she. She was dressed simply and well in a high-necked gray woolen gown and jacket with long white muslin sleeves buttoned at the wrist. In a cordial manner, she held out her

GEORGE SAND (1804–76) *was the literary idol of EBB, who named the heroine of her novel in verse* Aurora Leigh *after the writer, whose real name was Aurore Dupin. Years before she met Sand in Paris, EBB wrote two sonnets to "Thou large-brained woman and large-hearted man, / Self-called George Sand."*

small, well-shaped hand. Elizabeth took it in her own, and with that spontaneous passion that at times leapt from her letters, she stooped and kissed George Sand's hand.

"Mais, non! je ne veux pas!" George Sand remedied this act of homage by kissing Elizabeth's lips.

George Sand was a bit too heavy for her height, with shiny black hair parted and pulled back into a bun. She wore no head covering, which was the Parisian way. Elizabeth had seen photographs of her in ringlets and thought they would be better to deemphasize her overfull cheeks. Her complexion was a lusterless olive. "The upper part of the face is fine," with "dark glowing eyes as they should be." But the lower part of the face was disappointing. "The beautiful teeth project a little, flashing out the smile of the large characteristic mouth; & the chin recedes. It never could have been a beautiful face, Robert & I agree, but noble & expressive it has been & is."

No affectation, no coquetry "(& not a cigarette to be seen!)." She sat among two or three young men who listened to her. She spoke rapidly, low, without emphasis. She was not animated, but under her quiet, "an intense burning soul."

On their way out, Sand kissed Elizabeth again, and excused herself from returning the Brownings' visit because of work. She automatically invited them back the following Sunday. Out of love for his wife, Robert, who couldn't stand the society around Sand, escorted her there three times. The two or three respectful men sitting by George Sand turned into "crowds of ill bred men who adore her" in between "a puff of smoke and an ejection of saliva." The crowd was "ragged Red"— that is, socialist, mixed with lower theatrical types. Elizabeth pictured Sand as standing above her admirers, alone and melancholic, as the overdramatic theater people, some in costume, flatter her, go down on their knees to her, "tu" her. Elizabeth would go down on her knees to her as well, if she'd leave off these admirers "& be herself as God made her. But she would not care for my kneeling—she does not care for me." Elizabeth didn't take it personally. "Perhaps she does'nt care much for anybody by this time—who knows?"

George Sand slipped out of Paris without once visiting Elizabeth at home. Elizabeth was not proud; she eagerly went to see Sand in the middle of winter, when she usually did not budge from her rooms. Sand's health had not been very good lately either. Nothing Elizabeth attempted around her literary lion turned out right. She tried to share, besides politics and art, another subject of common interest—weak lungs.

"You should have seen the disdain with which she looked at my respirator—I took it out of my muff to show it to her—because her chest is not strong, & though better since she came to Paris, she has had a great deal of cough & was bled for this the other day—

" 'Oh,'—said she—'life wouldn't be worth the trouble of such precautions.' "

Elizabeth tucked her respirator back in her muff.

George Sand's eyes were still brilliant, her white uneven teeth still outflashed them when she smiled, "—only so rare a smile!"

This lady's smile seemed not to go everywhere. And she must have sensed Robert's disapproval of her casual way of holding court among the Reds and the thespians. He treated her with an exaggerated courtesy, which she may have understood as a criticism or considered as boorishly British—or both. When the two met by accident at the Tuileries, they walked the length together, and talked. But there was a coldness in their relationship that Robert referred to as a freezing over as soon as ice was broken. It probably didn't help that this unusual woman, as irregular in life as in features, was put on a literary and political pedestal by his wife.

Whatever discomfort he might have had in accepting what he considered his wife's overvaluation of George Sand, it was George Sand who received his rather judgmental approbation. On these social occasions, he certainly was the reluctant husband. Browning could get angry—not at people he loved, but at those he saw putting people he loved in false positions.

On their first trip to England, before they watched the coup from their window, this proclivity helped Robert to encourage his father toward an extremely unwise position. The Brownings had returned to London as publicly as they had left privately, with Wilson, with Flush, who had grown old and (according to their upstairs neighbor Eliza Ogilvy) smelly, and with the newest member of their entourage, their son, verging on the terrible, but to his mother terrific, twos. The trip to England had not been delayed solely by Robert's reluctance after the death of his mother. On February 12, 1850, Elizabeth wrote to Arabel that "the attack at the beginning of the winter was neither more nor less than a miscarriage." This time "I was sure of it." And at the end of July 1850 the poet had the last of her four miscarriages, and the worst.

SARIANNA BROWNING
(1814–1903). *The poet's sister
was an intelligent and lively woman
who devoted her life to her family,
taking care of her parents, and then,
after her father's death in 1866,
joining her widowered brother's
household in London, where she was
both a companion and a great help
in managing his daily affairs until
the end of his life.*

She lost a hundred ounces of blood, and it took her months to get back her strength. Then, even after almost five years away, the trip to England was decided on finally because Arabel couldn't get to Paris. At the time Elizabeth's brothers were still not reconciled.

It was so difficult for Robert to return to his old home at New Cross, now that his mother was dead, that he visited there alone at first, to adjust slowly to the place. Staying there, sleeping over, was out of the question.

His imagination sanctified the past. But he came home to his living family. Sarianna and her father had dealt with death firsthand, and Browning Senior was out of mourning. His father had already become enamored of a neighbor, a Mrs. Minny Von Müller, and was writing her passionate love letters. The widow did not send them back for the elder Robert Browning to burn. The homecoming: the mourning son, the courting father, the lively sister, Sarianna, caught between two passionate extremes. If the unworldly and guileless elder Browning broached the subject of a new woman in his life, one can imagine his minimizing it in relation to his son's shock. How much did Sarianna know, and how much did she disclose to her sensitive brother? One remembers her tact in sending him three notes in the midst of her grief, to prepare him for his own. One doubts the situation was ever

handled directly; it had the aspect of a Browning Senior caricature—
Poet's Return. After his son had reached some small peace with his
memories, his daughter-in-law and his only grandson arrived. Grandfather and Wiedeman got along famously, and that relationship turned
out to be both timely and convenient, keeping talk of Mrs. Von Müller
at bay.

It was in Paris during a visit from the father and Sarianna that the
issue surfaced. Both father and son had a penchant for debating theological and philosophical questions, so perhaps the elder Browning approached his relationship from the point of view of the issue that
greatly perturbed him. His new friendship had run smoothly until
Mrs. Von Müller had confided in Browning Senior that while still a
young woman she had married her second husband before she knew for
certain that her first husband was dead. This weighed on the elder
Browning's conscience and led him to write to her that she had been
"guilty of crime or gross error." Later he retracted and apologized. Perhaps in Paris he sought his son's advice. Should he continue to court a
woman who had married her second husband without being certain
her first had been laid to rest? He might have then noticed that his son
was so shocked by the mention of a courtship that he hadn't time for
the niceties of the theological threads. Browning Senior found himself
backtracking, seizing not on thoughts of remarriage but on the lack of
character of this kind of widow manqué. And his son rushed to help
his father shed whatever unholy hold Von Müller had forced on him.

The affair was not handled clearly—or cleverly. The father fudged.
The son? Well, Robert vented all his anger on the widow. And he put
it in writing. In a letter she received on November 1, 1851, Browning
wrote that " 'his father had informed him of the manner in which she
had annoyed him and of the persecution he had undergone.' " Shortly
after this she received a letter from Browning Senior, "withdrawing his
proposal" because of her youthful misconduct. His proposal? Did the
son know they were engaged—or did he believe that was part of some
sinister persecution?

Mrs. Von Müller and *her* son sued the elder Browning for breach of
promise. The case went to court. It was only during the legal proceed-
ings that Robert found out just how many letters had passed between
the two. His angry righteousness turned to pain. Through his letter
and his advice he became a prime mover of his worst nightmare: a
public scandal that hit the papers, a profane blot on the memory of his

mother, and a situation that put his rather guileless and eccentric father in the position of looking like an old fool.

And perhaps that was the good news. The bad news was that
Browning Senior lost the case, the judgment ruinous, over eight hundred pounds. To escape it and the humiliation, Robert's father moved
out of England. He was accompanied by his daughter, the child who
had stayed home. Sarianna settled in Paris, where she kept house for
her father. Browning Senior was freed from tedious bank work and was
eventually on pension till he died. Sarianna was in a sense forced out of
the house at New Cross. During those years of exile, which her bookish
and eccentric father learned to enjoy much more than she, did she ever
regret her beloved brother's homecoming?

On both ends of the Paris stay, there were trips to England.
And hopes for reconciliation with Moulton Barrett. Elizabeth wrote
to him once more, and Robert, according to her, wrote him an irre-
sistible letter.

Which he resisted, and sent back to the Brownings in a package.
In it were all the letters his daughter had written to him since her
wedding trip—not only returned but unopened. Some of them had
around them the black bands of mourning. Even this did not tempt
Moulton Barrett to read, to see if something in his daughter's life was
terribly wrong. He enclosed with these a letter so unremitting, so conscious of the pain it would cause, that Elizabeth, at the time a parent
herself, was even better able to see how deep this rejection was. She did
not believe, if he could still, after six years, be so hateful toward her,
that he had ever really loved her.

Elizabeth and Robert's reconciliation with George Barrett, and on
a lesser note with her other brothers, must have been helped, at least
slightly, by the marriage of her sister Henrietta to their third cousin
William Surtees Cook on April 6, 1850. It had been during the
Brownings' courtship that Surtees drank some tea left in Henrietta's
cup. Placing his "ugly mouth, where her pretty lips had been," he realized, "This is Love—." And a few days later he noted in his diary, "Her
father's consent before marriage is hopeless." He would "run away with
her when I am a Captain, if she will."

Five years later Henrietta did not leave Wimpole Street, as had
Elizabeth, before she and Surtees did what her brothers considered the
right thing. Their cousin wrote to Moulton Barrett, properly asking
for his daughter's hand. Moulton Barrett called the letter an insult.

The logic was that these two adults were going to marry no matter what the father might say. Therefore, as brother Alfred (Daisy) put it in "a 72-stanza epic depicting the event":

> *With hurried footsteps light as air,*
> *The errant damsel flew,*
> *Fast down the well-known winding stair,*
> *Nor paused to say adieu.*

Henrietta was over forty. Daisy, ten years younger, but a particular friend of the couple, wrote "to tell Henrietta of the aftermath of her elopement, of the 'grand battle scene in the drawing room' " after her father was informed, and to assure her that " 'nothing which any of us heard tonight has in the least shaken us in our belief that you were in every way justified in the course you have taken.' "

Surtees was related through the mother's side of the family, and the Graham-Clarkes were cold to the couple because the officer hadn't much money and he also seemed to have trouble finding a good commission. Henrietta couldn't get from the country to London to see the visiting Brownings. Still, she and Ba wrote. With Henrietta, Elizabeth shared thoughts about straitened finances that she felt might be lost on Arabel. With Arabel she shared certain concerns about Henrietta's streak of recklessness. The fact that Arabel was childless did not stem Elizabeth's flow on the issue of child rearing. On the way to France and England in June 1851, Elizabeth wrote from Venice of a motherly concern, Henrietta's disdain of baby caps, in relation to her infant son.

Venice had struck Elizabeth with force. "I have been in a sort of rapture ever since we arrived . . For the sake of it I would give up Florence, and twenty Parises besides." Only the deteriorating health of Robert and Wilson would finally spur her to leave. She alone, drunk on beauty, remained strong. Eliza Ogilvy was in Venice with the Brownings, and she remembered the very long walks she took with Elizabeth. "I think those were the longest walks I ever knew her [to] attempt. She very much depended for strength on a daily dose of ether in some peculiar mixture prescribed for her. One day the child got hold of the medicine after the maid had measured and poured it out. He drank it off, and great was the alarm, but it did not hurt him."

Around this time Robert won a rare victory concerning child rearing on the issue of baby caps. "Wiedeman wore a light cap with the

WILLIAM SURTEES COOK (1813–87) AND HENRIETTA BARRETT
MOULTON BARRETT (1809–60). *EBB's sister married her cousin, four years
her junior, on April 6, 1850, when she was forty-one and was immediately
disowned by her father.* "He never once, e'en in a dream, / Gave ear to lovers
tune," *wrote the couple's confidant, brother Alfred.* "No thoughts *would
make the heart repent, / Or feel for Surtees Cook."*

full borders for above a year, and until yesterday he *always wore the same
under his hat* & would continue to do so, only that Robert & I had a
quarrel about it yesterday & Robert had the upper hand," she wrote to
Arabel. "Robert wants to make the child like *a boy*, he says (because he
is a man)—and I because I am a woman perhaps, like him to be a baby
as long as possible. I maintain that he looks prettier, too, in the cap
under the hat, but I yield the point & Wilson consoles me by declaring
that he looks pretty anyhow."

For some reason, "it vexes Robert when people ask if he is a boy or
a girl—(oh, man's pride—) and he will have it that the lace caps & rib-
bons help to throw the point into doubt."

So Robert won, although Elizabeth viewed his idea of masculine
identification as misplaced pride. Her idea of a child's sexuality was
classically pre-Freudian—a child has no sex—as well as being specifically Barrettian. One remembers the Hope End portrait of the young
Elizabeth as a winged creature, too young and angelic to have grown a
lower half to her body: "The truth is that the child is not 'like a boy,'

and that if you put him into a coat and waistcoat forthwith, he only would look like a small angel travested. For he isn't exactly like a girl either—no not a bit. He's a sort of neutral creature, so far."

She kept him as neutral as she could. He had long curls that, for all Robert's coercing, she would never have the heart to see cut in her life-time. "Jasper" was the color assigned her son's hair in her poetry, glints of red and brown among the gold. She also dressed him poetically, as a Renaissance prince with brimming hats and velvet frocks. This might not have been as peculiar as it seems. The idea of Renaissance garb was all the fashion among the Anglo-Florentine artists. Robert did not like it, but his major fashion victory was his statement on baby caps.

In this belief in the neutral child and in her lack of separation from him, and in her delight in extending his babyhood, she was her father's daughter. But in other ways, she went far beyond the restraints of her own childhood. Her great belief was to let her child come to language and education and the forms of religion in his own good time. She believed an activity was good for a child in direct relation to its annoyance of an adult. A child should laugh, run, play hard, make noise. She didn't create pleasant lies for a child's ear when asked a direct question. And contrary to the fundamentals of British educa-tion, she did not send her child away from home for education. She be-lieved it a good thing to spoil the child—to reward, and to disapprove, with kisses.

Her son remembered her as a woman full of joy, and it was in this spirit that she raised him. But the excesses of attention that he was used to by the time they reached London, and Wilson's visit to her own family, tied Elizabeth down—the first time she'd taken the full brunt of progressive child rearing. When Wilson returned, the mother found she missed being awakened by her child at six. Browning worked around the edges of this upbringing, bringing in discipline through the music that he taught him, and at times succeeding in sustaining a reasonable punishment for a misdeed. In a carriage one day, the child's head rested on his father's leg. A traveler commented, "Your father spoils you." To which the child looked up and answered, "Oh no, my mother spoils me."

All of his wit, his hypersensitivity, his "baby-lonian" baby talk, of Italian, mixed with a little French and less English, was captured by his mother for posterity in letters, many of them cut down by less doting male editors. She wrote to her brother George from revolutionary Paris,

ROBERT WIEDEMANN "PEN"
BARRETT BROWNING (1849–1913),
by Euphrasia Fanny Haworth. The
only child of the poets. This pencil
and colored-crayon drawing by an
old friend of Robert Browning's was
done ca. 1851, after RB was able
to persuade his wife to take their
son out of his baby caps.

"As to Wiedeman, he is in ecstasies at the sight of the soldiers, &
the sound of the music. If you ask Wiedeman if he likes the revolution,
he says—'Less' (yes!) 'buono, buono!' " And to "Vive Napoleon," being
taught him by his French nurse, "he adds out of his own head, 'Bwavo,
bwavo!' (bravo)."

"Wiedeman" invented his nickname. In attempting to say his name
(in goodness knows what accent), his tongue caught and he came out
with something like "Pen," and later this turned into "Peni" and
"Penini." "Wiedeman" took second place once more, Robert Wiedemann Barrett Browning.

Bwavo Penini!

It was as Penini that the child returned to the Casa Guidi. After
their long stay in France the Brownings were greeted by a welcome
calm, their own apartment, their familiar furniture, their cozy sur-
roundings, all in excellent repair. Subletting had worked out well;
they'd even gained some months of free rent themselves. Elizabeth
planned more home improvements that would allow them to sublet at
a higher price when they went to Rome. In the spring of 1853 the
Brownings were happy to be back, and in a spirit of a second honeymoon, settled down to each other and to serious writing.

Their plans to go to Rome fell through once more, because of illness there, and because John Kenyon forgot to send the biannual fifty

pounds. In grandfatherly fashion, he had sent a hundred pounds a year since Pen's birth. But spring in Florence compensated. "People do always best, relying on themselves," Elizabeth wrote. "For my part I thank God for a very, very happy winter—so happy! Money-affairs never trouble *me*."

Along with Penini and Wilson, the couple took an open carriage to see the sunset from the neighboring hills. Elizabeth was strong enough to climb "to the top of Fiesole (leaving the carriage)" and to enjoy the view from "an old wall which made me giddy to sit on—and I got scolded for having a 'weak head,' an expressive phrase." When Penini looked over the wall and saw the "velly pretty" clusters of purple lilies, his mother suggested tying a rope around him and letting him down to pick them, then hoisting him back up. He'd only say "less" if Wilson was tied up with him, too.

"A ministering angel" in the form of a daring teenaged Italian girl insisted on fetching them for the child. She clambered over the side and picked the flowers. Pen was in ecstasies, and his happy father gave the girl two pence half penny English, which she considered princely. On the way down the hills, in the glow of twilight, Pen saw roses he wanted to add to his bouquet, but the coachman wouldn't stop, "which damped his joy a little—as is the way of all earthly joy, even when people go to Fiesole."

There were not only family outings. The proliferation of the railroad expanded romantic possibilities. The couple made a plan to leave "respectability and Penini behind us," and have a day trip for themselves. They'd take a train to Pistoia and Prato and have dinner at their whim at some cafe or other. "Like two lovers," Robert told her.

The lovers traveled to Bagni di Lucca for the summer, far from the cholera at Rome. But, it would turn out, not escaping close proximity to their noisy neighbor in the Pitti Palace. The Grand Duke had left the heat of Florence and had taken the old house on the top of the mountain, the very one they stayed in after Penini's birth, when Browning was mountain climbing and mourning his mother. Penini's nursery was turned into one of the Duke's drawing rooms. Right before they left Florence, they met Elizabeth Clementine and William Burnet Kinney. It was unusual for the Brownings to call on people (other than George Sand) first, particularly so close to their departure for the summer. But William Kinney would have the latest political news. He owned and once edited the Newark, New Jersey, *Daily Advertiser*, and had come to Turin to be the American minister to the court of Victor Emmanuel II of the House of Savoy, which ruled Piedmont. He and his wife were on a short visit to Florence; that short affair would turn, by the next year, into a long love.

Elizabeth was rewarded for her visit by hearing that Victor Emmanuel II liked her portrait of his father in *Casa Guidi Windows*. It was more than personally pleasing that the King of Piedmont was reading her work and had praised it to the American minister. By 1853, while the Brownings (and the Grand Duke) packed for their summer in the cool hills, the hopes of a united Italy rested no longer in Rome, where the republican government had fallen, or in Austrian Tuscany, but "in noble Piedmont," as Elizabeth had predicted in her poem.

Nor was Elizabeth's portrait of the King's dead father particularly flattering. Charles Albert was praised for dying well. If, as they say, he didn't live well, the "sin" passed, for he was redeemed by cannon smoke. He died in exile in Portugal after the Italian cause was defeated at Novara: "Taking off his crown," Charles Albert allowed one to see "A hero's forehead."

> *Shaking Austria's yoke . . .*
> *His last words were upon his lonely bed,*
> * 'I do not end like popes and dukes at least—*
> *Thank God for it.'*

It appeared that the son no more than the father liked Popes or Grand Dukes. He was willing to live the way his father died, for the Italian cause. This message was almost worth the annoyance of a return visit by the Kinneys on the actual eve of the Brownings' departure to the Bagni di Lucca for the summer.

Elizabeth Kinney, who had been a newspaperwoman, kept a journal. She had reservations about Barrett Browning's looks at first. The great poet appeared older than Mrs. Kinney imagined, her voice weak because of the illness of the lungs. Her idol would have looked younger and more attractive if she exposed her high cheekbones, and wore her strange and unfashionable heavy fingercurls away from her emaciated face. Then the upper part, "her great dark soul eyes," might predominate even more, keeping one from her overlarge mouth. To this observer, she still had the saving grace, at least, of looking like a poet.

ELIZABETH CLEMENTINE KINNEY
(B. 1810), *poet, essayist, journalist, was
the grandchild of the colonial American poet
Aaron Cleveland and the mother, by her
first marriage, of the "banker poet" Edmund
Clarence Stedman. She settled in Florence
in 1853. Happy to leave Turin, where her
husband was the U.S. ambassador to the
House of Savoy, she wrote that the city
"opened to me as a fountain in a moral
desert with its arts, its poetical, hallowed
associations. . . . I am no longer the slave of
'high life,' " but "chose my friends from the
congenial few who resort to Florence as we
did, to drink at her fountains—not to be
infected by her pools." Among the friends
she chose were Hiram Powers and the
Brownings, her "favorite Florentines."*

The more youthful Browning, the son of a woman with the squarest
head in England, had a round head placed squarely on his shoulders.
His full head of black hair was laced with gray, as was his beard. He
was impulsive and quick in speech, entertaining, as wiry as a cricket.
But he had a quality Mrs. Kinney would regret, and others would
praise—in the words of Walter Scott's biographer, he didn't look like
any damned literary man.

A year later the Kinneys returned to Florence, and they and the
Brownings became good friends. Elizabeth wrote to Arabel, "Mrs.
Kinney is a pretty woman with torrents of ringlets, & dresses perfectly—clever, literary, critical, poetical—just as you please . . . rather
over-lovely & not over-refined . . but a favorite of mine through her
truth & frankness, besides her warmheartedness towards ourselves. We
often spend the evening at tea time with them." By that time, Mr.
Kinney was "the ex-minister at the court of Turin—He is an admirable, thoughtful, benevolent person, as liberal in politics as an
American diplomat is bound to be & much more religious. Also he
agrees with me textually about Louis Napoleon . . . indeed [we] . . .
agree upon most subjects—excepting Swedenborg."

It was during tea that the Brownings had a conversation about

George Sand that underlined how alike their attitudes were compared to any private reservations. Their point of view shocked Elizabeth Kinney, who recorded it word for word. The conversation about Sand is in progress, caught by the former newspaperwoman.

"And I kissed her beautiful hand," Robert Browning said.

"Pray, who is her lover now?" Mrs. Kinney asked archly.

"I can't say, since she has a new one every day."

"What! Is she so bad as that? I supposed she had never loved but one—certainly but one at a time."

Browning, that lively, impulsive speaker, wry as a cricket, chirped, "*One?* good heavens! 'their name is legion.' Put three ciphers to your one and that will not include the sum total of her loves."

"And *you* kiss the hand of such a woman—Robert Browning does this?"

He looked at Mrs. Kinney with an air of surprise: "Yes, & *Elizabeth Barrett* Browning does the same, in respect to one of the greatest geniuses God ever made!"

"Well, well," Mrs. Kinney responded, "the greater the genius, the greater the shame of yielding that body, which should be sacred . . . to the 'lust of the flesh': to me George Sand is the worst of women."

"Don't say that!" Elizabeth exclaimed, getting up enough of a voice to continue. "She is not a *bad* woman, but, on the contrary, a good & charitable one."

"Then what your husband has said of her is not true."

"If it *be* true," Barrett Browning answered, "it is only because she has fallen under the dominion of a sensual appetite, which she cannot control; but it is no more than gluttony, or intemperance; I *pity* her, more than I blame her for it. Her *mind* is none the less godlike."

Mrs. Kinney sighed; her heart was so swollen with indignation she could not speak. How could that pure spirit, Elizabeth Barrett Browning, entertain such an idea? Still, she was not a prude. She was willing to concede a point. If George Sand had been led astray by an uncongenial husband, why, then, perhaps one could excuse an indiscretion, an unlawful love—

"*Love!*" both the Brownings interrupted in unison. "She never loved anyone but herself."

Ecco Roma

ALL ROADS lead to Rome, but for seven years the Brownings' way was being paved with good intentions. It was not until the end of 1853 that they finally arrived, singing. It had been a glorious eight-day journey, replete with sightseeing. Those spectacular Umbrian hills, more like rolling mountains, where St. Francis once walked a penitent in bare feet, and which became the background for many a Renaissance painting. Assisi, Terni. Perhaps part of the fun for Penini was sharing his mother's first time. "For the child was radiant & flushed with the continual change of air and scene." A budding patriot, he had been told that dangerous weapons were not allowed in by the Roman police, so he had plans of "tissing the pope's foot," so he could keep his toy gun.

The Brownings went right to their apartment at 43 Via Bocca di

PEN'S SKETCH OF HIS FATHER. *RB's knightlike qualities as perceived by his four-year-old son.*

Leone. How could they help but be in the highest spirits? Not only had they finally arrived in the Eternal City, but their good friends, the American sculptor William Wetmore Story and his wife, Emelyn, had not only found them a suitable apartment but had lit the fires and the lamps for them. After their long trip, they walked into a warm and glowing third-floor apartment, cozy and welcoming as home. No rooms to find, no chills in the late autumn, no odd or predictable tourist nightmares. The Storys, Americans with whom they'd vacationed in Bagni di Lucca, and who lived in Rome and knew it like a book, had ensured their comfort. They had probably heard of this apartment through their countryman and old friend, the painter William Page, who lived in the apartment below with his second wife, Sarah, and their children together and by her first husband.

The Storys had two children, Edith, eight, and Joe, six. Joe was named after his grandfather, an eminent lawyer from Salem, Massachusetts, who had risen to associate justice of the United States Supreme Court. During the summer at Bagni di Lucca, the two families and their children had laughed and played and created theatricals together. Joe was just a year or so older than Penini, and the two boys got along famously. There was even a thrilling donkey ride arranged by the Storys in the mountains, which Penini paid for the next day with a sore behind.

On the first night in Rome, the Brownings had a chance to thank the Storys for their kindness in arranging this warm welcome. As Elizabeth put it, that night "we had a glimpse of their smiling faces."

The next morning, before breakfast, there was a knock at their door. A manservant stood there with little Edith Story and a message. Her brother, Joe Story, was in convulsions. "Too true!" Edith was left with Wilson, and the Brownings rushed to the Storys, who were living on Piazza di Spagna. Their first full day in Rome was spent at the deathbed of Joe Story. "For the child never rallied . . never opened his eyes." He was dead by eight in the evening.

While they were with the grieving parents and dying child, little Edith had become ill at their apartment and could not be moved. Their downstairs neighbors, the Pages, had a room for her. They took her and put her to bed. It was a gastric fever that can go to the brain, the fever that had just killed her brother. The Storys' English nurse appeared to be dying of it as well, and downstairs, Emma, the Pages' youngest daughter, was sick with the same symptoms.

If Elizabeth could have, she would have caught her child "up in my arms & run to the ends of the world, the hooting after me of all Rome would not have stopped me. I wished—how I wished . . for the wings of a dove . . or any unclean bird . . to fly away with him & be at peace." She had lost her head, that's how her husband put it. "There was no possibility but to stay."

The physicians solemnly assured her there was no contagion possible; otherwise she would have at least sent her child to another house. The doctors proved correct, and the two children and the English nurse survived. "Roman fever is not dangerous to life . . simple fever & ague . . but it is exhausting if not cut off . . and the quinine fails sometimes."

In the weeks that followed, the Rome that Emelyn Story and Elizabeth saw from the Storys' carriage was the road to the Protestant cemetery. Elizabeth steeled herself to accompany the poor stricken woman, who sat calmly in her seat. Given the circumstances it would be "worse than absurd" for Elizabeth to faint: "I flinch from corpses & graves, & never meet a common funeral without a sort of horror. When I look death-wards I look OVER death—& upwards . . or I cant look that way at all."

One can see this in her poem "A Child's Grave at Florence," written soon after the birth of Penini. Reading the title of the poem from Rome, Father Prout thought the poets' infant had died—as he later had the brimming tactlessness to tell them. But no, it was the child of an active, blooming woman, Countess Sophia Cottrell. In the poem, the daughter that died, Alice, is called Lily:

> *Of English blood, of Tuscan birth,*
> *What country should we give her?*
> *Instead of any on the earth*
> *The civic Heavens receive her.*

Prout should have read further:

> *—Oh, my own baby on my knees,*
> *My leaping, dimpled treasure,*
> *At every word I write like these,*
> *Clasped close with stronger pressure!*

Too well my own heart understands,—
At every word beats fuller—
My little feet, my little hands,
And hair of Lily's color!

Then the poet looks over the grave.

Love, strong as Death, shall conquer Death,
Through struggle made more glorious:
This mother stills her sobbing breath,
Renouncing yet victorious.

The compensation for the grieving parents is bitter:

Well done of God, to halve the lot
And give her all the sweetness;
To us, the empty room and cot,—
To her, the Heaven's completeness.

Then the poem concludes quickly, and neatly, with a lily symbolizing "death's ANNUNCIATION" held in a smiling angel's hand.

Life was not as neat, and Elizabeth didn't deceive her only child when he asked about his friend Joe. She explained to Penini that Joe had died on earth and his soul was in heaven. Pen thought of his friend often, aware that Joe's body was lying under the cypress trees, the points of which he could see in his excursions in Rome.

When another dear friend to Penini, the Brownings' manservant Ferdinando, complained of being ill, Penini told him he hoped he wouldn't die. Ferdinando, not in a good mood, answered that perhaps it would be better if he did; after all, then he could go to paradise.

Pen was more than willing to join him there, just as he'd been willing to be lowered from the old wall in Fiesole, if another were tied together with him. And he knew how death could be accomplished: "I should do like Joe—eat a quantity of fruit & take no medicine, and then I should die too & go to you, & they would put wings on our backs and we should fly about wherever we like."

Thus the child of the poets structured his own compensation. His religion was formed from his heart and his imagination and from what he picked up along the way. He received no formal religious education, he was taught no dogma. He was much too young to understand any of that, and in no way, his mother was adamant, was he to be force-fed. But his Christian parents were good examples, and he daily witnessed his mother's morning prayers. Just as the Brownings' love was nurtured by their respect of each other's free will, their religion was rooted in faith. Their child would come to God at his own pace. After all, God exists. And so do death and love.

Such an ominous beginning to the Roman stay—the song they came singing turning to dirge. Anxiety was compounded by little Edith's relapses. Finally the Storys took her out of town. On the way to Naples, fearing the worst, they called on Robert Browning, asking for his comfort on their trip.

Robert to leave Elizabeth and Pen in Rome to follow death? The Storys should have left Rome earlier and obeyed the doctor's orders. Quinine, quinine, quinine was called for. Elizabeth stuck by her advice in letters to the worried mother, even defending the famous physician they had fired—not that she'd suggested they keep him once they had lost their trust. She was harshly honest in these letters. She was not happy that Robert made this overnight trip. In the end, she was, as she wrote to Emelyn, more than compensated by the good news of his not being needed once he got there. Little Edith rallied, and Robert Browning returned home.

AMERICAN MARBLE CUTTERS AND YANKEE TITIANS

WILLIAM WETMORE STORY would become a close and lifelong friend of Robert Browning. The American lawyer had artistic tendencies since youth. The writing that most pleased his relatives, however, was his two books on *Contracts,* still known at Harvard Law. At Harvard as well there's a marble statue of his father, Judge Joseph Story. Today students think nothing of propping a cigar between its Carrara-white fingers. But it was the statue that brought Story to Rome. Torn for years between art and the legal profession, he was commissioned to do a memorial statue after his father's death. He accepted on condition that he sculpt it in Italy. Perhaps his family thought this time he'd get Rome out of his system. In England, a father could be proud of a son who didn't want to "work," who wanted to be a gentleman and a poet. In nineteenth-century America, for a scion of an illustrious New England family, a family man himself, to go off to Italy, write poetry and sculpt, and take an interest in Swedenborg and spiritualism, not as a hobby but as a career—well, it was insane. W. W. Story did in fact have a nervous breakdown. What soothed his ragged nerves was following his heart.

Unlike the Brownings, he did not have to pursue art in Italy by dedicating himself to clever economies in an inexpensive clime. Story was rich. By 1856, after his mother's death, he would succumb to the siren's song and establish himself and his family permanently in Italy. He would live on the *piano nobile* of the grand Palazzo Barberini, built according to Gianlorenzo Bernini's designs. His landlord would not send bowls of oranges. The landlord was a Barberini, an aristocrat whose family gave Italy popes while they stripped the marble from the ruins in the Forum and from the Colosseum to build their palaces. The

Barberini were as enterprising and as busy as the bees on their coat of arms. The Romans, who are as ironic in wit as they are in their acceptance of the madness of this world, had a saying since the sixteenth century: First came the Barbarians and then the Barberini. And after them the cultured American expatriates, such as William Wetmore Story, who had the money to rent their noble second floors.

Of middle height, active in mind and body, friend of the Lowells and of Longfellow, a robust man of good conversation and wide interests, he was physically not unlike his friend Browning. Distinguished perhaps by accent, by an amazing growth of beard, and by the advantages of wealth—put to ideal uses. Story was principled, outgoing, intelligent, but not devious or ambiguous in a European sort of way—the type of American the novelist Henry James would write about. In fact, James became Story's biographer.

In the mid-nineteenth century, to be a "stonecutter" one had to come to Rome. It wasn't just for the marble in the hills of Carrara that Michelangelo once chipped away at till he found its inner form. It was the way of life, the climate of art and ideas, the cafes, the teachers, and the Italian artisans, inexpensive to hire, and trained generation after generation to their work, who did the actual cutting out of the artist's grand idea.

A woman artist could work in Italy as well. There were no life modeling classes in which she could draw from a nude in the United States. Story's friend Harriet Hosmer was the first American woman stonecutter. In Boston, when her doctor father asked if she could attend anatomy lectures at the Boston Medical Society, officials were shocked. In Rome, Hosmer studied with the English sculptor John Gibson, wore men's clothing when she wished, and rode her horse on the Pincio. She was a short, vivacious woman. "Oh—there's a house of what I call emancipated women—a young sculptress—American, Miss Hosmer, a pupil of Gibson's, very clever and very strange—and Miss Hayes, the translator of George Sand, who 'dresses like a man down to the waist' (so the accusation runs). Certainly there's the waistcoat which I like. . . . She is a peculiar person altogether, decided, direct, truthful, it seems to me. They are both coming to us to-night." Hatty Hosmer was to become a great friend of the Brownings. A woman artist who lived on her own, who was not dependent on marriage or men. Another model for Aurora Leigh.

The promise of freedom—in the personal liberation of their mar-

WILLIAM WETMORE STORY (1819–95). *The American lawyer, poet, and sculptor was the son of Joseph Story, a founder of Harvard Law School and U.S. Supreme Court Associate Justice. After he gave up law, he moved his family to Italy to pursue an artistic career. He became the lifelong friend of Robert Browning, who in 1860 sculpted in Story's Roman studio with him.*

PALAZZO BARBERINI, ROME. *The grand* piano nobile *of this imposing mansion was the home of W. W. Story and his family for most of their years in Rome. The Storys were a hub of the expatriate British and American artistic community, often holding amateur theatricals for their children in which Browning took part.*

riage, in the possibility of a unified Italy—expanded to include the open and imaginative lives of the Brownings' artistic American friends. One of the earliest friends had been Hiram Powers. This American stonecutter living in Florence was famous for his *Greek Slave*. In the whitest marble, his full-length standing nude was as flawless as an air-brushed centerfold. Her arms were softly bound in front of her—to attest to the fall of freedom in Greece. It's difficult today to imagine the symbolic force of this statue.

To view nudes in the mid-nineteenth century was aesthetically sophisticated and morally advanced. Elizabeth would tease Wilson, who was so shocked by the nudity of the classical statues in the Uffizi Gallery that she could not stay. Barrett Browning was advanced. When she looked at the *Greek Slave* in Power's studio she saw it as "white thunder," an appeal against white slavery as earnest and intense as her appeal against black slavery in "The Runaway Slave." Its nudity was divine.

She was no John Ruskin. That Victorian art critic and friend of hers extolled white marble, but ran from his marriage bed, shocked by

THE GREEK SLAVE *by Hiram Powers* (1805–73) *was created by the American stonecutter in 1838, a year after he settled in Florence. The statue was exhibited on a revolving pedestal at the 1851 Great International Exhibition at the Crystal Palace in London to universal acclaim. EBB had first seen the work when she arrived in Florence in 1847 and immediately wrote a poem on its power as an antislavery manifesto. In her sonnet, "Hiram Powers' 'Greek Slave,'" she may have set the tone for viewing this neo-classical nude as clothed in virtue.*

what he saw when a real woman disrobed. In fact, his wife had to get a doctor's report in retaliation. There was nothing wrong with her body—except it wasn't bald marble.

The sensuality of nudity, mortal love between two naked lovers, would be portrayed by Barrett Browning in *Aurora Leigh*. For her, Hiram Powers's work must have incorporated a harmony between freedom in art and politics, between the naked and the ideal, that she could not only look at unabashedly, but could champion. The statue was "passionless perfection." In America, far from the classical tradition of a headless and armless past, this statue went on tour. People paid to take a look at the naked woman in chains. Were they staring at "Art's fiery finger," attempting to break up "the serfdom of this world?"

> *Appeal fair stone,*
> *From God's pure heights of beauty against man's wrong!*
> *Catch up in thy divine face, not alone,*
> *East griefs but west, and strike and shame the strong,*
> *By thunders of white silence, overthrown.*

For Elizabeth, Powers's work was full of revolutionary force. No less, in Rome, in the mid-fifties, one saw example after example of white silence, nudes or partially draped classical figures, that retold the old stories and pointed to the ideal.

There was a painter in this group of American stonecutters who would be portrayed in one of Browning's greatest monologues. He was the Brownings' downstairs neighbor in Rome, William Page, called in his day the American Titian. Roman society was so lively that Robert began, at his wife's urging, to go out at night. Elizabeth herself went to a few soirees, but generally she stayed at home. Sometimes the painter William Page would come upstairs and they'd talk about spiritualism, which interested them both. His second wife, Sarah Page, did not join them. She was, during those evenings, pursuing her own interests.

Page was a middle-aged man, balding, bearded, serious. A rather lean man, full of enthusiasm about the nature of art. But he had a weary look. He and Robert Browning became extremely good friends. Both loved to theorize about the arts. And Page had such ideas, such theories. He staked his art on them. He believed that the great Venetian painter and colorist Titian had intentionally rendered his subjects in subdued grayish tones. Those portraits of princes, those flesh tones of his sumptuous nudes, were all meant to be in "twilight" colors. He did not believe that time had discolored them, that age caused the varnish on top of them to darken. The mid tone of gray was the universal color, and Titian had known it. In accordance with his theory, Page, the American Titian, underpainted.

In the spring of 1854, Robert Browning sat for his portrait at a pivotal point of the painter's life, and at a time when he had just discovered another theory—a new scientific way of measuring the proportions of the human body. Page was inspired by a favorite authority of the Swedenborgians, the Book of Revelation. Twenty-five years later he would remember that in reading Revelation, a remarkable statement struck him that helped him to figure out proportion in his paintings: " 'And he measured the wall thereof, an hundred and forty and four cubits, according to the measure of a man, that is, of the angel.' "

The idea of a mathematical formula divined from Revelation which would give a standard for the modeling of any human figure appealed to the Anglo-American community of artists and writers living in Rome at the time. "At an early day I told my countryman, Mr. W. W. Story, the sculptor and author, of the hints I had gathered from St. John and the use I had made of them."

Years later, Browning would encourage Page to publish his discoveries on human proportion in an English journal, and he helped Page to remember when he had first made the observations. It must have been before 1855, because Browning used them in his poem "Cleon," published in *Men and Women*:

> *I know the true proportions of a man*
> *And women also, not observed before.*

And Elizabeth had put them in her novel in verse, *Aurora Leigh*.

> *Erect, sublime*—the measure of a man
> *And that's the measure of an angel, says*
> The Apostle.

Browning steered away from telling Page he had used imagery from that discovery in another poem in his collection. In "Andrea del Sarto: Called 'The Faultless Painter'" he mentioned

Four great walls in the New Jerusalem
Meted on each side by the angel's reed

In that poem, another theory of Page appeared as well:

You smile? why there's my picture ready made,
That's what we painters call our harmony!
A common greyness silvers everything,—
All in a twilight, you and I alike.

Andrea del Sarto, the Renaissance painter, sits near the window of his studio as daylight wanes and speaks to his silent and unfaithful wife. His whole life is autumn, all "a twilight piece."

My youth, my hope, my art, being all toned down
To yonder sober pleasant Fiesole.

Most of the details of this poem, which scholars have attributed to the poet's reading about the life of the Italian painter, do not come from history. Del Sarto's life masked William Page's. Both painters had beautiful and difficult wives who also served as models. Del Sarto's Lucrezia was greedy and domineering. She wasn't the moonfaced, silent, serpentine woman who appears in Browning's poem, although she was, as was Page's second wife, an extremely beautiful young woman married to a middle-aged painter.

Browning veered from del Sarto's life by giving the Lucrezia in his poem a lover, a "cousin" who had gambling debts. Browning's Lucrezia regarded her husband's art as a means of paying off these debts. Her past lovers were legion:

My face, my moon, my everybody's moon,
Which everybody looks on and calls his,
And, I suppose, is looked on by in turn,
While she looks—

One remembers the Duke in Browning's "My Last Duchess," saying of his wife, "she liked whate'er / She looked on, and her looks went everywhere." And one recalls as well the moonfaced beauty, hair parted in

SARAH DOUGHERTY PAGE
(CA. 1849) *by William Page.*
The second wife of the American
painter. She did not share her
older husband's intellectual and
artistic interests, causing much
gossip in the American expa-
triate community in Italy, and
eventually ran away with a
young Neapolitan nobleman.
"Page and Cirella, a man and
a wisp of straw," wrote RB,
who loved and respected the
painter. Sarah became the real-
life model for Lucrezia in RB's
"Andrea del Sarto."

SELF-PORTRAIT (1860–61)
by William Page, who was
called the American Titian
in his day. Page was a close
friend of RB—his theories
about art greatly interested
the poet—and of EBB, with
whom he shared a belief in
Swedenborg. As RB sat for his
portrait by Page in Rome in
1854, he was a daily witness
to Sarah Page's affair with
Don Alfonso Cirella.

the middle and away from the face, in Page's portrait of his second wife.

Sarah Page was quite promiscuous. James Russell Lowell subleased the Brownings' apartment in the Casa Guidi during the winter of 1851–52 while the Brownings were in Paris and the Pages were in Florence. Lowell had witnessed Sarah's behavior. Her flirtations with the Austrian officers and her attentions to a Captain Neuhauser, "who used to play chess with Page," caused so much gossip among the Anglo-Florentines that the Pages moved to Rome. Page's wife never called him away from France as Andrea's wife did, but she certainly caused him to leave Florence. Lowell was a very good friend of his countryman W. W. Story and kept him informed. And Browning became a daily witness to the disrupting marriage while he sat for his portrait.

Only after its completion did Browning tell W. W. Story of the portrait: "I hate keeping secrets—but this was Page's, not mine—he even wished my wife to be kept in ignorance of it—which, of course, was impossible." During the sittings Browning could not help but see the open relationship Page's wife was having with an Italian friend of Story's, Don Alfonso Cirella, son of the Neapolitan Duke of Cirella. He was "a handsome spirited young fellow of about 21 years of age," according to Story's letter to James Russell Lowell. For a year Sarah had been with Cirella in the most open way. "He was at her house morning noon & night, & in the constant habit of dining with the family. I do not know how Page could be ignorant of their liaison, which formed the topic of gossip in American & Italian circles" during the season in which the Brownings were Page's upstairs neighbors.

In Browning's poem, Andrea is in his studio, his model and wife sits with him, and the twilight harmony is pierced by her lover's (cousin's) whistle. Between March and May 1854, Browning sat fifty-four times for his portrait, never for less than an hour and a half, and generally for two hours. During that time Sarah and Cirella were in and about, conducting their affair in the most open manner. The situation was much more blatant than in the poem, where adultery was suggested by a "cousin's" off-stage whistle. Life, like a Page portrait, had to be toned down.

Browning witnessed his friend, with his noble mind—"noble" is the adjective most applied to Page—passively accepting his wife's betrayal. Still, Browning as well as Story could say of Sarah Page: "she was kind & good & affectionate to us & to our child and we kept it in mind!" As well they might. It was Sarah Page who opened her doors to little Edith when Joe died of gastric fever, and nursed Edith and her own child when both came down with the same disease. Elizabeth, too, noted a specific kindness to Penini in March 1854—on his fifth birthday: "Mrs. Page, the wife of the distinguished American artist, gave a party in honour of him the other day. There was an immense cake inscribed *'Penini'* in sugar; and he sat at the head of the table and did the honours."

Sarah Page's temperament differed from the shrewish Lucrezia whom del Sarto married. Lucrezia scared her husband's students away with her sharp tongue. Hardly the quiet Lucrezia of Browning's poem, which cleverly began with a disclaimer: "But do not let us quarrel any more." And what Browning's Andrea accused his wife of was not willfulness but utter indifference to his art. His tone builds to an irritability that almost jumps out of the poem:

> *But had you—oh, with the same perfect brow,*
> *And perfect eyes, and more than perfect mouth,*
> *And the low voice my soul hears, as a bird*
> *The fowler's pipe, and follows to the snare—*
> *Had you, with these the same, but brought a mind!*
> *Some women do so.*

Such a woman, a woman of intellect, would urge her artist-husband to live for:

> *'God and the glory! never care for gain.*
> *'The present by the future, what is that?'*

But not everyone can be married to Elizabeth Barrett Browning.

The Brownings left Rome that summer and would not winter there again until 1858, but they maintained the closest ties with the Storys and with Page. That summer Don Cirella was at Albano, where Page leased a house for Sarah and the daughters while he remained in Rome. Story wrote to Lowell, "a most admirable arrangement for the two lovers & a most unfortunate one for the husband." When they returned, Cirella went home to Naples, and in December, "Sarah procured a passport . . . said to Page, that she was going to Albano &

disappeared." Because of difficulties with the passport, she had to return to Rome, which she did, using a false name and taking her own place, where she waited for a visa to Naples. Page found out she was in town, rushed to her, and begged her to return. She was very determined and did not listen to any of his arguments. In a day or two she disappeared again, to join Cirella in Albano.

Story told Lowell, "It is mere madness on her part—he is nine years younger than she—and will assuredly cast her off at some time. I do not in the least think that he was the seducing party. She fell in love with him—and led him on from step to step." Sarah was "determined to leave Page with some one or other (as I know) and had made overtures to other persons, at least to one other person . . . and there are tales of her which are the worst that can be told of woman. I hope they are not true." And, as in Browning's poem, there were rumors that "she has left considerable debts behind her."

Browning wrote to the Storys in December, "our greatest misfortune being in this sad business of the Pages . . . I fear Page is left deeply involved in debts of her contracting." Not hearing from Page, Browning wrote to him in the middle of January 1855. The heartfelt sympathy the poet felt for his friend was one that would translate itself into the more objective world of poetry: "This is only a word for my own sake—don't think it wants or needs answer of any kind." He just wanted to assure his friend "of my constant remembrance and affection." And tactfully, "I have heard very little about you, but fear you are harassed & out of health. How little we can do for each other in such conjunctures! Let me say what I feel, & understand why I say it. I have turned over in my mind the probabilities & prudence of a run up to Rome, just that I might see you—but it can hardly be. At the same time, I am not in apprehension as I should be did I know you less. No more is laid on any of us than he can bear. You must be an example to weaker men: and what gifts you have, and will ever have! I shall write no more now, out of the fulness of heart, this word *would* come, as I said. God bless you dear Page!"

A difficult letter to write. More difficult still was that the rupture in Page's life imitated a rupture in his art. A year before Sarah ran off, Elizabeth wrote to Anna Jameson from Rome of the wonderful portrait Page had just completed of their mutual friend, the actress Charlotte Cushman. It is "soul and body together." However, "Critics wonder whether the colour will *stand*. It is a theory of this artist that time does

ROBERT BROWNING (1854) *by William Page. Page sent his portrait to RB,*
but by the time it arrived in Florence, it had cracked and faded. Browning wrote,
"We love you and your art the more as we look at it the more—
I can say for my wife and myself" (September 9, 1854). Still, he sent the
portrait back to Page for repair. Its ghostlike quality has survived
subsequent attempts to restore it.

not *tone,* and that Titian's pictures were painted as we see them. The consequence of which is that his (Page's) pictures are undertoned in the first instance, and if they change at all will turn black."

When Browning's portrait was completed, Page made another of his noble gestures: He presented it as a gift to Elizabeth. He "painted a picture of Robert like Titian then like a prince presented it to me." Robert wrote of it to W. W. Story, whose sculpture he never praised as extravagantly, that it was "the wonder of everybody—no such work has been achieved in our time, to my knowledge, at least. I am not qualified to speak of the likeness, understand—only of the life and. effect, which, I wish, with all my heart, had been given to my wife's head, or any I like better to look at than my own."

He wouldn't have to look for long. In September he sent his portrait from Florence to Rome to have a crack repaired. By May 1855 the portrait was much lighter, the crack hadn't reappeared, and Browning was keeping it in the sun. He planned to take it with him to London and Paris. However, by October 29, 1855, he wrote to Dante Gabriel Rossetti: "I have taken you at your word—you will receive my portrait forthwith. You must put it in the sun, for I seem to fear it will come but blackly out of its three months' case-hardening. So it fares with Page's pictures . . . 'Kings do not die—they only disappear.' "

Ironically, the portrait that would begin to darken within a year of its completion had almost immediately cracked. A short time after Browning sat in Page's studio and witnessed Page's marriage disintegrating, he became the observer of Page's painting disintegrating as well. In the next century, after having been cleaned in 1949, the portrait once more turned black. Its ghostly appearance must have affected Browning. It offered a painful parallel to Page's life.

At evening tea with Mrs. Kinney, Browning might impatiently insist that there was no relation between George Sand's morality and her art. In a poem he wrote a few years later, Andrea del Sarto's perfect technique was an artistic fault that was related to a moral fault. Del Sarto's obsession with style impeded him from striving for meaning in art and also allowed him to succumb to his wife and to become morally culpable in his dealing with the French king. But the flaws in Page's life and his art sprang from a noble and more generous nature. Such "faults" must have perplexed and worried Robert Browning. Why was dear noble Page so afflicted in life and in art? The impetus for the poem itself, one of Browning's greatest, came out of the poet's attempt

CLASPED HANDS OF THE BROWNINGS *by Harriet Hosmer. The only way EBB would "sit" for this unique portrait was if Hosmer personally supervised casting the hands in plaster, which she did in 1853 at the Casa Guidi.*

Your soft hand is a woman of itself,
And mine the man's bared breast she curls inside.
                    —RB, "Andrea del Sarto"

to make some order—some sense—out of this painful and unanswerable question. One thing was sure. Both del Sarto and Page would have risen higher in their art if their wives' beauty had extended to their souls.

What if they had had loving marriages, had wives who led them from concerns about daily life and material things, putting an emphasis on artistic accomplishment? What if their wives had brought into marriage "a mind! Some women do so"? Against Browning's own worries about providing for his family as he wrote *Men and Women,* Elizabeth Barrett Browning held him to higher goals.

'God and the glory! never care for gain.
'The present by the future, what is that?'

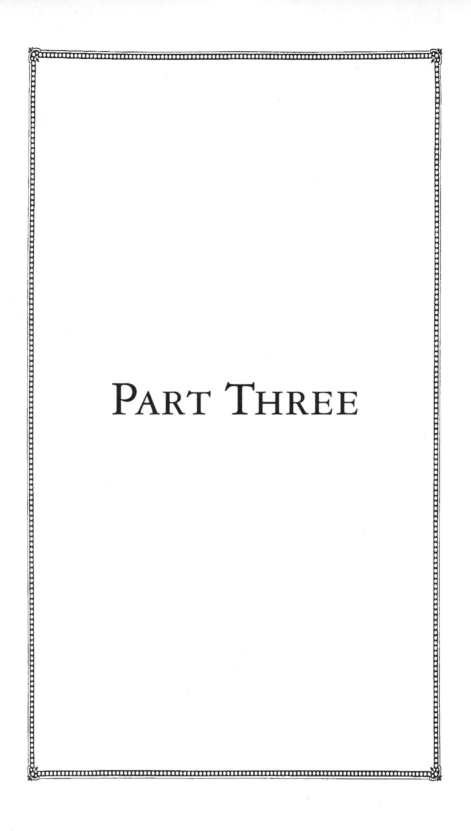

PART THREE

Spirit drawings produced by either EBB or Sophie Eckley during one of their private séances in Rome.

"Such a Wild Step"

In January 1855, Pen Browning walked into the salon of the Casa Guidi, where his mother sat. She was working on the manuscript of *Aurora Leigh*. He was going out for a walk, accompanied by Elizabeth Wilson (his "Lili") or his beloved Ferdinando, or both. Pen, close to his sixth birthday, was dressed fancifully and elegantly as always, probably in velvet pants and a fine blouse with lace embroidery. His hair was long and flowing, as it would have been in the days of Renaissance princes. He already had his hat on, perhaps one with a feather on it. According to his mother, he looked "radiant."

Before the child left the house, he would always come to her with a parting speech, imitating his father, who never went out or even to his room to write *Men and Women* without asking his family to " 'wish him good fortune.' " In Peni-babble this translated into "Dod bless you" or "Tate tare of yourself" or, closer to the master himself, "I wish you dood fortune in the house."

Today he said simply, "Dod bless you darling pet mama! I'm going out."

To which his mother responded, "Do you love me, Peni?"

"Oh yes—all the world—more than the world! all the stars."

"Would you be sorry if I went away?"

"I never would let you go."

"But if I were to die!!"

"Oh—don't *speak* about it."

This was said with such an expression of pain on the child's face that the mother was instantly seized by remorse. She tried to mitigate her words by talking "fast" about "all sorts of pleasanter trips" that the family might soon be taking—together.

This wickedness, this "stupidity," she related to her sister Arabel, who once slept in her room at Wimpole Street. Arabel had remained unmarried and at home, while her more gay-hearted and robust sister Henrietta, as well as her talented and ill sister Ba, went on to marriage, child rearing, and eternal expulsion from the heart and house of her father. In looks, Arabel most resembled her oldest sister, Ba—the thoughtful face weighed down as well by too many finger curls. It was an open face like her famous sister's, plainer, the eyes less vivid, but the lips as full. In temperament she shared the serious and the religious nature of Ba, turned not to poetry and the artistic life but to charitable works and to a Christianity steeped in the nonconformist beliefs of their childhood. It was a good thing that Elizabeth had been thoughtful enough not to ask Mr. Stratten, that clergyman who consulted the wishes and ideas of his children, to marry her and Robert close to a decade ago. The father would never have allowed Arabel to continue to worship at his chapel. And it was there that the pious Londoner gained sustenance throughout her life.

Arabel Barrett Moulton Barrett devoted much time and effort to the Ragged Schools she helped found for the poor, downtrodden, and prostituted girls of the London slums. At home she was an obedient daughter until the end. And after the end—her father's death, that is—she finally had her chance to make her own life. But for certain things, it would seem, it was too late. A strong woman in her own right—"the union of *gentleness with decision*," Joseph Milsand called it—she also bore the curse of many a duteous son or daughter. Inexplicably at times, cruelly at others, she was often overlooked. Even Elizabeth, who loved her so dearly, often relied on her to make reservations in London and Paris, often assumed that Arabel, too, would agree that Arabel's own life was easier than Henrietta's, and often took her for granted. But after all, they were sisters and Barretts. Both were able, to each other, to speak up. And Robert? Well, he was Robert Browning, double underline. He very much appreciated Arabel's worth. He told his wife he loved Arabel as much as, if not more than, his own sister. And in this familial relationship, too, time would show the authenticity of his words.

On January 10, 1855, on the very day Elizabeth told her sister of her "stupid" conversation about her own death with Pen, her old friend and correspondent Mary Russell Mitford died at the age of sixty-seven. From then on, really since the first days of her marriage, Elizabeth's

unpublished letters to her sister Arabel—more than 225, half of them
at the Berg Collection at the New York Public Library and half in family hands—offer the most intimate account of the poet's life. It was to
Arabel that the poet revealed her soul—and her working habits.

Robert Browning was completing the two volumes of his poetry
to be collected as *Men and Women,* and Barrett Browning was working
on *Aurora Leigh.* "Robert and I do work everyday—he has a large volume of short poems which will be completed by the spring—and I
have some four thousand five hundred lines of mine—I am afraid six
thousand lines will not finish it." To assure their regular working
schedule, they gave instructions that they would not receive visitors
before three.

On September 12, 1854, she wrote to her sister, "Married today
eight years." Pen brought her flowers; Ferdinando and Wilson helped
him arrange them. "Then Robert had a gift for me, after the precious
love undim through all these years, a beautiful malachite broach." He
knew how she admired malachite.

Circumstances had favored the couple: love, friendships, a child.
The future was still ahead of them. Robert's poems were magnificent
and clear. He would be appreciated this time. Elizabeth was writing
directly and truthfully about modern life. The world of conformists
and conservative critics would not be ready for her views. She didn't
care. She no longer had to imagine the world, she was living in it—
giving voice to and influencing it through her art.

Still, that "stupid" conversation with Pen. To someone who knew
her as well as Arabel, it must have hinted at illness and morphine. The
winter of 1854–55 was unusually cold in Florence, and Ba developed
what she described to Arabel as "a little more cough . . . just in the
morning—you know my cough is always *there,* waiting like a lion in
his den & ready to work on provocation." Robert's prescription was to
get her to take asses' milk before she went to bed, and people said she
was looking much better.

That was as sick as she would ever get by letter home. Actually, she
had had the worst attack of her old illness—the congested lungs, the
coughing, the pain in the side, the difficulty in breathing—since her
marriage. The lion stirred once more during some of the most active
and happiest times of her life, and he prodded his ally, Elizabeth's oldest foe—morbidity.

This was just a glimmering of morbidity among happier preoccupations with domestic life and child rearing. The Brownings were still educating their child at home. Wasn't Robert's real education within the compass of his own father's library? Didn't Elizabeth keep the little glove of her father, who had been ripped from colonial life at Pen's age to England for education?

Now Henrietta was teaching her son mathematics. Too much disciplined learning could cause the child to break down, to run a fever. It was just not healthy. Elizabeth herself had been a child prodigy. Was she speaking from her own experiences as she exhorted her sister, with an intensity tinged with fear, to allow little Altham's mind to develop naturally? Elizabeth would not teach Pen to count to a hundred just because his cousin Altham could. In Rome she told him straight out, "I will never teach you that."

"Then I must go to Papa."

And what did Papa do, "out of spite," according to his wife? Why, Robert "gave him the theory of counting to a hundred, directly."

In politics, tutored, Elizabeth told Arabel, not by her but by Ferdinando, Pen had become an Italian patriot, as were both his parents. But he developed as well an anti-British stance that foreshadowed the full blooming of his mother's perspective and appalled his father. When the Brownings' friend Isa Blagden said, "I'm proud of being English," Pen responded, "But *you're only* a woman, *Isa!*" Elizabeth was struck by the degree to which he felt "his advantage of belonging to the male sex." It "quite startles me."

That he had made a point of his maleness at the age of six was probably as psychologically healthy as it was politically incorrect. Elizabeth had extolled his angelic qualities when he was an infant and she was reading Swedenborg. The daughter of Edward Barrett Moulton Barrett was still in no great hurry to see her beloved child grow up—too fast.

No wonder Robert, the most sexually unbiased of men and the great friend of Anna Jameson, Adelaide Sartoris, Harriet Hosmer, and Charlotte Cushman, was shocked not by his child's masculine bluster but by his disturbing lack of John Bull. He argued with his son on the issue of British patriotism. "As for me I can't help laughing," wrote Ba to her sister. She attributed Pen's anti-British stance to his linguistic superiority to those in the Anglo-Florentine community who couldn't speak proper Italian: "The English always will shut their *mouses* when they speak."

PEN BROWNING, *ten years old, Rome, 1859. Elizabeth could not bear to have his hair cut and liked to dress him fancifully. Robert inscribed this copy of the photograph, "Penini with his eyes squeezed up against the Roman sun, May 24, '59."*

In Pen's formative years the Brownings' contrasting views of child rearing would not be that confusing to the child. He knew when to go to his father and when to go to his mother. As progressive and at times radical as Elizabeth's child-rearing views were, and as concerned as Robert was for his Florentine child to become British (whether or not he wore knickers), as a married couple these two poets, rather unconventionally, offered balance.

And Pen offered his parents an added incentive for leaving Florence: to visit aunts and uncles, and at least one grandfather, who hadn't seen the radiant child since he was three. A more immediate reason was to get to England in time to expedite the publication of *Men and Women,* due to be issued by the end of 1855. The couple planned, as much as they ever planned, to repeat the pattern of their trip four years earlier, visiting London on either end of a long stay in Paris.

Once more they made the decision to keep the Casa Guidi. Their last months in Florence had been filled with painters and cleaners sprucing up the apartment. The money it took was well worth it. They "have not paid too much for making our apartment quite perfect . . too perfect almost to leave! . . & fit to receive anybody in the shape of an occupant." They'd sublet at a good rate, and since they planned to return to Florence in a year or so at least for a little while, they would have a pleasing apartment should they decide to live there longer.

Just before the Brownings left Florence, a singular escapade of Elizabeth's was recorded by Elizabeth Kinney. Kinney wrote that she, Harriet Hosmer, and Elizabeth Barrett Browning were together when Robert told them of some fine paintings in a nearby monastery not open to women. Harriet Hosmer "jumped up and exclaimed, 'But we *will* see these pictures!' " Characteristically, she suggested they dress like schoolboys, in "full pleated frocks reaching to the knees, and fastened at the waist by leather belts, with loose trousers *à la Turque,* cloth caps, etc.,—and go as male pupils of Mr. Kinney and Mr. Browning, they to pass as our tutors."

" 'Good!' cried Mr. Browning." If Mr. Kinney agreed, he would, and "our grave husbands approved." Hiram Powers was let into the secret and helped in "getting up" the disguises, which included boys' wigs. "Mr. Powers declared that no one would suspect that we were not youths, Mrs. Browning about nineteen, and I fifteen. But Hattie Hosmer, being short and stout, looked like a fat boy . . . and very peculiar!"

HARRIET HOSMER
(1830–1908) *by William
Page, ca. 1855. She was
the first American woman
to come to Rome to study
sculpture. Determined to
become a professional, she
arrived at John Gibson's
studio with two daguerreo-
types of her work and a
certificate of proficiency in
anatomy from the Missouri
Medical College. She later
formed a close friendship
with both of the Brownings,
who were charmed by her
puckishness and wit.*

They met for the adventure and dressed at the Casa Guidi. "Mrs. Browning completed her toilet first, and really looked handsome in it. For the first time I saw her without those dark, heavy curls she always wore half concealing her cheeks, and the wig of short straight hair improved her looks; excitement gave her usually pale face a fine color, and her large black eyes an unwonted brightness." But then she did something "crazy" as the others finished dressing. Elizabeth Kinney and Hattie looked out the window and found that rather than waiting inside the gates of the palazzo for the carriage, there was "Mrs. Browning walking slowly on the square up and down! It must have been an extra dose of opium that pushed her to such a wild step!"

Disguised as a schoolboy, her hair pulled back, as handsome as Bro when they were both young, she wandered dazed beneath her own window. Did her costume bring her back to that day at Hope End, before her illness, when the brother she loved and whose tutor she had shared was sent away to school, leaving her alone in her study of the classical languages and with her knowledge that the world he entered was fraught with dangers?

Watching her from Casa Guidi windows, Elizabeth Kinney exclaimed, " 'What shall we do!'

" 'Why, go to her!' answered Hattie. 'We mustn't leave the great Elizabeth alone in such a state!' Hattie rushed down into the street and took Mrs. Browning's arm to conduct her back. . . . By that time our strange appearance began to attract attention, when all at once Mrs. Browning, seeming conscious of the situation, began to cry, and whispered in my ear,

" 'Oh, Mrs. Kinney, we shall be in the Bargello!'—(Jail)."

It was all so ludicrous that "Hattie and I burst into a laugh. This excited observation still more, and we should have been the center of a crowd had not our husbands driven up in a hack and taken us in, just in time. But Browning was as pale as death with fright, and declared that now he would not venture to carry out our plan, as no doubt we had been discovered, and that the police might follow us, and the whole matter be exposed in the papers, with our names. Mr. Kinney laughed at his fears, while Hattie took fire and called him a poltroon and other hard names. Mrs. Browning cried, I laughed," and Browning refused to visit the monastery.

On the eve of leaving Florence, Elizabeth wrote a very long letter to her father. It had been almost nine years since she and Robert married secretly and she had left Wimpole Street without telling him. Surely there was at least a possibility, after all this time, and all this life, that there could be some sort of reconciliation.

The signs were not favorable. Even before the Brownings' arrival, the father was talking about taking Arabel out of London on vacation that summer. But the siblings still made their plans in the old secret way. "Arabel," Ba wrote, "if Papa keeps more in the house than he used to do, next summer you can come to me, but I can't go to you. Neither can Penini . . Only we must smuggle him in to see dear Minny [the housekeeper]—that must be."

By the middle of May, between writing and hearing Penini's lessons first thing in the day, she was readying and packing Pen's wardrobe, including twelve pairs of trousers with embroidery on each: "he's expensive, that child . . and I'm vain about him." Keeping Pen elegant wasn't always easy. At a full-dress country party right before they left Florence, while out riding a pony with the other children, he filled his pockets with strawberries. His mother would not have known if Peni hadn't boasted of it. She was able to scoop out his pockets with a spoon before he brushed up against and ruined other people's clothes. "Such a mess!" His mother said, "Oh Penini, how could you do such a thing?"

"But I didn't sint they would *melt,* dear Mama."

But strawberries were the least of the Brownings' annoyances that May. Just as they were getting ready for their trip, Elizabeth Wilson announced that she and their manservant wanted to get married! Perhaps Pen had been prophetic months before; on his parents' eighth anniversary, grappling with the difference between anniversaries and birthdays, he asked Wilson, "Dear Lili, when is *your* wedding day." Robert was usually opposed to mixed marriages, but in this case, he considered Ferdinando's sympathies so wide that it was not an impediment. And Wilson had lived in Italy so long that she considered herself half Italian.

These unions between Italians and foreigners might have gained a patriotic status as well. The American intellectual Margaret Fuller had come to Rome in 1848 from where she sent vivid dispatches of the early days of the Risorgimento to the New York *Tribune*. Her notices paralleled the events Elizabeth Barrett Browning wrote about in *Casa Guidi Windows* and in many ways captured a similar point of view. Fuller was also preparing a history of the Revolution, which she considered her best work. Completely devoted to the cause of Italian unity, she fell in love with the younger Marquis Giovanni Angelo Ossoli and had a child by him. Presumably they married, though there might have been obstacles to a legal ceremony. After the fall of the Roman Republic in 1849, Margaret Fuller moved to Florence with her family. Before her return to America with Ossoli and her child, on her last night in Florence in 1850, she had visited the Brownings and presented a Bible to Peni from her little son, inscribed prophetically, "In Memory of Angelo Eugene Ossoli." Margaret Fuller had presentiments about the ocean voyage on the *Elizabeth* which she expressed to Elizabeth, who had lost her brother on a calm day at sea. The poet recounted to Arabel that Fuller turned "to me with that peculiar smile which lightened up her plain, thought-worn face, 'I accept as a good omen that our ship should be called the *Elizabeth.*' "

By the time Fuller got to Gibraltar she sent a note to the Brownings that the captain had died of smallpox and had been buried at sea. "You know me & my cowardice, Arabel—'Do burn it,' " she implored Robert. In August 1850, as Elizabeth was recovering from her fourth and most dangerous miscarriage, she could tell, as she always could, that Robert was attempting to keep some bad news from her. For two days Robert had avoided telling her that which had horrified him.

Fuller's fears had been founded. For the *Elizabeth* sank at the very end of the voyage home. Margaret Fuller, her husband, and her son all drowned within sight of land.

The manuscript of Fuller's history of the Revolution, which would have added dimension to the Anglo-Americans' concern for liberty and for the unity of Italy, went down with them. Elizabeth Barrett Browning became the poet of the Risorgimento; another woman, one who considered herself married to an Italian, the American thinker Margaret Fuller might have become the chronicler of those events had fate allowed.

Jesse White, the British feminist, had come to Italy and married a politically engaged Italian. As Jesse White Mario, she toured England giving lectures on the Italian revolution, taking a view opposite that of Elizabeth Barrett Browning. Though she admired the poet, White continued to uphold Mazzini and had other views that Elizabeth denounced in her letters.

The mixing of Anglo-American and Italian, Protestant and Roman Catholic, was not all a matter of Sarah Page running away with a nobleman many years her junior. For the Brownings, the concern over Wilson and Ferdinando was not the mixed marriage but the possible loss of a couple who had served their needs so well.

Elizabeth thought Wilson might wait till England to marry and have her family present, but the couple married in the English church in Florence and planned a Catholic wedding in Paris.

England was of special interest to Elizabeth in the spring of 1855. From it she was receiving exciting news that supported her fervent belief. She wrote to her sister Arabel with glee: "Now, listen, all unbelievers in spirits! You cant survive much longer, so make the most of your life." Spirits who could be summoned by mediums, and whose presence could be heard in the rapping on tables, the tilting of tables, and the mysterious presence during séances of disembodied hands had its beginning, in 1848, in . . . upstate New York. It was America's contribution to that revolution in religious values that occurred during the Victorian period.

After the new biblical criticism from Germany had disproved the divine authorship of the Bible, casting doubt on previously held religious certainty, not all Victorian intellectuals ran about London in despair, wringing their hands and contorting their prose with shouts of the everlasting Nay! "God is dead" was not shouted from every rooftop. Nor did all believers in the face of science and the theory of evolution turn nostalgically to the past or return to a stubborn form of traditional orthodoxy—or become High Church or go over to Rome. From Victorian roots, hybrids flowered. For example, the works of the eighteenth-century Emanuel Swedenborg recirculated, and many in the Brownings' circle, Powers, Page, Story, believed in the spirit world he envisioned. His work *Conjugal Love,* which described an afterlife not unlike life, when married couples were united as one mind, was known to the Brownings, studied early in their marriage. For some the loosening of orthodoxy expanded possibilities. It was not surprising that this optimism swelled in the United States, where mid-century congregations of five to ten thousand spiritualists could be found meeting in Boston in the music hall on a Sunday. By the spring of 1855, séances and spiritual rappings ran rampant in the well-to-do and stately homes of England. And it was an American friend of the Brownings, the discerning and pioneering collector of Italian art James Jackson Jarves, who first sent Elizabeth the good news.

Robert Browning took a skeptical attitude on the spiritual rappings, spurred on perhaps by his wife's immediate will to believe. Yet he, as well as his wife, considered the wealthy young Jarves "rather a cold man—& honest." Jarves was heir to what would later be called the Boston and Sandwich Glass Company. He had traveled to and written about Hawaii before coming to Italy. There he saw American tourists attempting to grapple with Italian culture. He became a writer on art who believed he had a mission to carry thoughts about art and the artistic life back to the United States. Even before he arrived in Italy, his own marriage had turned very bitter. Still he did not believe in divorce. "We must all bear our own sin, and in some degree our neighbors' also," he would write. (He did not consider himself the biological father of his last child by Elizabeth Swain Jarves.) "Marriage can be made self-corrective by viewing it in its true sense, as a school in which to train the virtues for heaven. If its trials are sore, so are its years few."

On his way back to America, without his wife, Jarves, whose invaluable art collection would be bought in his lifetime by Yale University, planned to stop in England and attend a séance with a young psychic who had become all the rage, Daniel Dunglas Home (or "Hume" as it is pronounced and as Elizabeth spelled it). Jarves himself had not had any personal experiences with the spirits, though he tended to believe in them, given both his parents', and particularly his mother's, enthusiasm. Robert, respecting Jarves's clear head at the time, told him on parting, "'If you *see anything*, write to us, and I will receive your testimony.'" With that, off Jarves went to England with his friend J. R. Tilton, the American artist who lived in Rome.

No letter came. "'I told you so,' Robert said. 'He's an honest man. He has seen nothing & won't write. I knew he wouldn't write. These things always slip through.'"

Robert spoke too soon. Jarves's letter, when it arrived, was such an explosive account of Home's power that in Florence for weeks nothing else but the letter was "talked of, everybody snatching it from everybody, reading it, copying it, dreaming and discussing over it."

The description Elizabeth offered Arabel was her own "I told you so" to her more orthodox sister. She couldn't quote the letter verbatim, as it was still going the rounds, yet: "He has seen a heavy table with a French lamp on it lifted into the air, without a finger touching it—the same table tilted up on end . . the lamp kept in its place unmoved . . contrary to all laws of gravitation—same table made so light he could lift it with a finger—same table made so heavy that all the persons present tugging at it, couldn't stir it an *inch*. (This, in different private houses.)"

Then there were the spiritual hands. Elizabeth tried to re-create his words, "'As surely as I clasped your hand at parting . . . I clasped the hand of a spirit . . .'" They were "'hands of different sizes'—'softer & more thrilling than any woman's'—'conveying an inexpressible pleasure'—the 'softest & most loving tenderness of touch.'" These "hands did everything you asked them to do—untied a lady's apron-string & carried the apron across the room . . . struck playfully or patted tenderly the person present—took Mr. Jarves's handkerchief & knotted it in so ingenious a manner as would be hard for a man's craft. Then there was music—an accordion was played upon exquisitely in a full light," played "more exquisitely than a mortal could play it. That may or may not be an exaggeration."

She did not want to overstate. "I must tell you that altho he felt the hands, clasped them, felt the fingers, was aware of their various size & pressure, yet he himself saw them indistinctly—a sort of floating cloud each hand was to him—but the other persons present, all of them, including Mr. Tilton our unbeliever, saw the hands of the spirits as *perfectly & clearly as they saw their own*. Then the house was shaken as with an earthquake . . with the perpendicular & lateral movement . . until the master of it begged for quiet—he was afraid of the consequences to the walls. The whole ended in trance & prayer on the part of the medium—magnificent in character—'like Dr. Channing' says Mr. Jarves who had heard him."

Though this would seem to have been enough spirits for one day, Mr. Jarves and Mr. Home decided to sleep together: "The demonstrations being often interesting on such occasions. . . . (You see Hume is known to Mr. Jarves's family—he is quite a gentleman—related to the Earl of Home—& is said to be a most interesting young man . . refined, frank, affectionate, pious . . & rather like Mr. Ruskin in personal appearance.)" The sleeping arrangement proved fortunate. Sounds began immediately. "The demonstrations were so violent as to frighten Hume who crept close to me for protection," Jarves wrote to a friend. Elizabeth reported to Arabel, "The spirits walked round the bed with distinct footsteps—drew the curtains backward & forward, lifted up the heavy fourposter bed into the air . . & did everything Mr. Jarves asked them to do *except one* for which there seemed to be a reason. They said they wd. try to do it, but they failed. He saw, but dimly, a full-length spirit upon the occasion." And if that were not enough, extraordinary revelations were made to him, "not only upon his own affairs but upon matters connected with people in Florence—& two or three ladies here are in agonies because something is hinted which may refer to one of them. Well—what do you say?"

Robert said, "We can't any of us sit down & conclude that the man whom we saw the other day, cold & sensible . . & skeptical about Mr. Kirkup's pet medium Regina . . has gone suddenly mad." He said, "Upon the whole, I can't make up my mind to believe it is a delusion." He would hold his judgment until "he sees with his eyes." But in the meantime, "if it's spiritual, I'm inclined to think it devilish," which to his wife "is the most cruel conclusion I ever heard. I protest against such conclusion." For her part, "I don't believe in the least degree more since I read his letter, simply because I believed entirely, previous to reading it." She and Robert and their friend Isa Blagden would go to a séance while they were in London over the summer—and the pious Arabel must go, too. "Won't you? Only we won't sleep with Mr. Hume, we have agreed, unless you should particularly desire it."

In June, before Elizabeth reached England, she wrote to Arabel from Paris that her sister had been very wrong not to go to a séance with Home in London when she had the opportunity. "I want to impress upon you the fact, that a spirit out of the body doesn't pretend to more infallibility than a spirit in the body. What you go to receive is the *proof of access from the spiritual world*, not to receive instruction in doctrine." When Elizabeth arrived in London, "Certainly you *shall* see Hume. I *will* have it so." Did she forget that Arabel was a Barrett, too? Both sisters held to their convictions.

But would the Brownings ever get out of Paris? The trip from Florence had been filled with problems. They had left on the outbreak of cholera and Elizabeth had been afraid. On ship, Pen had fun, but Robert again was sick. In Marseilles her brother Alfred was in the hotel, and had booked a room near their own. "Robert accused me of a want of sisterly affection because I insisted on washing my face and breakfasting before I sent for him—but if I hadn't, I certainly should have dropped down in a fit at the first word of greeting. So we breakfasted—& then we sent Penini in alone with a slip of paper."

Uncle Alfred was in high spirits and might have been doubly pleased to be greeted by his sister's pixielike child. The fifth Barrett son (aka Daisy) at the age of thirty-five was on his way to France to visit and marry the woman he loved, his cousin Elizabeth "Lizzie" Barrett, thirteen years his junior.

Though he came from a big, close, letter-writing family, he apparently did not know that Ba had already heard of his matrimonial plans from Arabel. He didn't confide in her; instead he talked of the country house he had rented in France on a six-month lease, "furnished with plate and linen" and costing only twenty pounds. He was in the happiest of moods, delighting in the "liberty of the French government." Another republican in the making, it would appear.

Alfred's closed mouth and his sister's breakfast before greeting him might have stemmed from an unspoken difference. Ba was not a champion of his plans: "depend upon it, Arabel, he comes here to meet & marry Lizzie—that's certain. I am very, very sorry."

Why? The next seven and a half lines of the letter are crossed out. We are in the realm of family secrets. Alfred certainly had been in close quarters with his young cousin. When he was in his early twenties, Lizzie lived as part of the family at 50 Wimpole Street. Ba drew "A Portrait" of Lizzie Barrett at the age of ten, collected in her *Poems* of 1844. She quoted Ben Jonson: "Our name's Elizabeth." The poem painted a physical and psychological portrait that might make us a bit un-

GEORGINA ELIZABETH "LIZZIE" BARRETT, 1843, *by Alfred Barrett Moulton Barrett. Lizzie was ten years old and living at 50 Wimpole Street when her twenty-three-year-old cousin Alfred did this watercolor. Her mother was mentally ill and could not take care of her, so as a child she lived with the Barretts of Wimpole Street.*

ALFRED BARRETT MOULTON BARRETT (1820–1904), *pencil and watercolor by his brother Octavius, June 1845. The tenth child of Edward Barrett and Mary Moulton Barrett, "Daisy" was disinherited when he married his cousin Lizzie, thirteen years his junior.*

easy today, when we know so much of the intricate family reasons of why a beautiful young child might seem overwise, unchildlike, and compliant.

> *Oval cheeks encolored faintly,*
> *Which a trail of golden hair*
> *Keeps from fading off to air:*
>
> *And a forehead fair and saintly,*
> *Which two blue eyes undershine,*
> *Like meek prayers before a shrine.*
>
> *Face and figure of a child,—*
> *Though too calm, you think, and tender,*
> *For the childhood you would lend her.*
>
> *Yet child-simple, undefiled,*
> *Frank, obedient, waiting still*
> *On the turnings of your will.*

What was this compliant child doing living in the Barrett household? Her father's military and Jamaican interests kept him abroad, and her mother, Mary Turner Barrett, was unstable and unable to care for her daughter from the earliest years. There were whispers of insanity and alcoholism.

In Paris in the summer of 1855 it might have been Mary Turner Barrett who showed up to visit the Brownings—her daughter's sister- and brother-in-law—"smelling intolerably of spirits—both mentally & bodily. The tone of her conversation made me ashamed of her relationship to me—Don't repeat this to anyone." Better yet, Arabel crossed her name out, too.

Lizzie's father, Captain George Goodin Barrett, was the youngest of the four illegitimate children born to two earlier Barrett cousins— one being Samuel Barrett, the favorite son of Edward of Cinnamon Hill. Samuel's illegitimate children by his cousin Elizabeth Barrett Waite Williams were generously provided for until maturity in his father's will. The youngest son, Captain George Goodin Barrett— Googie—was welcome in his cousin's house on Wimpole Street. Ba complained in her letters to Robert of his doing Jamaican business downstairs while Lizzie was upstairs with her.

The marriage between Daisy and Lizzie did take place, at the embassy in Paris shortly after his sister predicted it. In August, from London, she wrote to dearest Alfred, "I little thought when we parted at Marseilles, that you would bring me another sister before we should meet again. May God bless you & *her*, dear Alfred, & make you happy to the utmost of your hopes."

Daisy informed his father before he married. As he told Sette, "I have written to the Governor, not according to my wishes, but out of regard to *hers* [Lizzie's]. She insisted upon my shewing respect to him who is nominally 'My father' & so I wrote in such a strain, I thought best suited to allay the dreadful injury I was about to inflict. I regretted having to make such a parade, but what I regretted still more was the consequent annoyance it would create among you all. He has I suppose been outrageous—& his society necessarily disagreeable."

Sette, too, hoped his brother would wait, at least until some of his debts were paid off. But by August 2, the day after his marriage, Daisy wrote to Henrietta that "the dread deed has been done. I am a married man—." And he told the sister he was closest to, "You must know my dearest Henrietta that I have loved Lizzie for years—for a long, long time we have been engaged." Lizzie and Daisy had begun taking walks with Henrietta and Surtees just before the Brownings met, in 1844—Lizzie was eleven and Daisy was twenty-four.

There was so much interbreeding in this marriage of double cousins, so much concern about the mother's insanity, so many memories not only of 50 Wimpole Street but of Jamaica and of illegitimacy and mixed racial birth and of contested wills that this particular marriage might have struck an even more bitter chord to Moulton Barrett, who could not seem to escape the curse of generations. He cut his son out of his will in a codicil.

After the marriage Elizabeth would fret about Alfred's foreign assignments, which left his young wife alone for too long a time. Lizzie Barrett was young, pretty, frivolous, in need of interesting experiences. "I fear much that it is merely outside prettiness with her—only she is so very, very pretty, that one would fain give the outward credit for the inward." In her sister-in-law's view Lizzie was not one to be kept for too long on the vine. What happened to the serious child to whom she had read and who'd had dreams of her own? Whatever Elizabeth's doubts about Lizzie's stability and Alfred's debts, meeting her brother, while they were both at Marseilles and right before his marriage, at the exact moment when she was heading toward England and hoping for some reconciliation with her father was quite inopportune. Would her father mistake her opinions on this issue, would he think she had encouraged this match? This time there were justifications for reservations that went beyond her father's irrationality and his cruel and primitive way of cutting pain away—and his children with it. Ba took a pause before seeing Alfred in Marseilles, and her brother didn't breathe a word of his intentions. She was "very, very sorry" about the marriage, and whoever excised the reasons she gave Arabel for it was discreet.

In a practical matter, the fact that Alfred had left London turned out to be a big help. Two of the Brownings' boxes were lost at Marseilles. Elizabeth ascribed it to traveling on the thirteenth and to Wilson and Ferdinando being rather distracted at this juncture. All of Elizabeth's concern centered on Pen's wardrobe. Served her vanity right that his Browning grandfather and his aunt Sarianna would see the child in the bedraggled clothes on his back—hardly the little prince, as she told Arabel. Only in postscript to Daisy was there any mention of the "ms notes to a book," tucked in among the finery. But it was Elizabeth's "way to hope against stone walls," even "in the face of Robert's despair." She thanked her brother for finding and sending both boxes on to Paris "very, very much. . . . It has taught us some wisdom, & we are not likely ever to lose our boxes again, whatever we may do with our wits."

But not only missing property kept the Brownings in the City of Light. "We are not married yet," and there were difficulties. A mixed marriage between a Roman Catholic Florentine and a British Protestant was a difficult political affair. The Anglican service had been performed in Florence. But to get married in the Roman Catholic Church, one had to vow the children "should be baptised & educated as Catholics." Wilson couldn't lie. She *could* promise that if "the children *chose* to be Roman Catholics, the mother won't hinder them." They had to resolve this issue in Paris, for they were only "half married."

It was not because of religious scruples that a church wedding had to be performed. In Tuscany "(in Piedmont they order it better) there is no legal marriage, except by the act ecclesiastical." So the couple could not return to Florence as husband and wife unless they were married by a priest. Only Wilson was bound. Wilson "has shed tears enough," and Ferdinando was willing to convert, "to profess protestantism, renounce his country and act up a fiacre (of all vocations adopted through melancholy!) in Lyons." The couple were desperate for a resolution, and the Brownings were using all their influence to find one.

At the same time, Elizabeth had her own worries about the union, "because I am human . . . & thinking rather of myself than of her." Robert says, " 'Of course you cant separate a man & his wife'—Well—I suppose we cant—And yet my Penini who wants somebody to take care of him & be with him always—what's to be done with him. As to his sleeping in a room by himself, it's out of the question. I suppose he must have a crib in my room. I cant fancy what to do. If he wakes in the dark, he cries instantly."

Finally, Robert got to the Archbishop of Paris. The formula they decided on was that Wilson "has agreed to *submit to her husband's wishes* on the point of the children—and if they don't exact an oath from her all will be safe. . . . I have just had a note from Mdme. Mohl who has been kindly active in our behalf, to the effect that the emperor himself could not wring from the church better terms." So the couple would not have to live in Lyons and the Brownings and the Ferdinando Romagnolis could finally travel to England. "We" were all married at last.

To lie would have been inconceivable, even if it meant that not to lie would make a return to Italy problematic. But there was more behind the couple's high emotions in Paris than the Brownings could guess at the time. Wilson was pregnant.

The Brownings did not find out until they were in England, and Elizabeth was shocked. The woman with whom she entrusted her child, the woman for whom the exact wording of her wedding contract was important. . . . If one expected a more open reaction from the writer who was now creating Marian Earle, one would be wrong. Marian Earle gave birth to an illegitimate child, but she was still "pure," the victim of poverty, British society, and rape. The woman poet who kissed George Sand's hand was very upset by Elizabeth Wilson Romagnoli's pregnancy and the lies involved. She had to focus on all that Wilson had been to her in the past in order not to judge.

One is reminded of the brothers Elizabeth herself left on Wimpole Street nine years earlier with a letter to explain her own secret marriage. Being kept out of a secret in any situation in which one has had a part is being played the fool. The deeper issue was trust. The trust was violated and so was her respect for this woman who traveled with her. Flush had died in Florence the previous winter, so old and mangy that even his devoted mistress was able to let him go. And the woman who had attended her courtship and marriage and her son was no longer the person Elizabeth once thought she was. Back in England, before the advent of the cruel east wind, helping her husband with his proofs of *Men and Women* and her son with his new adjustments, another wind was blowing, and it wasn't balmy. There had been clues all year. In 1855 the Brownings were subject to the winds of change.

"Who's There?"
The Ealing Séance

Daniel Dunglas Home was an agent of change. The Brownings arrived in London on July 12, 1855, and Ba was immediately informed that Anna Jameson's earlier account of the medium's travels to Italy was in error. In fact, the young American of Scottish descent was still in town, staying at the Ealing home of two of Anna Jameson's friends, Mr. and Mrs. J. S. Rymer. The wealthy couple was treating the medium like a son. They hugged and kissed him, and he often nestled against them in a childlike manner. The behavior was remarkable, yet to the Rymers, Home's type of lisping affection might also mediate a communication from beyond the grave. In his séances at their house he had been able to bring them in contact with the rapping spirit of their own dead son, Wat. British reserve collapsed between the couple and the medium, and so did emotional separation. No rush to Paris, where the emperor called, or to Florence, where the Anglo-American community waited. No rush? Why, Home, barely twenty, had been in England only since early April, and his fame had already spread among the wealthy, the powerful, and the literati. The séance Jarves reported to the Brownings in Florence occurred in mid-May. Mrs. Trollope and her son Thomas read about it and took a quick trip from Villa Trollope to England for a look-see. Not that they believed. (It would be some months before Home would get to Florence and levitate in their living room.) Still, on June 19, along with the Rymer family and Charles Dickens, their disbelief was shaken.

In Paris in late June, Thackeray's daughters had reported to the Brownings that Thackeray had had an experience with Home that had made them terribly frightened about " 'the spirits'—'hoping it may not be true!!' Mr. Thackeray saw Hume a fortnight ago, had no visible

DANIEL D. HOME (1833–86). *A wood-cut—attributed to the spirits—of the most famous medium of the nineteenth century and the toast of European aristocrats and artists. Home was born in Edinburgh, Scotland, but moved with his family to Norwich, Connecticut, when he was nine. RB considered him a fraud and after EBB's death satirized him in "Mr. Sludge, 'The Medium.'" RB had often argued with EBB about spiritualism, and in the long poem had the pleasure of catching Sludge cheating, something that never happened in life. Sludge defended himself the way EBB defended unsavory mediums:*

> What's a "medium"? He's a means,
> Good, bad, indifferent, still the only means
> Spirits can speak by; he may misconceive,
> Stutter and stammer—he's their Sludge and drudge,
> Take him or leave him. . . .

manifestations," but he felt a spiritual presence about him, pulling and pressing him. "In his astonishment . . what do you think he did? . . he began to swear—gave out a volley of oaths—and then, by a reaction, turned intensely sick. . . . His daughters say he doesn't know what to think; it was altogether astonishing." Such reports! And here were the Brownings at Ealing eleven days after their arrival in England, ready for the séance that Ba anticipated with as much gusto as she had meeting George Sand on her last long trip in 1851.

"Ah, dearest Madonna," Elizabeth would remember, writing to Anna Jameson, the compiler of the Madonna in art, "We arrived at Mr Rymer's by daylight & Hume, showing us the pretty garden, said that he would prepare a garland of flowers, and that afterwards he would ask 'the spirits' to put it on my head—You know [or peradventure you dont know] the American knack of making beautiful wreaths of flowers . . with a skill & grace quite peculiar. A very pretty wreath was made then, & laid upon the table."

The séance itself occurred after dark at nine. Robert Browning had promised to send back a full account of it to a fellow nonbeliever, Elizabeth Kinney, who had promised to keep his words to herself. It was a long, detailed letter, which did not conflict with Jarves's experience, except that details were recorded carefully, evidence strictly observed—as in a police report. The séance began with "some noises, a vibration of the table, then an up-tilting of it in various ways." Then there were more noises and raps, "which were distinguished as the utterance of the family's usual visitor, the spirit of their child 'Wat' who died three years ago, aged twelve."

The rappings stopped; the "circle was too large." The spirits picked out those who were to go, leaving Home, the Rymers, their living son and eldest daughter, two family friends, and the Brownings. The poets were the only outsiders. Once this circle was established, the spirit of the dead twelve-year-old Wat grew less shy, and Wat touched as he had previously rapped. His parents felt the spiritual hand of their boy, and Elizabeth's dress was uplifted near the waist by that same inquisitive spirit. It happened twice. "The spirit then announced (by raps in answer to questions) that it would play the accordion" and that it would show Robert Browning its hands. The lights were all extinguished. "A hand appeared from the edge of the table, opposite to my wife & myself" and it "rose & sank—it was clothed in white loose folds, like muslin, down to the table's edge—from which it was never separated." His wife wrote to her sister Henrietta that she put up her "glass to look at" it, "proving it was not a mere mental impression." The only difference in the couple's account was tone.

Then Home asked Elizabeth to leave her husband's side and take the chair by him. She got up in the dim room and did what the medium desired. A larger hand appeared. Robert reported it pushed the wreath the American had fashioned off the table, "then picked it up from the ground" and brought it to her. The hand then seemed to crawl up Home's shoulder in order to place the wreath on the poet's head. In the hushed circle of nine, in the dark room, the spirits crowned Elizabeth Barrett Browning in laurels.

"The particular hand which did this was of the largest human size, as white as snow, and very beautiful," Elizabeth told Henrietta. "It was as near to me as this hand I write with, and I saw it as distinctly. I was perfectly calm! not troubled in any way, and felt convinced in my own mind that *no spirit belonging to me* was present on the occasion." No dead Bro.

The detachment she gained from this realization allowed her to speak directly to the stranger spirit, requesting the hand to take the wreath from her head and to give it to her husband. The crown was brought to Browning from under the table. Browning reported to Mrs. Kinney, "I was touched several times under the table on one knee & the other—and on my hands alternately—(a kind of soft & fleshy pat)—but not so that I could myself touch the object. I desired leave to hold the spirit-hand in mine, and was promised that favor—a promise not kept, however." Browning was only allowed to hold the accordion that the spirits played under the table. He observed the spirits were freer under the table than above, though he could not see the trick by which the wreath was placed on his wife's head.

The medium then "observed that he supposed the hand with the wreath was that of a particular relation of my wife's—raps to confirm this opinion: the alphabet was put in requestion to discover the *name*—(someone calling 'A. B. C.' &c., & the raps indicating the letter)—it was given successively as William, Frank, Charles, Henry—misses all. Hereupon Mr Home went into a trance & began to address Mr Rymer, in the character of his dead child—in a sort of whisper, at first, to represent a child's voice, but with Mr Home's own inflexions, peculiarities, and characteristic expressions—beginning 'Dear Papa,—is not God *good*,—isn't he *lovely?*' "

"The talk affected the parents, as you may suppose,—there was nothing pleasant to describe." After that the medium rose and "saluted the company with upraised arms,—(we had light enough to see this) and began to speak, apparently in the character of 'the spirits' collectively,—instructing us on the legitimate objects of this work of investigation—and hardly can you conceive a poorer business." Whereas Jarves could hear the invocation of the spirits through Home as worthy as Channing's preaching, Robert Browning heard the charlatan. What other people had reported as eloquent, beautiful, and poetic, Robert Browning observed as being a poor business.

Elizabeth agreed. "I think that what chiefly went against the exhibition, in Robert's mind, was the trance at the conclusion during which the medium talked a great deal of much such twaddle as may be heard in any fifth rate conventicle. But according to my theory (well thought-out and digested) this does not militate at all against the general facts. It's undeniable, and has been from first to last, that if these are spirits, many among them talk prodigious nonsense, or rather most ordinary commonplace."

Home seemed unable to allow the misnaming of those close to Elizabeth, the rapping out of "William, Frank, Charles, Henry," to stand. Elizabeth understood that spirits could make mistakes and was obviously relieved that none close to her was present at the moment to rip through her detached delight. But Home had blundered in front of Robert Browning. With upraised arms, the self-conscious Home allowed the spirits to speak through him. Browning reported their apologetic garble: "that there had been four spirits over my wife's head pouring rays of glory from a sort of crown, or something and that 'we could have given their names but that you (my wife) were intently considering them, and would have called the answer thought-reading.' "

After this, the Brownings and the two female friends of the family were asked to leave while Home conferred with the Rymers. After a quarter of an hour they were called back in. Home still seemed determined to win over Robert Browning. Four strong spirits lifted the table so that Browning could see the process in the light. "I looked under the table and can aver that it was lifted from the ground, say a foot high, and more than once—Mr Home's hands being plainly above it. It was tilted,—and the lamp remained—I am not sure whether there was anything remarkable in *that*,—its base being heavy." Mr. Rymer remarked on how the spirits were holding the lamp on the tilted table.

But still Robert was not impressed.

"I called attention to the fact that a silver-pen rolled readily—the cloth notwithstanding—and said 'will the spirits now prevent the rolling of *this*?' "

This skepticism went beyond the pale. His hostess's daughter was seized by an impolite spirit and from her trance demanded: "Do not put that question! Have you not seen *enough*?"

And so it ended. Browning did not seem to realize that his incredulity had been recognized. "I ought not to omit the sitting was conducted in exact conformity to Mr Rymer's suggestions, which though polite were explicit enough,—that we should put no questions, nor desire to see anything but what the spirit might please to show us. I treated 'the spirit' with the forms & courtesies observed by the others, and in no respect impeded the 'developments' by expressing the least symptom of unbelief—and so kept my place from first to last." His unconsciousness of how his behavior appeared to others led

to an uncharacteristic conclusion—he blamed his wife: "I should like
to go again and *propose* to try a simple experiment or two, but fear it is
already out of my power,—my wife having told one of the party that I
was 'unconvinced.' "

Home knew that already. He was nothing if not supersensitive to
criticism—particularly that of older men. He very much wanted this
philosopher-poet to accept what he saw with his own eyes. And
Browning knew it would have been inexcusable for him at that family
séance to grab at the hands the Rymers took to be those of their
dead child. Yet he had missed the only opportunity he'd have to
expose Home. In fact, the poet did try to arrange for another séance
a few days later. When his request was refused, Browning became
furious.

Still, Home wanted to be a friend of the poets. He came to call on
them, escorted by the Rymers. The visit provoked a heated quarrel between the Brownings. After nine years of marriage the couple came to
an issue that could not be resolved through compromise. In this disagreement, Robert could not be led to higher truth by his wife. Between spirits and humans there might exist only a gauzy veil, but on
the subject of Home, between Robert and Elizabeth, there existed a
stone wall.

Browning was not about to receive Home. The man repelled him.
This twenty-year-old who "declares he has 'no strength at all'—
(why?—even if it were so!) and affects the manners, endearments and
other peculiarities of a very little child indeed," calling the Rymers
papa and mama and kissing all the family, is in actuality "a well-grown
young man, over the average height, and, I should say, of quite the ordinary bodily strength: his face is rather handsome & prepossessing,
and indicative of intelligence,—and I observed nothing offensive or
pretentious in his demeanour beyond the unmanlinesses I mention,
which are in the worst taste."

Elizabeth grew nervous, agitated. Not see the waiting Home? It
was rude; it was unnecessary. This was a social visit. Wait! No, he
wouldn't. He would greet the medium as he deserved. She tried to
calm Robert. When Robert went to Home she was by her husband,
telling Home she was sorry, so sorry.

Although the twenty-year-old acted like a child and proclaimed
his lack of manly strength, he was taller than the poet and half his age.
Browning's rage surprised the medium. When Home raised his hand

to shake Browning's, the poet refused. Browning told him that if he didn't leave immediately, he'd throw him down the stairs.

Home left immediately, but he didn't hold a grudge (not Mr. Sludge). He couldn't understand it, he'd tell all of London. He liked Robert Browning so much; he wanted to be the poet's friend.

The couple could not have picked a more public altercation. Back in London less than a month, Robert Browning had thrown D. D. Home out of his house to Elizabeth Barrett Browning's consternation. This gossip of the day probably changed emphasis in time, just as the spiritual hand that crowned Elizabeth at the séance became identified as Dante's. "It is really a pity to contradict the story about Dante's hands," she wrote to Anna Jameson. "I should have been enchanted to have had such a coronation." What about that wreath, that thorny memory? Why, Ba brought it back to Florence and kept it in her bedroom in the Casa Guidi as it dried and got dusty. It took Browning two more years before he threw it out the window. And one can imagine the issue the couple were discussing in private, when the desiccated garland hit the cobblestone street.

But the issue itself was not cut-and-dry. At the time it was not spiritualism Browning was disavowing as much as Home. Why, even Elizabeth Kinney, who shared Browning's disbelief, would go to a séance of Home's when he arrived in Florence a few months later. When she saw "accordions fly through the air, playing as they went," she became, temporarily, an ardent believer. Browning would not discredit her experiences. They simply weren't his. His rage was not at belief. He had missed his opportunity to expose Home, to reach out and feel those spiritual hands—to grab them, to see if they were indeed on a string or on a person. Show his wife the truth. But that reach had exceeded his grasp. No wonder he was so enraged after the séance with Home. For the first time in their married life, Robert found himself alone.

But any thought that Robert would be an average husband, or a tyrannical one who forbade his wife, was ill founded. By October 31, 1855, the Brownings were back in Paris expecting a visit from the famous novelist Bulwer-Lytton, now Sir Edward, and his son the poet Robert Lytton (pen name "Owen Meredith") when who should appear, "judge of my consternation . . . Mr Jarves himself!" The room "seemed to swim with Hades let loose." Rather than threatening to throw this bedfellow of Home down the stairs, "Robert met him & he Robert in as friendly a manner . . as if there was no spiritual world." Of course there was no *talk* of the spiritual world as they chattered about "Florence friends." When the Bulwer-Lyttons arrived, Ba made tea and then had a chance to talk with Jarves on the side. He said something softly to her, to which she replied, "Oh, I don't dare to ask you."

Jarves looked over toward Robert "with a half smile, gently, not in vexation, . . & then said . . 'I know—And I have so much to tell you, so much, so much.' "

In a whisper he told her he could now see the spirits as plainly as he saw her. They woke him up at night sometimes, and he could hear the spirit voices. "It seems to be a mediumship of a high order." But before Mr. Jarves could tell her all, Robert called her to the general conversation, and Jarves left. To Arabel she commented, "When you say I am not submissive as a wife I am sure I don't know what you mean—it seems to me I deserve the gold medal for passive perfection . . except in thought & conscience . . which cant be made passive if one happens to have any."

The dutiful wife was then startled when Robert whispered to her across the tea table, " 'Speak of the spirits.'

" 'No,' said I . . I don't like to do that.' "

She realized that Sir Edward had heard of "the whole explosion in London in all its details." So she didn't speak because "I did not choose that he should suppose me capable of the indelicacy of throwing the conflicted subject in the face of my husband before people, without his special permission . . and Robert's whisper had been inaudible to Sir Edward." She went off to talk with the younger Lytton when they both realized that father and husband were "in the thick of the spirit-controversy.

" 'Oh', said Lytton to me . . 'I do wish they would talk of something else.' (He was so afraid of a quarrel.) Not a bit of it."

In fact, "Robert recounted his observations . . how he wasn't permitted to touch the 'hands,' how he thought they were operated by strings . . ."

Bulwer-Lytton then replied. He was a handsome, young-looking man, with "a quantity of light curly hair (not a touch of grey) and moustaches." He spoke with "a slight excess of emphasis . . but full of information & fluent & even brilliant in expression."

" 'The first time I held a hand I believed it was Home's own—& I thought within myself . . "Now, shall I expose this young man." Then

I considered—He is young, he doesn't do the thing for money . . I will rather take him apart presently & speak quietly to him on this ill-proceeding. In a moment, however, the indignation overcame me, & I said aloud, "Mr Hume, that was your hand!" He rose up from the table exclaiming against the wrong I did him by such a suspicion. He went to the window & shed tears hysterically & I followed him & soothed him,—begged him to come back & to allow me to satisfy my natural doubts by holding his hands in mine. He said he would do anything I chose. He came back. I held his two hands in mine—& the three spirit hands proved themselves to me that they were not his. One great hand, rough like a mariner's—one soft smooth delicate woman's hand, of which I felt the veins and the polished nails—and one child's hand that played with mine, was caught & let go. There was no child in the room. I cannot believe there was a trick at all.'

"Robert listened to it all."

In a much lower voice his son told Ba what he had heard about Home in Florence. Home was staying with the Trollopes, and "Mrs. Trollope says she has seen him lifted into the air & whirled round the room, with her own eyes." Nothing unusual. "The manifestations in America are said to be more & more wonderful."

Robert Lytton was wise to whisper. Imagine Robert Browning being told Home was whirling in the air around the Trollopes' villa. Levitating or in a circle, in his long career Home was never found out. In the twentieth century it was Harry Houdini who attempted to debunk him. Houdini constantly sought to make spiritual contact with his mother, who had been the most important person in his life. He argued with the arch-spiritualist Conan Doyle about Home, and wrote an exposé as well. It was Houdini's contention that Home was no medium but a master magician, like Houdini himself.

In his blood Browning knew Home for a trickster—one who stayed among the rich by offering them the rappings of their dead young sons. Some say it was because Home always performed within a family circle of believers that outsiders had trouble catching him or were too polite (as Browning thought he had been) to try. Years later, Maggie Fox would confess that she and her sister had begun the whole phenomenon of spiritual rapping as youngsters in Arcadia, New York, through their ability to make raps with their feet. But by then she was out of luck and an alcoholic, and later recanted her recant.

Browning despised Home, but in 1855 he was open to spiritualism.

When the Lyttons said they were going to a French medium the next day, turning to Robert, Sir Edward asked, " 'would you like to go?'

" 'Yes,' said Robert in a moment. 'And would *you?*' " he asked Ba.

"I looked at my liege lord & was permitted to say my natural 'yes.' "

The French girl turned out to be a weak medium.

After that séance, Robert said to his wife, "You see I am not ashamed of acting against my own resolutions."

She was able to answer truly "that it was one of the noblest things in him, not to be tenacious in either wrong-saying or wrong-doing. And so we were the best of friends in the world with regard to spiritual matters."

Still, "At the same time, at the same time, Arabel, I shall never mouth the subject, unless it is first mouthed." Nor make mention of Home in letters: "He will be convinced one day, this Robert of mine, . . but it wont be by me, or by my means."

Many of the intellectuals, artists, and liege lords of the day whom the Brownings knew were fascinated by and believed in the spirits. Harriet Beecher Stowe was an example at the head of Ba's list of believers who had logical minds. Yet those closest to Ba didn't believe: her husband, her sister Arabel, her brother George. Henrietta's disbelief wasn't given equal intellectual weight. They were wrong and Ba was right, and the wonders of spiritualism produced letter after letter.

While the Brownings were in London Arabel was whisked away by her father to vacation at Eastbourne. "How I miss you dear, dearest Arabel!" the poet wrote on the flap of the envelope on October 2, 1855. "I shall always think tenderly of the risk you ran for me, in coming to London." She would have spared Arabel, gone to her instead with Pen, but she didn't want to leave Robert in the midst of his proofs "when I can really be of use to him."

That summer Moulton Barrett saw his grandchild for the first and only time. It was one of the occasions when Pen was at Wimpole Street visiting his aunt Arabel and uncle George. "George was playing in the hall with him and he was in fits of laughter. Papa came out of the diningroom and stood *looking* for two or three minutes." Then Moulton Barrett asked George, " 'Whose child is that?'

" 'Ba's child.'

" '*What is the child doing here?*'

"Not a word more—not a natural movement or quickening of the breath."

I hate the dreadful hollow behind the little wood

ALFRED TENNYSON READING MAUD. *Black ink and sepia wash by Dante Gabriel Rossetti, September 1855. Rossetti was one of the guests of the Brownings in London who heard Tennyson read* Maud *and RB read "Fra Lippo Lippi." Sarianna Browning noticed Rossetti sketching as Tennyson read. The sketch later hung left of the fireplace in the Brownings' salon at the Casa Guidi.*

Arabel, upset at her father, had sworn she would not leave town while her sister was there. But she did succumb, her rebellion manifest in a secret trip to London. There was a reason beyond proofs why the Brownings wouldn't visit her at Eastbourne: "As to Robert, you must learn that he sees snakes and crocodiles in Thames water *without* the microscope—he sees in every drop of good every possibility of evil— and as to money-matters, the idea of being in a difficulty is absolutely horrible to him." Speaking Barrett to Barrett, Elizabeth asked her sister to indulge her husband in his avoidance of the expense of traveling. "It's horribly difficult (as I know) for rash people like you & me to sympathize with cautious people like *him*—cautious as to spending money at least—"

When Arabel did visit, she walked in on an uneasy household. John Kenyon had once more forgotten the half payment on the hundred pounds he had sent the poets each year since the birth of Pen. The scene with Home was still in the air, and Ba herself was unhappy in London now that dear Arabel was banished. Moreover, Pen was sleep-

ing with his mother and given to wild fits of extreme temper, understandable given his separation from Wilson's constant scrutiny and focused concern. The poets were not only working over the proofs of *Men
and Women* but at the same time attempting to keep social obligations
with all of London who wished to see them. Sociability was a particularly good idea, given their long exile and the imminent publication of
Robert Browning's first new collection of poetry in ten years. Still,
Arabel also walked in on a very special literary evening when Tennyson
read *Maud* aloud and Browning read "Fra Lippo Lippi."

Good aunt as well as good sister (and rebellious daughter man-
quée), Arabel brought Pen back to Eastbourne with her, allowing the
Brownings to concentrate on the proofs: "Robert misses Peni almost
as much, I think, as I do. It's the bird of the house, fled." Though
Pen ruffled his feathers at times, he also enjoyed himself, requesting
to stay a few days longer once perched. This time the radiant only
child was the center of attention of his aunt and many unmarried uncles. The whole flock had been shooed from London while Grandpa
Barrett stayed on at Wimpole Street, supervising yet another thorough
cleaning.

THE ALMOST
MIRACULOUS YEAR

WITH THE BIRD of the household on vacation, the Brownings could concentrate on Robert's proofs—their only reason for remaining in London. They had high hopes for *Men and Women,* these two volumes of Browning's new poetry. The intensity of their expectations had a history stemming back to their earliest love letters. Long before Ba met him in person, his future wife had begun to have a profound influence on Robert's work. She wrote at the beginning of the correspondence, "Yet I believe that, whatever you may have done, you *will* do what is greater. It is my faith for you." He too believed his best work was ahead of him, and agreed. She answered, "I really did understand of you before I was told, exactly what you told me. Yes—I did indeed. I felt sure that as a poet you fronted the future—& that your chief works, in your own apprehension, were to come." Elizabeth was aware of her own sharpness of intuition, a certain psychic power. She spoke with authority on Browning's future greatness and fame, and such prophecy inspired the younger poet—he was being appreciated as he appreciated himself in his deepest dreams.

In Robert's second letter to his future wife, he acknowledged her greatness. She was able to do what he could not. "You speak out, *you,*—I only make men & women speak."

But that was his greatness, she replied. "You have in your vision two worlds—or to use the language of the schools of the day, you are both subjective & objective in the habits of your mind. You can deal both with abstract thought & with human passion in the most passionate sense." And then she urged him to change direction. Up until then his inclinations were those of a dramatist. His works were performed (if not always understood) in London. "A great dramatic power may de-

ROBERT BROWNING, *by Dante Gabriel Rossetti, 1855. Browning sat for this portrait while he was in London preparing his masterpiece,* Men and Women, *to go to press. EBB wrote to Arabel, "I wanted Rossetti to exhibit it, but he wouldn't, being resolved to save himself for the great portrait he means to have of us two together next year—As to me, I shall have no time for much sitting for pictures, therefore if he wants me, he must snatch me."*

velop itself otherwise than in the formal drama; & I have been guilty of wishing, before this hour . . . that you wd. give the public a poem unassociated . . . with the stage, for a trial on the popular heart."

She had "a fancy that your great dramatic power would work more clearly & audibly in the less definite mould," away from "the theatre which vulgarizes . . . the modern theatre in which we see no altar!" She believed his "monodrams" and what later generations would call his dramatic monologues were more appropriate to his vast talents. She suggested, often subtly, and confidently, that in these poems, not in his stage dramas, his greatness would be recognized. He seemed, as always, ready to profit by her wisdom. He never again wrote for the stage.

Not only did she predict his direction but her own as well. She told him in that second letter that she was aspiring to "a monodram of my own," but that "her chief *intention* just now is the writing of a sort of novel-poem—a poem . . . completely modern . . . running into the midst of our conventions, & rushing into drawingrooms & the like 'where angels fear to tread' . . . & speaking the truth as I conceive of it, out plainly." She was waiting till she could make up the right story on which to base the work. Ten years later the poets were reading proofs of Browning's two volumes of dramatic monologues. After these were sent to the printer, they would return to Paris and Barrett Browning would complete her novel in verse, *Aurora Leigh*. These works were milestones of their marriage as well as of the cultures they represented.

Among the fifty poems in which *Men and Women* speak were many on which much of Browning's contemporary reputation is based. They were all dedicated to his wife in a poem written in London on September 22, 1855, just as the proofreading was completed. The title of the poem of dedication came from the love letters, from the way the poets had in those days of discussing their love and what they were going to do about it, by insisting they weren't going to discuss it, they were just going to say—

One Word More
To E.B.B.
1855

There they are, my fifty men and women
Naming me the fifty poems finished!
Take them, Love, the book and me together:
Where the heart lies, let the brain lie also.

Though many of the following eighteen stanzas may not ring as crystal
clear on first reading as the poets had hoped, the passion Browning felt
for his wife, and the exultation he felt at the completion of his master-
work, were movingly evident.

> Love, you saw me gather men and women,
> Live or dead or fashioned by my fancy,
> Enter each and all, and use their service,
> Speak from every mouth,—the speech, a poem.

The speech, a poem, not a *play,* it might be emphasized.

> Hardly shall I tell my joys and sorrows,
> Hopes and fears, belief and disbelieving:
> I am mine and yours—the rest be all men's,
> Karshish, Cleon, Norbert and the fifty.

"I am mine and yours." Could a good marriage be described any more
succinctly? Could the privacy of marriage be described any more succinctly? Now the subjective poet:

> Let me speak this once in my true person,
> Not as Lippo, Roland or Andrea,
> Though the fruit of speech be just this sentence:

The sentence is a quatrain in which he tells Ba:

> Pray you, look on these my men and women,
> Take and keep my fifty poems finished;
> Where my heart lies, let my brain lie also!
> Poor the speech; be how I speak, for all things.

"Poor the speech" of this man who can only make men and women
speak. It was she, E.B.B., their love, their marriage, her noble art that
spoke for the best in him. In this dedication, he saw her as he had always seen her, as an exalted person and great artist. Finally, there's "one
word more" in "One Word More."

Every creature on earth is given by God "two soul-sides," one to
show the world and one to show the woman he loves. He exposed that

unseen side as the poem concluded. She was his "moon of poets." There was the visible side of the moon: "Thus they see you, praise you, think they know you!" On that side, Browning stands with the adoring public "and praise you / Out of my own self, I dare to phrase it."

> *But the best is when I glide from out them,*
> *Cross a step or two of dubious twilight,*
> *Come out on the other side, the novel*
> *Silent silver lights and darks undreamed of,*
> *Where I hush and bless myself with silence.*

"One Word More" was finally a love poem. And that love glided past Daniel D. Home, money matters, and words to the other side of the moon.

There were many reasons for Robert Browning's expectations about *Men and Women*. From the crème de la crème of British literary society, from Rossetti to Carlyle to Tennyson to Ruskin to Jameson to Barrett Browning, great things were expected from Robert Browning. Not to mention that his old friend Domett had named a street for him in New Zealand, as well as one for Carlyle and Dickens, long before Browning was as popular as the other two writers.

Later critics would concur that "Browning had reason for his early confidence, for he had produced his finest collection of poems thus far." And all the commercial signs had been good. The trade had subscribed heavily, which meant the bookshops had ordered the volumes. The first edition was almost immediately sold out. The Americans wanted reprint rights, which also meant they might pay and might not pirate the edition. Browning's confidence was buoyed.

But beyond the public side of the moon, there were the dreams that went back to the magical days of the courtship. These dreams had become so imbued in the texture of the couple's married lives as to have taken on the guise of fact. Robert Browning had completed the dramatic monologues that would be clearer than his earlier work and that would win him fame and, with it, God willing, royalties enough to make him at least co-supporter of his family. Elizabeth Barrett Browning had helped him to clarify his artistic intentions and had led him beyond concerns of money and material well-being toward the creation of the poems themselves.

On November 17, 1855, the prestigious *Athenaeum* reviewed *Men and Women*: "These volumes contain some fifty poems, which will make the least imaginative man think, and the least thoughtful man grieve. Who will not grieve over energy wasted and power mis-spent,—over fancies chaste and noble, so overhung by the 'seven veils' of obscurity, that we can oftentimes be only sure that fancies exist?"

An unremembered critic's two sentences as opposed to a great poet's greatest ten years of work? No contest. Browning's hopes were dashed on publication day. *Men and Women*, in print and studied today, was out of print in about a month, after selling a first edition of fewer than two hundred copies.

The Brownings were in Paris at the time; the magnitude of the defeat of Robert's expectations was gleaned gradually. Elizabeth Barrett Browning was hard at work on *Aurora Leigh*. "Oh, I am so anxious to make it good," she wrote to Anna Jameson. "I have put much of myself in it—I mean to say, of my soul, my thoughts, emotions, opinions; in other respects, there is not a personal line, of course." Of course. "It's a sort of poetic art-novel." That was the end of February. On May 2, 1856, she wrote to her dear Madonna that Robert was encouraging her, though he had seen only six out of eight books. To the early advocate of women's rights, she went on, "Oh, I do hope you won't be disappointed with it—much! Some things you will like certainly, because of the boldness and veracity of them. . . ." Even after she had developed her "plan" she was true to her early "intention" of holding the mirror up to conventional life. This was to be the best of her life's work. She had helped her husband at the point where she could, going through his proofs; she had borne the season in London, that city that she dreaded; now her focus was on the completion of the ever-flowering *Aurora Leigh*.

Despite ill health it was a period of intense work and creativity—for her. The Brownings shared a publisher, Edward Chapman. From Paris, Robert wrote to him about *Men and Women*, asking Chapman about money matters and "if the book continued to do well." He had seen notices of his book and on December 17 wrote, "Meanwhile don't take to heart the zoological utterances I have stopped my ears against at Galignani's of late. 'Whoo-oo-oo-oo' mouths the big monkey—'Whee-ee-ee-ee' squeaks the little monkey." The critics aped each other. He looked forward to the French review by his dear friend Joseph Milsand in January. A French review? Chapman must have thought that too late and in the wrong language.

ANNA JAMESON *by John Gibson. In the last five years of her life (1855–60), the prolific writer was often in Italy, where she was a respected member of the British and American expatriate community. Her husband, from whom she was estranged, had died in 1854, leaving his property to another woman. Jameson's friends took up a subscription that guaranteed her an annuity of £100.*

Browning celebrated the new year of 1856 by writing to Chapman, "Now do, do pray dear Chapman, let us have the Christmas account to put a little life and heart into the end of this bleak month." What a bleak month it had been for *Men and Women*: "I have read heaps of critiques at Galignani's, mostly stupid and spiteful, self-contradicting and contradictory of each other." Would it hurt sales? "You must tell me," he wrote to Chapman, "if I am ever to know." And like publishers before and after him, Chapman kept quiet. On April 12, 1856, Browning ended a letter plaintively, "Goodbye, my dear Chapman, I don't tell you much but you tell me nothing at all."

And on April 21 there was a transformation in Robert Browning's substance and style in dealing with Chapman. "We are very glad that another edition of E.B.B.'s *Poems* is wanted, and have turned over the various matters in our minds which you desire us to consider." He threw himself into the arrangements for the publication of his wife's past poems and for *Aurora Leigh*, using the first person plural as have husbands before and after him who've become business managers for their artist wives. "As to my own Poems—they must be left to Providence."

After the failure of *Men and Women*, Browning went back to his most obscure poem—one published fifteen years earlier, before he knew his wife—*Sordello*, which he attempted to revise. That was in late February. By April he had taken up drawing. His wife equated it with her novel reading: "He can't rest from serious work in light literature, as I can; it wearies him, and there are hours on his hands, which is bad both for them and for him. The secret of life is in full occupation, isn't it? This world is not tenable on other terms. So while I lie on the sofa and rest in a novel, Robert has a resource in his drawing; and really, with all his feeling and knowledge of art, some of the mechanical trick of it can't be out of place." When Browning returned to Italy, the hours still weighed heavily. He continued working from the nude in life-drawing sessions in Florence, and later sculpted with W. W. Story when they were together in Rome.

In those letters to Chapman, Browning's snapping tone at the stupidity of the critics became raw and uncomfortable, self-conscious and grating—as if something unexpressed were gnawing at his innards. A dream from the courtship was over. The future had not been won by present work. Throughout the fifteen years of his marriage, Browning would remain the obscure poet. There would be something in the savage-conciliatory tone of "Mr. Sludge, 'The Medium,' " his satire of Daniel D. Home, that would suggest it was begun in this period. Yet his next volume of poetry would not appear until 1864, three years after his wife's death.

A dream was over for Elizabeth Barrett Browning as well, though she couldn't have realized it until they were back in Italy. She loved for love's sake, as she wrote in the sonnets. She had also married a poet king, her superior, Robert Browning double underscore. But the pomegranate poet had lost heart.

Arabel and the "Untles"

In late June 1856, when the Brownings returned to London from Paris, the situation of the previous summer was simply reversed. Elizabeth was completing and transcribing *Aurora Leigh* and Robert was supervising the proofs. The London visit was much more comfortable this second summer, thanks to John Kenyon. The Brownings were staying at 39 Devonshire Place, the home of their cousin and supporter, while he was on the Isle of Wight. Kenyon was an old man by then, and his health was failing. The previous year the Brownings had stayed a few extra days in London to visit with him. This year they would travel to see him for the last time.

Moulton Barrett was still intractable. His oldest child continued to visit Wimpole Street on the sly. In July, a defiant Elizabeth jotted Henrietta a note from "Wimpole Street, sitting at Arabel's table while she goes down to see Trippy in the dining room, I take her pen, and ask you to keep me company." The note cuts off when "Arabel shrieks out I shall be too late." But Papa didn't come home in the middle of this brazen act of rebellion. When he heard that the Brownings were back in London staying at John Kenyon's, he sent Arabel and the family to Ventnor—on the other end of the Isle of Wight—on a moment's notice. During her secret visit to London the previous year, Arabel may not have seen her anxious brother-in-law at his best, but she was learning to sympathize—more than Ba could understand at the time—with caution, not only on the matter of spiritualism but on money matters as well. Arabel had wanted to defy her father the previous summer. Now she wanted to again but didn't. Instead, she appealed directly to the frugal Robert Browning to bring his family to her in exile. Elizabeth wrote: "We came off from London at a day's notice, the Wimpole

Street people being sent away abruptly (in consequence, plainly, of our arrival becoming known), and Arabel bringing her praying eyes to bear on Robert, who agreed to go with her and stay for a fortnight."

The way his grandfather Barrett whisked his aunt and uncles from his mother now captured Peni's attention: "It has naturally begun to dawn upon my child that I have done something very wicked to make my father what he is. Once he came up to me earnestly and said, 'Mama, if you've been very, very naughty—if you've *broken china*!' (his idea of the heinous in crime)—'I advise you to go into the room and say, "*Papa, I'll be dood.*"' Almost I obeyed the inspiration—almost I felt inclined to go."

At Ventnor, "Poor Arabel is in low spirits—very—and *aggrieved* with being sent away from town," Ba wrote to Julia Martin. She shrugged off Arabel's grief at being exiled, and told her old friend, as well as her sister, that the air would do her good. Not only that, *"happiness is more an intellectual habit than the product of circumstances,"* she lectured Arabel. By October she did admit to a physical liability of Ventnor to "dearest, darling" Arabel. "Do you know, it does seem to me that sea air always makes your legs swell."

Arabel had not been well the last winter and worked much too hard "in London with schools and Refuges, and societies." Elizabeth disapproved of all of this social work. Her sister "does the work of a horse, and *isn't* a horse." One wonders if Aurora Leigh's harsh opinions about those who sacrifice themselves for the poor owe their roots to Arabel's dogged work for others. Arabel needed, her oldest sister prescribed, "a new moral atmosphere—a little society. She is thrown too entirely on her own resources, and her own resources are of somewhat gloomy character. This is all wrong."

A few months earlier, on July 4, 1856, Arabel Barrett Moulton Barrett had her forty-third birthday. A good time to take a tally. She was the sister of a famous poet, the youngest daughter in a large family, and the one daughter who had stayed home. She may have had a romance at Torquay, but after that tragic season she had slept on the sofa in her sister's room during all the years Ba was an invalid on Wimpole Street. She had done her duty to her siblings and to her father. Now she was a middle-aged woman. This was the second summer in which she was ordered to leave town by her father. Commanded to leave her charities, her chapel, her visiting relatives from Italy, her city; to leave her life. On both occasions she had said she wouldn't obey but she had.

ARABEL BARRETT MOULTON
BARRETT (1813–68). *The
youngest sister of the poet, who
slept in her room on Wimpole
Street and who was Elizabeth's
closest confidant after her marriage. "My comforter, Arabel, you
always were," EBB wrote to her
sister after the death of their
father.*

By obeying, she was learning something new and frightening about
her situation.

When Ba and, after her, Henrietta disobeyed Moulton Barrett,
they left the house on the arm of a husband and the promise of a new
life. Both now had households and children of their own. She missed
the company of those sisters. What would happen to Arabel if she disobeyed her father—not about marriage, but about where she spent the
summer? She had done nothing to offend her father, but as the years
passed her freedom had become more and more dependent on him.
Perhaps it took her being forced to abandon town to make her realize
how tenuous her situation in life really was. At Ventnor, Arabel told
Ba she realized that she could be kicked out of the house at Wimpole
Street at any moment, on the slightest provocation. That winter in
London, perhaps while tending her father, who had not been well, she
began to think of what she would do. She could become a companion,

she told the poet. She was artistically inclined. She wondered if she could "apply herself among the wood-engravers." She was actively preparing herself for the eventuality of being disinherited.

No wonder she did not go to Paris when the Brownings were there, even though her own father had suggested it. On October 31, 1855, Elizabeth wrote to Arabel, "If Papa had not himself proposed the going to Paris, it would have been altogether different—but, as it is, he is just as likely to be displeased with you for seeming to care nothing about profiting by his suggestion, as not—very likely indeed to say, 'They *never* accept *my* suggestions.' " But that suggestion of the father's could very well have been a trap. Go to Paris. See your sister. Do as you like. Isn't that what he had told Elizabeth years earlier when she applied to go to Pisa for her health? And she hadn't gone. She had known better.

Arabel was confronting the bleak possibility of being disinherited on a whim (or on the slightest provocation). Her brothers wouldn't be able to help her without being disinherited themselves, and her sisters had family and money problems of their own. She was also, culturally, a sophisticated Londoner; that was her city, and she had no inclination to go to warring Tuscany or papist Rome, even though Ba wanted her to visit them in Italy. Ba's suggestions to Arabel might have been heartfelt—don't work so hard, go to a séance, visit us in Paris, come to Florence—but the encouragement was not for Arabel to be Arabel, but for Arabel to change, to live more like Ba. No wonder Arabel looked "dull" and sad at Ventnor. It was one thing to need a vacation, another to be commanded to go away. The legitimate great-granddaughter of Edward of Cinnamon Hill was not that far from the destitute girls she helped at the Ragged Schools. She might be a charitable and well-to-do spinster who had never earned a wage in her life, but at any moment she could be forced out into the streets.

Perhaps Robert understood her anxieties more than her sister did. Her father was banishing her from the people she loved, and she could not stop him. It was Robert Browning she applied to, whom she prayed to, tears in her eyes. She didn't want to go into this exile from the people she loved. It was he who immediately responded. Perhaps not all Barretts could afford to be as reckless in spirit as Elizabeth earlier assumed Arabel to be. Perhaps the interest on the four thousand left by one's grandmother and the four thousand left by one's uncle had to be added to the credits column in order to balance the books. Arabel

Barrett Moulton Barrett was one of the many unsung sisters of the nineteenth century. Her situation was not as dramatic as that of Elizabeth Barrett Browning or Henrietta Barrett Cook, both of whom left 50 Wimpole Street. But what this sister faced offered good reasons for a mid-age crisis. Her brothers had vocations, her sisters had husbands, and her father had complete control over her economic fate.

Later that summer, Arabel didn't dare to meet the Brownings at Taunton when they visited Henrietta and her family, "because she knew that if her father should come and find her absent he would never forgive her." In September, from John Kenyon's house on the northern end of the Isle of Wight, Elizabeth wrote to Henrietta about the planned trip: "Arabel and I talking of this, she said and swore she would go, too, if she *could,* without fear of an arrival from London. I have written to tell her when we go—and perhaps, perhaps—But no, I don't dare to think of it. Robert says it's very wrong of me even to wish for it. But I'm wrong obstinately. I'm wicked—I do wish it—Only I don't hope much. I left her in bad spirits, distressed and angry at being sent to Ventnor, and determined to dislike it accordingly."

While the father had stayed in London, the Barrett siblings had had a wonderful time. Arabel and Ba, George and Henry and Occy. "What a very happy fortnight we had together! And how good they all were to me & mine! and how I never never shall forget it! . . . I feel as if I had been home again, the first time for ten years. How I love you all!" Home was still what it had always been for the brothers and sisters: a good time behind the father's back.

Elizabeth's sisters had supported her marriage, and now the brothers, too, seemed reconciled. They certainly didn't turn away from their elflike nephew any more than had Alfred, who had feted him at Marseilles. They had their work cut out for them. His rebellious uncles at Ventnor gave the seven-year-old Pen a British education: "Also, little Pen made his way into the heart of 'mine untles,' and was carried on their backs up and down hills, and taught the ways of 'English boys,' with so much success that he makes pretensions to 'pluck,' and has left a good reputation behind him."

On one occasion Pen went up to a boy of twelve who had taunted him, and exclaimed, " 'Don't be impertinent, sir,' (doubling his small fist), or I will show you that *I'm a boy!*' " The twelve-year-old may have doubted this, given Pen's Renaissance frock and long curls.

"Of course, 'mine untles' are charmed with this 'proper spirit,' and applauded highly. Robert and I begged to suggest to the hero that the 'boy of twelve' might have killed him if he had pleased.

" 'Never mind,' cried little Pen, 'there would have been somebody to think of *me*, who would have him hanged' (great applause from the uncles).

" 'But *you* would still be dead,' said Robert remorselessly.

" 'Well, I don't tare for *that*. It was a beautiful place to die in— close to the sea.'

"So you will please observe," Elizabeth summed up for Julia Martin, "that in spite of being Italians and wearing curls, we can fight to the death on occasion. . . ."

Happy memories of a reunion at Ventnor, of a first and last time.

SURPRISE ENDINGS

AURORA LEIGH was published a year after *Men and Women*. The novel in verse Barrett Browning believed would fly in the face of convention did so. But it was also an immediate and resounding success. Society seemed ready to read about Aurora Leigh, a woman artist who chose her art over a man, her cousin Romney Leigh, an idealistic socialist, and Marian Earle, a young girl from the lower class who was the loving mother of an illegitimate child born of treachery and rape. It seemed ready to acknowledge the excesses of the drawing room and to reach out to the poverty-filled London streets, where women prostituted themselves to stay alive. The reader was also treated to a view of lower-class life in which brutish parents prepared their girls for the life of the street through harshness, contempt, and greed. Romney's well-meaning socialism set against this view of human nature was parodied throughout.

The difficulties of being a woman—whatever the class—in the real world seemed of immediate concern to readers. The woman poet, Aurora Leigh, sang not of Italian politics but of modern life. And a wealth of experience and wisdom was tied to a charged and suspenseful, page-turning plot. "That divine book," Robert called it. "I am surprised, I own, at the amount of success," Elizabeth wrote to her sister-in-law in November 1856. "Golden-hearted Robert is in ecstasies about it—far more than if it all related to a book of his own."

By January 1857, the book was already in a second edition, and she wrote to Arabel that the American reviews "are ecstatical—I am said to have 'put down all my faults & have gone miles beyond myself in all ways'—The Americans especially delight in the scene in the church & the dialogue of the fine people." One American "can't under-

CHARLOTTE CUSHMAN *by William Page, ca. 1853. In Rome, the American actress and friend of the Brownings performed excerpts from EBB's well-received novel in verse,* Aurora Leigh. *Known for her roles as Romeo and Hamlet, she met the Brownings in Paris in 1852 when she and a female companion had "made vows of celibacy & of eternal attachment to each other—they live together, dress alike." EBB wrote, "it is a female marriage. I happened to say, 'Well, I never heard of such a thing before,' " to a friend who answered, " 'Oh, it is by no means uncommon.' "*

stand how an Englishwoman could so perfectly see & represent English peculiarities as I have done in this book." The intellectual and artistic detachment from England did nothing to separate her from a major emotional concern there: "Tell me if Papa has made any observation about the second edition of 'Aurora.' I think so much of these things in reference to him—but I dare say he is absolutely indifferent to me and my writings.

"In Florence the poem has found great favour. People say 'it magnetizes them,' though it wasn't written by the spirits after all," as had been rumored. The English bookseller there told Robert "he had been foolish enough to order only a few copies—which had been sold instantly, so that he had had to send for others." It had to be the story and bold plot that moved people. The poetry? "I never will believe that the masses are moveable by mere poetry." After all, look what happened to golden-hearted Robert's poetry little more than a year before.

The poet Leigh Hunt wrote her a twenty-page letter. The poem so moved her American publisher that he cried. And the American actress and friend of the Brownings, Charlotte Cushman, "is giving or about to give 'readings' of 'Aurora' in Rome."

However, "on the other side . . . there's a party in England holding up their hands at the scandal of a woman's writing such a book. And Mrs Ogilvy tells me that 'the mamas won't allow their daughters to read it'—Well the daughters must be very young—& my comfort is that they will grow older."

The enormity of the success could also be gleaned from the fact that a woman so self-effacing would write so much about *Aurora Leigh* in one letter. Still, there were things "my shyness won't let me repeat."

Robert took up the slack, writing to their publisher Edward Chapman of Ruskin's praise of *Aurora Leigh* as being "the greatest *poem* in the English language." Ruskin said Elizabeth was second only to Shakespeare, but in the realm of pure poetry she surpassed Shakespeare himself. When people "write & talk of the 'jealousy' of authors & husbands, let them look at him!" Ba wrote to Arabel of Robert Browning.

At the time of *Aurora Leigh*'s enormous success, Robert Browning came into his own money. It had nothing to do with the sale of his poetry but with the death of a dear friend. John Kenyon died in December 1856. At first it looked as if the poets had been passed over. "Robert has come in," Elizabeth wrote to Arabel from Florence, "& there is *no letter.* He still expects one, he says. It may come (I say) but it is not likely. . . . Of course I would not write of these things to any but yourself." But this time Robert was right; notice of a bequest did finally arrive. The Brownings were left eleven thousand pounds. Robert inherited the major share, sixty-five hundred pounds. Kenyon had divided the inheritance with his usual sensitivity to the couple. No one could ever say again that Browning lived off his wife.

Although Kenyon's legacy to the Brownings has always been assumed to be a boon for which they were unequivocally grateful, they had misgivings.

Arabel wrote asking her sister if she had been disappointed by their share of the inheritance. "No, Arabel, I may truly say I was not 'disappointed'—On the contrary—for I imagined we were passed over. But as you ask me, I will confess frankly to you that we should not have *disliked* the Devonshire Place house." That was where the Brownings had spent the previous summer. Although "we could not have lived there—it wd. have been a branch to light upon when we went to London,—& we should have had pleasure in keeping things together

as a memorial. Never mind . . . we both feel that what has been actually done for us was most sufficient & kind."

After that visit with Arabel and the "untles" the previous summer,
the Brownings had in fact traveled to the north of the Isle of Wight to
be with John Kenyon at his summer place. The family was led by servants to where the ill man sat waiting for them in the drawing room.
"So frightened I was at the idea of seeing him that my heart beat to
take my breath away." When John Kenyon saw these favorites of his,
his spirits revived: "I put my arm round his neck & kissed him once,
twice . . & over perhaps. I was [touched] to be there & see him—over-
joyed to see him so much better than I expected. . . . Thinner he is certainly. . . . He is thinner & paler—& he stoops more. . . . The only real
malady is the breath," a condition which "he has been liable to all his
life." Once more, Elizabeth attempted to look over death.

In the grand, quiet house with its view of parade and sea, she read
proofs and with Robert's help prepared *Aurora Leigh* for the press. Solitary Pen, away from his "untles," blew the ivory whistle Kenyon gave
him, went out in the coach-box, and in his own room played " 'minister'—reading the Bible aloud from a pillow on his table."

But there could have been no real doubt that Kenyon was dying. "I
never witnessed suffering of so distressing a kind, before. It was like a
prolonged death agony." There was that "peculiar look in the eyes
which you cant mistake." Kenyon's struggle for breath made him say
"he *desires death*—death, to have rest in it." And there was no doubt
that Kenyon's will was on both the Brownings' minds—in terms of
provisions for Henrietta. "Robert spoke warmly of dear Surtees—he
took an opportunity of doing that: but, you see, everything was determined in a hurry and agitation, and between wanderings of mind, at
last." The Brownings' disappointment was only for her. "For ourselves,
if we had expected anything considerable, (but, as you know, we did
not) there would have been some disappointment on our own part. As
it is, we are very thankful and contented. I only wish the same had
been done by you."

"But oh," she would write to Arabel, "that it had been more for
Henrietta, oh that it had. And how strange, when you come to think,
. . that it *was* not! To you, the need is not likely to come, in spite of
imaginary contingencies Arabel; but a few thousands to Henrietta
would have been a great help."

Henrietta's inheritance of one hundred pounds was hardly worth her father's refusal to give Kenyon's solicitors Henrietta's address. But Moulton Barrett was very angry about being left out of the will. Elizabeth wrote to Henrietta, "Arabel represents papa as much vexed. If the principle of relationship had been recognised *at all, (which it was not)* he had his *undoubted* claim."

Sitting in the Jamaican coffeehouse, Moulton Barrett must have heard from others, if he wouldn't read it himself, of his daughter's two-paragraph dedication of *Aurora Leigh* to their Jamaican cousin. It began: "The words 'cousin' and 'friend' are constantly recurring in this poem, the last pages of which have been finished under the hospitality of your roof, my own dearest cousin and friend." And it ended with his daughter sending their cousin "this book, the most mature of my works, and the one into which my highest convictions upon Life and Art have entered; . . . you have believed in me, borne with me, and been generous to me, far beyond the common uses of mere relationship or sympathy of mind. . . ." She signed it from under Kenyon's roof, "39 Devonshire Place: October 17, 1856."

In private, Elizabeth Barrett Browning's tribute to Kenyon was even warmer. From Florence, two months later, at a time when she was sure she had been passed over in Kenyon's will, she wrote to Arabel, "In the last ten years he has put himself in the place of my own father, in taking care, for me & mine, that we do not want. We should have wanted much, except for him. His last act with regards to that book of mine" was proof to Elizabeth that he appreciated her dedication to him. The same act was also quite fatherly. Just before his death John Kenyon bought forty-seven copies of *Aurora Leigh* and distributed them among his friends.

Still, would Moulton Barrett have paused over the auspiciousness of his daughter's public dedication? It might not have been a bad idea, during all those years his cousin came to Wimpole Street, to have once invited him to stay for dinner.

A more immediate loss to the Moulton Barrett household occurred in February 1857—the death of Treppy, Mary Trepsack, the daughter of a slave mother and planter father who had been adopted by Edward of Cinnamon Hill. Her passing marked the passing of an era. Her end was very difficult. She had grown "so mortally ailing & decrepit & joyless" in her dotage. But as Ba wrote to Arabel, with Treppy, "so many tender memories of years full of love are also swallowed up & disappear, that the heart faints within us to think them over." She thought

260

DARED AND DONE

of putting Pen in mourning, but "I had not the heart for it." She described her own dress: "Crepe sleeves & collar, black net & long ribbon for the hair—the black cloth jacket & silk skirt (without crepe trimming) will do, I think. Is that what *you* will wear? I wish to be right in these respects because it seems to me that this dear spirit would care . . ."

The dear spirit's distribution of her meager effects was a slap in the face to Arabel. Elizabeth wrote on April 3 to let the silver cup left her to stay where it was, "and if Papa should say a word on the subject, I enjoin on you or others to answer that . . . *'she would rather not have it.'*"

Elizabeth was so angry at this departed spirit "that it cancels the tender gratitude which I ought to feel." Good reason she had. Her sister Arabel, the daughter who remained at home and had tended to the ancient woman, was left with not one silver glint of acknowledgment. "All we can say is—*may it have been pure madness*; for other excuses are impossible."

Not only was Arabel ignored, but the only possible justification for the madness was canceled. "How strange that George, who was always accused in common with you, should have been forgiven apparently at last. Perhaps because of his having been of use in business." One wonders what that accusation was. Treppy had grown paranoid in later years, often thinking the Barretts were trying to poison her.

Elizabeth was certainly on the side of her sister this time, but her understanding of Arabel was limited. The symptoms of Arabel's new illness astounded her, that feeling "of being squeezed to death by the chest in an iron vice. . . . I have felt that for years & years—but why *you* should, I don't understand."

There had been a bequest for Pen, too. A watch and a parrot. His mother knew Pen would like to have the parrot. She wanted to tell him that Aunt Arabel would take care of it (who else?) and he could visit it when he was in England. Robert, however, didn't want Pen to know a thing about the bequest. His scruples did not come from anger at the way his sister-in-law had been mistreated. Instead, they came from misgivings that reveal his mixed feelings about having been the benefactor of Kenyon's will at all. Houses were not on his mind. He emphatically did not want the child to know of any bequest, any possible benefit derived from the death of another human being. His reason? "A belief in the wickedness of human nature deep within him." He didn't want to pass this on. And he could not help but remember a vivid image that had appalled him since his first trip to Rome when little Joe Story died. He never got it out of his mind, having seen the eight-year-old Edith Story after the death of her brother: "Robert cant forget Edith Story's walking about proudly in her poor little brother's red shoes."

Barrett Browning's enjoyment of her success was marred by the death of John Kenyon and the lack of success of Robert's *Men and Women*. Still, for all of her private nature and timidity in a crowd, she had wanted fame. From the age of eight her works had been published, first within the family, then without. She had always felt she had a mission in life and that to be a poet was a sacred vocation. Now she had written the long work that best expressed her mature intentions, a work she held so important that she would have herself judged by it alone. And within a few years it would go into five British editions. But her father had recently been ill. An attempt through Julia Martin to reconcile him to his married daughters had failed, and the thought of him "has been hanging like a stone about my heart for ever so long,—now when I ought to be elated & delighted I suppose at the success of my poem." Instead, "how little happy this reaching in a degree, what has been with me an object in life, has made me. If there was nobody to be uneasy about, how different it would feel, I say to myself. Robert, at least is happy. . . ." And her unease was founded. Four months later a third death robbed her of any joy in her greatest accomplishment.

On April 17, 1857, a month before his seventy-second birthday, Edward Barrett Moulton Barrett died. An hour before his death he dismissed Arabel and her aunt "with a cheerful or careless word about 'wishing them goodnight.' " His last words were connected with sleep and being made comfortable for the night. He was suffering from what Arabel wrote to inform Elizabeth was a minor illness—it actually was erysipelas (St. Anthony's fire), an acute skin disease that could spread and poison the blood. George wrote the next day to inform the Brownings of the end.

"So it is all over now," Robert wrote to Julia Martin on May 3, "all hope of better things, or a kind answer to entreaties such as I have seen Ba write in the bitterness of her heart." How could one understand his father-in-law's unyielding rejection of his married children? "There must have been something in the organisation, or education, at least, that would account for and extenuate all this; but it has caused grief enough, I know; and now here is a new grief not likely to subside very soon." He quickly added that his wife was reacting reasonably: "she does not reproach herself at all; it is all mere grief, as I say, that this should have been *so*; and I sympathise with her there."

But mere grief did turn to self-reproach. By the following month she wrote to Arabel, "my soul is bitter even unto death." Her father had died "without a word, without a sign. It is like slamming a door on me as he went out." She continued to believe "that what he did & the extreme views he took" were taken conscientiously, the result of "a false theory—He did hold by the Lord & walk straight as he saw." But "As for me, in these days of anguish I have wished—

"Well there is no use now of writing what—but I did love him. . . . Certainly I would have given my life for his life—yet he went without a word." She had her compensations: "Robert is perfect in tenderness," and "It has helped me, . . writing this letter." For Arabel knew that "my misfortune is that I cant always cry freely, which makes one turn into stone." In Elizabeth's case this inability turned into a specific life-long reaction, "that hysterical choking which prevents swallowing." She became physically unable to eat.

Elizabeth could not even write a letter outside of the family until July 1, when she told Julia Martin, "There has been great bitterness." That was natural, she understood. But there had also been "some recoil against myself, more, perhaps, than is quite rational." Morbidity returned. "My temptation is to lie on the sofa, and never stir nor speak, only I don't give up, be certain."

She spent time on her sofa imagining the dark interior of the house on Wimpole Street. In her mind she walked through all those rooms again. As she brooded in Florence, passing hours of uneasy nostalgia, realizing that she and her father could never be reconciled, her siblings in London were busy. As quickly as they could, they planned to leave 50 Wimpole Street. Their haste after their father's sudden death was extraordinary. Arabel wanted to have her own house and live alone. George was thinking of giving up law and moving to the country. Some brothers returned from Jamaica, others went to Jamaica. There was no greater testimony to the economic hold the father had on the children than the rapidity with which they seized their freedom. Ironically, as they fled Wimpole Street, their oldest sister was once again drawn toward it. "They won't break up everything at once in Wimpole Street—they can't, I should think, though I know nothing."

But for Arabel a lifetime of submitting to the wishes of another was over—even if the strong Barrett voice this time was that of her oldest sibling. Ba wanted Arabel to come and stay with her and her family in Italy, and not just for a short while—for a few years perhaps. That's exactly the kind of fate the stoic Londoner might have envisioned for herself when she thought it quite likely that any day her father might arbitrarily cut her out of his will.

There had always been order in the Barrett household—an undisputed way of doing things that conformed to the father's wishes. Rebellious children circumvented him when they could, but they paid lip service. On April 17, 1857, that reign ended. How the other Barrett children grieved we do not know, but in action they were united. The minute each person was free to do things his or her own way, liberty tore the house down quickly. Reform was more difficult for Barrett Browning to accept within the family than within her own poetry or her politics. Still, six weeks after Moulton Barrett's death, his oldest daughter seemed to have made peace with the new regime. Of course Arabel should do precisely what she wished. "You see I was at the moment a little disappointed," she explained to Henrietta, "but that is over; and from the first I have known that every human being who is able to choose a life should do it for himself and herself as he and she *sees*, and not as another sees."

AFTER HER FATHER'S DEATH Ba's advice to both her sisters was unbridled. It might have been that she was now the oldest in the family, that she had just written an enormously respected book which flowed with her own ideas. It might have been a way of forgetting for a moment the finality of the breach with her father. There was a frantic quality to her unasked-for advice. Arabel should get out of London at first, take her time, spend a long summer with Henrietta by the sea. Come to Italy in any case. If she were going to take a house, why in London? She should live in the country. She shouldn't put so much into the Ragged Schools. The London air, the social work, it was ruining her health. On August 4 she wrote to Henrietta, "Isn't Arabel vexed with me? Tell me the truth."

After Arabel moved to her own house she thought of adopting a child. Here was one "subject on which I *cannot* advise." But it did bring back the days when the two single sisters shared a dream. "Do you remember our fine plans for the Foundling hospital? Now, I wouldn't have a child except my own."

Rather incredulously to contemporary eyes, but not to the readers of Victorian novels, Arabel would have liked to adopt her sister Henrietta's only daughter, Mary. Ba saw nothing wrong with this plan, if it could help Surtees financially as well, though she was not surprised that Henrietta refused. Still, about Henrietta giving up her daughter, "people send their children to school—& this would not be worse as far as regards separation, & how much better otherwise?" Arabel's next idea was to adopt a cousin's, Sam Barrett's, child, Emma. Ba felt Mary would be a much better choice: "Apart from other reasons, you could always send her home, if you cared to go anywhere without carrying her on your back. But what can one say against poor Henrietta's wishes."

Arabel did take Emma in and asked Elizabeth for advice about keeping her. "Dear, how can I 'advise' you about Emma? . . . If the child is a comfort to you, keep her—if she burdens you, part from her at once. I agree quite that if you keep her you should not send her home [on vacation] at this time, but whether you shd. keep her or not is a matter of personal feeling—I dare say her parents will be disappointed, but that is not the question at all—only it will become one if you do not decide quickly."

The giving of all the unasked for (and asked for) advice in the world couldn't help Elizabeth get over the death of her father. Five days before the first anniversary of his death, on April 12, 1858, she wrote a revealing account of her mental state. She was quite ill, but this time, she told Arabel, her bad winter was "not with my chest. The fact is that last summer when I wanted repose to recover from a great shock, I couldn't get it—& my usual strength didn't return the whole year."

Well, the summer of 1858 would be different; she would see Arabel once more. After that: "I have sworn to Robert to go with him not to Jerusalem, but to Egypt next winter. I am not equal to Jerusalem & the camels, but a water-journey of six or seven months" might be possible. "Robert made me swear because he distrusted my wishes & intentions, I think.—" Her husband wouldn't have made her swear if she were in the throes of physical malaise. Going to Egypt might have been just what Browning needed to inspire him to write again and to shake his wife from her gloom. But the thing about her gloom was:

"I don't brood, in your sense, intentionally—I should be dead by this time if I brooded. I worked at the sort of work I could do even last year—(& worked off the back of a German dictionary)—Robert said he really 'respected' me for my application. But if one gets up and walks across the room, then comes . . . what I call, myself, 'brooding,' though it is not intentional . . not at all."

Any physical movement at all triggered depression: "I struggle against habitual sadness as against corruption & ignorance, & against ingratitude besides. But I have a horrible vibrating body. If I am un-easy in mind for half an hour, I am unwell; & then, being unwell makes me uneasy again. It acts and reacts."

Exactly the condition she was in when Browning first saw her on her sofa at Wimpole Street and assumed she was unable to walk. What might look like self-will or invalidism from the outside was a lifelong battle—body and soul—with habitual depression. Struggle against it she did, and with humor: "I go out regularly in the carriage now, & we have delightful drives through hedges of maybloom, the almond trees & peach trees blooming on the other side. Still I don't get strong as I might do, & shall presently, I dare say,—though I have doubled my cod's liver oil, taking two tablespoons a day. See how virtuous I am, Arabel. I don't do everything I like, I assure you."

"MY FIG TREE," *drawn by EBB on October 7, 1860, in Siena.*
Browning noted after her death that this was the last time
she sat under it.

PART FOUR

Admitting Impediments

IN THE ELEVENTH YEAR of their marriage, a woman came between the Brownings—and Robert couldn't threaten to throw her
down the stairs.

If Elizabeth's insistence on the validity of D. D. Home maddened
her husband at times, and gave the couple their most serious disagreement, Home was still in the realm of the abstract, an issue, not a man.
Sophia May Tuckerman Eckley, the beautiful, rich, poetic, and "pure"
American, came right into the Brownings' lives. A cousin of Louisa
May Alcott on her mother's side and an extremely wealthy woman on
her father's side, she wrote unbodied, overallegorized poetry as well
as her own theologically introspective travelogues. The Brownings met
her, her husband, David, and their child—Pen's age—Doady during
the disastrous summer after Moulton Barrett's death when they were
vacationing at Bagni di Lucca.

That summer of 1857, Elizabeth could not get the rest she needed
to recuperate from her father's death. The poet Robert Lytton, who followed the Brownings to the Baths, became dangerously ill. Much of
Robert's time and that of the Brownings' friend Isa Blagden was spent
nursing him until the crisis passed. In the middle of these duties, Wilson suffered a bad pregnancy and had to leave service quickly. The
Brownings were lucky to find a fine Italian woman, Annunziata, to replace her. Ferdinando stayed with them, a continuity in Pen's life.
Then, at the end of September, Pen fell ill, and what looked like
measles or scarlet fever turned out to be a slight case of gastric fever.
"Robert blamed me for looking like a terrified ghost. Could I help it?"
Browning must have been terrified that this new shock was going to
add to his wife's increasing morbidity. Pen realized it as well: The sick

eight-year-old cautioned his mother, "Don't be unhappy about me. Fancy it's a boy in the street, and be a little sorry of course, but don't be unhappy." Such a son was worth twenty Aurora Leighs, his mother wrote, and she repeated his words in more than one letter.

By then the issue of the red shoes had been settled. As the boy recuperated, he wrote to his aunt Arabel—and here he sounded like a little boy again: "I hope that you will keep me my Parrot till I come to see you."

Browning's recreation at Lucca amid his responsibilities combined his two solaces, riding and climbing to the top of mountains. Sophie's husband, David Eckley, rode with him on the day that "Robert's horse fell over a precipice of sixty feet, head over heels—A tree broke the fall. Robert rescued himself (by the grace of almost a miracle) by catching at a crag of rock, when the ground gave way beneath the horse's hoofs. . . . I was not told of it until another day. Think of what an escape—I might be writing to you at this moment (or rather not writing to you) without a husband & without a child! Therefore thank God for me my beloved Arabel. I feel a good deal shaken all together, but I am not ill."

The trip to Egypt that Browning had insisted his wife swear to was made more viable by their new friendship with the Eckleys, who planned to travel there in the fall of 1857. They talked about it with the Brownings over the summer at Bagni di Lucca, trying to persuade the couple to join them—a suggestion that appealed to Robert but that Elizabeth obviously rejected. She regretted her decision, and by February 1858 wrote to Sophie Eckley, "If you knew how repentant I am of not going with you! If I *had*, I should have lost some cold things besides the weather here," which "is nearly killing us all." Robert and Pen had been sick, and in politics, Felice Orsini, in January 1858, attempted to kill Napoleon and his wife as they drove up to the opera house. "I myself feel crushed in body and spirit."

Still, she was able to leap into friendship with Sophie, via mail. She could share something with her that she could not share with Robert (or Arabel)—the spirit world. In December she wrote to Sophie that Jarves saw "Hume in Paris at his own rooms in the Champs Élysées, & saw the splendid gifts showered on him. Hume said he received no money, . . but that benefaction was showered on him from persons unnamed:—that, for instance, he found his tailors' bills paid, & so with other bills." On June 30, 1858, just as she left for Leghorn on her way to France in an attempt to regain her health by the sea in company with her in-laws and Arabel, Elizabeth told Sophie that Home's Russian bride brought with her 25,000 crowns' worth of dowry. The spirits were treating him well.

As for her own news, "I am very tired, & not very bright, at leaving our Italy—but we are coming back, we are coming back, I say that to myself." And in this letter the poet defines her relationship with Sophie: "Love me, pray for me, you who are to be (it is settled) my 'sister' of the spiritual world."

It was settled. The love of her spiritual sister for Elizabeth was reflected in her parting gifts. Sophie, recently returned from her travels, said goodbye with a brooch, a ring, Damascus slippers, a rosary from the Holy Sepulchre, a traveling bag, and some accessories, such as collars and sleeves. Ba, in a letter to Arabel, characterized the gifts as "overpowering." Still, she thanked Sophie for the "voyage bag" she had sent "in time to replace one given to me by my sister Henrietta soon after my marriage, & now dropping to pieces. This bag is also from a sister—How I thank you, *darling.*" Browning would come to refer contemptuously to Sophie's "wallet of wares." But now, in return for her kindness, Elizabeth sent Sophie a locket, and Browning seemed to be willing to part with a strand from his true cross: "Robert gives you the hair (because it is his)," meaning of course hers.

That summer by the sea in dismal Le Havre, surrounded by relatives, neither of the Brownings was happy. At its beginning, Elizabeth had not only to prepare Arabel for the commercial town and her in-laws, but for the fact that she could hardly walk. "I don't walk as well as I did—but that will come. At present you see I am out of the habit of it, seeing that walking (even if I had been strong enough muscularly) was extremely bad for me—and I have done no more than walk about the house, you know, for months & months—Now I creep through the opposite houses by a way Robert has found to where I can look at the sea & sit down, so that this is a beginning of walking. You will see me looking well." Arabel was shocked by this letter. "Dear, by some extraordinary awkwardness I seem to give you an impression of being ill when I mean to tell you I'm well. . . . I improve immensely & Robert says I could do more if I chose—which is quite true. But I'm afraid of tiring myself, because it might throw me back again. . . . I *am well.*" This recovery would be aided by her time with her sister both at Le Havre and Paris, though she wrote to Sophie that "In the Baths of

Lucca you hide yourself in the woods, you lose yourself in the mountains and you are not vexed" as one is at commercial and ugly Le Havre.

Robert found the daily life at Le Havre "dull," and wrote to Isa Blagden, "You seem to have been passing your time pleasantly,—at least with amusing people." His family obligations and Ba's health ate into his writing time, not that it much mattered. "I go mechanically out & in and get a day through—whereof not ten minutes have been my own—so much for your 'quantities of writing' . . . I began pretty zealously—but it's of no use now; nor will the world very greatly care." As the time at Le Havre neared its end, Robert wrote to Isa on September 11, 1858, "the place has been wholly 'unfructuous' to me, unless Ba's and Peni's health turn out to be particularly the better for it." It was a matter of place: "I wish we had gone to Nouville." They were off to Paris.

Sophie Eckley added to Robert's discomfort in Le Havre. She had commissioned a portrait of his wife that had the scent of a memento mori. Browning was forced to write to her about the portrait, which her "kindest of kind hearted husbands" had paid for. It gave David his highest reward, "the pleasure he promised himself in giving you this particular pleasure." David Eckley's obsequiousness to his wife's every demand was at least as unnerving as William Page's passivity to his second wife's lovers. Browning never failed to mention it. Browning had been upset by Sophie's idea of leaving the portrait to Pen. She had forced him to think of his wife's death. "Dear Mrs. Eckley: what you say about its [the portrait's] 'final destination' is meant as *only you* mean such kindness—and I shall not be hindering any kindness of yours; only diverting it into its more fitting channel . . . without referring to eventualities which are in the hands of God, let your own dear child keep one day what may remind him of a face he will have forgotten—and let it remain in America. I dont care to write much about this but, let it be so!"

Neither of the Brownings was impressed by the finished portrait by Michele Gordigiani. Elizabeth wrote to Arabel that he made her "a large buxom matron with a torrent of black ringlets at each cheek" and in parentheses: "(When Robert saw Gordigiani's portrait at his return, he gave it up at once.)" By then, January 22, 1859, they were in Rome, and Robert Browning would probably have liked to give up Mrs. Eckley as well. Yet his wife had made up her mind that Sophie was an angel, a rose, a spiritual sister, the purest of all women.

SOPHIA MAY TUCKERMAN ECKLEY (1821?–74) *with her older half sister,*
HANNAH PARKMAN TUCKERMAN (1805–59). *The beautiful Sophia,*
with a characteristic white rose in her hair, was the daughter of Edward
Tuckerman of Boston and his second wife, Sophia May. She was left a fortune
at her father's death. A poet and traveler, as her mother had been before her,
Sophia Eckley became EBB's spiritual sister and Robert Browning's nemesis.

Sophie's only fault was having too high an opinion of Ba. The poet was conscious of Sophie's off-centered idealization that never before in her life would she have characterized as love. But now? "And I love you, dear. You have done me real good with your sweet pure harmonious spirit."

In Elizabeth's letters to her spiritual sister, there is at times a theatrical tone that doesn't ring quite true. Or perhaps it is that the two friends are inventing the nuances of their private language. On July 12, 1858, she wrote of her recovery: "Also, I am far less languid—& my eyes dont look quite so much out of caves of blackness at night after the fatigues of the day." She ended her letter, "Dearest Sophie, *my sister*, may God love & bless you dear." And from Le Havre, "*Literally* I love you." That was just at the beginning of the 121-letter correspondence that Elizabeth would one day wish she could get back. But try as her husband might to open her eyes, she insisted they were wide open. On the subject of the spiritual world, the spiritual sisters were much more awake than he. "Because, you see, dear, dear, my own medium is what suits me." Sophie Eckley would become Ba's own medium, keeping the "constitutional evil" of her depression at bay.

Back in Florence after the summer of 1858 in France, Elizabeth found her spiritual sister awaiting her. "You know the Eckleys," Elizabeth wrote to Arabel, "& that Sophie had taken it into her enthusiastic head to fall into a sort of love with *me* (spiritual concordances & other worse reasons). They are rich people." Now the fantastical, storybooklike Eckleys absolutely insisted that the Brownings travel with them to Rome in their two lavish pumpkins and that they send Ferdinando and the heavy luggage by sea. "The advantage [of their carriages] would be great to us, both as a cheapness, & the comfort—in that easy conveyance with good springs & cushions."

But even the friendship of the very wealthy could not stop the snow, and if there was unmelted snow on the mountains, they would not be able to make the trip. The Eckleys decided not to go to Rome either. They were stationed in Florence just waiting on the Brownings. Whatever the Brownings did, they would do.

"Arabel!—since I began to write this letter it has begun to rain."

The Brownings and Eckleys left, along with two children, two teams of horses, drivers, and a pony.

It wasn't that Elizabeth and Robert did not see the particularities of the Eckleys quite clearly. "Such a woman & such a man are forever ex-

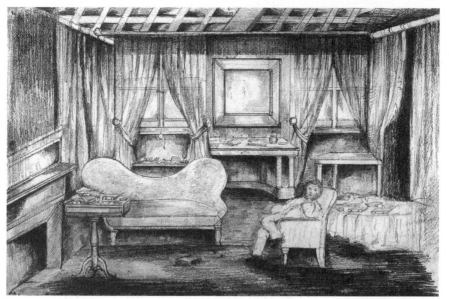

43 Via Bocca di Leone, Rome. *A drawing found in the album in which Sophia Eckley kept EBB's letters. The Brownings sublet this apartment in 1853 and 1858. During the 1858–59 season in Rome, the Brownings were in almost daily contact with Sophia and David Eckley.*

ceptions among men & women. I myself did not before I knew them, believe such things & such people could be," Ba wrote to Arabel. David Eckley's love of his wife moved him "as God's love should move us all— Literally, what she loves *he* loves . . with a sort of child's devotion—a desire to give away everything out of his pockets to prove what his feeling is—with tears in his eyes & a trembling in his voice—well it is strange." Not only that, "he lays his head under our feet & begs us to walk over him. Not because she tells him to do it, observe, but because she feels so herself. It is strange." Robert Browning was struck by the symbiotic nature of the Americans' relationship, and by the way in which David didn't have to wait to hear his wife's wishes verbalized before he carried them out. The Brownings accepted his groveling largesse, and the two husbands continued a friendship that seemed based on long horseback rides together. On the trip to Rome the wives sat inside one of the carriages having their own conversation: "The spirits made signs several times to Sophie & me on the journey."

One wonders why they didn't signal them to watch out for the road. The horses had a dangerous slip or two. But the great adventure was with the two oxen-team drivers "who came to take the two carriages up a mountain. The drivers began to fight, & one of them pulled out a knife & prepared to stab." Robert Browning reacted quickly. The poet rushed in between the two angry men and prevented the stabbing, during which he was thrown down.

"Oh, papa, papa!—come away, papa! Oh, the naughty man is killing papa."

His wife didn't shriek the way her son did, "but did the next best & fainted—or all but fainted. It really was frightful." There were bandits on the road as well, but, perhaps fortunately for them, they stayed clear of Robert Browning.

The minute the Brownings got to Rome and settled at 43 Via Bocca di Leone, Robert went downstairs to the apartment of a dear friend from the time of his last stay in the Eternal City five years ago. William Page, the American Titian, had remarried. "The new wife said he was ill in bed—but as soon as he heard of Robert's coming, he got up & dressed and came to throw himself in Robert's arms."

Page's third marriage was a stable one, though he was pained through his life by the newspaper notices of his moonfaced second wife, Sarah, who continued to use his name. After her young Italian lover left her, Sarah rejected her first idea of entering a nunnery and went on stage in America instead, taking the name Augusta Page. Later she married a notorious member of the Tweed ring, and when the ring was exposed in the press, she fled with her husband to Paris.

Engaged by her new friendship with Sophie, Ba was well enough to give crowded teas: "People get warm (in other than a physical sense) by rubbing up against one another." There were many friends in Rome: the Storys, the Pages, Harriet Hosmer, Charlotte Cushman, the Cartwrights, Odo Russell, Frederick Leighton, Lord Oswald. Not a few of them were spiritualists. But it was Sophie Eckley who added fresh confidence to Elizabeth's belief in the spirits.

By Christmas the daily contact with Sophie was evident in her greeting to her real sisters and brother Stormie, whom she kissed "through the air." She told them: "Perhaps you may see my 'nerve-spirit' sitting at your Christmas dinner!—Yet dont, because you will see tears in the eyes of it, though a true loving smile on its lips."

Christmas gifts, receiving gifts in general, had become a problem. Nowadays when Sophie asked Ba if she liked something they'd seen together, she immediately said "no" to ward off receiving it. The ploy didn't usually work; at times Pen got the gift. But Sophie wasn't the only gift-bearer. At Christmas, Elizabeth was given some very expensive brooches, two of which were from people she didn't love. The one from Sophie she accepted out of love and because of love, though it made her uneasy. She wrote to Sophie that her "beautiful cameo" was meant for Sophie's "own marble throat." The gift produced what is rare in the poet's letters: unctuous prose. She fretted over the gifts. "Tell me Arabel, how is one to accept gifts from persons one doesn't love, & how is one to refuse them to persons one would avoid quarreling with?" One of those that she apparently did not love was the wife of her husband's best friend, William Wetmore Story. She returned the cameo she received from Emelyn, telling her she had just accepted an identical one.

Sophie's never-ending gift-giving was upsetting to Robert Browning. "Naughty dearest Sophie," Ba responded to one unnamed but obviously lavish present.

"Don't take it. It's too much," Robert told her.

"It's too much, & I *will*," answered Ba. The rationale was that "There is a name & a thought! you—" and that is not to be devalued. Still, "dear, dearest Sophie, let this be the very last thing of this kind that you overwhelm me with because you give me pain—" Yet there was a double message because, "No, I won't say more—I love you, dear, dear, much, & I take it from you for love's sake."

Browning watched the expensive love pour in.

Throughout the long season in Rome, the spirits showed themselves through Sophie's mediumship. On March 29, 1859, Ba assured her real sister, "I'm not 'going mad' Arabel oh no. . . . Intercourse with the unseen makes me calm & happy—full of hope & understanding of the two worlds." The next six and a half lines might have exceeded Arabel's limitations; they are heavily crossed out. Robert Browning couldn't cross anything out. He saw his wife revive physically and mentally through her relationship with Sophie. He once had the power to bring his wife to the real rivers and mountains—to life. Now this beautiful and strange American woman, who both Brownings agreed was protected from life through the velvet trappings of wealth, was making his wife calm and happy, showing her a world that didn't exist.

Elizabeth's morphine use may have increased during this time after her father's death, adding to her calm, or else its effects were simply more noticeable. People talked about it, and it got into print on more

than one occasion. Julia Ward Howe was one American woman not
charmed by the Brownings. She felt the couple had slighted her when
she was in Italy, and she consoled herself in her 1857 volume of poetry,
Words for the Hour. These words could be sung to the music of her most
famous work, "The Battle Hymn of the Republic":

> *I hear you do not praise me, Barrett Browning, God inspired*
> *Nor you Robert with your manhood and your angels interlyred.*

Revenge was hers in another poem in the volume, "One Word More
with E.B.B." The nasty poem included stanzas which told the reader
that Julia Ward Howe would say no to drugs, even if drugs brought
with them poetic heights.

> *I shrink before the nameless draught*
> *That helps to such unearthly things,*
> *And if a drug could lift so high,*
> *I would not trust its treacherous wings;*
>
> *Lest, leaping from them, I should fall,*
> *A weight more dead than stock or stone,—*
> *The warning fate of those who fly*
> *With pinions other than their own.*

Robert was outraged. In Rome he made a special trip to see Howe's sister, the wife of the sculptor Thomas Crawford and mother of the novelist Marion Crawford—"to show her how much I despised her sister."
Then and through the rest of his life, he would never suffer in silence
even the slightest disparaging of his wife's name.

Elizabeth was much more tranquil. The allusion was to a " 'name-
less drug' dear, & not morphine," she wrote to Sophie. With an understanding of the reading public's love of symbolism, the poet thought
the literal meaning might not be understood. But even if it were, she
was "not a bit" angry. Why should she be? It had been "perfectly true,
so far, that life is necessary to writing, & that I should not be alive except by help of my morphine." In the same letter she told her friend, "I
have had too many poison arrows in me to care for a harmless word like
this. I am not like YOU, Sophie . . used to walk on velvet & breathe
only the breath of such roses . . as you send me, dearest, kindest friend.

How beautiful." Perhaps her morphine opened her even more to Sophie.

If all Robert Browning could do was watch, watch he did. Two years after his wife's death, he wrote to the Storys that he had always known Sophie to be a liar. So this new lie of hers, that her husband had been unfaithful, "does not astonish me one whit nor in the least degree add to my acquaintance with that very peculiar mind which I had reasons of my own for thoroughly studying long ago: I dare affirm that I know that character in enough of its ins and outs, turns & twists,— and you, of course, remember that I *did* know it of old—those who did *not,* have all this novelty to learn & admire."

By April 30, 1859, Sophie was hearing loud voices. They followed her to church. She and Ba did automatic writings together, meaning that the spirits wrote through them, directing their hands. They also attempted communication through mental telepathy when they were apart. In their private séances together, Ba never heard voices herself. Her friend was the stronger medium. Yet as strong a medium as she was, the beautiful Sophie "is very shy & timid of being associated with these phenomena—," Ba explained to her disbelieving sister in London. "Not like me, Arabel, who have none of that sort of shame about me. If it's truth at all, it's God's truth—& why should a man or a woman be ashamed of it?" A good question. Robert Browning most likely pointed out to his wife: If it's truth at all, why should Sophie Eckley be ashamed?

But she and Sophie knew that a new world order was on the way. Love was once more pulling her by the hair; this time it was not only telling her she was alive, it was telling her she was right.

Although the two women at times communicated "through the air," they corresponded by letter as well. When Sophie asked the poet if she would be able to forgive her if she did something wicked, Elizabeth answered that the possibility of her wickedness was beyond belief. In Rome, when she was confined because Pen was unwell, she asked, "Have you had any sign from the spirits? You do not say. You are afraid of naming them to such a traitor as you have found in me. Is it so?" Perhaps Elizabeth had talked to others of Sophie's powers despite her friend's shyness. She certainly wrote to her sister and talked with her husband. The next day, Pen was better. "Dear you interest me very much," the poet wrote, encouraging her shy friend, "Tell me more, more, as you know it, for there is nothing to me of such grand & at the same time, intimate significance, as this subject." She might as well have written, just pour it on, give me exactly what is needed.

Browning knew that his wife's nature was such that she found it impossible to believe that the people she loved could possibly lie. But he also knew she helped inspire, was complicit, in Sophie Eckley's deception. His wife, the *testa lunga,* had made up her mind.

Elizabeth's spiritual activities with Sophie did not exclude Christian worship with Robert, though one doubts it reassured her youngest sister concerning her sanity. "And when spring approached I was wicked enough to go with Robert (you now prepare to excommunicate me Arabel!) to the catholic services & no where else! I cant bear the fatigue of a succession of services on sunday, & I did prefer St Peter's & the like & have enjoyed few modes of worship so much as the gathering together in the solemn twilight of the aisles, with the sublime music floating upwards with my prayers. In fact Arabel, both I and Robert liked it extremely." Her son "went with us sometimes," but by now he was old enough to attend the English church always. "A child requires something less vague than his own thoughts."

While Elizabeth and her soul sister consulted the spirits, Robert and David Eckley met every morning before dawn, at a quarter after six, and rode. Robert wrote to Isa Blagden, who was then in Spain, that "we go all about Rome, up & down, in & out, the worst & best of it, so that I can see it thoroughly on the outside & like it *so* much—so much more than last time." The future author of that great Roman murder story *The Ring and the Book* was pursuing both halves of his Rome. Also, twice a week he would draw at the home of the painter Emma Landseer McKenzie. And at night he went into society. "I am far better & stronger than last year—tho' sufficiently bothered by a cold I caught at the theatre the other evening—which is getting better."

If Robert had a spiritual sister, it was Isa Blagden. Blagden did not get along with Sophie. This good friend was the kind of person who was usually a welcoming hostess with a sympathetic ear. A small woman in her forties at the time, dark, lively, and of Indian and English blood, she was one of those expatriates who had learned to live creatively on little money. As "our lady of Bellosguardo," she did this above Florence in the fourteen rooms of Villa Brichieri, employing two servants and keeping a carriage. A minor novelist and poet, she often shared expenses with another woman, and in her novel *Agnes Tremorne*

THE TERRACE AT BELLOSGUARDO. *Isa Blagden's villa was situated in the hills of Bellosguardo, from which one had not only a "beautiful view" but reprieve from the heat of the plain of the Florentine summer.*

she had written of the single life, "I think few writers lay sufficient stress on the large space which a true friendship . . . holds in the lives of two single women, and what exquisite enjoyments are derived from it. In the personal intimacy which exists in such a relation, there is entire comprehension and knowledge of each other. This is seldom attained, even in the holiest and truest marriage."

It was a view with which Elizabeth might have agreed when she had urged Arabel to set up housekeeping with a like-minded single friend of hers as a rewarding alternative to keeping the young Emma: "It has seemed to me sometimes that you and Miss [Rafael?] might have agreed to live together—you agree in so much—& what you want in certain respects, she has—so that I should have been glad rather—only one person cant arrange for another."

The Brownings' friends included many independent women. It may not have been a simpler age, but love was certainly less differentiated before Freud. Children were sexless, and the most lavish endearments in correspondence and person were often considered the call of the soul. While we are literally compelled by our textbooks to raise an eyebrow and clear our throats, the Victorians went on enjoying their freedom.

Robert's friendship with Isa Blagden seemed to have had some of the quality of his friendship with Anna Jameson, except that Isa and Robert were about the same age. In their friendship and correspondence there was a pattern that would run through the poet's later life. He was to have many interesting women friends to whom he was attached in deep sympathy, mutual interest, and affection. He would have many women friends—and one wife.

In the last years of her marriage, Elizabeth supposed that after her death her husband, being a man, might be capable of some "feeble bigamy." Feeble she knew it would be. And bigamy? For both Brownings, yes. Whether one locates it in their Christian faith, their love of Dante, or their reading of Swedenborg's *Conjugal Love,* they had faith that they would meet again in the afterlife. They believed their marriage was eternal. After Elizabeth's death, Browning would put this quote from Dante's *La Vita Nuova* in her Bible: "I believe and I declare—Certain am I—from this life I pass into a better, there where that lady lives of whom enamored was my soul."

His wife turned out to be as prescient as she could be on the question of his feeble bigamy. As a widower he once thought of a second marriage, to Lady Ashburton, who seems to have proposed it. He emphatically assured Lady Ashburton that his heart lay buried in Florence and such a marriage would be for his son. In so doing he took a lifelong enemy rather than a bride.

Many have commented, including his wife, on how handsome and well Browning appeared in the last years of his marriage. And in Rome he took diplomatic and aristocratic and intellectual society by storm. Everyone did then and always would love an evening with Robert Browning. Some later critics have suggested that perhaps a man in his prime, married to a woman six years his senior who was becoming increasingly reclusive, might have had a roving eye. . . . Well, that was just not to measure the extraordinary inner nature of Robert Browning. It was simply viewing a marriage from this side of the moon. On the underside was what Browning would one day call a familiar blot on his picture of the past—that thorny white rose, Sophia Eckley. Between 1857 and 1859 it wasn't Robert, it was Elizabeth Barrett Browning who played with fire.

Isa Blagden no more than Robert could convince Ba to be wary of Sophie. Instead, Ba tried to convince Isa of Sophie's worth. Sophie wasn't haughty, as Isa thought, but "shy, & hates strangers & mixed so-

ciety." She never called on anyone first, but she had called on Isa. Sophie "thinks you passed her once or twice in the street—she knows you
were as cold as ice to her at Casa Guidi—and after all she writes,
wishes to be on cordial terms with you. She told me so! & bade me to
tell you. She is a very peculiar person, impressionable & susceptible to
the last degree—but of a pure, sweet, & noble nature, which you
would comprehend if you came near enough."

It would only be back in Florence, as the Eckleys prepared to leave
for the summer season, that Elizabeth became cautious. She sent Sophie a gift and a note to read after the Eckleys left for the Baths of
Lucca. Perhaps she'd paid some heed to her husband's misgivings—or
her own. The note was as chillingly prophetic as it was loving: The
poet loved her spiritual sister enough to tell her "the simple truth—
you have done too much for me, thought too much of me—I have had
to be on my guard against your kindness, as I might be against other
people's malice."

The trip back to Florence at the end of May had been a particularly
joyful one. Napoleon and his troops had arrived in Italy, the Grand
Duke had once more fled, and it looked as if, with France's help, Victor
Emmanuel II, the House of Savoy, would rout Austria. Once more the
Italians captured the rapture of 1848, but with hindsight. This was
just as the Brownings' friend Massimo d'Azeglio, the great Italian patriot and Piedmont's minister to England, had prophesied when he visited them in Rome.

As the Brownings entered Tuscany, the tricolored flag of Italy was
once more being displayed. How exciting it was for Pen to see it:
"Here's a flag—& there & there!—dear papa, dear mama, do look."
When the Brownings neared Florence they saw the French troops en-
camped close by on the Cascine meadows. Robert and Pen took off
their hats and yelled out "Viva" from their carriage. And when they
entered their city, it was "winged" with the tricolor from every window. The bright colors, the festive mood, the songs, and the morale
must have reminded the couple of the exhilaration they witnessed
from their windows on their first anniversary. "This time we know our
own minds," Ba reported, echoing d'Azeglio, and "the feeling toward
France & the Emperor is beautiful to see. It is an enthusiasm of gratitude." The camaraderie was exhilarating; there were shouts and songs.
The Italians called out "Viva la Francia" to the French troops, who returned it with the French chorus "Vive l'Italie."

Back in Florence, Elizabeth missed a visit with Sophie one day because she thought her friend would have arrived earlier if she were coming. As a result, Elizabeth joined her husband and son, and the three drove to the Cascine meadows to visit the French camp and gossip with the soldiers. The British poets and their child shook hands with the men. One soldier in "an effusion of tenderness turned and kissed Peni," who thought it "so very kind." It was like a kiss from Napoleon's lips. Such was the camaraderie of those spring days.

Barrett Browning wrote a poem of this time when beautiful, well-dressed Tuscan ladies went into the field to dance with the common French soldiers who were stationed there. She pictured the times as the times really were. Joy and hope seemed everywhere. Sadness seemed to have deserted the poet. She wrote on the eve of Italian unification that she had never been happier in her life. And from the Brownings' terrace, the one they had paced at night at the beginning of their marriage, two flags were draped, the French and the Italian.

The Brownings were united in their Italian patriotism. Robert even admitted that the British government as well as the *Times* had been up to no good. He subscribed what he could monthly and even got Pen to concentrate on his lessons by rewarding him with his own money to give to the cause of unification. But Robert had done more, as had his wife. They had put their money into Tuscan bonds when one had no idea of the political fate of Tuscany. One can almost hear poor Mr. Kenyon rapping. But where Robert's heart lay his funds lay also. "We shall hold on," wrote Elizabeth, the poet of the Italian Risorgimento, "& funds like peoples, will rise again."

IN JUNE the French and Italian troops routed the Austrians from Magenta. On June 27 Elizabeth wrote to Arabel, "The sort of excitement we live in here you can scarcely imagine to yourself. Other wars have to do with commerce & political theories—this has to do with life, love, national salvation. The people have tears in their eyes through profound feeling. The poorest & most ignorant study the maps & count the advances & retreats, as if each had a personal enemy at his shoulder."

The Brownings and Pen weren't considered English at all, she was proud to tell her sister. That's what "an intelligent Italian assured me the other day . . & I believe it to be perfectly true, for we have not lived here in a corner, on account of our poetry . . & besides I have heard of my rages this spring from more than one quarter. They let us through the custom house with scarcely a question. . . . A friend of ours (by the way) was considerably amused, on coming to Florence & enquiring about me at the door of Casa Guidi" to have the answer from Ferdinando, " 'Sta molto bene è *contentisima*': as if the state of my health was mainly dependent on the state of war—!—So, as long as the Austrians keep away, you need not spend an anxious thought on us indeed."

There was truth to these lighthearted words. "I used to have *literal physical* palpitations over the newspapers—tears in my eyes, sobs in my throat." For Elizabeth, "The war must end well."

Now in Florence as the war went well, Elizabeth's anxiety turned into a new form of excitability and happiness, and the poet went full force from the sofa into society: "I never in my Florence life was so dissipated as just now—I feel stirred up to the dregs of me, & go here & there, to hear & talk & look into other people's faces for sympathy. I cant rest, I am so excited." Why shouldn't she be excited? She instructed Arabel as to the meaning of the victory at Magenta: "What you should see in this . . the arm of God has been with us from the beginning, . . to make Austria mad, in order to destroy her life in Italy."

She even accompanied her husband to the theater and recorded that theaters in Florence were empty because of the preoccupation with the war. "I heard the great actor Salvini saying lately that the real tragedies had excluded the false ones."

By now the Brownings might have been considering their summer plans. But "I should have much disliked being away from Italy at this crisis, as a matter of feeling," she wrote to Arabel. Furthermore, it was a good time "to be in the neighbourhood of our coupons," she jested to her frugal sister, referring to the interest on their Tuscan bonds. "If the Grand Duke, the tender parental grand Duke had bombarded Florence, as he desired or even if Austria came up now & bombarded us, the risk to coupons would be considerable, you see. Not that we are or have been in the slightest alarm. Only our interests are here . . just as our hearts are on the cause."

When Robert met their friend the minister of finance on the street, he enthusiastically took both his hands and congratulated him on the prospects of Italy. Excitement was so well justified that perhaps even Browning didn't think of the effect a possible reversal might have on his wife. Ba informed her sister-in-law that in Florence, "it is as if each one had a personal enemy in the street below struggling to get up to him. When we are anxious we are pale; when we are glad we have tears in our eyes. . . . You [people in France] *talk* about our living or dying, but *we live or die.* That's the difference between you and us.

"We shall live, however. The hope is rising into triumph."

Though the Eckleys went to the Baths of Lucca and the Storys were at Siena, the Brownings stuck to their Florence in the heat of the revolution. Then, like a lightning bolt out of a starlit night, Napoleon abruptly agreed to an armistice. In a finger's snap the Peace of Villafranca was signed on July 9, 1859, a little more than a month after the Brownings returned to Florence. Sudden death. Only it wasn't a father, it was Tuscan hopes that died.

> *My little son, my Florentine,*
> *Sit down beside my knee,*
> *And I will tell you why the sign*
> *Of joy which flushed our Italy*
> *Has faded since but yesternight:*
> *And why your Florence of delight*
> *Is mourning as you see.*

Knowing that Prussia might be joining Austria to fight, seeing the casualties and the lack of active Italian soldiers, Napoleon compromised. Austria would yield Lombardy to Piedmont; France would eventually absorb Savoy and Nice. But Tuscany? Once more the Grand Duke would return.

Elizabeth managed to write to one person, her sister in the spirits: "But I have been miserable about public affairs, couldn't keep the tears away from my eyes for days & days, wasn't fit to write or sleep or eat or do anything.

"I was in despair in fact."

So was Florence.

The poet was "enraged with the whole world meaning England, Prussia & Russia—Selfish, wicked policy which has undone us. . . . You can see I cant help harping on it. My heart is sore." She scarcely alluded to the spirits. She had grown "very bitter, very skeptical, very fierce," she told her spiritual sister. "One doesn't fall down from a star with impunity."

WALTER SAVAGE LANDOR
(1775–1864). *A pencil sketch of the
octogenarian by W. W. Story. The
Romantic poet and author of* Imaginary Conversations *was an early
champion of RB's work. In the 1840s,
when EBB mentioned RB in a poem,
Landor wrote a poem about* Bells and
Pomegranates *as well. It compared
RB to Chaucer. In Florence years later
RB became the official guardian of the
querulous old poet who tried everyone's
patience, including EBB's.*

IT WAS BROILING HOT in Florence when Elizabeth wrote Sophie this
letter. But "at this time of crisis, it seems scarcely possible to live away
from this place of action & information."

In fact, she was staying in her city by herself. "Robert is not *here*—
think of that! He is at Siena!!!!"

At a moment when Robert had to be worrying about the effect this
latest political blow would have on his wife's health, Walter Savage
Landor, in his eighties, descended from the outskirts of Florence, giving "up his family for good and all!" For the last week he "has been
spending the greater part of every day with us. At last he comes to a decision to go to Siena. Robert couldn't let him go alone & set off
in company with him at seven this morning in order to settle him
as comfortably as the circumstances admit of his being settled, &
then of course to return quickly—but he cant be back till tomorrow at
soonest—The Landor family made a stormy attempt to besiege their
Head in this house—but Mr Landor however, stated, that, if his
beloved wife entered the door he would throw himself out of the window, she had nothing to do but to go away without further attempting
to see him."

Browning went to Siena, where the Storys were kind enough to admit Landor temporarily till Browning could settle him. Wilson, who had lately had her own bouts of madness, now rented rooms, and the poet would make arrangements for Landor to board with her. But his visit had another object as well. While he was there, he and the Storys picked out a summer villa for the Brownings. It was important to get his wife away from the disappointments and the broiling heat of Florence, and the poet had no intention of joining the Eckleys at Lucca. His newfound guardianship of Landor might have indeed strengthened his case. In her next letter to Sophie, Elizabeth told her that "Robert in the act of depositing Mr Landor at Siena saw & was so enticed by a certain villa that he has taken it for two months—we go, in a week, if I am able to move."

If she were able to move. "Dearest Sophie—dear—I have your second note & am going to write things which will not please you." First, she had been ill. Second, she and Robert were going to Siena for two months. About her illness, "It had been a very bad attack on the chest partly from cold, I dare say, & partly from late excitements acting on the circulation during the extreme heat. For two nights & days I suffered almost strangulation—which is quite passed—only I cant talk, or scarcely *speak* without being the worse for it." She required "absolute quiet" and "change of air." She was not supposed to write at all, but did so in order for Sophie to know she was getting better. "If Robert wrote you would tink [*sic*] me worse than I am—& I would not have you uneasy."

The handwriting in this letter to Sophie had degenerated. It might have been the mark of an aged woman attempting a scrawl after a debilitating stroke. "I have been ill." It would be impossible to look at the letter without imagining the worst. Someone of Sophie's inclination might have assumed it was automatic writing from a tortured ghost. The difficulty the poet had in *physically* forming the words is apparent. "May God bless you & love you. Wouldn't it have been well to have died with my Italy? But I hold on to hope, to hope. . . . Your loving Ba."

Wouldn't it have been better to die with Italy? The poet of the Risorgimento was next to death. Leaving Florence at all became a desperate attempt, a last option, to save her life. On July 30, she was carried out of the Casa Guidi, she was carried into a railway carriage, and then at Siena she was carried into the Hotêl Algride. Isa Blagden took it on her own to wire ahead to the Algride and to the Storys to alert them to her friend's condition. And one of the few foreign doctors who had stayed in Florence, the Prussian patriot Dr. E. G. T. Grisanowski, followed after the poets by train and ministered to Elizabeth for two days and nights at Siena. He would take no recompense. She had become Tuscany's own dirge.

And when she could sleep in between the pain in her chest and the lack of breath and the wretched coughing, "I dreamed lately that I followed a mystic woman down a long suite of palatial rooms. She was in white, with a white mask, on her head the likeness of a crown. I knew she was Italy, but I couldn't see through the mask. All through my illness political dreams have repeated themselves, in inscrutable articles of peace and eternal provisional governments. Walking on the mountains of the moon, hand in hand with a Dream more beautiful than them all, then falling suddenly on the hard earth—ground on one's head, no wonder that one should suffer. Oh, Isa, the tears are even now in my eyes to think of it!

"And yet I have hope . . ."

Dr. Grisanowski helped Robert pick a suitable villa before he left Siena. Back in Florence he added his own voice to the Tuscan chorus about the great English poet who was dying with Italy.

Only she didn't die. Once again she was to rise slowly from the ashes of physical and mental defeat.

Robert, between nursing his wife day and night, becoming Landor's legal guardian, and hearing Pen's lessons, had to cope with Mrs. Eckley. Why hadn't the Brownings joined them in Lucca?

Events had become so life-threatening that it is easy to overlook the domestic compromise the Brownings must have reached before Elizabeth became ill. Robert Browning had refused to spend the summer at the Baths of Lucca with the Eckleys.

Ba had written that they were going to Siena because her husband had fallen in love with a villa. Then why were they at the Villa Alberti instead? On August 2, Robert gave Sophie one excuse too many: The proprietor had raised his demands, and Dr. Grisanowski preferred the small, more hygienic villa. Still, "I am very glad that we decided to come here . . . I have a dread of the damp dead heat I remember at Lucca in the middle of the day. Let Ba but get well and strong, as I trust will soon be the case, and I shall be thankful to Siena indeed." For "This has been a sad interruption of her continued increase of health and strength since the spring."

This did not satisfy Sophie. When she wrote to the Brownings on August 4, Browning assumed she had not received his letter: "Ba has been very ill—more ill than you suppose, if you think her capable of writing to bid you goodbye from Casa Guidi. . . . Her strength was absolutely *gone*—she was carried downstairs, carried into the railway carriage, carried up to bed in the Hôtel—and she left Florence in so pitiable a state that Grisanowski set off by the next train and spent two days at the Hôtel with us to be of any use he might; he selected for us, not the beautiful Villa I had set my mind on but the least commodious of all that were to be let, on hygienic grounds for the quality of the air obtainable in it."

But why weren't they at Lucca?

"I am very satisfied that we should have gained less in your gay place—tho' we certainly *should* have gained your neighbourhood, and all the delight that it implies. But you will have understood by this time how matters really stand. I trust that we shall meet again soon happily and be able to discuss the respective advantages of Lucca and Siena."

On August 9, Elizabeth wrote to her friend: "Dearest Sophie, here I am . . . on the right side of the earth." She had to explain another slight. Not only hadn't she written from the Casa Guidi again after the letter with the ghostly handwriting; she hadn't communicated through the air: "Dear *I spoke to you*—but my voice was so hoarse & inward that you did not hear. I said, God bless you, Sophie." She was better now, though "I am very weak—so weak that to walk across the room without an arm sets me reeling & liable to fall."

On to the important matters: "As to Lucca, dear, I could not have borne the journey to Lucca. . . . We required immense courage to come even here—If you had seen the state in which I was deposited in the railroad!" As to Sophie's health: "But you—you have suffered from indigestion? I am sorry. You should take more exercise—did you not agree it was better?"

Sophie Eckley had a single-minded concern the summer her friend almost died. Why didn't Ba want to be in Lucca with her? What were people telling her in Siena? Had Ba found her out?

Even in the midst of his wife's illness in Florence, when she didn't think the villa he had chosen would do, Robert had written to Story that they hoped to find another villa in Siena that would afford them two months of happiness. Two months of happiness away from Sophie Eckley. Robert Browning had had as much as he could take of her. In Siena and without the Eckleys the intimacy between the couple seemed to grow stronger. Robert had been "perfect," Elizabeth would write in letter after letter.

As ELIZABETH BARRETT BROWNING slowly healed, viewing the eternal Tuscan landscape and breathing the clear air, her husband often sitting in silence by her side, she came to admit the truth about her spiritual sister. Earlier that summer in Florence, Elizabeth had written to Sophie that Sophie had an "exaggerated apprehension of what I am. . . . If you could see me as I am & yet love me, I should be much easier." But the poet herself had an exaggerated apprehension of her American friend. We see this in her poem "Where's Agnes?"

> Had she any faults at all,
>   'T was having none, I thought too—
> There seemed a sort of thrall;
>   As she felt her shadow ought to
> Fall straight upon the wall.
>
> Her sweetness strained the sense
>   Of common life and duty;
> And every day's expense
>   Of moving in such beauty
> Required, almost, defence.

In Siena it would appear that one person brought her the truth about Sophie. Whoever it was, it was a message and a messenger she couldn't dispute. Less than four years before, she heard from Elizabeth Kinney in Florence that D. D. Home's "moral character" had failed and that Hiram Powers had excluded him from his house. She wrote to Powers to ask him if Home's "sorcery" was also "trickery." For "the opinion of a quiet, cautious philosophic observer like yourself, would be incalculable to me." A detached onlooker, no Robert Browning, informed her that Sophie's mediumship was an absolute fraud, just as

AUTOMATIC WRITING. *This scrap, preserved among three others in Sophia Eckley's album of EBB's letters to her, was most possibly an example of the automatic writing the two women privately experimented with in Rome in 1858–59.*

her husband had told her . . . and told her. Once, she had faced that her father loved her less than she thought; now it was time to look again at the truth.

And to break the bond. She wrote Sophie a letter that she considered harsh and devastating. But reading it, one might agree with Sophie, that it was "kind." The poets never shared the letters they wrote to others, but this letter Elizabeth gave Robert to read.

"My dear Sophie, as I told you before I *believe in the spirits*—nor do I mean to express a doubt that the *spirits* have written through you and me—On several occasions also, words have apparently been written in reply to mental questions of mine, and names been given, which could not have been in your mind! But then, observe, they were in my mind—and they were only *apparently written* as I say: I mean they were legible rather to me than to you—which means very faintly legible."

More to the point were the long messages written down by Sophie supposedly coming from spirits of those related to Ba. Her father? Bro? Her mother? Treppy? John Kenyon? Her dear uncle Samuel? Her dead brother Sam? Her grandmother and namesake? Edward of Cinnamon Hill? Whomever they were from, these messages seemed to prove that American was spoken in heaven (and hell): "The form of expression was distinctly unlike those beings, in fact, I should say *impossible to them!* Again & again, for instance, there have been slight American-isms—turns of phrases which are not usual among the English."

Of course this proved nothing against the American medium: "throws not a shadow of suspicion on the medium's 'integrity,' (need I say that?) but was & is an indication to me that my particular spirits were not present nor speaking."

The poet took her share of the blame. "Certainly, when you have wished to leave off the writing, I have sometimes urged the continu-ance of the experiments. That is perfectly true." One can see Robert nodding. "I wished to push the experiments to the utmost extent of the power we had. But you must be aware that beyond a certain line, there was nothing. I had no personal proof of anything but some invol-untary writing . . which *never of itself* & without distinct characteristics could satisfy me. The 'sounds' are twenty times more satisfactory to me, as I have often told you—but the sounds never occurred with us—never: though with you alone, you said they were always occurring."

Sophie had told her "you are sure of my having had communica-tion with spirits belonging to me. How can *you* possibly be sure, if *I* am not sure? There has been *no* testimony worth a straw to me—though I kept my mind open & ready for the possibility to ripen into a certainty—Sometimes for a moment it touched a probability—but never beyond."

Why, just ask Robert: "My husband is my witness that I told him at the time, when he asked me the question 'whether I believed in cer-tain identities,'. . that 'I kept my belief in a balance, believing in the *class of facts,* & in the *possibility of getting identities proved,* but not consid-ering them proved in my case so far.' " No, Elizabeth Barrett Brown-ing had never herself made contact with her dead.

"Always I shall be eager to hear any experience on the subject which is & must remain one of deep interest to me. But the *writing* seems to me of no practical use, at least such writing as you and I produce—and I have made up my mind to try it no more. I think there are spirits who communicate—nay I *believe there are*: but the question of identity is quite different, & there is no sort of proof that any spirit connected with myself ever intimated his or her presence through your mediumship, either to you or to me. In fact, I grieve to say that the proof is the other way, as I apprehend it. It is my great loss. Too happy I should be to believe otherwise. For minutes together

I have struggled to believe it—but thought has always been too strong for belief & desire."

She parted from Sophie. "So much I have said, dearest Sophie, that you may understand where & how the question rests with me. There is nothing to regret in having tried a long series of experiments—but then there *would* be, if ever I began it over again, after once seeing them to an end."

Could Sophie salvage the friendship? According to Robert, she never even tried. "When Mrs. Eckley found herself discovered, she never made an effort to recover her place in Ba's liking—not to say love, still less esteem: she just asked leave to come and see her sometimes,—by way of hiding the separation from people."

After the rupture Elizabeth wrote to Sophie: "Ever dearest Sophie, what am I to say? That you were very wicked & that I pardon you, or that I was very wicked & you must pardon me. Really considering what passed, it looks to me as if the wickedness of us two was mixed up." After all, "I meant no harm, you meant no harm—now did you?"

At the end of this note she reached for an analogy from the mathematics Pen was studying: "You are a dear darling friend. After the long sum, there's the *quotient* . . . don't they call it? I mean the figure at the bottom,—the result."

The "result" she factored candidly to Arabel when in 1861 the Eckleys and the Brownings were once more in Rome. "I have seen her only three times this winter—I am very cold—but there's no quarrel—She asked me to forgive her—I said . . If she had injured me it would be very easy to forgive—but what was impossible was to feel the same to a person in whom one has lost faith. I said it quite mildly. She asked me to kiss her & say God bless her—and I did both. Afterwards—she conducted herself precisely as if nothing wrong was between us—The fact is (it's horrible to say. . .) she wants to *pass for being my friend,*—& would eat much dirt for that fair distinction. I never was more deceived in a woman. The least touch of real feeling, though expressed in a good honest fit of crossness would comparatively have saved her with me. But the calculating want of delicacy & sensibility are too disgusting to my whole nature. There's a piece of scandal for you my own Arabel."

The scandal turned into a poem, "Where's Agnes?" According to Browning, his wife had thought of making the poem completely specific, a true "Where's Sophie?" She disguised "the circumstances for my sake—who always said, 'For the husband's sake,—and because *you* deserve some punishment in the matter.' " It was he who published the poem for the first time in the collection of his wife's works he edited after her death.

In the startling image that opened the poem, the deceived lover who narrates it imagines that it would have been better had someone come to report not Agnes's treachery but her death. This messenger would have said:

> *'I saw her, I who speak,*
> *White, stiff, the face one blank:*
> *The blue shade came to her cheek*
> *Before they nailed the plank,*
> *For she had been dead a week.'*

This gruesome depiction of Agnes dead and moldering would have been better than the truth that Agnes was corrupt morally—her soul "turned mere dirt."

> *Why, if he had spoken so,*
> *I might have believed the thing,*
> *Although her look, although*
> *Her step, laugh, voice's ring*
> *Lived in me still as they do.*

But, "my Agnes false? such shame? / She?" Much, much worse. By the end of the poem, anger and disillusionment veer inward and the deceived lover asks, "Who's dead here? No, not she: / Rather I."

The result of Agnes's deceptions? No more "fluctuant curves" for this believer in ideal womanhood. "No more roses!—hard straight lines." The "Poplars, cedars, cypresses!" that end the poem are a harsh tribute to masculine logic (and Robert Browning) on the issue of that "white rose," Agnes. And both images point to death.

In the poem a lover is deceived by a beautiful, seemingly stainless woman. In life, the poet often referred to Sophie's having fallen in love with her. Her own letters to Sophie at the time sound as if she were a younger woman experiencing a schoolgirl crush. "Of course the letters are nothing but what it is natural Ba should feel for 'Agnes' in her supposed perfection of purity," Browning would write to Isa Blagden almost seven years after his wife's death, when he finally read the entire collection. He made no distinction between Agnes and Sophie. There was none. In the same letter he remembered Sophie's appearing in London to offer her condolences after his wife's death, "bathed in tears." "I could not, for the life of me, feel angry—any more than the poor fellow, in 'Madame Bovary,' " with the man whom, after his wife's suicide, he finds, by a bundle of love letters, had seduced his wife."

When Ba wished she could get her letters back, realizing that Sophie would show them to people, "I used to reply (for she mentioned her belief more than once)—'of course she will parade them, and you must make up your mind to it.' " Now you laugh at the " 'love, the honesty you were once confident in.' " It was Ba's own fault: " 'You should have believed *me* so far at least as to use your own faculties and so get to believe for yourself.' " Almost seven years after his wife's death, "So I say still—with hardly any additional pain."

In a much lighter moment, in Paris at the end of the Le Havre trip, when Ba was once more well enough to go out shopping by herself, she lost her purse through absentmindedness on the way to a shop to buy a hat. Pen ran home to tell his father. Both assumed he'd be very annoyed, but instead, by the time she got to their place, he was coming out of the door with more money. She wrote to Arabel, "There was Robert perfectly magnanimous & forgiving, coming to pity & bring more money. It was very, very good of him. Still, as I say, he is human, & I expect to [be] reminded of it three times a day to the Day of judgment."

Browning's sole charge against Sophie was "that she cheated Ba from the beginning." But his charge against his wife: "I say, in the bitterness of truth, that Ba deserved it for shutting her eyes and stopping her ears as she determinedly did."

He accepted Sophie "as a familiar blotch on a picture of the past," he could write to Isa, rather calmly. But he could also blow up in a letter to Story after hearing of her lies against poor David, her husband. He talked about that "dunghill" once again. The other day, he told Story, he "solaced" himself by placing "two portraits of her, one on each side of a delicious drawing 'in the costume of Truth.' " One can imagine him alone in his study in England, his Italian days behind him, with two portraits of Sophie, the Liar, dressed elegantly as she dressed, on each side of a nubile, naked Truth. "I should like above most things to have a good talk with her: no hurting *me,* alas!" But he never would talk—or rage—to her face.

In 1869, Browning visited Sophie in London to read the book that contained all the letters his wife had written to her. "Much such a collection as I expected,—and leaving off abruptly, where I was certain it would: the first leaf records the fact that at the present owner's death it belongs to me,—or, I being dead, to Pen. She repeated her offer that I might take it at once: I should have been harsh,—or rather foolish to do so,—for under these circumstances known to many people, any other bequeathment of the book would bring far more disgrace to her than the publishing would bestow glory: I have little doubt she has *shown* them to far more people than she confessed to,—but I believe she never intended for a minute to print or sell anything."

Why didn't Browning take the book at that moment? Is it possible that he couldn't bear to have it in his sight? Was his anger such that he still felt Sophie's possession was something his wife deserved?

He never burned any of those letters after Sophie's death in Arques, France, in 1874. They were left, along with the love letters, to Pen. After Pen's death they went to the Moulton-Barretts, and they were sold at auction at Sotheby's in 1937 as part of the estate of Elizabeth's nephew Harry Peyton Moulton-Barrett. They are now in the Berg Collection of the New York Public Library. The letters have been taken from the album, which is also at the Berg. The stripped album is poignant. The letters are strange. There's a dried flower among them— picked from the grave of Keats—the type of gift Ba often wished for herself instead of Sophie's lavishness. They've never been published, nor has there been much of an attempt to quote from them. In a minor way they are the dark side of the Brownings' love letters. It was no feeble bigamy, this affair of soul between Sophie and his wife. His wife needed that which did not exist, and when her husband could not give it to her, she fell in love with someone who could. Browning, in spates, neither forgot nor forgave. He was as human as his wife. If the poets were right in their belief that they would meet again, then this was one grievance Robert Browning brought with him to Judgment Day.

WE POETS OF THE PEOPLE

JUST AS Elizabeth Barrett Browning's mental health would become much more precarious after her father's death in the spring of 1857, her physical health became much impaired after the attack on her lungs—and perhaps her heart—in the heat of Florence in the summer of 1859. Still, her Phoenix-like ability to rise from the ashes was humorously recorded in her letters. And in Rome in 1859–60, her will to live was revived once more, particularly as she realized that the Treaty of Villafranca had not ended Italian aspirations. Large parts of Italy were in fact uniting under the House of Savoy in Piedmont, and Cavour was somehow harnessing Garibaldi, who hated him for, among other things, allowing his birthplace, Nizza, to become Nice. Fully aware that falling from the star of political idealism had spun her into physical decline, she vowed to moderate her hopes. She wrote to Julia Martin that she would be more careful this time: "As to Italy, I have to put on the rein to prevent myself from hoping into the ideal again. I am on my guard against another fall from the chariot of the sun."

People wondered at the Brownings' going to Rome during these dangerous times. "If a revolution in a good sense would happen there, it would be welcome to me," Ba wrote to Arabel. And prices were certainly lower in 1859–60. Once more privy to diplomatic and revolutionary sources, Elizabeth told Julia Martin that "things look magnificently, and if I could tell you certain facts (which I can't) you would admit it. Odo Russell, the English Minister here (in an occult sense) . . . came to me two days ago and said, 'It is plain now, The Emperor is rather Italian than French. He has worked, and is working, only for Italy.' " Both Brownings were close to the heart of Italian affairs in Rome. And if Robert had separated from his wife on the matter of Sophie Eckley, he came closer to her than ever before on political matters.

An International Congress on the Italian question was to be held in Paris in January 1860, and, finally, Cavour had been chosen to represent Italy, which by itself championed the cause of the government at Piedmont, the House of Savoy.

Right before the Congress, on December 22, 1859, a pamphlet, "Le Pape et le congres," was published in Paris, and the ideas were attributed to Louis Napoleon. The pamphlet held that the Congress should urge that the Pope's territory be confined to Rome, and that Romagna, separated de facto, should not return to papal domination. It would seem that the old idea of a loose confederation of states under the figurehead of the Pope was giving way and that, in Garibaldi's words, *Italia sará*. Italy will be. When Austria asked the Emperor if he intended to advocate the principles in the pamphlet, he said he would, and Austria withdrew from the Congress. It was postponed indefinitely, only to take place in Elizabeth Barrett Browning's last book of poetry, *Poems before Congress*. But initially the poet thought she was participating in a historical event:

> *We, poets of the people who take part*
> *With elemental justice, natural right,*
> *Join our echoes, also, nor refrain.*

Her poetry became not the echo but the voice. It was she rather than Cavour who represented Italy. In doing so she addressed Napoleon:

> *An English poet warns thee to maintain*
> *God's word, not England's . . .*

Her poem to Napoleon captured the political exultation of the time:

> *Shout for France and Savoy!*
> *Shout for the council and charge!*
> *Shout for the head of Cavour;*
> *And shout for the heart of a King*
> *That's great with a nation's joy!*
> *Shout for France and Savoy!*

All the poems were based squarely on the historical situation and were full of the life of the times—if only one knew the times or trusted the poet's voice: the disappointment of the Treaty of Villafranca, the tricolored Italian flag being brought into St. Peter's at Christmas, the disappointment—in male voice, no repeating old mistakes here—at the Grand Duke's returning yet again to Florence, the aristocratic Italian ladies dancing in the Cascine with the French foot soldiers, the Milanese ladies, patriotic and bejeweled, visiting the wounded in the hospitals. Once more Barrett Browning was the poet of the Italian Risorgimento—a true unacknowledged laureateship.

Trumpeted in America at the time, where they were printed as *Napoleon III in Italy, and Other Poems*, they were harshly condemned in England. Despite the British antipathy to their French neighbor (though they were delighted that Napoleon wished to confine the Pope), the uproar against these poems by the author of *Aurora Leigh* was much more vituperative than the Brownings expected. For not only did the public misunderstand, but the critics were quite unrelenting.

Robert Browning was furious, yet one negative review gave him unbridled delight. The British *Spiritual Magazine* to which his wife subscribed reported that she had been "Biologised by infernal spirits since *Casa Guidi Windows*." They had seen the hand not of Dante but of "Moloch," in her latest work. "Robert shouted in triumph at it, and hoped I was pleased, and as for myself, it really did make me smile a little, which was an advantage, in the sad humour I was in at the time."

The more mainstream reviews objected to politics being the subject of poetry, they objected to unfairness to England, and they objected to such poems being written by a woman. The reviewer for the *Saturday Review* believed "that women ought not to write about controversial issues of the day but should confine themselves to their household duties and that if they had to go out of their homes, they should become nurses, like Florence Nightingale." This might have given Elizabeth confirmation. She believed, and had told Anna Jameson, that for all of her valor, Nightingale was appreciated because she stayed within the range of woman's work as approved by men.

One has to wonder what the fate of these impudent, self-willed, psychologically fueled, idealistic, and fiery political poems would have been had they been written by a man of similar stature. Would shocked critics have said of them that the Italian cause had found its visionary voice? Or that wide humanity had found its champion? For Barrett Browning was not ultimately a nationalist. Her concern was for "Italy and the World":

> No more Jew nor Greek then,—taunting
>   Nor taunted:—no more England nor France!
> But one confederate brotherhood planting
>   One flag only, to mark the advance,
>   Onward and upward, of all humanity.

As her publisher had predicted, the uproar did not hurt sales, and as *Aurora Leigh* went into a fifth edition, *Poems before Congress* went into a second.

Two poems in the collection, the poem to Napoleon and "A Curse for a Nation," a poem against slavery in the States in which England's insularity and corruption were also pointed out, infuriated John Bull. But it was the tone of her Preface to this slim volume that led the way. There was a certain bitterness in it and a certain condescension to the English reader. Had Barrett Browning been looking for a fight?

She began by telling the British reader, "These poems were written under the pressure of the events they indicate, after a residence in Italy of so many years that the present triumph of great principles is to be heightened" by its comparison with what she, in 1849, "witnessed from 'Casa Guidi windowes.' " So far so good. She felt compelled to go further, as she had in so many letters home. "Yet if the verses should appear to English readers too pungently rendered to admit of a patriotic respect to the English sense of things," she would not excuse it by her long residence abroad or by her love of the Italian people. Why should she put the idea of her own lack of patriotic respect into her public's mind? Why should she suggest what followed might be too strong for them? The answer was simple. It was because she loved truth and justice, " 'more than Plato and Plato's country, more than Dante and Dante's country,' " and, in her own words, "more even than Shakespeare, and Shakespeare's country." Reading the Preface first, one now had a focus for the interpretation of the following eight poems. It, as much as her support of Napoleon, fueled the fire.

That anti-British stance of hers, which she enunciated in letter after letter, was a political statement. There was no doubt that the

London *Times* was narrow, that England was for Italy's unity only if it didn't have to pay any dues. And time would prove what the Brownings knew, that Queen Victoria was secretly on the side of her Austrian cousins.

After her father's death, the poet's unrelenting bitterness in her letters toward England's policies was remarkable. Her son was her "Florentine." The last thing in the world she would wish for him was narrowly British roots. Pen spoke Italian at home, read German, and at times called his British mother "a foreigner." "Never mind," she wrote to Arabel, "perhaps England will be proud" of Pen one day, "and he shall be 'a citizen of the world' after my own heart & ready for the millennium." Until that day when the spirit world and the human world united and all nations became one, as she phrased it to her son in "A Tale of Villafranca":

> *They say your eyes, my Florentine,*
> *Are English: it may be.*
> *And yet I've marked as blue a pair*
> *Following the doves across the square*
> *At Venice by the sea.*

She was as proud as she could be that the Florentines didn't consider her or her family British. And her neighbor Eliza Ogilvy recorded that never once in their years of friendship had the poet spoken of her family's "forbears" or traditions: "One might know Mrs. Browning for years, and never hear of one of her 'forbears.'" No charming anecdotes about the benevolent slaveholder Edward of Cinnamon Hill that were often told by Treppy. In fact, no mention of Jamaica, from where all of her "forbears" came.

After her death, Browning brought his son back to England: "Of course Pen is and will be English as I am English and his Mother was pure English to the hatred of all un-English cowardice, vituperation, and lies——." Nicely put, but how purely English was she?

What was it that she kept trying to tell her very British sister Arabel as she mocked Britain in letter after letter? What was it she was saying to George when she told him that he, along with England, had fallen not into any madness of great wits, "but the low consequence of some feline bite——You understand nothing." What was it she attempted to throw in the face of her British public in her Preface to

Poems before Congress? The tone of it was not the tone of the poetry, yet it very well may have done the reputation of that poetry harm. Insular Britain would suppress the freedom of a noble people for its own benefit. It was tyrannical and unbending in its self-interest. Insular Britain no more understood or sympathized with Liberty outside its domain than her own father had. Her view of England's politics had its own logic and sense, but her anger at England, her frustration and her contempt, contained painful recriminations that never would find their rightful channel.

Her father would never acknowledge his grandchild; well, why should she acknowledge raising the first legitimate great-great-grand-son of Edward of Cinnamon Hill? In life, as in art, Pen was her Florentine. Until the millennium, she had found the country of her soul.

The sibling who stood up for her volume this time was, surprisingly enough, Stormie, the shy stutterer who always took the side of the underdog, although he would never approve of his sister's secret marriage to Browning, seeing it to the end of his long life as a betrayal of his father. "Arabel tells me that you praise my last book—which is very extraordinary for an Englishman—Oh Storm—If you were to see, if you were to read, if you were to know, how I have been abused in England." She sent that letter to Jamaica, where Stormie (Charles John, his Moulton grandfather's namesake) and Sette (by then quite obese) handled (or mishandled) the family's diminishing fortunes.

Well might Stormie applaud such a poem against slavery as his sister's "Curse for a Nation." Four months before his father's death, he had had in Jamaica by Elizabeth Barrett, a woman of color, a daughter, Eva. ("Eva" wasn't a Barrett name; was it a reference to *Uncle Tom's Cabin?*) In February 1860 another daughter, Arabella, was born. He and his two children were given conditional baptism in the Catholic church. As early as 1853, Elizabeth heard rumors that Stormie had converted to Roman Catholicism. A few years after his sister's death, in 1863, Stormie married his mulatto children's governess, "a well educated brown woman of good class," Anne Margaret Young. Had his father any hopes of avoiding legitimate heirs of mixed blood, they were posthumously undone. Stormie, with that quiet civility of his, erected a monument instead at Cinnamon Hill, Jamaica, where his father had been born. "About eight feet high with a Cross at the top," its inscription read:

To The Memory

EDWARD MOULTON BARRETT

Proprietor of those Estates
who died in London
A.D. *April 17, 1857*

R . I . P .

THE TRIP BACK to Florence from Rome that June in 1860 had none of the ebullience of the previous year's return. Elizabeth compared her state with that of Pen's pony; they were both "unusually fatigued" during the picturesque six-day journey. "I am not as strong since my illness last summer."

Elizabeth wondered if a new treatment, something beyond conventional medicine, would help her. Homeopathy had helped cure Robert's biliousness, but he had had to give up wine. "Oh—if it were not for my contradictory drug which I cant do without," she lamented more than once. Homeopathy particularly appealed to her, for "I have a profound disbelief in the power & knowledge of medical men." Who was more an expert than she? "Such heaps of new drugs &—old, as I took when I was ill. Drops here, pills there—& so many bread crumbs in effect, as Robert observed. The medical art is the merest blindguessing, I am certain. Homeopathy is a road broken in the right direction, though one cant always travel by it, when under previous obligations as I am."

The contemporary reader can't help wondering what might have happened if, even at this late point in her life, the poet had been able to go through a slow withdrawal from morphine and been able to substitute for it proper food and exercise. Would that have been homeopathy enough? This is not to contradict the poet's notion that her morphine kept her alive. It had in effect kept her heart from bursting out of her chest, and it very well might have had a beneficial effect on her damaged lungs. As brave as she was at facing the truth once she saw it, her elixir had had the ability to bring her relief and sleep—for over forty years.

Returning from Rome, she found herself "under previous obligations" and stuck to her morphine and her travels. Even if she increased doses of both, the prescription was wearing thin. And luck was not with her.

That June of 1860, in a weakened physical state, she received the first hint of another personal tragedy. From Florence she wrote to both of her sisters, who were in London. But Henrietta was not there on holiday; she was there to consult good doctors. "Dearest Henrietta & Arabel, I see you both together,—and a word dropped by Arabel shows me Henrietta not well, suffering pain." The cause of the pain was hinted at in a way that allowed Elizabeth to connect it with some type of gynecological problem "very common in these latter days." Quiet and cheerfulness were necessary, wrote the older sister, advice once more keeping fear at bay. Henrietta should get a nursery governess to take care of her children for a few months. Rest was what she needed. "I am sure my dearest Henrietta should lie on a sofa all day & not walk or stand—isn't that so?" The prescription would suit someone who was attempting to avoid a miscarriage. Perhaps that was what Elizabeth was led to believe. At the same time, the youngest brother, Occy, and his wife, Charlotte, had just had "their new joy." That Henrietta didn't wait until after the child's delivery before going up to London to consult the doctors signified that she must have been quite ill. "Although, after all, no one can help a woman very much in that hour, it always seems to me." Ironically, that same Charlotte would die in childbirth a few years later.

Ba had at this first hint of her sister's illness a dark presentiment. She knew her own anxiety caused her to exaggerate and blacken her feelings, but still this news of Henrietta's seeing doctors in London made her feel once more "as if there was a stone around my neck somehow." Robert attempted to reassure her, but wondered if she was self-willed in her worry. At every whisper as well as every crisis since her father's death, she had, against her own intentions, looked toward despair.

Henrietta, for whose birth the slaves in Jamaica did not get a half holiday (as they would have, had Henry been born), was only three years younger than Elizabeth. She had always been the outgoing sister, the one who had taken risks. She had been prettier, healthier, more lighthearted than the others. Her older sister had been close to death most of her life. Henrietta's younger sister, Arabel, worked hard for others at the Ragged Schools and suffered from pain in the face—perhaps a neuralgia—as well as breathing difficulties that resembled Elizabeth's as she grew older. The middle sister was caught between Art and Piety on either side and ill health on both and had skipped out to the country to lead her own normal life. She had a good marriage, three children, though her cousin Surtees, who had courted her with such steady persistence, seemed not to have gotten the select commissions he had wanted. The family did not have much money. They had their life. And they had absolutely no intention of giving their daughter to Aunt Arabel, no matter how favorable the economics. With Henrietta, healthy, lively, perhaps not as deeply reflective as her two sisters, Elizabeth had been able to share all of her maternal advice, pouring it out to her married sister in letter after letter. A specialty was the evils of too much childhood education. Henrietta's oldest boy, Altham, who would become Pen's friend, had been taught to count to a hundred, whereas Pen had to make his way past mother to father to imitate that feat. Altham was sent to school, was made to memorize, was taken out of baby hats too early . . . Neither sister would live long enough to see the result of her system.

But just the thought of Henrietta going first! In any large family it's typical for each child to have a role. Henrietta's role certainly wasn't to get sick. It was easy to take for granted Arabel's duteous and pious nature. She'd work herself to death. One understood, as well, Ba's fortitude, her resilience against all odds, her eccentric poet's temperament, her stubbornness. What did one take for granted about Henrietta? Her normal domesticity, her life!

Back once more in Siena the summer after her health and her relationship with Sophie crumbled, Elizabeth's sadness turned to morbid self-accusation. And any normal happiness was interrupted by the thought that at that very moment her sister might be in pain. Ba, unlike the fortunate Arabel, could not nurse Henrietta. Convinced not to go to England in her own weak state of health, she saw herself as completely useless. The only power she had was "at the end of my pen."

And by now the author of *Aurora Leigh* held her poetry against herself. Praise was abhorrent. "Thanks from a stranger for this or that have sounded ghastly to me who can't go to smooth a pillow for my darling sister. Now, I *won't* talk of it any more." And she didn't. She went on to Italian politics, spiritual concerns, the blessed quiet and lack of society in Siena outside of the Storys, Isa Blagden, and Landor. The struggle for balance, for Christian optimism, continued. But she did not see anyone; she stayed home. She told George to tell Henrietta that "I am with you in my soul, in my power of loving & suffering." And she gave advice. "One thing is clear," that "to lull the pain she *must* take opiates—because pain does *actual* harm—wears out the memory system. Sometimes the narcotic in a pill agrees less than in a liquid state—which is the case with me always. Then morphine agrees better than opium—Has she tried morphine?"

As for Robert, when he was not tending his wife or Pen or the octogenarian Walter Savage Landor, or Wilson, or socializing with his small group of reachable friends—he rode.

In October, when the Brownings returned to Florence, the waiting for news on Henrietta's obviously deteriorating condition became unbearable, although Ba snatched at the one small light—that at the time Henrietta's pain had lessened. But still, as she had written to Euphrasia Fanny Haworth in August, "an internal tumour," which the London medical man called " 'an anxious case.' We all know what that must mean." On November 17, Robert wrote to William Story in Rome that he had just received the "worst news" about his sister-in-law, and he had decided to leave Florence at once. The end was in sight, "& what the effect would be on Ba, of mental & physical suffering together, you may imagine—so I am determined to get her off tomorrow." He told his wife it was her duty to go to Rome before it became too cold to travel, keeping back the even colder news. The trip was meant to alleviate her mental state more than her physical state, to give her close to a week without a chance of a letter.

They arrived in Rome to no news. Mail was misdirected. Things were chaotic. Any day now the Pope's last city could join the rest of Italy in a burst of gunfire. It was not until December 3 that the Brownings received George's notice that Henrietta Moulton Barrett Cook had died on November 23, 1860. On their very first trip to Rome the Brownings had been greeted, within twenty-four hours, by the death of young Joseph Story. Now they were once more greeted by death. Henrietta left a grieving husband—one who loved her to the point of always considering her in spirit and liveliness eighteen—and three children younger than Pen Browning, who was in his eleventh year.

The dark veil of depression that the poet fought less and less successfully all summer came down over her head. On her honeymoon trip, Frank Mahony had complained of how she put down her veil before meeting him, the famous Father Prout. If she had seen next to no one in Siena, she saw no one in Rome. Robert kept the world, even Pen, at bay. As much as she loved her child, one finds no indication that she felt she had to stay alive for him. She felt less and less that she contributed to his life.

Robert watched as she turned inward. He kept telling her she should go out, that this isolation should not last. She kept agreeing with him. Only she didn't move from her apartment on Via Felice— Happiness Street. Her inability not to grieve devastated her. She became more and more convinced that her grasp of her faith was shallow and that she was unworthy.

She had written to Arabel almost a year after the death of her father: "Did I tell you ever that cheerfulness was a christian duty? I should rather have said, (if I did not say) that it is the proof of a higher spiritual life, I think so still. So much I think so, I would compound for less knowledge as the price of it. I would rather be mistaken in dogma, than downcast as a habit of mind. I think this is *always* a proof of a low spiritual state and a reason for looking back to see where the life has been wrong or the tenets unscriptural. I think that if we can't do God's work cheerfully in this world, we shall not do it cheerfully in the next."

Not only her Christianity but spiritualism enforced this faith. "You know I don't believe in any sudden dropping at death into joy or pain. After death, After death, [*sic*] there is the continuance as well as consequence of the life here. If Christ has not redeemed us, He never will. If we are born again here, the new life has begun in us already—and if we do not like *that* here, it is a bad sign. This is my persuasion."

The persuasion ran deep. When Sophie Eckley's sister died, Ba wrote to Sophie from the Casa Guidi, "She is nearer you, you *know*, than she would be if alive. Do not disturb her where she is, by unreasonable sadness,—but rather by faith & assurance draw her 'nearer & nearer.' And still nearer, till the re-union for ever." And as for Sophie's duty to her husband and her son: "You must put the light in the old house windows for them, & not let them lose their way in the wood."

But the poet was no longer able to light her own way.

Generally a wry yet cheerful quality prevailed in her letters. But the unpublished letters to her sister Arabel document the private story. Browning often tried to shield her from the writing of letters when he felt they were harmful to her health, and the tone of the letters she wrote to Arabel in December 1860 after Henrietta's death suggests they were written in solitude. Her handwriting became progressively

EBB WITH "BRO" AND HENRIETTA (CA.1818) *oil by William Artaud (top), and* HOPE END, *a photograph of the siblings' childhood home (bottom). By 1860 the past was a ghostly memory for Elizabeth Barrett Browning. After the death of her sister Henrietta, she could not regain her Christian optimism in the way she had after the death of Bro.*

longer and sloppier as she wrote. Some parts were scratched out and some written over, oddities in her correspondence. All her letters were spontaneous conversations, heart-to-heart. These were tinged with morphine.

The loose handwriting hadn't the spidercrawl of death upon it, as it had in Florence during the illness that brought on her decline. She seemed to be getting high as she wrote. "There is pressure from within" for her to write to her sister. "I think of you, oh I think of you. As you said, we are drawn closer together, Arabel." This did not mean that the bond with Henrietta had slackened. "She is only in the next room—though for me I cannot see her or hear her—others might." As her handwriting degenerated, she remembered the onset of her anxiety about Henrietta: "Dear, I was frightened through all that illness—from the beginning—that little light soft hint you gave pierced me through like a knife. And Robert thought me foolish & that I really did *want* some evil to cry about." Robert "did not understand. And then besides, because he loves me it was anxiety about me, he struggled to present the bright side of things."

She regretted not having gone to England to be with Henrietta, though Robert told her "it is quite wrong of me to be sorry that I did not go. He would have let me go if I had persisted—only he would have deeply disapproved, he says—and I was influenced by his opinion & yours too—Now I can't help feeling some bitterness about it—only *that's* foolish of course. But all our grief is foolish, if we could see aright."

The problem was that the poet could not see aright. Her deep Christian faith, her reading of Swedenborg, and her belief in the spirits convinced her that Henrietta "is as in the next room—that the change too, is not great. There are so many things I believe which are comforting—And yet, *or* how it is." Here she stumbled as she re-created her feelings: "It is like some precious wine poured into an ill-tempered cup—this cup of my nature—and the moment this is set down to the fire—cup breaks—wine runs out."

High and distraught, she testified to her moral weakness. "Because I am so unworthy Arabel—the word is made for me—'I believe—help—my disbelief.'" Earlier in December, when her erratic handwriting also showed the effect of the morphine, she had written, "I am very unworthy. You know I was always. I believe in the spiritual, but the mortal takes hold of me & strangles me. Robert says I am put to shame sometimes by the Theodore Parker people who believe in the voice of God within them only—not in our Lord Christ's, and yet manage to keep up in face of great disasters."

She could not find the comfort her faith should offer, her Christian optimism. Something must be lacking in her. Something must be wrong in her life or in the tenets of her beliefs.

"Dearest dear, I ought not to name myself—but if you knew what the last three weeks or more have been to me—what that journey was—Looking back it seems as if the blood of my heart MUST be left in stains on the stones of the road. Here it is all very still—And Robert takes care of me, & keeps away every face, & I am much, much better through his tenderness. I helped Peni to prepare his Latin testament for the Abbé today—so you may see how well I am."

Yet she herself was the precious wine pouring out of her broken spirit as she asked her questions: "Did the illness come on suddenly as it seemed to me? When she went to London was there alarm? I dig into the dark with my poor heart in wondering at these things. Did she never speak to the children—in reference to what was coming." She had been more specific in another letter: "Tell me one thing. Was it *cancer*—? did *she* think *it* would end so from the beginning? did nobody give much hope?"

While her handwriting seemed to be suffering extra strain, she again wrote while she was alone. She had been able to keep a thought still in her head, she told Arabel, "Which proves that I am not quite base & suicidal, eating my own poisoned heart because I will." If Robert were not out, "he would send his true love. He was very much touched by your words about him—yes touched to tears. He loves you dearly. He said he would do more for you than for his own sister—and I believe it."

As for Elizabeth, she had always had a very special love for Arabel, and she asked Arabel to love her and pray for her before her handwriting, perhaps along with that thought she was holding, became indistinct.

In another letter to Arabel, Elizabeth sent her the one thing that had helped her grief since Henrietta's death. It was an abstract from a letter she had received from Harriet Beecher Stowe. Without having any idea of Henrietta's death, the author of *Uncle Tom's Cabin* wrote about the solace she had just received from having contacted the spirit of her own dead son. "It did me more good (her letter did) than anything which has happened, & so I couldn't hold it for myself though to you it may probably seem a pure piece of insanity." One doubts Arabel forwarded it to her brother-in-law, as Elizabeth had suggested.

"You will not have liked my last letter perhaps—you don't feel with me in some things! It might be wise to be silent, but I love you so that I can't keep out of sight points which lie habitually near in me to the region of love." It had been the first letter she received from Stowe, and "it struck me as at least a strange coincidence that she should have been impelled just now & just in such terms to write me this letter." Add to that, she'd just heard from Mr. Jarves in America. She took both as signs: "It looks as if it were meant that I should take comfort and I do take it."

She rose up to meet her faith: "I think that some of it came thus Arabel—that in the first shock, we get distracted." We "cant disengage our feelings from the earth—I hope it has been more a stupidity of mind than anything else in me, & that as the eye sees clearer it makes no tears." For certainly we would be able "to communicate if the defect were not in *us*."

Meanwhile, "I have seen nobody yet—which Robert says is wrong & must end—& of course must—but here in Rome if one opens one's door, one opens it to everybody. The quiet has been the best thing for me. Now I read. Reading is so part of my life that I suffer horribly when I dont read. The soul eats itself."

A few weeks later she received a letter from Surtees which Robert absolutely would not allow her to read. "He says it is a sort of letter which must have done good to the writer—full of the deepest tenderness & grief—but that it would simply 'tear me to pieces' & he can't consent to give it to me. I resisted & entreated for some time—It looked like a selfishness & want of love to be spared so—But Robert was positive. He said there was nothing new. . . . Therefore he must oppose himself to my being exposed to fruitless agitation. For me, I am sick of being 'spared' & useless." So useless was she that she had allowed all letters about Henrietta's illness, from the beginning, to be filtered through her husband. She blamed herself for her weakness—was it lack of love to need to be spared so? As she had written to Arabel earlier, "If I could envy you whom I love so, *anything* Arabel, it is your bitter melancholy life of the last five months—What a thing to look back on? You helped what a human being could—you were there—you saw the last. There is a deep pure benediction over you &

in you—& you have it as a joy forever." The ink here was blotched. By tears from the sister writing or by the sister reading these words?

"Have you thought at all . . . of taking little dear Mary?" Ba asked Arabel in another letter. "For the child's sake. I feel the propriety of it strongly, and I can't help believing that he [Surtees] will yield soon. His own mother will press it on him—for women understand such things better than men." Victorian women, apparently. "I can't write of those children—my heart & eyes fill."

By February 1861 Arabel had decided to return Emma to her parents. Keeping her had been "a mistake from the first, you will be right in being decided at last & not renewing. If you had been very fond of the child & acted out of the fulness of your inclination instead of things being pressed on you, it would have been different. . . . But to be called to the duties & responsibilities of a mother without a mother's love is hard. . . . At the same time . . . I cant blame the parents for being extremely disappointed—I am sorry for them & for the child." Still, Arabel must stand firm: "hold yourself free to receive Mary." Surtees Cook, however, would never give his daughter up.

As for herself: "I am pretty well & I eat & I drink." This time the "hysterical choking" that came from her inability to cry had lessened, she had earlier told her sister, so in a sense she was forced to eat. Still, "I am little contented with myself indeed. It seems to me that I am not earnest earnest enough to get the right good out of anything." The repetition of the word *earnest* which ended one line and began the next is a rare repetition found in the long correspondence. When Oscar Wilde wrote *The Importance of Being Earnest,* he played with more than a given name. He spoofed the Victorian emphasis on spiritual earnestness—the ultimate soundness of the individual's faith and the worthiness of her soul. "I feel right for a moment & then let the feeling go. Pray for me to believe better & hold fast more."

An earnest Christian, particularly one who incorporated into Christianity Swedenborgian and spiritualistic beliefs, would hear her sister in the next room. She could not. She felt she had been soul-to-soul with her sister, feeling her pain in Siena as Henrietta suffered in London. But after her sister's death, she could no longer locate her. Neither could she see people, move from her chair, from her room, get on with her life.

In Elizabeth Barrett Browning's letters to Arabel, in the handwriting, in the morphine highs, and in the tortured conscience, one sees the depth of the poet's pain. *"As for me,* I'm made of brown paper & tear at a touch."

But she never ceased to struggle against depression. "Sometimes one gets self disgusted & rolls oneself in the dust," she wrote to Arabel, "—but with me it's chiefly when I am tired (from one rough reason or other) of sitting up. Sometimes I feel as if I had ever so much light on my face & saw more than most people—& that's not humility—is it? What vexes me again is, that light or not I stumble & fall, as certainly as others whom I have taken on myself to call blind." In this letter from Rome, perhaps in February 1861, she encouraged her sister to "go to the Strattens" to moderate her own mourning. For "Nothing is more true to me than that *gloom* is an immoral thing . . . and as to solitude, I *know* it to be full of temptation." She gave Arabel her best advice: "Dancing is better for the soul than fasting, I believe."

WE *KNOW* EACH OTHER

THERE IS NO DOUBT that Robert Browning was a man who nurtured others. Look at his care of Robert Lytton during his illness, his guardianship of Walter Savage Landor. The care he took of John Kenyon when he could. Also in London he had been very solicitous of Lady Elgar and helped to feed her after her stroke. The shadow side of this need to be of use to those he loved would later fall on his son, on whom he would try to impose his own standards. He would try to "help" Pen to become the British gentleman Pen didn't want to be. He never tried to help his wife be anything other than herself.

And concurrently, in those days, he stayed himself. He could not bank a fire warm enough to dispel depression; what he could do—of an anxious temperament himself—was try his best not to fall into gloom as well. Though he had once told the woman he loved that he was sick of society and wanted nothing more than to stay by her side day and night, he had found society again, particularly in Rome and in the cool shadows of Bellosguardo where Isa Blagden held court. Robert Browning, even in the dark final days, lived his own life.

Elizabeth was very grateful for this. She was no Sophia Eckley, needing to know why a note wasn't written, or why the person she loved had other friends or accepted other gifts. There was none of that self-serving possessiveness which Robert once parodied as many couples' idea of love. What Browning's social life meant for her was that during these desolate spells of isolation and struggle, she had one less thing to punish herself about.

But what did Browning's social life mean to Browning? He was almost fifty years old in 1860 and had written no new poetry for five years. He knew his wife was comparing him with Tennyson, who worked on a daily schedule. Did he still consider himself a poet? When he looked back over his marriage, what did he see? As a younger man he had taken the greatest risk of his life. He had married a woman from a wealthy family, a poet of reputation, an invalid, and brought her to Italy without thought of the repercussions to him had she died en route. The one vulnerability of their early marriage was that people would say—and they did say—that he was living off his wife. The Brownings were no more in the class of the Barretts in England than the Tittles had been in Jamaica. It could not be lost on him that he had run off with the great-granddaughter of Edward of Cinnamon Hill. He had since his marriage executed all of the duties entailed with grace and compassion. "And knowing this, is love, and love is duty."

In the early years of the marriage, still learning from the woman and poet who, like Dante's Beatrice, was there to show him the way, he had given up playwriting. He had concentrated on his dramatic monologues, wherein his fame would lie, in her opinion. He had summed up all the lived life of the first half of that marriage in two volumes of poetry that were, in both Brownings' opinion, clear this time. But complexity was the very root of Browning's genius. What he took from life he examined from every angle, and he found in his men and women objective correlatives for ideas and emotions which could be quite raw in his life. For example, knowing he hated Daniel Dunglas Home (and Sophia Eckley) in life has made some critics assume he hated the American medium Sludge in verse. In fact, he was as fair to Home as he said he was to Cardinal Wiseman when he used him as a prototype for Blougram. In "Mr. Sludge, 'The Medium' " he saw more than Home; he saw the type and how the type related to time and place. He was able to detach in poetry, see things whole, beyond the limitations of his own ego. The impetus to the creation of a character might be loathing and hate, but an artist cannot hate his or her created character. The complexities of *Men and Women* were beyond the grasp of narrow England at first, though America understood what was different, what was new.

Still, from the age of forty-five until his wife's death, when he was fifty, he may have sketched out ideas, but he hardly wrote poetry. In Florence he attended life-drawing classes. Weekly he took a good long look at naked flesh. His wife was in such ill health during these years and Pen was sleeping in their room—it seems probable that there was a curtailment in their sexual life. But not in Browning's sensual life. In the last year in Rome he sculpted every day with William Wetmore Story at the latter's studio. The fleshy, the sensual, the delights of the eye—those were the exquisite pleasures Italy had to offer the Englishman. By now the Brownings had decided to stay in Italy, had in fact almost bought a villa in Florence toward the end. If it hadn't been for the cold winters, they would have.

If his countrymen had recognized *Men and Women,* perhaps he would have had the inspiration to keep on writing, believing as his wife did that what he saw in Italy was accessible to all men and women. As it was, the inspiration that acceptance can fuel was not forthcoming. He needed Egypt, Jerusalem. He made his wife swear they would travel—at least to Egypt. But that was not to be—nor did he, after her death, go without her.

What of the early romantic love had proved illusion for him? They weren't writing poetry together every day. And after *Poems before Congress* neither was writing. His aim had been to learn from his wife constantly. Yet there were many things he could teach her about the true nature of certain people. Only her Barrett stubbornness was as strong as she had warned him in her second letter. There was no saving his wife from her erroneous opinions—or her temperament or, finally, from her father. At fifty he couldn't do what he thought he had done at thirty-three—save her life.

And at fifty he might have appeared to himself what he later tried to keep his son from becoming—something of a dilettante. Sketching, modeling, playing the piano, discoursing with his friends, not to mention some high-spirited antics late at night.

He could look back at his marriage and see that things had not worked out as he and Ba had envisioned.

He was still dapper: "Robert is looking remarkably well and young—in spite of all lunar lights in his hair," Elizabeth wrote to her sister-in-law at the end of March 1861 from Rome. "He is not thin or worn, as I am—no indeed—and the women adore him everywhere far too much for decency. In my own opinion he is infinitely handsomer and more attractive than when I saw him first, sixteen years ago— which does not mean as much as you may suppose, that I myself am superannuated and wholly anile, and incompetent therefore for judgement. No, indeed, I believe people in general would think the same exactly."

Still, she wished he were writing rather than sculpting. "But Robert waits for an inclination," so the "active occupation" of modeling "is salvation to him with his irritable nerves, saves him from ruminating bitter cud, and from the process which I call beating his dear head against the wall till it is bruised, simply because he sees a fly there, magnified by his own two eyes almost indefinitely into some Saurian monster." The truth is, "He has an enormous superfluity of vital energy, and if it isn't employed, it strikes its fangs into him. He gets out of spirits as he was at Havre. [She knew what he tried to keep from her.] Nobody understands why—except me who am in the inside of him and hear him breathe. For the peculiarity of our relation is, that even when he's displeased with me, he thinks aloud with me and can't stop himself. And I know ultimately that whatever takes him out of a certain circle (where habits of introversion and analysis of fly-legs are morbidly exercised) is life and joy to him."

She understood Robert to the extent that she lived inside of him and heard him breathing. Robert was no less reticent to tell his brother-in-law George: "I shall only say that Ba and I know each other for time and, I dare trust, eternity:—We differ *toto coelo* (or rather, *inferno*) as to spirit-rapping, we quarrel sometimes about politics, and estimate people's characters with enormous difference, but, in the main, we *know* each other, I say."

That was the pride of their years of love. Whatever had altered, trust had not. They breathed with each other's breath. At the beginning they saw the other as a brilliant poet, an amazing intellect, a compassionate and strangely similar heart. They learned their differences through the years. Neither gave over to the other. Each remained a complex and thrilling person. An exciting person to know, a different person to know. As early as December 1851, Ba wrote to Arabel about her and Robert's disagreement about Napoleon: "You know I do think for myself (if the thought is right or wrong) and I do speak the truth (as I am capable of apprehending it) to my husband always. Also, we agree absolutely always on the principles of things—& therefore it is, that what you used to call 'our quarrelling' is an element of our loving one another, & a very important element too."

No wonder they were so proud to proclaim their knowledge to their in-laws. To know each other on the other side of the moon was for each the accomplishment of their love. They didn't say they knew what was best for each other. Ba might have wanted Robert to write, but she knew that was what Ba wanted, not Robert. And Robert might have wanted Ba to admit that Home was a fraud, but suppose after his death Ba were to make "a present of the £4000 to Mr. Hume, the day after receiving it,—what then? Could I prevent her?"

Mrs. Jameson had died in 1860, another sadness for the Brownings. She had always argued against the impractical nature of poets— and that they certainly shouldn't marry each other. But the Brownings never tried to create the other in his or her image. They were far away from the marriage of David and Sophia Eckley—a marriage that ended in bitterness.

Their true accomplishment? Knowing each other as each was, not as each would like the other to be. And being proud of and trusting that holy knowledge right to the end.

Many a critic appears ready to punish the couple for not having lived happily ever after, but having lived real lives. Without comment, in *Robert Browning: A Portrait,* Betty Miller ended her section on the "Death of Elizabeth" with this quote:

" 'The general impression of the past,' wrote Robert Browning a few years later, 'is as if it had been pain. I would not live it over again, not one day of it. Yet all that seems my real *life,*—and before and after, nothing at all: I look back on all my life, when I look *there*: and life is painful. I always think of this when I read the Odyssey—Homer makes the surviving Greeks, whenever they refer to Troy, just say of it, "At Troy, where the Greeks suffered so." Yet all their life was in that ten years at Troy.' "

Yes, life had been painful. His mother's death; his own questioning, nervous temperament; the lawsuit against his father; money worries; the constant responsibilities of marriage and fatherhood; the failure of his best poetry; Ba's relationship with Sophia Eckley; the long, sad decline and loss of the woman who was the great love of his life . . .

But what we can glimpse of the other side of the moon is much more compelling. After all, what was so extraordinary in the Brownings' marriage was that these two complex individuals both believed the years they spent in Italy together, her last years and his middle years, were the only years in which they really lived. Daring to marry secretly and to leave England to fend for themselves, they had actually brought each other to life.

La Vita Nuova

IT WAS CLEAR to Robert Browning that his wife was in decline. In Rome that last season she did absolutely nothing—only went out for three or four short drives during the six months they were there, and never walked two steps out of her room. Her dosage of morphine increased; movement triggered depression.

The photo of her with Pen in Rome in 1860 showed her as she was toward the end, her lips stretched long, resembling a smile, her head tilted to the side, her look knowing. The broad leathery face, the wide lips, the skin tight over the bones . . . She didn't look her fifty-four years; she didn't look ill as much as she looked somehow preserved, encapsulated. She believed she had the blood of West Africa in her. In this picture, next to her long-haired fairy prince of a son, her unidealized, exotic features are captured, contrasting sharply with her hooped skirt and her silly curls.

In the London winter of 1846, now so long ago, random luck had championed the lovers. The unusual springlike weather allowed Elizabeth Barrett the time she needed to regain her health. It had been a period of "lovers' luck" when not only had the elements favored the couple but their visits continued without interruption by the curious or by the vindictive. And after their marriage, the first anniversary was celebrated by the Italians striking out for liberty underneath their very windows.

If the trip to Rome in 1860–61 brought with it the personal loss of a sister, the trip back to Florence brought with it a tragedy for all Italians, who were now so close to unity. On June 5, 1861, on the Brownings' first day back in Florence, Camillo Benso di Cavour, the great diplomat and architect of a unified Italy, died at the height of his power at fifty years of age, after a short, violent illness.

CAMILLO BENSO DI CAVOUR (1810–61), *at the Congress of Paris in 1856, the architect of the Italian Risorgimento, the great diplomat of the House of Savoy. His sudden death was another mortal blow to EBB.*

    This great Piedmontese statesman was worth any amount of Barrett Browning's praise. Cavour was born in 1810, the younger son of an old and illustrious Absolutist family. From his academy days through his stint in the military, both his parents complained that his liberal views and liberal friendships were destroying them. At eighteen he wrote to his older brother words that are reminiscent of Barrett Browning's autobiographical essay when she was just fifteen: "I would die a thousand times for my country or for the good of the human race." However, the future diplomat appended, "if I believed it would truly benefit it." A short and plump man, he was round-faced as a youth. By the end of his life he had a dark receding hairline and graying whiskers that outlined his face and met under his strong chin. This gave his weighty face an oblong cast. His round spectacles seemed wedged between overhanging brows and pronounced cheekbones, and they magnified narrowed, questioning, very clear eyes. Clarity was a part of Cavour's genius. He knew exactly what he wanted: liberty for Italy under a constitutional monarch from the House of Savoy. His diplomatic skills allowed him to examine the possibilities inherent in any political situation, no matter how volatile and unpredictable, to see in what ways it could be turned toward this goal. He had negotiated brilliantly with Napoleon. He had been indispensable to King Victor Emmanuel II, and to Italian hopes.

Along with the Brownings and much of liberal Europe, he realized that the hopes for Italy were with Piedmont, just as Barrett Browning predicted at the end of *Casa Guidi Windows*. To follow Mazzini's Republican rhetoric and demand revolution all through the peninsula was to court anarchy and ultimate suppression. Had he, rather than Elizabeth Barrett Browning, represented Italy at the Congress that never materialized, he, too, would have shouted (or skillfully negotiated) "for France and Savoy!"

Now, "the head of Cavour," which had steered "the heart of a King," was past thinking for Italy. Elizabeth wrote to her sister-in-law, "If tears or blood could have saved him to us, he should have had mine. I feel yet as if I could scarcely comprehend the greatness of the vacancy. A hundred Garibaldis for such a man. There is a hope that certain solutions had been prepared between him and the Emperor, and that events will slide into their grooves. May God save Italy."

The Italian patriot and the Brownings' friend Massimo d'Azeglio had a similar reaction, as quoted by Cavour's biographer: " 'Poor Cavour!' wrote Massimo d'Azeglio amid his tears, 'I realize how much I loved him. I might well enough have died, who am no longer of any use. These two days past I seem to be dreaming, and I pray God to aid Italy; and one idea has at last given me a little calm. If Providence wishes to save Italy—and I believe it does—it will save her even without Cavour.' "

Immediately on Cavour's death Napoleon III officially recognized the Kingdom of Italy—a solution Barrett Browning predicted. But would Italy stay together? Would the Veneto and Rome be won without Cavour?

In Florence after this dreadful blow, Elizabeth kept to her rooms. She did not leave the Casa Guidi nor did Robert urge her to go out. He did suggest that she take the air and exercise indoors. "Our terrace is green with quite high trees—daturas & others—& the smell of lemon

blossom comes through the open window," she wrote to Arabel in July
1857. And Sophia Peabody Hawthorne recalled that the first time she
met the Brownings, Robert offered her a pomegranate from the tree on
the terrace. In the first years of their marriage, the Brownings would
go to the long and narrow terrace of the Casa Guidi and walk up and
down, talking for hours at a time under the stars. Now, when Robert
suggested that his wife get up and walk up and down one time to commemorate those days, Elizabeth made an attempt to get from her chair
to the window, but could not.

Robert would mark his wife's decline from the Peace of Villafranca
and the illness that attended it. The six-month trial of "daily waiting
for news from Henrietta" and then Henrietta's death "rendered her
weaker—weaker—she did *nothing* at Rome . . . yet, on the other hand,
her cheerfulness . . . made everyone say 'how wonderfully she recov-
ers,—she will soon be strong again, another *quiet* summer and *then.*' "
Cavour's death hammered another nail into inevitability.

Isa Blagden, Our Lady of Bellosguardo, was a saint to the Brown-
ings during these scorching June days. She went back and forth from
Bellosguardo to Casa Guidi, staying with Elizabeth at times, helping
Robert, and taking care of Pen.

Elizabeth's isolation seemed to be having the desired effect. But
the hot weather affected her health in a new way. She told her husband,
"My cough has got well at once, as is always the way in such weather,
but, curiously, it begins to affect me, as usual." Browning's response to
this sign of pulmonary illness was "Let us go at once." They began to
talk of where they would spend the summer. The choice would be
made according to the requirements of Elizabeth's health. The very
conversation, like so many in the past, might have stirred hope. The
old reliable prescription.

There were clues in notes to a letter she didn't finish to Ruskin
that she may have been resolving some spiritual issues at the time.
Ruskin had been writing to her of his own crisis of faith. His letter of
May 13, 1861, struck a sympathetic note. He told her: "I am fighting
through all kinds of doubt and wonder: and have no strength—cannot
look things in the face." She had asked him for a photograph. "You
shant have anything of the kind." When he looked at his own face, "I
can't conceive why I'm so ugly, but I *am* so ugly." He had lost his belief
in his church; his friends had deserted him. "I am stunned—palsied—
utterly helpless—under the weight of finding out the myriad errors

that I have been taught about these things: every reed that I have leant on shattering itself joint from joint—I stand, not so much Melancholy as Amazed."

Elizabeth understood his difficulty, but she had escaped the shock of the "myriad errors" of Christian doctrine. "It is because the bonds of some traditions of religious teaching were loosened in me formerly & gradually during my long sequestration from the external communion of churches. I have long seen that the foundations of all the visible churches were giving way . . . that the scholastic forms which contain essential truths were splitting into atoms . . That an oak planted in a flower pot must shatter the vessel, if it lived & grew; that if Christianity were a vital principle it must develop." Why, her spiritualism was based on this development.

Ruskin was caught at a juncture where he could not tailor new clothes for his beliefs. Even "the greatest physical science discovery . . . since Newton's time," maybe "the greatest of all time," that the "Sun's made half of iron," couldn't divert him from his troubles for more than a moment. Perhaps he'd go somewhere in Switzerland and "grow currant bushes & red daisies," spend his days walking and digging "till I've recovered tone of mind." He had "a horrible feeling just now of having no home."

The poet responded, "Your sad letter drew me into a sad sympathy for you. Seeming to myself to see more clearly than you say you do, and feeling certainly a stronger cheerfulness . . ." A stronger cheerfulness.

On June 20, Robert went out to read the newspapers at about six or seven o'clock in the early evening, and Isa Blagden came to stay with Elizabeth. It had been another hot day; the windows had been shut—Italian fashion—to keep out the heated air. In the hours before twilight, however, as the sun waned, there was usually a breeze in the air that accompanied the even light and the chirping of birds that are hallmarks of those hours. The windows of the Casa Guidi were opened to let the breeze in.

During these early evenings it was usual for the poet to have a chair placed for her in the doorway between the rooms to catch the cross-drafts. Isa argued against it, but Elizabeth said, "Oh, the cushion at the back of the chair prevents my suffering."

Browning came in from his newspaper room, and the three had tea. Then his wife remarked, "I think I have a sore throat."

The next day seemed ordinary, although Elizabeth told Robert she

JOHN RUSKIN, SELF-
PORTRAIT. *Ruskin believed
that portraiture was good for
art if the man it portrayed
was virtuous. In the early
1860s, he suffered from a
crisis of faith and lost many
of his friends, but not EBB,
to whom he could confide his
despair in intimate detail.*

had a cold. That night the coughing began to become serious, and she
was restless and sat up often. In the morning, when Browning wasn't
with her, she took two "Cooper's pills" to prevent the attack she
thought imminent. Again, nothing unusual happened during the day,
but she was so sick toward night that she asked her husband for a blister to be applied and some wine, for the congestion in her chest. The
"Cooper's pills," the mixture of half stout and half porter to which she
didn't often resort, seemed to have too much of an effect. At ten in the
evening Browning ran to the chemist's for the blister, applied it,
poured the wine. By one o'clock in the morning her sufferings intensified; there was an accumulation of phlegm that she could not cough
up. Browning left her with Annunziata, the servant who had long
since replaced Wilson, dressed, and ran to Dr. Wilson, a physician who
had a reputation for maladies of the chest. With great difficulty
Browning aroused the porter and the doctor, who followed him back to
the Casa Guidi. By now Elizabeth was worse, the congestion unre-

lieved. She labored to breathe. Dr. Wilson was a specialist. He wrote two prescriptions to go to two different chemists, and off into the night Browning and the porter of the Casa Guidi rushed. The poet returned, and a sinapism was put on his wife's breast and back while hot water and mustard were put on her feet. She didn't respond. The doctor stayed until five in the morning. Finally the attack was over, and hopes for her recuperation revived. Still, she had not slept for two nights, spending each "in violent exertion" attempting to breathe.

In the short days after this attack, Elizabeth would always report that the symptoms were "a little better." The doctor examined her carefully, however, and reported "with a very serious face, that one lung was condensed (the right) and that he suspected an abscess in it." Still, Dr. Wilson was aware of her history, of how she had for years pulled through. He couldn't predict what would happen, except to say, "It would require a long time to get well."

Browning sifted through these factors and told some of them to Elizabeth, who was well enough to have her own opinions, repeating them through his report. "It is the old story—they don't know my case—I have been tapped and sounded so, and condemned so, repeatedly: this time it is said the right is the affected lung while the left is free—Dr. Chambers said just the contrary. This is only one of my old attacks. I know all about it and I shall get better." Not only that, but this attack of asthma, Elizabeth told her husband, was not as bad as the one that brought them to Siena two summers ago. She'd get well. But most likely an abscess had already broken in her lung.

From then on, Browning carried his wife into the drawing room every day, where she sat in her nightgown in her own chair in the airiness of the room. "She read the newspapers, a little—saw nobody of course," and went to bed about seven. Browning sat up most nights; in the last week he remembered lying down by her only once, or perhaps it was twice. He was up so often to tend to her that he simply stopped going to bed. She didn't seem to notice. By then they had brought a small bed into the drawing room and put her in it and "she began to doze very much." But she dozed restlessly and seemed unaware that her husband was not in bed on a sofa behind her.

Dr. Wilson had prescribed nourishment, even wine, imitating in effect Frank Mahony's cure of years ago in these same rooms. "But Ba never could or would try to take solid nourishment: she had strong brodo (clear soup) but would take nothing else." It went on like this,

ELIZABETH AND PEN
BARRETT BROWNING,
*photograph by Alessandri;
Rome, 1860. "This is simply
to introduce Penini & me,"
EBB wrote to Arabel on June
14, 1860. "I don't please
myself, being vain {after} the
manner of women, & not being
pleased to look either black or
old. But it's made up to me in
Penini, even in the vanity.
He's lovely—isn't he—."*

ROBERT BROWNING, *photograph by
Alessandri; Rome, 1860. Browning had
said that there were no two pictures of him
that looked alike. His good state of health,
implemented by homeopathic cures, was in
sharp contrast to his wife's.*

twice a day his wife telling him she was feeling better, though the symptoms remained unfavorable. Though she could hardly speak anymore, she was as cheerful as ever. "It would be nothing," she repeatedly told Browning. A week after she sat in the cross-breeze and developed a sore throat, she drank some asses' milk with success. She had a better night, always with "much expectoration however, and her feet swelled a little." Robert allowed Isa Blagden to come and to kiss her. Elizabeth managed to whisper, "I am decidedly better," and Isa thought she was.

On Friday she seemed to rally, for not only did she take her asses' milk and brodo, but she had some bread and butter. Another positive indication: The Brownings began once more to discuss where they were going to live. The Casa Guidi had grown too small. They seemed to be clutching onto their lives as they realized that for both of them the Casa Guidi "had suddenly grown distasteful . . . noisy, hot, close—poor place we had liked for fourteen years!"

Robert said, "It would be best to take a Villa—you decide on Rome for the winter, and properly,—what good of coming in the summer to a town house you cannot stay in?"

She said, "Ah, but I can't leave Florence, I like Florence,—you would like to establish ourselves in Rome."

"No," Browning said, "there's Villa Niccolini, for instance—that would just suit."

"That would suit—try, enquire." She seemed so intent on his taking action immediately that he moderated.

"There's no hurry," he told his wife. "We can get in there at once if you like—and it will be just as cool as Siena, with the convenience of being near the city."

"Oh, that's not it—we must change the air now, that is my one chance,—I meant, that if you take it for three years you can send up our furniture and we can enter at once in it when we return next Spring."

It was her only chance. The woman who sublet the Casa Guidi so often, and was instrumental in not giving it up, was suddenly ready to flee as quickly as she could. The excited rush was light-headedness. Robert named it and Elizabeth agreed. She was having strange thoughts, she told her husband. And she was taking more morphine. Rather than the tricolored flags of Italy that lined the streets of Florence and that she portrayed in her poems, she now saw the reverse: Hungarian colors hung from the windows.

ELIZABETH BARRETT BROWNING, *May 27, 1861, photographed by Alessandri a month before her death. On June 11, 1861, she wrote to reassure Arabel concerning her health: "How I look like myself you will see by my photograph, sitting for which was my last wise act at Rome."*

When Isa Blagden came at eight on Friday, Elizabeth took up her glass and said, "Oh, I not only have asses' milk but asses' thoughts—I am so troubled with silly politics and nonsense."

Isa told her some of the good news of Bettino Ricasoli following Cavour and having the ability to deal with Napoleon. This interested Elizabeth so much that Robert had to impose. "No talking, come, go Isa," he said, and pushed her out.

Isa told him later that when his back was turned for a moment to pour out medicine, Elizabeth whispered, "Did you say Ricasoli said his politics were identical with those of Cavour, only they took different views of the best way of carrying them out?"

"Yes."

"Ah, so I thought."

Isa was pushed out, convinced her friend was getting better. The doctor confirmed it with "perhaps a little better." Then Elizabeth Romagnoli, Ba's once-devoted Wilson, came and stayed for a half hour while her former mistress readied herself for bed, brushing her own hair. Wilson left convinced she was better. But the other servants were sure that Wilson was "a bird of ill omen," and Pen got wind of this.

"Are you really better?" he asked his pet mama when he went to say goodnight to her.

"*Much* better."

He asked her the same question and received the same answer three times.

Browning and the doctor discussed Elizabeth's aversion to food. Robert had a very strong fowl jelly made and had it placed on ice in case his wife would have some during the night. She refused. Browning himself didn't know if the food would do her any good. "The weakness came from other causes, and *these* were important—the other could be easily got rid of."

He sat up with her Friday night. She took her medicine, her morphine, she coughed and dozed constantly. "If I spoke she looked, knew me, smiled, said she was better, and relapsed."

By three o'clock in the morning the dozing made him very uneasy. She said, "You did right not to wait—what a fine steamer—how comfortable!" It was the slightly increased dosage of the morphine acting on her weakened body, he thought.

Browning called for Annunziata and told her to get some hot water.

He sent the porter for the doctor. He told his wife to sit up, and she was able to do this with some help. He put her feet into the hot water. "Well, you do make an exaggerated case of it!" she said. But then she said, "My hands too," and put them in another basin of warm water.

Her husband asked her, "You know me?"

"Know *you*." She looked at him smilingly, happily. "My Robert, my treasure, my beloved." She kissed him and kissed him. "Our lives are held by God," she told him.

Robert's response was more of the earth. "Will you take jelly for my sake?" (She hated the jelly.)

"Yes."

He fed her a spoonful of it, then another. He poured some into a glass, and she drank it all.

She put her arms around her husband. "God bless you, God bless you," she kept repeating. And between this blessing she kissed him and kissed him, and when he laid her back down in the small bed, she continued to kiss the air with her lips and several times she lifted her own hands in front of her and kissed them.

Fear came over him. The intensity of this devotion—why at this moment, unless?

"Are you comfortable?" Browning asked.

"Beautiful."

Then she motioned to have the jelly wiped from her hands. Browning sponged her hands for her, and she slept. He knew it was the end. He felt he had to raise her. He took her in his arms, supported her head with his own, and felt the struggle and the cough begin and end without relieving her chest. A second abscess had broken, piercing her trachea. Yet there was no pain; there were no sighs, just a silent fight. Her head fell to his arm, and he thought she had fainted. But then there was the least knitting of her brows.

Four-thirty in the morning, June 29, 1861. Annunziata cried, "This blessed spirit has passed."

LEFT TO HIMSELF AT CASA GUIDI, his son under the care of Isa Blagden, Robert Browning re-created the death of his wife in a letter to Sarianna and his father. As he made arrangements for the funeral and the burial, he caught himself thinking, "I will ask Ba about that." On the day of the funeral he scarcely noticed that the shops on their street had closed for it and that the morning and evening Italian papers had been full of the news and the mourning. The coffin was allowed to be carried through the streets on its way to the Protestant cemetery, a singular honor. There were two crowns of laurel and white flowers on it. In a sort of flash at the grave site Robert saw Italian men crying like children. He recognized the poet Francesco Dall'Ongaro and the historian Pasquale Villari among the many. He went straight from the cemetery to Isa's villa—"and presently in the evening came the astonishing sight" of an unexpected comet that had "reached its nearest point to the earth on the *29th*," the day of Elizabeth's death, and now, on the night of her funeral, blazed "over half the sky." He saw the comet from the hills of Fiesole, aware that it was going off rapidly and that within a week or so it would be millions of miles away.

The Municipality of Florence would erect a tablet to Elizabeth on the Casa Guidi. Its Italian translated:

> *Here wrote and died*
> *Elizabeth Barrett Browning*
> *Who in her woman's heart reconciled*
> *A scholar's learning and a poet's spirit*
> *And whose poems forged a golden ring*
> *Between Italy and England*
> *Grateful Florence*
> *Sets this memorial*
> *1861*

A week after her death, Minister Ubaldino Peruzzi, one of the most respected men of the new Italy, called on Browning to tell him "the Italians all were anxious" he should not leave Florence and "that Pen might continue to be 'a Tuscan.' "

If Pen had to go for a year or two, he should come back. "We want those who were friends in our ill days to share in our coming good fortunes—every thing will be open to him!"

But Browning and his son were leaving. It was only after Browning had had Pen's hair cut, had dressed him as an ordinary boy, and was ready for the voyage that would lead him back to London that his delayed "paroxysm of grief" welled up. In front of Isa Blagden he found himself gasping uncontrollably, "I want her, I want her." Grief and rage, panic and surprise. "I want her."

PEN BROWNING *on his horse, Stella; Rome, May 1861.*
"Imagine his ecstasy Arabel when I told him that Robert has
actually bought the pretty Sardignian horse for him," EBB
wrote her sister from Siena, October 1859. After his mother's
death, his father took the twelve-year-old and his pony to live
in England. But EBB had known her son. He returned to
Italy permanently after he married.

Later, in the French countryside, he would wake up only to the knowledge that Ba was dead, not to where he was or what he was doing. Once awake, he would struggle to bring the scraps of his life into focus. When he slept, he slept well, escaping a perilous despair.

The night he wrote to his family, however, Browning was not without his wife in the Casa Guidi. Elizabeth Barrett Browning was in the next room. He blessed his "dearest papa and sis" and told them not to worry about him. He saw the rest of his life dedicated to his son. "I have some of her strength, really, added to mine." He was now ready to end his letter and go to his wife, "my Ba, for ever." He walked into the next room.

Browning sat up with her that final night, just as he sat with her on so many other sleepless nights. But his wife was not coughing or struggling to breathe. Death had removed all signs of physical pain. The hollows and lines had been filled in. The conflict of conscience had been erased. Her own passage to the next room was as imperceptible as she always believed death to be. Not only her husband but those who viewed her had trouble believing she had crossed over.

Leaving her side finally, he added a postscript to his letter: "How she looks now—how perfectly beautiful!" Her final serenity was a great solace to him. Her kissing him with such passion, her blessing him before she died. That youthful face of hers looked so happy. On those lips was such a living smile.

A WORD MORE

BROWNING NEVER REMARRIED; his widowerhood lasted for twenty-eight years. He didn't allow a biography of his wife during that period. When people asked about her ancestors, he told them he had never discussed the subject with her, as he avoided areas that caused her pain. John Ingram approached Christina Rossetti in 1888 to write about Mrs. Browning, but she would not go against Mr. Browning's wishes even though the fifty pounds offered was attractive to her. It is doubtful that his sister, Sarianna, would have approved a life of Robert right after his death in 1889 if she hadn't wanted a third party to negate the issue of African blood. Privacy was important to the family. When Sarianna realized that her brother's recorded voice was played after his death, she was shocked at the impropriety.

During his widowerhood Browning's need for privacy became absolute. Though he destroyed all the letters of his youth that came into his possession, all the letters to his family, he could never destroy his wife's letters to him—and by extension, his to her. What to do with them? He could not decide. He left their fate to his son. Pen, by then not unused to controversy, published them in 1899. Browning knew his wife believed that "death would be deader" without letters. Perhaps that's why he didn't interfere with the Sophia Eckley correspondence. He fretted about the revealing letters to Arabel, half of which are still in family hands. He considered his wife's belief in spiritualism the one flaw in a brilliant mind—a flaw the public might seize upon and exploit. In fact, Elizabeth Barrett Browning's reputation declined as time passed, just as his grew. By his trying to keep her real story from the public, much of her life became embroiled in sentiment and myth.

G. K. Chesterton would write at the beginning of the twentieth century that, at his wife's death, a door closed in Browning that would never open again. To open the door, to see how Browning managed and mismanaged the education of his son and his relations with other women, to take a look into the heart of the widower poet is a whole new story. A whole new life really. He wanted it to be as different as possible from what had come before, and his wish was granted.

Men and Women is now considered his masterpiece. And in the eight years after his wife's death he produced two outstanding works that had their roots in his old life with her in Italy: *Dramatis Personae* (1864) and *The Ring and the Book* (1868–69). His reputation increased, but poetry alone did not make him famous. He appreciated the irony of his ascent. He wrote about it to Julia Wedgwood, a woman who abruptly cut off their friendship in 1865 when she realized that the spiritual ménage à trois she was having with Robert and the memory of Elizabeth was going to cause her much more pain than pleasure. "I lost something peculiar in you, which I shall not see replaced,—is that stated soberly enough?" Robert wrote to her on March 8, 1869. He had no idea why she ended the friendship. But on to other issues. "Yes, the British Public like, and more than like me, this week, they let their admiration ray out on me, and at sundry congregations of men wherein I have figured these three or four days, I have seen, felt, and, thru' white gloves, handled a true affectionateness not unmingled with awe—which all comes of the Queen's having desired to see me, and three other extraordinary persons, last Thursday: whereupon we took tea together and pretended to converse for an hour and twenty minutes; the other worthies, with the wives of such as were provided, being Carlyle, Grote and Lyell."

But Browning's wife was present on the day he met Queen Victoria. On March 17, 1869, his sister, Sarianna, wrote to Annie Egerton Smith, "The interview with the Queen seems to have made a sensation, every body is talking of it—but I must tell you one little circumstance which occurred—Robt. saw her take Lady Augusta aside, and talk to her for some time in a low tone, and he perceived from her looks that she was speaking of him—Afterwards he found out that she was asking Lady Augusta whether it would be painful to Robert's feelings if she were to speak to him of his wife,—for she was longing to express the deep admiration she felt for her, but would not do so if it might give him pain. Lady Augusta replied that she thought not, so then the Queen talked a great deal of her to him, in terms of thorough appreciation."

Robert Browning's constancy to the memory of his wife became part of his public persona. Elizabeth Barrett Browning always maintained that the fame of a poet never was based on pure poetry. Browning's poetry was appreciated for what it had to say. It was his Christian optimism (as the public interpreted it) that was sought after. He was seen as a teacher, a seer. Yet sixteen years after his wife's death, he had a crisis that was at the very heart of his faith.

On September 13, 1877, Browning had a chance to review his belief that he would rejoin his wife after death. On the day after what would have been the Brownings' thirty-first wedding anniversary, he and his sister and their dear friend Annie Egerton Smith, half owner of the Liverpool *Mercury,* were vacationing together in the Alps at a chalet called La Saisiaz. He and Annie took a walk partway up La Salève, the mountain they planned to drive to the next day. They had a lively conversation on that walk. The latest issue of the *Nineteenth Century* had been delivered. In it was a dialogue "On the Soul and Future Life." Immortality was argued for and against by prominent men, churchmen and agnostics, logical positivists and Comtean Socialists. Rational inductive reasoning was employed to discern scientifically if immortality was a belief or a fact. On the day after the anniversary of what Elizabeth had called her great compensation day, the one day a year the Brownings had celebrated as their sacred day, Robert Browning, playing devil's advocate at times, brought himself and Annie back to his essential Christian belief in the immortality of the soul. And with that lively, intensely philosophic mind of his, he was able to do it on the back of the latest, most up-to-date, most fashionable method of scientific discourse of the late 1870s. He seemed quite pleased with his logic, had a pleasant evening with his sister and their friends, and went to sleep looking forward to the next day's drive.

In the morning, he woke up early at La Saisiaz, bathed, and waited, but Annie Smith didn't come out of her room. "I looked through an opening in the curtain, and saw her kneeling on the ground—which her poor head had touched. I called my sister, who ran in—cried to me—and brought me to her side. She was quite warm—but dead. . . . She must have died *standing* and fallen as we found her. So, have I lost one of the most devoted friends I ever had in my life."

The shock of it overwhelmed him. Ten years before, quite unexpectedly, Arabel Barrett had died in his arms; sixteen years before, Elizabeth. Elizabeth Barrett Browning, too, was buried in a foreign land among foreign onlookers. Vulnerable, shaken, unable to sit still waiting for burial instructions to be telegraphed, Robert once more bolted, assuaging grief the way he had done after his mother's death, by climbing to the mountain's top. On Mt. Salève the issue now became " 'was ending ending once and always, when you died?' "

> Is it fact to which I cleave,
> Is it fancy I but cherish, when I take upon my lips
> Phrase the solemn Tuscan fashioned, and declare the
>   soul's eclipse
> Not the soul's extinction? take his "I believe and
>   I declare—
> Certain am I—from this life I pass into a better, there
> Where that lady lives of whom enamored was my soul.

The phrase from Dante, "the solemn Tuscan," were the words Browning inscribed in Elizabeth's Bible after she died. Did he still believe Dante's words? Was Annie gone forever? Would he meet her again? Would he meet the great love of his life again?

At sixty-five, gray-bearded and portly, now as famous in his own time as he would be in future time, looking like the dinner guest the young novelist Henry James watched closely and found so inscrutable, he chose for one moment to shout his faith on Mt. Salève so as to hear it in his own ears. As a young man he had once gone to Italy to follow in the footsteps of Shelley. His great enthusiasm for Shelley faded only after he learned how shabbily the poet had treated his first wife. Now he had climbed to the mountaintop, hoping, despairing, shouting out his faith to mankind in the pose of a Rousseau, a Byron, a Shelley.

But he knew this was in vain. It was the life he led, the chances he took, the beliefs he held, the love he ardently accomplished that were important. "All our life is some form of religion, and all our action some belief," he'd written to Elizabeth Barrett. What mattered was the heart's whisper, the life's example, not the Romantic pose, the loud shout. "Truth is truth in each degree / Thunderpealed by God to Nature, whispered by my soul to me," he'd conclude in La Saisiaz.

Thirty-one years before, he had written to his wife of one day that he would never forget her courage in marrying him. "What is a belief?

My own eyes have seen—my heart will remember!" His audience might believe Robert Browning interpreted the ways of God to man. They might pluck "God's in his Heaven, all's right with the world" out of Pippa's mouth and put it in his. But he was as contemporary a man as any in the *Nineteenth Century.* When he spoke as Andrea or Blougram or Mr. Sludge or this one time as Robert Browning, there were no certainties. At best, there was faith, there was love, there was courage. There was the way one lived one's life.

> *Dared and Done: at last I stand upon the summit, Dear and*
> *   True!*
> *Singly dared and done: the climbing both of us were bound*
> *   to do.*

Alone once more, Browning began his poem on the mountaintop. The personal parts recapture the past with love; the philosophic parts are thorny and difficult to read. He would later say of *La Saisiaz* that he could "proceed to nothing else till I had in some way put it all on paper." The long work offered him what all of his poetry appeared to offer his readers: hope and consolation.

NOTES

SELECTED BIBLIOGRAPHY

ACKNOWLEDGMENTS

INDEX

NOTES

Dates in brackets or with question marks are as they appear as catalogued or in print.

INTRODUCTION

page 3 "dear Miss Barrett": All quotations from the love letters between EBB and RB are taken from *The Letters of Robert Browning and Elizabeth Barrett Browning, 1845–1846,* edited by Elvan Kintner in two volumes. Often the quotes will be locatable through dates given in the text. When not, they will be identified in the notes by author, volume number, and date as in the following note. See Bibliography for full citations.

"and I love you too": RB, 1, Jan. 10, 1845.

6 "I never wanted them": RB, 1, Feb. 26, 1845.

7 "more admirable for being beyond": EBB, 1, Jan. 15, 1845.

8 of the young Browning: John Maynard, *Browning's Youth.*

DEATH OR LOVE

14 greenish glow: See Althea Hayter, *A Sultry Month,* pp. 66–67.

"Small face & sundries": EBB to Haydon, *Invisible Friends,* edited by Willard Bissell Pope, Jan. 1, 1843.

16 disease of the spine: See *The Brownings' Correspondence,* edited by Philip Kelley and Ronald Hudson, vol. 1, *Supporting Documents,* pp. 325–27. All further reference to this correspondence will be as Kelley, followed by volume number and page.

17 with antibiotics: I want to thank Professor Corrine Davies for a conversation we had about bronchiectasis at the EBB Conference at Baylor University, November 4–6, 1993. She had come to a conclusion similar to my own, having seen a relative suffer from this disease, and mentioned that when having an attack the patient could not eat and lost about thirty pounds. EBB never ate when ill, something her father attributed to stubbornness. It might have been a physical symptom. In my opinion, this disease or some form of acute bronchitis (as her descendant Captain Gordon E. Moulton-Barrett suggested) plagued EBB.

19 "a sign of suffering": EBB, 11, Aug. 27, 1846.

21 "mean for me": RB, 1, Oct. 23, 1845.

22 "clearly against" the father: EBB, 1, Jan. 26, 1846.

23 "one by one": EBB, 1, Aug. 20, 1845. Her characteristic " . ." has been changed here in one place to dashes so as not to be mistaken for an ellipsis. "Exact" substituted for Kintner's {ask > exact} for clarity.

page 23 by his long hair: W. S. Seton-Kerr supplied his own memories of Edward Barrett to John H. Ingram, Esq., in a letter of Dec. 15, 1888, that is at Wellesley. He told Ingram, "I knew Edward Barrett very well." He looked back to his diary. The weather had been "fine" on the day of the accident. "Edward Barrett's body was found as you say, nearly a month afterwards." He told Ingram, "It was recognized by his hair which was very long at the back. . . ." There were other signs as well.

24 busts of the poets: Hayter, *A Sultry Month*, p. 57.

25 "you know best": RB, 1, Oct. 23, 1845.
expressly autobiographical: *La Saisiaz* was written in 1877 after the sudden death of his friend Annie Egerton Smith.
"deader from henceforth": EBB, 1, Feb. 15, 1846.
"not my fault": EBB, 11, Sept. 18, 1846.

26 "and down over you": RB, 1, Nov. 16, 1845. One ellipsis converted to comma for clarity.

30 "Come then": EBB, 1, May 15, 1845.

31 "so few pleasures": EBB, 1, May 23, 1845.
"so adroitly": RB, 1, May 24, 1845.
"your suspicion should . . . clear up": RB, 11, Mar. 30, 1846.

32 "so much good": EBB, 1, May 23, 1845.

35 "Arabel thought I was dead": EBB, 1, Jan. 15, 1846.

36 "washed his hands of me altogether": EBB, 1, Sept. 25, 1845.
"I should be *here*": RB, 1, postmarked Sept. 25, 1845.

37 "clear conception of them": RB, 1, Jan. 19, 1846.
"accepted like the rest": EBB, 1, Oct. 11, 1845. In terms of keeping her siblings in the dark, EBB wrote compellingly to RB in the same letter of Jan. 15, 1846, in which she describes Moulton Barrett's violence against Henrietta: "My brothers, it is quite necessary not to draw into a dangerous responsibility: I have felt that from the beginning, & shall continue to feel it—though I hear & can observe that they are full of suspicions & conjectures, which are never unkindly expressed. I told you once that we held hands faster in this house for the weight over our heads. But the absolute *knowledge* would be dangerous . . . with my sisters it is different, & I could not continue to conceal from *them* what they had under their eyes—and then, Henrietta is in a like position—It was not wrong of me to let them know it?—no?—"

Lovers' Luck

39 "into April": EBB, 1, Nov. 10, 1845.
" 'miraculous' as the rest": EBB, 1, Jan. 15, 1846.
" 'so glad to see me' ": EBB, 1, Jan. 18, 1846.

40 "more or less of it": RB, 1, Feb. 4, 1846.
"all this to you": EBB, 1, Feb. 4, 1846.

41 "not think such a thing": EBB, 1, Nov. 12, 1845.
"less need for the opium": RB, 1, Feb. 24, 1846.
"pretend to advise": EBB, 1, Feb. 12, 1846.
"not persuade me": EBB, 11, Apr. 3, 1846.

42 "I shall end my letter": EBB, 11, Apr. 7, 1846.
"Your Ba": EBB, 11, Apr. 7, 1846, Tuesday evening.

43 "a child's game": RB, 11, Apr. 8, 1846.
"more darkness, more pain": EBB, 11, Apr. 8, 1846.

page 44   "admission and retraction": RB, 11, Apr. 10, 1846.

"whom I love wholly": RB, 11, Apr. 10, 1846.

45   "even to tears": EBB, 11, Apr. 12, 1846.

"with the strongest": Unless otherwise indicated, all quotations from *The Letters of Elizabeth Barrett Browning to Mary Russell Mitford* come from the three volumes edited by Meredith B. Raymond and Mary Rose Sullivan and are noted EBB to MRM followed by volume number and date. In this case, it's EBB to MRM, vol. 11, Oct. 31, 1842.

"nor aught else": RB, 11, Apr. 12, 1846.

who was a cousin: Meredith B. Raymond, who is preparing a study of John Kenyon, informed me that Kenyon's grandmother and Edward Barrett Moulton Barrett's grandfather, Edward of Cinnamon Hill, were sister and brother.

48   "possibility of such things": EBB, 11, Apr. 12, 1846.

49   "singing song for song": See Kintner, 1, n. 7, p. 273. Landor sent the poem to Browning in appreciation of his *Bells and Pomegranates*. It "came to sound like prophecy to the two poets when they were planning their marriage and escape to Italy." So, after November 1845, when Robert received it and showed it to Elizabeth, they made reference to the siren's call through the correspondence.

"between the leaves": EBB, 11, May 1, 1846.

"now doesn't it": EBB, 11, Apr. 16, 1846.

"expect it": RB, 11, Apr. 16, 1846.

50   "dare to do it yet": EBB, 11, June 30, 1846.

51   "London in Triumph": Kelley, vol. 6, n. 143.

"butt of laughter in *Punch*": Kintner, 11, p. 810.

came to his: Kintner, 11, p. 810.

"Dearest dearest!—": RB, 11, June 23, 1846.

53   "none of us be moved": EBB, 11, June 23, 1846.

"a great man": EBB, 11, June 26, 1846.

"mortified self love": EBB, 11, July 9, 1846.

"instruct you": RB, 11, July 6, 1846.

54   "for next summer": Kelley, vol. 6, p. 144.

55   "melancholy teaching": EBB, 11, July 6, 1846. In the letter of June 30 quoted on page 55, EBB's characteristic two-point ellipsis [. .] has been deleted for clarity.

56   "a young man": EBB, 11, June 21, 1846.

"to make any difference": EBB, 11, Aug. 17, 1846.

"inclined to go to sleep": EBB, 11, June 21, 1846.

58   "comes nothing": EBB, 11, Aug. 5, 1846.

59   " 'the man of the pomegranates' ": EBB, 11, July 15, 1846.

60   "*But* HOW": EBB, 11, July 28, 1846.

"been married to-day": RB, 11, July 29, 1846.

"*would do as well*": EBB, 11, Aug. 31, 1846.

61   "in or out of the house": EBB, 11, Aug. 2, 1846.

62   "beyond my power": EBB, 11, Aug. 28, 1846.

63   "distinct from the other": RB, 11, Aug. 30, 1846.

64   "a spendthrift doctor": *Letters of EBB to MRM*, introduction, vol. 1, p. xxviii.

65   "this Papa of mine": EBB to MRM, 11, Oct. 27 (28), 1842.

66   "darling Flush's destiny": EBB, 11, Sept. 2, 1846.

"too much for failing": EBB, 11, Sept. 2, 1846.

68   "give you up to-morrow": RB, 11, Sept. 4, 1846.

"that is true": EBB to MRM, 11, Sept. [16], 1843.

page 69   "as Mr. Taylor": EBB, 11, Sept. 6, 1846.
             "everything with you": RB, 11, Sept. 10, 1846, Thursday morning.
             "not unfavourable": RB, 11, Sept. 10, 1846, 4 p.m. Thursday.
      70   "my heart will remember": RB, 11, Sept. 13, 1846.
      71   "which failed to *me*": EBB, 11, Sept. 13, 1846.
      72   "over our heads": EBB, 1, Jan. 15, 1846.
      73   "it is my hope": EBB, 11, Sept. 14, 1846.
             include the number 50: See EBB, 11, letters of Sept. 15 and 16, 1846.
             "what could be the matter": EBB, 11, Sept. 16, 1846.
      74   "a large one": RB, 11, Sept. 17, 1846.

RIDING AN ENCHANTED HORSE

      75   "persuading her to rest": Anna Jameson wrote five letters to Lady Noel Byron in
             England describing her trip from Paris to Pisa with the Brownings and her niece
             Gerardine. These autograph letters are dated Paris, 22–23 September, 24 September,
             26–29 September; Avignon, 7–9 October; and Pisa, 15 October 1846. They are at
             the Pierpont Morgan Library, MA 1325, and are quoted with the kind permission of
             the library.
             "my wife EBB . . . RB": Unpublished letter from EBB to her sister Arabel, dated
             "Paris. Sat. Hotel de la Ville de Paris." One hundred thirteen unpublished letters of
             EBB to her sister are held at the Berg Collection, New York Public Library, and are
             quoted by the library's kind permission. Referred to as EBB to Arabel, Berg, date.
             More than 115 from EBB to Arabel letters are still in family hands, and passages are
             quoted from them by the kind permission of Captain Gordon E. Moulton-Barrett.
             These letters are referred to as GEM-B, followed by the date.
             painter of miniatures: See Clara Thomas, *Love and Work Enough,* to which I am in-
             debted in this section about Anna Jameson's family.
      78   "dreadfully anxious about me": EBB to Arabel, Berg, Sat., Hotel de la Ville de Paris.
             Except when indicated otherwise, all quotes from EBB in Paris are from this unpub-
             lished letter to her sister.
      81   "so anxious and terrified": The letters to her two sisters are from *Twenty-Two Unpub-*
             lished Letters of Elizabeth Barrett-Browning and Robert Browning Addressed to Henrietta
             and Arabel Moulton-Barrett, and will be referred to as *Twenty-Two Letters,* with date, in
             this case, Oct. 2, 1846.
             "considering my solitude": EBB to MRM, 11, May 24, 1843.
      83   "beyond them all": EBB to MRM, 111, Friday, Sept. 18, 1846.
             "mistake during a trance": All letters to Julia Martin are from *The Letters of Elizabeth*
             Barrett Browning, edited by Frederic G. Kenyon, 2 vols., and are listed as Kenyon,
             volume number, and date—in this case, Kenyon, vol. 1, Oct. 20?, 1846.
      85   "so many good wishes": *Twenty-Two Letters,* Oct. 2, 1846.
             "relation or friend": EBB to Arabel, Berg, Sat. Hotel de la Ville de Paris.
      86   "in such . . . danger": EBB to Arabel, Berg, Oct. 1846.
      87   "between you two": *Twenty-Two Letters,* Oct. 2, 1846.

"THE RUNAWAY SLAVE"

      88   "I am sure": *Twenty-Two Letters,* Nov. 24, 1846.
             "in my life": Kenyon, 1, Nov. 5 [1846].
      89   "prose or rhyme": EBB to Henrietta, *Twenty-Two Letters,* Jan. 7 [1847].

page 90   "dish of oranges": EBB to MRM, 111, Dec. 19 [1846].

"'you are *transformed*'": EBB to Julia Martin, Kenyon, 1, Oct. 20?, 1846.

"as much as is prudent": RB to Arabel, Berg, Feb. 8, 1847.

"in eight days": EBB to Arabel, Mar. 6–9, 1847, *Browning Institute Studie*s 5 (1977).

"any other family in England": Kenyon, 1, Nov. 5 [1846].

"sorrow they can desire": *Twenty-Two Letters,* Nov. 24, 1846.

91   "Everyone, except *you*": *Twenty-Two Letters,* Jan. 7 [1847].

92   "dealt with tenderly": Berg, Feb. 24, 1847.

93   his master's plantain: The manuscript "Austin was a Creole negro slave" in Richard Barrett's hand is in the Berg Collection. It is reprinted in *Richard Barrett's Journal,* edited by Thomas Brott and Philip Kelley.

99   Jeannette Marks: I am indebted to Jeannette Marks's *The Family of the Barretts* and have made use of her study all through the Jamaican part of this section. Her papers are held at Wellesley College, her alma mater. Her preliminary studies and type-scripts of *The Family of the Barretts* are ample evidence of her painstaking and schol-arly method. At times it seemed to me that her typescripts were less opaque than her printed book. John Maynard, in a footnote, suggested that her conclusions about Robert Browning's blood were a matter of believing what she wanted to believe. But she meticulously went back over two hundred years of documents in Jamaica in re-searching the book—a book dealing with colonization, slavery, and mixed blood that was ahead of its time—even for its author.

Jeannette Augustus Marks (1875–1964) taught at Mount Holyoke College, where she was named Kennedy Professor of English Literature in 1921. She was a prolific author of fiction, poetry, and drama as well as scholarly articles and books. *The Fam-ily of the Barretts* (1938) won the Silver Musgrave Medal of the Institute of Jamaica. Among her other studies were *Thirteen Days,* which chronicled the Sacco and Vanzetti trial, and *Genius and Disaster: Studies in Drugs and Genius.* She was influential in the Little Theatre movement. Should anyone become interested in her life and work, the Special Collections of the Margaret Clapp Library at Wellesley College has "150 boxes, 62–63 linear feet," of her papers in the process of being catalogued.

100   "from the date hereof": Marks, *Family of the Barretts,* p. 255.

Elizabeth Barrett Waite Williams: Her four sons by her cousin Samuel Barrett (Ed-ward of Cinnamon Hill's son) carried on the family tradition of using the same Chris-tian names. These illegitimate sons were Samuel, Richard, Edward, and George Goodin Barrett.

"a free negro woman": Marks, *Family of the Barretts,* p. 211.

101   were quadroon: From 1785 to 1794, George Goodin Barrett had six quadroon chil-dren with Elissa Peters, and he had already manumitted them from his father, Ed-ward of Cinnamon Hill. They were Thomas, William, Ann, Maria, Samuel, and Richard. Marks, *Family of the Barretts,* p. 221.

Samuel (her uncle) and Sarah: He did have one other legitimate grandchild, his granddaughter by his son Henry, another Elizabeth Barrett, who died in 1830.

"during widowhood": Copy of the will, Berg, NYPL.

102   "own immature perceptions": Margaret Forster, *Elizabeth Barrett Browning,* pp. 5–6.

103   executor of his will: Marks, *Family of the Barretts,* pp. 222–23, 250.

105   "their own bodies": Copy of the will, Berg, NYPL.

106   had black blood: Marks concludes: "The transitions pivoting on the name Moulton are inescapably suggestive. E.B.B.'s statement might explain the following state-ment from *What the Negro Thinks*: 'It is carefully recorded that highly creditable (sic)

records associate the names of Pushkin, Dumas, Elizabeth Barrett Browning, and even our own Alexander Hamilton with the Negro race.' Dumas and Robert Browning, yes! Elizabeth Barrett, no! On the Barrett side she inherited, so far as the documents show, no blood of the negro. Indeed Charles Moulton's own connections may have helped to build up this idea about his granddaughter Elizabeth Moulton Barrett" (p. 313).

But in the love letters, EBB herself documented her grandfather's blood. Even if she were in error, the poet herself believed in the lineage of the slave, evident in her features and dark skin.

In typescript Marks wrote, "It is a fact that in the will of Charles Moulton all Moulton relatives seem to have disappeared. To no brothers, sisters, uncles, aunts, or even cousins does he refer. As the head of the family of the Moultons, said to have been among England's greatest, the scantiness of the one reference to him in the Jamaican newspapers is as strange as his seemingly solitary position. There was not even the obituary usual for anyone of any position in the Island life" (p. 72). Wellesley, Marks archives, typescript, record group 4.

page 106   "from generation to generation": EBB, 1, Dec. 20, 1845.

107   her African blood: Her dark complexion, which she noted in her description of herself to Haydon ("I am 'little and black' like Sappho"), is mentioned in a description by the young Anne Thackeray that is quite similar: "She is very small, she is brown, with dark eyes and dead-brown hair, she has white teeth and a low, curious voice." Anne Thackeray Ritchie, *Records of Tennyson, Ruskin, and Browning,* p. 240. On June 15, 1854, Thomas Chase described "her dark complexioned face," whereas Robert Browning had "a rather dark complexion." A picture might be worth a thousand words, but it is interesting to realize the liberties taken in every oil and watercolor image of Elizabeth Barrett Browning in terms of skin color. Surely she was not the only sitter so treated. Portraits, it would appear, could once be as selective as memoirs. For the quotations above and for an interesting discussion of related issues, see Michael Meredith's introduction to *Meeting the Brownings*, pp. 9–14.

108   Richard Barrett: For a sympathetic reading of Richard Barrett (1789–1839), see the introduction to *Richard Barrett's Journal*, edited by Thomas Brott and Philip Kelley. He was a captain of the Royal Horse Guards as well as being a member of the Jamaican House of Assembly, where he rose to Speaker of the House. His journal of his trip to the United States and Canada shows him as the strong advocate of slavery that he was. That he was murdered, poisoned, in Jamaica on May 5, 1839, is called a family supposition in the introduction, but it was widely suspected at the time. On May 12, 1839, the *Falmouth Post* in "Death of the Hon. Richard Barrett, Speaker of the House of Assembly" stated he "had been transacting business when he was taken seriously ill, and removed upstairs to the lodgings of Miss Catherine Shaw, where he shortly afterwards expired." The paper understood "that two inquests were warned by the Coroner (Mr. Evans) but for reasons unknown to us, the Jurors were not sworn to view the body nor did they in any way whatever investigate the cause of death." The body was illegally removed from the lodgings after Miss Shaw was informed that an inquest would be held. "It is bad law . . . Mr. Barrett, we understand, had been walking about the town of Montego Bay within a few hours of his death in apparent health. . . . If this be not a case for a Coroner's Inquest," what would be. "But the mystery yet remains unsolved."

110   "the coloured people": F. J. Furnivall, "Robert Browning's Ancestors," *Browning Society Papers* III, p. 31.

page 111   Creole side: Furnivall's discussion of "Creole" in a footnote might be worth a footnote here: "(A Creole is, in the primary sense, a native, a person born in the West Indies or Louisiana, so that there are both Creole whites and Creole negroes. That the white and black blood got occasionally mixed, goes without saying; and the word Creole is often incorrectly used for Mulatto or Quadroon, of a person having a strain of negro blood, a dash of the tar-brush. That Miss Tittle had this dash was understood by some of Robert III's [RB's grandfather's] second family; and the eyes and colour of Robert IV [RB's father] confirmed it.) On the meaning of the word *Creole,* Mr. H. G. Bowen, Chief Accountant of the Bank of England, who is himself a Creole, as being born in the West Indies—but all whose family are of the pure Saxon type—says: 'The word in its original and limited sense was used in Spanish Colonies to describe Spaniards born in the Colonies, of parents born in Spain. The word spread to the West India Islands of all sorts, to the Southern States of America, and (I believe) to Canada, and there it first meant persons born in the colony, of parents born out of the colony: Hence, French Creole, English Creole, Creole Negro, &c. Thus Creole, which originally meant absence of "colour"—white blood as distinct from black,—now covers all shades.' " "Robert Browning's Ancestors," n. 2, p. 31.

112   "Dr. Furnivall wrote": Marks, *Family of the Barretts,* pp. 236–37.

"distinctive enough": RB to EBB, 11, [Thursday, Sept. 17, 1846].

"Hannah Kennion": Marks, *Family of the Barretts,* p. 235.

Browning said of Furnivall: To understand the relationship between the two men, and indeed the way the late nineteenth century looked to Robert Browning as an oracle, see two fine studies by William S. Peterson: *Interrogating the Oracle: A History of the London Browning Society,* and *Browning's Trumpeter,* an edition of the letters between RB and Furnivall, with an enlightening introduction.

113   "or nearly so": *Twenty-Two Letters,* Mar. 26, 1847. The following description of the miscarriage is from this letter. EBB's physician was Dr. John Cook.

114   "played with his life": *Twenty-Two Letters,* [Jan. 23–29, 1847].

115   "making it bitter": EBB to MRM, 111, Feb. 8, 1847.

PISA POSTSCRIPT

116   "crushed with gifts": Berg, Dec. 14 [1846].

"who could escape": *Browning Institute Studies* 5 (1977), p. 141.

117   "to do it": EBB to Henrietta, Dec. 19, 1846, in *Elizabeth Barrett Browning: Letters to Her Sisters,* edited by Leonard Huxley.

THE MARRIAGE OF TRUE MINDS: HERS

124   "kept well for us": EBB to Henrietta, Huxley, *Letters to Her Sisters,* Sept. 13, 1847. The entire letter is reproduced without cuts in Elizabeth Barrett Browning, *Casa Guidi Windows,* edited by Julia Markus, Appendix, pp. 65–69. This letter is quoted throughout in describing the demonstration. Quotations from the poem come from this edition.

129   "to render it exigent": See my introduction to *Casa Guidi Windows,* p. xx.

130   "clear as a flower": GEM-B. Letters from EBB to Arabel still in family hands are referred to as GEM-B. See note 75 on page 346.

"venuto da quel corpo": *Elizabeth Barrett Browning's Letters to Mrs. David Ogilvy,* edited by Peter N. Heydon and Philip Kelley, p. xxvii.

"& exclaimed aloud": GEM-B, Apr. 8–12, 1849.

132   "her poetic pitch": Henry James, *William Wetmore Story and His Friends,* vol. 11, p. 55.

"Italian Risorgimento": *The Golden Ring: The Anglo-Florentines 1847–1862,* pp. 76, 207.

133   "sentiments of *Casa Guidi*": William Irvine and Park Honan, *The Book, the Ring, and the Poet,* pp. 253–54.

134   called Anglo-Florentine: This is the opinion of the Italian critic Giuliana Artom Treves, whose *The Golden Ring: The Anglo-Florentines 1847–1862* is an excellent study of this community.

"Promethean soul": The poem appeared in the *Tuscan Athenaeum,* Nov. 20, 1847. The only complete file of the paper, minus a "Specimen Number" issued earlier, is at the New York Public Library.

"highest of them all": *Tuscan Athenaeum,* Jan. 8, 1848.

135   "leave for the battlefield": *Tuscan Athenaeum,* Mar. 26, 1849.

137   "perfectly clear this time": Berg, Oct. 7–11, 1848.

138   "too much": Kenyon, 11.

THE MARRIAGE OF TRUE MINDS: HIS

139   wrote to her sisters: *Twenty-Two Letters,* Mar. 9, 1849.

"when he was about half born": *Letters of Robert Browning Collected by Thomas J. Wise,* edited by Thurman L. Hood. Subsequently referred to as Hood, *Letters of RB.*

140   " 'as they were tied' ": *Twenty-Two Letters,* Mar. 9, 1849.

"even so": The preceding quotes are from EBB to Arabel, GEM-B, Apr. 8–12, 1849.

142   "lavished on me": GEM-B, Mar. 7 to Apr. 1, 1848.

"not to say decency": EBB to MRM, 111, Aug. 24 [1848].

143   "supreme being": *Robert Browning: A Portrait,* p. 145.

145   "Sir Charles Forbes": Beinecke Library, Yale University.

"1842 RB": Beinecke Library, Yale University.

"when half is wasted": *Robert Browning and Alfred Domett,* edited by Frederic G. Kenyon, May 22, 1842. (Hereafter referred to as *RB and AD.*)

147   "attainable or no": *RB and AD,* July 13, 1846.

148   "last thirty years": *RB and AD,* Mar. 1, 1872.

150   "of our terraces": Berg, May 10–11, 1848. By March 24, 1850, "We have taken a new room . . . a new drawing room with three windows, a most beautiful room to which our rooms open through a once condemned door; we pay two additional pounds a year for this." GEM-B.

151   "is black & white": EBB to MRM, 111, Oct. 10 [1848].

152   "great fault—conviviality": Blanchard Jerrold, "Introduction," in *The Final Reliques of Father Prout,* collected and arranged by Oliver York, p. 36.

"over the rail": Jerrold introduction, *Final Reliques,* p. 62, in a letter dated June 5, 1868.

153   "my black veil": EBB to Henrietta, Huxley, *EBB: Letters to Her Sisters,* May 16, 1847.

154   "unveiled prophetess": EBB to Henrietta, Huxley, *EBB: Letters to Her Sisters,* Nov. 23 and 24, 1847.

"bought yet": Berg, May 10–11, 1848.

"woke better": *Robert Browning and Julia Wedgwood,* edited by Richard Curle, Oct. 17, 1864.

page 155 "for spitting": The following description of an evening with Prout is from EBB to Henrietta, Huxley, *EBB: Letters to Her Sisters,* Nov. 19, 1848.

160 "to dazzle": *The Hierarchy* 38 (Dec. 1850), pp. 527–28.

"nature of the man": EBB to Henrietta, Huxley, *EBB: Letters to Her Sisters,* Nov. 19, 1848.

"happiness of Florence": EBB to Henrietta, Huxley, *EBB: Letters to Her Sisters,* Jan. 4, 5, and 6, 1848.

161 "injured him so far": EBB to MRM, 111, Apr. 30 [1849].

"woman's estate": EBB to MRM, 111 [July 18?, 1849].

"nourished he has been": RB to Henrietta and Arabel, *Twenty-Two Letters* [Mar. 9, 1849].

162 "change of plans": EBB to MRM, 111, Apr. 30 [1849].

"pay for plate": EBB to MRM, 111 [July 18?, 1849]. The description that follows is from this letter.

163 "from anybody else": RB to Sarianna, Hood, *Letters of RB,* July 2, 1849. The description of his condition that follows is from this letter.

164 "in the forests": EBB to MRM, 111 [July 18?, 1849].

165 "to the right": RB to Julia Wedgwood, Curle, *RB and Julia Wedgwood,* pp. 95–101, letters Nov. 1, 1864, and Friday morning.

"as they pleased": Berg, Jan. 12, 1851.

167 "slovenly appearance": Jerrold introduction, *Final Reliques,* p. 51.

"inevitable hypocrisy": Jerrold introduction, *Final Reliques,* pp. 200–201.

170 document of its times: For a full treatment of the relationship between the images of the poem itself and Mahony and Wiseman, see Julia Markus, "Bishop Blougram and the Literary Man," *Victorian Studies* (Winter 1978): 171–95.

THE ROADS THAT LED TO ROME

172 her brother George: "I was delighted, dearest George, to have your letter & shall be still more delighted if you will conquer your repugnance to writing, as to let me hear from you sometimes." This quote and those about Napoleon that follow in the text are from *The Letters of the Brownings to George Barrett,* edited by Paul Landis [Dec. 4, 5, 1851]. Subsequently referred to as EBB to George or RB to George.

173 "said George Sand—": EBB to George [Feb. 28, 1852].

"George Sandism": EBB to MRM, 111, Oct. 22 [1851].

"without seeing George Sand": EBB to MRM, 111, Feb. 15 [–16, 1852].

175 "burning soul": EBB to MRM, 111, Feb. 15 [–16, 1852].

"care for me": EBB to MRM, 111, Apr. 7 [1852].

176 "rare a smile": EBB to George [Feb. 28, 1852].

"sure of it": GEM-B.

179 old fool: See Irvine and Honan, *The Book, the Ring, and the Poet,* particularly pp. 282–83.

180 "you have taken": See "Elizabeth Barrett Browning and Her Brother Alfred," by Ronald Hudson, *Browning Institute Studies* 2 (1974), pp. 135–60.

"twenty Parises besides": Berg, May 16, 1851?

"did not hurt him": "Mrs. Ogilvy's Recollections," Heydon and Kelley, *EBB's Letters to Mrs. Ogilvy,* p. xxxi.

182 "neutral creature, so far": Berg, Venice, June 5 [1851].

183 " 'Bwavo, bwavo!' (bravo)": EBB to George [Dec. 4–5, 1851].

page 184   "never trouble *me*": GEM-B, Apr. 1, 1853.

"Like two lovers": The quotations for the preceding scene from EBB to Henrietta, Huxley, *EBB: Letters to Her Sisters,* May 14, 1853.

185   Elizabeth Kinney: For information about the Kinneys and for the quotations from Elizabeth Kinney's journals, I am indebted to the fine study by my former classmate Ronald A. Bosco, "The Brownings and Mrs. Kinney: A Record of Their Friendship," *Browning Institute Studies* 4 (1976), pp. 57–124. Mrs. Kinney's papers are in the Stedman Collection at Columbia University.

186   "excepting Swedenborg": Berg, Aug. 22, 1854.

ECCO ROMA

190   "way at all": All quotations in this section are from EBB to MRM, III, Jan. 18 [1854].

191   "wherever we like": EBB to George, Jan. 10 [1854].

AMERICAN MARBLE CUTTERS AND YANKEE TITIANS

194   "to us to-night": EBB to Henrietta, Huxley, *EBB: Letters to Her Sisters,* Dec. 30, 1853.

197   pointed to the ideal: Hiram Powers was a self-made man. In the first draft of her unpublished "personal impressions" of him, in the Stedman Collection, Columbia University, Elizabeth Kinney wrote, "I love to picture that rickety old farmhouse under the shadow of the Green Mountains, at Woodstock Vermont where Hiram Powers was born on July 29th, 1805. No special rejoicings at his birth indicated unusual signs of promise in the eighth child of a poor, hard-working family." After the death of his father, Powers moved to Cincinnati, where he modeled in wax for the Western Museum. "Genius enables everything it touches, and so his wax figures were not expressionless dolls but speaking men and women of whatever character," Kinney wrote. It was in Cincinnati that "a humble German sculptor" taught him to model from life. That the young man got to Italy at all was a credit to the American dream.

198   "of the angel": *Scribner's Monthly* 17 (Apr. 1879), p. 894.

201   moved to Rome: Joshua Taylor, *William Page: The American Titian,* p. 115.

"was impossible": RB to WW Story, June 11, 1854, in *Browning to His American Friends,* edited by Gertrude Reese Hudson. Subsequently referred to as Hudson, *American Friends.*

"American & Italian circles": W.W. Story to RB, Hudson, *American Friends,* Jan. 9, 1855.

202   "did the honours": EBB to Sarianna, Kenyon, II.

203   "& disappeared": W.W. Story to J.R. Lowell, Hudson, *American Friends,* Jan. 9, 1855.

"bless you dear Page": This unpublished letter of Jan. 13, 1855, at the American Archives of Art can be found in Julia Markus, "Andrea del Sarto and William Page," *Browning Institute Studies* 2 (1974), pp. 11–12.

205   "will turn black": Kenyon, II, Dec. 21, 1853.

"than my own": RB to W.W. Story, Hudson, *American Friends,* June 11, 1854.

"they only disappear": Hood, *Letters of RB,* Oct. 29, 1855.

"SUCH A WILD STEP"

209   might soon be taking—together: Berg, Jan. 10–11 [1855]. Quotations in this section not otherwise identified are from this letter.

page 214 "shape of an occupant": Berg, May 1 [–2], 1855.

by Elizabeth Kinney: The quotations in this scene are taken from Mrs. Kinney's account as quoted in Bosco's study cited above.

217 "dear Mama": Berg, May 15, 1855. The discussion about spiritualism below is also from this letter.

had horrified him: GEM-B, July 30, 1850.

219 by Yale University: Jarves's financial problems led to an auction of his collection on loan to Yale University. Yale bought it for $22,000, and it immediately added invaluable prestige and visibility to the developing university. For information on Jarves and for the quotations used in this section, see Francis Steegmüller's excellent study, *The Two Lives of James Jackson Jarves.*

222 "very, very sorry": Berg, June 25, 1855.

225 "utmost of your hopes": See Ronald Hudson, "EBB and Her Brother Alfred," *Browning Institute Studies* 2 (1974), pp. 135–60. Letters quoted are from this account.

"for the inward": GEM-B, Nov. 23, 1856.

226 "except by the act ecclesiastical": The letters from EBB to Arabel quoted in this section are from France, Berg, June 25, June 27, June 30, July 1, July 8, and July 10, 1855.

"WHO'S THERE?" THE EALING SÉANCE

230 "altogether astonishing": Berg, June 30 to July 1, 1855.

"upon the table": EBB to Mrs. Jameson, Berg, Rue du Colysee [1856].

231 "aged twelve": The quotations from the following description of the séance come from Robert Browning's letter to Elizabeth Kinney reproduced in Bosco's article and from EBB to Henrietta, Huxley, *EBB: Letters to Her Sisters,* Aug. 17, 1855.

235 Home left immediately: D. D. Home, in his *Incidents in My Life,* second series, p. 107, remembered, "I held out my hand, when, with a tragic air, he [Browning] threw his hand on his left shoulder and stalked away." After Elizabeth's death Browning published a brilliant satire of Home, "Mr. Sludge, 'The Medium.' " Though Home professed he could not see the slightest resemblance to himself in the poem, he attributed Browning's dislike of him to the poet's not having been crowned by the spirits as his wife had been at the Ealing séance.

"playing as they went": GEM-B, Dec. 16–17, 1855.

237 Houdini himself: A tip of the hat to the fine contemporary poet David Clewell, who shared his knowledge of magic with me.

238 "or by my means": Berg, Oct. 31, 1855. All the quotations above are from this letter.

"use to him": Berg, Sept. 10, 1855.

"two or three minutes": see Gardner Taplin, *The Life of Elizabeth Barrett Browning,* p. 297.

"of the breath": This quotation from EBB to Anna Jameson, Berg, "13 Dorset Street."

240 "house, fled": Berg, Oct. 2, 1855.

THE ALMOST MIRACULOUS YEAR

241 "faith for you": EBB to RB, 1, Feb. 3, 1845.

"were to come": EBB to RB, 1, Feb. 17, 1845.

243 "popular heart": EBB to RB, 1, Jan. 15, 1845.

was completed: EBB to Henrietta, Huxley, *EBB: Letters to Her Sisters,* Oct. 3, 1855.

245 "poems thus far": Irvine and Honan, *The Book, the Ring, and the Poet,* p. 335.

page 246   "fancies exist": Taplin, *Life of EBB,* p. 300.

247   "bleak month": The letters from RB to Chapman in the winter and spring of 1856 are published in *New Letters of Robert Browning,* edited by William Clyde DeVane and Kenneth Leslie Knickerbocker.

248   "out of place": EBB to Anna Jameson, Kenyon, 11, Feb. 28, 1856.

ARABEL AND THE "UNTLES"

249   "too late": EBB to Henrietta, Huxley, *EBB: Letters to Her Sisters,* July 1856.

250   "stay for a fortnight": EBB to Mrs. Martin, Kenyon, 11, Sept. 9, 1856.
"product of circumstances" and "your legs swell": GEM-B, Sept. 11, 1856, and Oct. 4, 1856, respectively.
"is all wrong": EBB to Mrs. Martin, Kenyon, 11, Sept. 9, 1856.

252   "the wood-engravers": Taplin, *Life of EBB,* p. 306.

253   "forgive her": Taplin, *Life of EBB,* p. 306.
"dislike it accordingly": EBB to Henrietta, Huxley, *EBB: Letters to Her Sisters,* Sept. 8, 1856. Taplin, *Life of EBB,* lists this letter as Sept. 19, 1856; Kelley, *The Brownings' Correspondence,* lists it as Sept. 18, 1856.
"How I love you all!": Berg, Sunday [Sept. 7, 1856].

254   "death on occasion": Kenyon, 11, Sept. 9, 1856.

SURPRISE ENDINGS

255   "book of his own": Kenyon, 11, Sept. 13, 1856.

257   "will grow older": Berg, Jan. 25, 1857.
of Robert Browning: GEM-B, Dec. 10, 1856.
"any but yourself": GEM-B, Dec. 10, 1856.

258   "sufficient & kind": Berg, Jan. 25, 1857.
"liable to all his life": Berg, Sunday [Sept. 7, 1856].
"rest in it": GEM-B, Sept. 11 and Sept. 21, 1856.
"done by you": Huxley, *EBB: Letters to Her Sisters,* Mar. 4, 1857.
"a great help": Berg, Jan. 25, 1857.

259   *"undoubted* claim": Huxley, *EBB: Letters to Her Sisters,* Jan. 10, 1857.
among his friends: GEM-B, Dec. 10, 1856.

260   "dear spirit would care": Berg, Mar. 20–21, 1857.

261   "red shoes": Berg, Apr. 3, 1857.
"is happy": GEM-B, Dec. 10, 1856.

262   "with her there": Kenyon, 11, May 3, 1857.
"one turn into stone" and "prevents swallowing": GEM-B, Apr. 1857, and GEM-B, Dec. 20, 1860.

263   "as another sees": Huxley, *EBB: Letters to Her Sisters,* June 2, 1857.

264   "I *cannot* advise": Berg, June 26, 1858.
"except my own": Berg, Apr. 12, 1858.
"Henrietta's wishes": Berg, Nov. 22, 1857.

ADMITTING IMPEDIMENTS

269   introspective travelogues: *The Oldest of the Old World* (London, 1860) was dedicated to her mother, who was a traveler to Egypt and the Holy Land herself and who became Edward Tuckerman's second wife. This book is the journal of Sophie Eckley's trip to

Egypt and the Holy Land from October 25, 1857, to May 6, 1858, at the beginning of her friendship with Elizabeth Barrett Browning. Barrett Browning advised her against publishing it, was skeptical of the theological passages, and wished Eckley had given more domestic detail. A copy of it exists in the Boston Public Library. It seems to this reader that time has lent the account a pleasant patina. Eckley's prose style seemed more concrete and focused than her style of poetry.

page 270   "I am not ill": Berg, Sept. 28, 1857.

"body and spirit": EBB to Sophia Eckley, Berg, Feb. 9, 1858. All of the 121 letters from EBB to Sophia Eckley are in the Berg Collection of the New York Public Library and are quoted with its kind permission. They are referred to as EBB to SE. Some letters are clearly dated; when they are not, they are referred to by the sequential number assigned in the Berg Collection.

271   "(because it is his)": EBB to SE, Berg, June 1858, letter number 12.

"looking well": Berg, July 30, 1858.

272   "are not vexed": EBB to SE, Berg, July 23, 1858.

"very greatly care": All of Robert Browning's letters to Isa Blagden quoted can be found in *Dearest Isa: Robert Browning's Letters to Isabella Blagden,* edited by Edward C. McAleer. This is an excellent edition with an informative introduction and exquisitely helpful notes that have been of use to this reader both generally and specifically in terms of Isa Blagden's work and David and Sophia Eckley's background and life. This reference is to the letter of Sept. 4, 1858.

"let it be so": RB to SE, Berg, Aug. 19, 1858.

"gave it up at once": GEM-B.

274   "harmonious spirit": EBB to SE, Berg, June 1858.

"it has begun to rain": Berg, Nov. 13, 1858 (?).

276   "in Robert's arms": EBB to Arabel, from 43 Bocca di Leone, Rome, Nov. 26, 1858.

"rubbing up against one another": Dec. 24 and 25, 1858.

"on its lips": Dec. 24 and 25, 1858.

277   "own marble throat": EBB to SE, Berg, letter number 39, written around Christmas, 1858, and labeled [Spring 1859].

"for love's sake": EBB to SE, Berg, letter number 71.

278   "despised her sister": McAleer, *Dearest Isa,* Jan. 7, 1859. For this dispute with Julia Ward Howe and the poems involved, see McAleer, *Dearest Isa,* p. 30, n. 36.

"help of my morphine": EBB to SE, Berg, letter number 43.

279   "to learn & admire": Hudson, *American Friends,* Mar. 27, 1863.

"Is it so?": EBB to SE, Berg, letter number 120.

280   "as this subject": EBB to SE, Berg, letter number 121.

"his own thoughts": Berg, June 27, 1859.

"is getting better": McAleer, *Dearest Isa,* Jan. 7, 1859.

281   "and truest marriage": quoted in McAleer, *Dearest Isa,* p. xxii.

"arrange for another": Berg, Tuesday, Feb. [25, 1858].

283   "came near enough": EBB to Isa, McAleer, *Dearest Isa,* Feb. 15 [1859].

"other people's malice": EBB to SE, Berg [Summer 1859], letter number 45.

on the Cascine meadows: The day before, on May 29, 1859, in Siena, the Brownings presented the Eckleys with a note that EBB had jotted to record their trip to Tivoli together in April. "After a very happy journey," EBB added to it. In this handwriting "RB says the same very truly." Sophia Eckley put this in her album. Berg, Misc. Ms. and Drawings.

"Vive l'Italie": Berg, June 3, 1859.

page 284   "kissed Peni": This description from EBB to SE, Berg, letter number 66.
             "will rise again": Berg, Mar. 29, 1859.

      285   "must end well": This and the following quotations, Berg, June 3, 1859.

      286   "rising into triumph": Kenyon, 11, EBB to Sarianna, Florence [about June 1859].

      287   "attempting to see him": EBB to SE, Berg, Sunday [Summer 1859], letter number 47.

      288   "Your loving Ba": EBB to SE, Berg [Summer 1859], letter number 49.

      289   "yet I have hope": Kenyon, 11, Villa Alberti, Siena: Wednesday [July–August 1859].

      290   "since the spring": RB to SE, DeVane and Knickerbocker, *New Letters,* Aug. 2, 1859.
             "Lucca and Siena": DeVane and Knickerbocker, *New Letters,* Aug. 7, 1859. Both
             EBB's letter of Aug. 2 and this one are in the Berg Collection, NYPL.

      291   "incalculable to me": This letter of EBB to Hiram Powers, listed in Kelley's checklist
             as 56:12, 3 Jan [1856] from Hamilton's Cat., 29 Jan. 1976, is actually about D. D.
             Home and is now at the Pierpont Morgan Library. Whatever doubts EBB had about
             Home's character, she maintained in other letters that the human character faults of a
             medium in no way discredited the fact that the spiritual world existed and that spir-
             its could communicate with this world. Sophie Eckley's claim to mediumship, how-
             ever, had been bogus—"trickery"—from the beginning.

      292   gave Robert to read: This letter of EBB to SE, Villa Alberti, Siena, Tuesday [Summer
             1859], is number 52 at the Berg and is quoted at length.

      294   "separation from people": RB to Isa, McAleer, *Dearest Isa* [Mar. 19, 1868?].
             "the result": EBB to SE, Berg [Winter 1859], letter number 55.
             "my own Arabel": GEM-B, Mar. 15, 1861.

      295   "in the matter": RB to Isa, McAleer, *Dearest Isa,* [Mar. 19, 1868?]. This is the letter
             quoted below, written almost seven years after EBB's death.

      296   "Day of judgment": Berg, Sunday, Oct. 1858?
             "she determinedly did": RB to Isa, McAleer, *Dearest Isa,* Apr. 19, 1869.

      297   "hurting *me,* alas": Hudson, *American Friends,* May 2, 1863.
             "or sell anything": RB to Isa, McAleer, *Dearest Isa,* Apr. 19, 1869.

                          WE POETS OF THE PEOPLE

      298   " 'only for Italy' ": Kenyon, 11, Dec. 29 [1859].

      300   "in at the time": EBB to Miss E. F. Haworth, Kenyon, 11, Aug. 25 [1860].
             "like Florence Nightingale": Taplin, *Life of EBB,* p. 376. Also see his discussion of
             the critical reputation of the poem, to which I am indebted.

      302   "of her 'forbears' ": In "Mrs. Ogilvy's Recollections" in Heydon and Kelley, *EBB's
             Letters to Mrs. Ogilvy,* p. xxxiv. The expanded section reads: "Her cousins, the Peytons,
             abounded in family traditions, but one might know Mrs. Browning for years,
             and never hear of one of her 'forbears.' I attributed this greatly to old Mr. Barrett's
             sturdy Nonconformity; but I have since met well-born Dissenters with plenty of
             family legend."
             "vituperation, and lies—": RB to John Forster, DeVane and Knickerbocker, *New Let-
             ters* [July 1861].
             "You understand nothing": EBB to George [Apr. 18, 1860].

      303   " 'abused in England' ": quoted in Marks, *Family of the Barretts,* p. 629. Marks notes
             it is the only surviving letter between EBB and Stormie, and it was passed to her
             from his daughter Arabel Moulton-Barrett.
             "of good class": Marks, *Family of the Barretts,* p. 613.

      304   "R.I.P.": Marks, *Family of the Barretts,* p. 612.

age 304 "illness last summer": EBB to Miss E. F. Haworth, Kenyon, 11, June 16, 1860.

"as I am": In an earlier letter to Arabel on March 24, 1858, she had written that she and Robert had become homeopathists, and Robert was so much better in health and spirits "that the temptation to me is great, to make a trial of turning over my morphine—only I do feel shy of some illness, some sudden breaking down if I do it; the medium having come such a second nature with me after all these years."

305 "it always seems to me": Berg, written in June or July 1860, not June ? 1859? as labeled.

306 "*won't* talk of it any more": EBB to Miss E. F. Haworth, Kenyon, 11, Aug. 25 [1860].

"loving & suffering": EBB to George, Sept. [6, 1860].

307 "tried morphine": GEM-B, Aug. 25, 1860.

308 "their way in the wood": Berg, Friday, Casa Guidi [Summer 1859]. Sophie Eckley's half sister, Hannah Parkman Tuckerman, died on June 7, 1859.

the private story: At the Berg there are five letters and one fragment of a letter written after Henrietta's death: [Dec. 8?, 1860?], Jan. 8?, 1861, Tuesday 1861 (which I think was written around Jan. 15), May? 1861, May? 11, 1861?, and one sheet Rome?, May? 1861? They are all from Rome and are numbered 108 to 113 and will not generally be cited separately. Ten letters written to Arabel after the death of Henrietta are in family hands. The handwriting in GEM-B, Dec. ?, 1860, and Dec. 20, 1860, is very bad. These two letters and another very important one, Feb.? 1861, which contain information about the Mary/Emma situation, will not be cited separately in this section.

314 "tear at a touch": Berg, May? 11, 1861?

We *Know* Each Other

318 "life and joy to him": Kenyon, 11.

"we *know* each other, I say": RB to George, Apr. 2, 1861.

"important element too": GEM-B, Dec. 12–15, 1851.

319 "I prevent her": RB to George, Apr. 2, 1861.

"years at Troy": p. 217.

La Vita Nuova

321 "truly benefit it": William Roscoe Thayer, *The Life and Times of Cavour,* vol. 1, p. 17.

322 "May God save Italy": Kenyon, 11, June 7, 1861.

"even without Cavour": Thayer, *Cavour,* vol. 11, p. 493.

323 " '*quiet* summer and *then*' ": RB to Sarianna, Hood, *Letters of RB,* June 30, 1861. This letter to his sister, including an intimate description of his wife's last days and her death, is quoted throughout. It is the most thorough and moving of the many accounts of EBB's death, all of which substantiate what RB wrote in his first grief.

324 "Melancholy as Amazed": John Ruskin to EBB, Berg.

"a stronger cheerfulness": Berg, EBB notes to answer John Ruskin's letter. She did not live to finish it or send it.

A Word More

page 335 attractive to her: Three letters from Christina Rossetti to John H. Ingram on this subject are at Wellesley.

337 "in my life": RB to Mrs. Charles Skirrow, DeVane and Knickerbocker, *New Letters*, Sept. 15, 1877

SELECTED BIBLIOGRAPHY

UNPUBLISHED SOURCES

I have made very extensive use of manuscript material, especially unpublished letters, in this book; they are listed in the Notes and in the Acknowledgments.

PRIMARY SOURCES

Letters of Both Brownings

The Brownings' Correspondence, ed. Philip Kelley and Ronald Hudson, 2 vols. Winfield, Kansas: Wedgestone Press, 1984–(in progress).
The Letters of the Brownings to George Barrett, ed. Paul Landis. Illinois: University of Illinois Press, 1958.
The Letters of Robert Browning and Elizabeth Barrett Browning, 1845–1846, ed. Elvan Kintner, 2 vols. Cambridge, Mass.: Harvard University Press, 1969.
Twenty-Two Unpublished Letters of Elizabeth Barrett Browning and Robert Browning Addressed to Henrietta and Arabel Moulton-Barrett. New York: United Feature Syndicate, 1935.

Letters and Diary of Elizabeth Barrett Browning

Diary by E.B.B.: The Unpublished Diary of Elizabeth Barrett Barrett, 1831–1832, ed. Philip Kelley and Ronald Hudson. Athens, Ohio: Ohio University Press, 1969.
Elizabeth Barrett Browning: Letters to Her Sisters, 1846–1859, ed. Leonard Huxley. London: John Murray, 1929.
Elizabeth Barrett Browning's Letters to Mrs. David Ogilvy, 1849–1861, ed. Peter N. Heydon and Philip Kelley. New York: Quadrangle/The New York Times Book Co., and the Browning Institute, 1973.
Invisible Friends: The Correspondence of Elizabeth Barrett Barrett and Benjamin Robert Haydon, 1842–1845, ed. Willard Bissell Pope. Cambridge, Mass.: Harvard University Press, 1972.
The Letters of Elizabeth Barrett Browning, ed. Frederic G. Kenyon, 2 vols. New York/London: The Macmillan Company, 1894.
The Letters of Elizabeth Barrett Browning to Mary Russell Mitford, 1836–1854, ed. Meredith B. Raymond and Mary Rose Sullivan, 3 vols. Waco, Texas: Armstrong Browning Library, 1983.

Letters of Robert Browning

Browning's Trumpeter: The Correspondence of Robert Browning and Frederick J. Furnivall, 1872–1889, ed. William S. Peterson. Washington, D.C.: Decatur House Press, 1979.

Browning to His American Friends, ed. Gertrude Reese Hudson. London: Bowes & Bowes, 1965.

Dearest Isa: Robert Browning's Letters to Isabella Blagden, ed. Edward C. McAleer. Austin, Texas: University of Texas Press, 1951; reprinted 1977.

Letters of Robert Browning Collected by Thomas J. Wise, ed. Thurman L. Hood. London: John Murray, 1933.

New Letters of Robert Browning, ed. William Clyde DeVane and Kenneth Leslie Knickerbocker. New Haven, Conn.: Yale University Press, 1950.

Robert Browning and Alfred Domett, ed. Frederic G. Kenyon. New York: E. P. Dutton, 1906.

Robert Browning and Julia Wedgwood: A Broken Friendship as Revealed by Their Letters, ed. Richard Curle. New York: Frederick A. Stokes Co., 1937.

EDITIONS OF THE POETRY

Casa Guidi Windows, by Elizabeth Barrett Browning, ed. Julia Markus. New York: The Browning Institute, 1977.

The Poetical Works of Elizabeth Barrett Browning, with a new introduction by Ruth M. Adams. Boston: Houghton Mifflin Company, 1974.

Browning: Poetical Works 1833–1864, ed. Ian Jack. London: Oxford University Press, 1970.

La Saisiaz: The Two Poets of Croisic, by Robert Browning. London: Smith, Elder & Co., 1878.

BOOKS, ARTICLES, COMPILATIONS

Barrett, Richard. *Richard Barrett's Journal,* ed. Thomas Brott and Philip Kelley. Winfield, Kansas: Wedgewood, 1983.

Bosco, Ronald A. "The Brownings and Mrs. Kinney: A Record of Their Friendship," *Browning Institute Studies* 4 (1976):57–124.

Brandon, Ruth. *The Spiritualists: The Passion for the Occult in the Nineteenth and Twentieth Centuries.* New York: Knopf, 1983.

The Browning Collections: A Reconstruction. Compiled by Philip Kelley and Betty Coley. Waco, Texas: Amstrong Browning Library, 1984.

The Brownings' Correspondence: A Checklist. Compiled by Philip Kelley and Ronald Hudson. Winfield, Kansas: Wedgestone Press, and New York: The Browning Institute, 1978.

Forster, Margaret. *Elizabeth Barrett Browning.* New York: Doubleday, 1989.

Furnivall, F. J. "Robert Browning's Ancestors," *Browning Society Papers* III (February 1890): 26–45.

Griffin, W. Hall, and H. C. Minchin. *The Life of Robert Browning.* London: Methuen & Co., 1938.

Hayter, Althea. *Mrs. Browning: A Poet's Work and Its Setting.* London: Faber & Faber, 1962.

―――. *A Sultry Month: Scenes of London Literary Life in 1846.* London: Faber & Faber, 1965.

————. *Opium and the Romantic Imagination.* Berkeley and Los Angeles: University of California Press, 1970.

Hewlett, Dorothy. *Elizabeth Barrett Browning: A Life.* New York: Knopf, 1952.

Home, D. D. *Incidents in My Life,* second series. London: Tinsley Bros., 1872.

Hudson, Ronald. "Elizabeth Barrett Browning and Her Brother Alfred: Some Unpublished Letters," *Browning Institute Studies* 2 (1974):135–60.

Irvine, William, and Park Honan. *The Book, the Ring, and the Poet: A New Biography of Robert Browning.* New York: McGraw Hill, 1974.

James, Henry. *William Wetmore Story and His Friends.* 2 vols. Boston: Houghton Mifflin, 1903; reprinted by the Library of American Art, 1969.

Kaplan, Cora. Introduction, *Aurora Leigh and Other Poems.* London: The Women's Press, 1978.

Karlin, Daniel. *The Courtship of Elizabeth Barrett and Robert Browning.* Oxford: Oxford University Press, 1985.

Mahony, Rev. Francis. Introduction by Blanchard Jerrold. *The Final Reliques of Father Prout.* London: Chatto and Windus, 1876.

Marks, Jeannette. *The Family of the Barretts: A Colonial Romance.* New York: The Macmillan Company, 1938.

Markus, Julia. "Andrea del Sarto (Called 'The Faultless Painter') and William Page (Called 'The American Titian')," *Browning Institute Studies* 2 (1974):1–24.

————. "Bishop Blougram and the Literary Man," *Victorian Studies* 21 (Winter 1978):171–95.

Maynard, John. *Browning's Youth.* Cambridge, Mass., and London: Harvard University Press, 1977.

McAleer, Edward C. *The Brownings of Casa Guidi.* New York: The Browning Institute, 1979.

Meredith, Michael. *Meeting the Brownings.* Waco, Texas: Baylor University Press, 1986.

Miller, Betty. *Robert Browning: A Portrait.* London: John Murray, 1952.

O'Reilly, Bernard. *A Life of Pius IX,* 16th ed. New York: Peter F. Collier, 1878.

Orr, Mrs. Sutherland. *Life and Letters of Robert Browning.* Cambridge, Mass.: Riverside Press, 1891.

Peterson, William S. *Browning's Trumpeter.* Washington, D.C.: Decatur House Press, 1979.

————. *Interrogating the Oracle: A History of the London Browning Society.* Athens, Ohio: Ohio University Press, 1969.

Porter, Katherine H. *Through a Glass Darkly: Spiritualism in the Browning Circle.* Lawrence, Kans.: University of Kansas Press, 1958.

Ritchie, Anne Thackeray. *Records of Tennyson, Ruskin, and Browning.* London: The Macmillan Company, 1896.

Ryals, Clyde de L. *The Life of Robert Browning.* Oxford and Cambridge, Mass.: Blackwell, 1993.

Sherwood, Dolly. *Harriet Hosmer, American Sculptor 1830–1900.* Columbia, Mo., and London: University of Missouri Press, 1991.

Steegmüller, Francis. *The Two Lives of James Jackson Jarves.* New Haven, Conn.: Yale University Press, 1951.

Taplin, Gardner. *The Life of Elizabeth Barrett Browning.* London: John Murray, 1957.

Thayer, William Roscoe. *The Life and Times of Cavour.* Cambridge, Mass.: Riverside Press, 1911.

Thomas, Clara. *Love and Work Enough: The Life of Anna Jameson.* Toronto: University of Toronto Press, 1967.

Treves, Giuliana Artom. *The Golden Ring: The Anglo-Florentines, 1847–1862,* trans. Sylvia Sprigge. London, New York, and Toronto: Longmans, Green & Co., 1956.

Tuscan Athenaeum, October 30, 1847, to January 22, 1848, thirteen issues published in Florence. The only complete file is at the New York Public Library.

Ward, Maisie. *The Tragi-Comedy of Pen Browning.* New York and London: Sheed and Ward, 1972.

Ward, Wilfrid. *The Life and Times of Cardinal Wiseman,* 2 vols. New York and Bombay: Longmans, Green & Co., 1899.

ACKNOWLEDGMENTS

THIS BIOGRAPHY is the result of twenty years of interest in Elizabeth Barrett and Robert Browning, and I have the pleasure of many people and institutions to thank. For much of my historical work, which resulted in the first modern editon of EBB's *Casa Guidi Windows* as well as some of the background for "A Marriage of True Minds, Hers," I am grateful to the Biblioteca e Archivio del Risorgimento in Florence and the Museo di Firenze com'era. In Rome, I was assisted by the staff of the Museo Centrale del Risorgimento and the Biblioteca Nazionale. Once upon a time Giuliana Artom Treves helped me to locate pictures and generously answered questions, Dorothy Amisano assisted me and sent me material from Rome, and Frank R. DiFederico encouraged my work with enthusiasm and with his knowledge of Italy. The only appropriate words of thanks seem to be from *Casa Guidi Windows*: "If we tried / To sink the past beneath our feet, be sure / The future would not stand—." Or the present.

I decided to write a biography of the poets' married years because I wondered how that marriage fared. The rich resource of letters by and about the Brownings fueled this study and led me to track the poets' married life through their own words and actions. Four institutions particularly made this exploration a pleasure. The Berg Collection of the New York Public Library holds 113 unpublished letters of Elizabeth Barrett Browning to her sister Arabel and the unusual 121 unpublished letters between EBB and Sophie Eckley, among other riches. I thank the Henry W. and Albert A. Berg Collection, the New York Public Library, Astor, Lenox, and Tilden Foundations for permission to quote from them. The Margaret Clapp Library, Special Collections, at Wellesley College houses the love letters, much correspondence, including Christina Rossetti to John Ingram, and the papers of Jeannette Marks. I thank the library for permission to quote from them. The Pierpont Morgan Library granted permission to quote from Anna Jameson's letters to Lady Byron, MA 1325. The Armstrong Browning Library of Baylor University, which houses the largest collection of Browning letters and material, has aided me in every way and granted permission to quote from its collection and to publish many illustrations it generously afforded me. I am also particularly indebted to the Butler Library at Columbia University, the Beinecke Library at Yale, the Harvard College Library, the Schlesinger Library at Radcliffe, the Schomberg Center for Research in Black Culture at the New

York Public Library, the Rare Books Collection of the Boston Public Library, and Eton College. Further permissions to quote from unpublished letters appear in my notes, and I append a separate list of permissions to publish illustrations that have come from many generous institutions and individuals. I thank Philip Kelley for lending me many illustrations in his possession. And my bibliography stands also as thanks to so many scholars and critics who have written on the Brownings.

JUST AS I WAS about to submit my manuscript to copyediting, one of those enormous changes at the last minute occurred. The senior member of the Moulton-Barrett family, Captain Gordon E. Moulton-Barrett, allowed me to read and to take notes from the more than 115 letters from Elizabeth Barrett Browning to her sister Arabel that are in his possession. Not only that; he made photostatic enlargements of this grand correspondence so that I could read through it with greater ease. I am very grateful to him for his generosity and his support of scholarship. Having access to the entire correspondence of Elizabeth Barrett Browning to Arabel Moulton Barrett (an enormous correspondence—if published, I imagine it would amount to at least four volumes) has been a great privilege. It has also confirmed my opinion that Elizabeth's letters to her sister Arabel rank with the love letters in literary and historical importance. The correspondence is one of the jewels of the nineteenth century. I thank Captain Moulton-Barrett for his courtesy, for his permission for my quoting excerpts from the correspondence, and for many interesting conversations about the family as well.

Although so many people have supported this project, no one except myself is responsible for my conclusions or for the occasional (I hope) error that must accompany any work, no matter how well edited. I have attempted to lift Elizabeth Barrett Browning from certain myths, only because she showed me the way. Her real relationship to her father, her African blood, her painful battle with depression, and her relationship to Sophie Eckley, are in her letters. No one was more of a spontaneous letter writer than she, and at the same time no one was a greater advocate of allowing one's private words to be read at a later time. Letters and journals made "Death less deader," she wrote. Robert Browning might not have agreed. But he certainly emerges in his letters and in hers—and in all of his traceable actions, as who he was—a constant lover and devoted husband as well as a great poet. It is a quiet sign of his stature to say simply that this combination was and is unique. After his wife's death, Robert Browning's entire life changed. I hope to follow him in his "after life" and write that story one day.

I want to end these acknowledgments with my thanks to those who have supported me and encouraged me in this project. My editor, Victoria Wilson, has been a champion of this book since the beginning, and with that fine eye of hers immediately saw that the drawing by Robert Browning's father, which has at times been considered to be the earliest image of the poet, was really a drawing of his close friend Alfred Domett. My literary representative, Harriet Wasserman, has been an inspiration to my work year in and year out. My former thesis adviser and good friend William S. Peterson read this work for the first time in galleys and generously offered significant editorial advice. I thank him, as always, for his intelligent reading, his love of the printed page, and for his very high standard of scholarship which has served as a model for many of us who have studied with him. Roberta Maguire, also at the University of Maryland, read the galleys against my text and I thank her for her painstaking care and enthusiasm—both of which were invaluable to me.

Adrian Thompkins saved me from insanity one rainy day by making out my bibliography cards and helping me to locate certain references. My thanks to Frank Mattson, the knowledgeable curator of the Berg Collection, and to Stephen Crook and Philip Milito for so much help. At the Special Collections of the Wellesley Library, my thanks to Ruth Rodgers, the librarian, and her staff—especially to Jill Triplett for her assistance and enthusiasm. Warm thanks to Roger Brooks, director of the Armstrong Browning Library, and to Betty Coley and Rita Humphrey for every form of kindness while I was at Baylor University, as well as when I requested help by phone and letter. Michael Meredith, the librarian at Eton College, enthusiastically photographed some of the collection left the library by the recently deceased Edward Barrett Moulton-Barrett, allowing the reader many new images of the family. And I want to thank Jeanne Reinert for her hospitality while I was in Miami. I thank Hofstra University for awarding me research grants and special leave. I am most grateful to the National Endowment for the Humanities, from which I received a summer research and travel grant and later a Fellowship for College Teachers and Independent Scholars to complete this biography.

Certain friends have supported me in this project with their faith in my work: Richard Bausch, Diane Cleaver, Rebecca Goldstein, Oscar Hijuelos, John Lane and Miriam Levine, Rena Levitt and Stanley Konecky, Marjorie Markus, Michael Montlack, Bob Sargent, Susan Berns and John Rothchild, Mariolina and Zeno Zeni. There are so many of you who have added life to this project. I hope you'll all enjoy reading the book as much as I've enjoyed writing it.

INDEX

Numerals in *italics* refer to illustrations.

ILLUSTRATION CREDITS

Robert Browning's writing portfolio. Courtesy of the Armstrong Browning Library, Baylor University.

DEATH OR LOVE. Manuscript of Sonnet 1. Courtesy of the Pierpont Morgan Library, New York, MA 933.

MARY MOULTON BARRETT. Self-portrait of EBB's mother, ca. 1825. Courtesy of the Henry W. and Albert A. Berg Collection, the New York Public Library, Astor, Lenox, and Tilden Foundations.

SEPTIMUS and OCTAVIUS MOULTON BARRETT, by Mary Moulton Barrett. Courtesy of Mary V. Altham.

GEORGE, ARABEL, SAMUEL, AND CHARLES JOHN MOULTON BARRETT, oil by William Artaud, 1818. Reproduced by permission of the Provost and Fellows of Eton College; in the school library, Eton College.

THE BARRETTS AT WIMPOLE STREET, by Alfred Moulton Barrett, 1843, including Edward Barrett Moulton Barrett, 1847. Reproduced by permission of the Provost and Fellows of Eton College; in the school library, Eton College.

EDWARD BARRETT MOULTON BARRETT. Courtesy of Captain Gordon E. Moulton-Barrett.

RB'S FIRST LETTER TO EBB, January 10, 1845, pages 1 and 4. Courtesy of the Wellesley College Library.

EBB AS AN INVALID WITH HER DOG, FLUSH, by Alfred Moulton Barrett, 1843. Reproduced by permission of the Provost and Fellows of Eton College; in the school library, Eton College.

ROBERT BROWNING, from an engraving by J. C. Armytage in R. H. Horne's *Spirit of the New Age*. Courtesy of the Armstrong Browning Library, Baylor University.

EDWARD BARRETT MOULTON BARRETT, detail of an oil of EBB's father by Henry William Pickersgill. Courtesy of Captain Gordon E. Moulton-Barrett.

BENJAMIN ROBERT HAYDON, SELF-PORTRAIT. Courtesy of the National Portrait Gallery, London.

ROBERT HEDLEY. Reproduced by permission of the Provost and Fellows of Eton College; in the school library, Eton College.

MARY RUSSELL MITFORD, engraving after a drawing by P. R. Say, 1837.

FLUSH, by Elizabeth Barrett Browning. Courtesy of the Henry W. and Albert A. Berg Collection, the New York Public Library, Astor, Lenox, and Tilden Foundations.

50 WIMPOLE STREET. Courtesy of the Armstrong Browning Library, Baylor University.

ANNA JAMESON at age sixteen, from an engraving of a miniature by her father, the artist Denis Brownell Murphy.

EDWARD BARRETT OF CINNAMON HILL, miniature by John Barry, 1791. Courtesy of John Altham.

SAMUEL BARRETT MOULTON BARRETT, watercolor of Elizabeth's uncle. Courtesy of Mary V. Altham.

MARY TREPSACK, "TRIPPY" OR "TREPPY." Reproduced by permission of the Provost and Fellows of Eton College; in the school library, Eton College.

EDWARD BARRETT MOULTON BARRETT AS A YOUNG MAN. Reproduced by permission of the Provost and Fellows of Eton College; in the school library, Eton College.

MARY GRAHAM-CLARKE BEFORE HER MARRIAGE. Courtesy of Mary V. Altham.

MAP OF JAMAICA. Courtesy of Frederick A. Praeger, Inc.

JOHN GRAHAM-CLARKE. Courtesy of the British Museum.

ARABELLA GRAHAM-CLARKE. Courtesy of Mary V. Altham.

RICHARD BARRETT. Courtesy of Greenwood House, Jamaica.

ROBERT BROWNING, SR., the poet's father. Courtesy of the Wellesley College Library.

MARGARET TITTLE. Courtesy of the Wellesley College Library.

ROBERT BROWNING, the poet's grandfather. Courtesy of the Wellesley College Library.

JOHN KENYON, a sketch by Sir George Scharf from a portrait bust by Thomas Crawford, made in Rome in 1841. Courtesy of the National Portrait Gallery, London.

PART II

RB, photo; EBB, painting. Robert Browning, first known photograph. Courtesy of Michael Meredith. Elizabeth Barrett Browning, oil by Michele Gordigiani. Courtesy of the National Portrait Gallery, London.

THE BROWNINGS' DRAWING ROOM IN THE CASA GUIDI, an engraving after the oil by George Mignaty. Courtesy of the Armstrong Browning Library, Baylor University.

CASA GUIDI. Courtesy of the Armstrong Browning Library, Baylor University.

ITALIAN DESPOTS, from an old engraving.

DEMONSTRATIONS IN FLORENCE FOR THE RIGHT TO FORM A CIVIC GUARD. Courtesy of the Museo di Firenze com'era, Florence.

POPE PIUS IX, from an old engraving.

SARAH ANNA BROWNING. Courtesy of Wellesley College Library.

ALFRED DOMETT AS A YOUNG MAN, by Robert Browning, Sr. Courtesy of the Armstrong Browning Library, Baylor University.

ALFRED DOMETT, by George Lance, from an old engraving.

FLOOR PLAN OF THE BROWNINGS' APARTMENT, sketched by Elizabeth Barrett Browning in a letter to her sister Arabel. Courtesy of the Henry W. and Albert A. Berg Collection, the New York Public Library, Astor, Lenox, and Tilden Foundations.

CARDINAL NICHOLAS WISEMAN, from an old engraving.

"I LIKE TO BE DESPISED." *Punch,* December 7, 1850, page 233.

THE FRASERIANS, after an engraving by Daniel Maclise.

GEORGE SAND, by Eugène Delacroix. Courtesy of the Ordrupgaard Collection, Copenhagen.

SARIANNA BROWNING. Courtesy of the Armstrong Browning Library, Baylor University.

WILLIAM SURTEES COOK. Reproduced by permission of the Provost and Fellows of Eton College; in the school library, Eton College.

HENRIETTA BARRETT MOULTON BARRETT. Courtesy of Mary V. Altham.

ROBERT WIEDEMANN "PEN" BARRETT BROWNING, by Euphrasia Fanny Haworth. Courtesy of the Wellesley College Library.

ELIZABETH CLEMENTINE KINNEY. Courtesy of the Edmund Clarence Stedman Papers, Rare Book and Manuscript Library, Columbia University.

PEN'S SKETCH OF HIS FATHER. Courtesy of the British Museum.

WILLIAM WETMORE STORY, at his studio among his workmen. Courtesy of Peter de Brandt.

PALAZZO BARBERINI, ROME. Courtesy of Alinari/Art Resource, New York.

THE GREEK SLAVE. Courtesy of Yale Art Gallery.

SARAH DOUGHERTY PAGE, by William Page. Courtesy of Professor A. M. Hayes.

WILLIAM PAGE, SELF-PORTRAIT. Courtesy of Detroit Institute of Art.

ROBERT BROWNING, by William Page. Courtesy of the Armstrong Browning Library, Baylor University.

CLASPED HANDS OF THE BROWNINGS, plaster cast by Harriet Hosmer. Courtesy of the Schlesinger Library, Radcliffe College.

PART III

Spirit drawings produced by Elizabeth Barrett Browning or Sophie Eckley, probably during a private séance. Courtesy of the Henry W. and Albert A. Berg Collection, the New York Public Library, Astor, Lenox, and Tilden Foundations.

PEN BROWNING, photograph. Courtesy of the Armstrong Browning Library, Baylor University.

HARRIET HOSMER, by William Page. Courtesy of the Boston Museum of Fine Arts.

GEORGINA ELIZABETH "LIZZIE" BARRETT. Reproduced by permission of the Provost and Fellows of Eton College; in the school library, Eton College.

ALFRED BARRETT MOULTON BARRETT, by his brother Octavius. Reproduced by permission of the Provost and Fellows of Eton College; in the school library, Eton College.

DANIEL D. HOME, a spirit woodcut. Courtesy of Harry Price Library, University of London Library.

ALFRED TENNYSON READING MAUD. Courtesy of the Edmund Clarence Stedman Papers, Rare Book and Manuscript Library, Columbia University.

ROBERT BROWNING, by D. G. Rossetti, October 1855. Courtesy of the Fitz-william Museum, Cambridge.

ANNA JAMESON, portrait bust by John Gibson. Courtesy of the National Portrait Gallery, London.

ARABEL BARRETT MOULTON BARRETT. Reproduced by permission of the Provost and Fellows of Eton College; in the school library, Eton College.

CHARLOTTE CUSHMAN, by William Page. Courtesy of the National Portrait Gallery, Washington, D.C.

PART IV

"MY FIG TREE." Reproduced from *The Browning Collections* (1913).

SOPHIA MAY TUCKERMAN ECKLEY with her older half sister, HANNAH PARKMAN TUCKERMAN. Courtesy of the Henry W. and Albert A. Berg Collection, the New York Public Library, Astor, Lenox, and Tilden Foundations.

43 VIA BOCCA DI LEONE, ROME. Courtesy of the Henry W. and Albert A. Berg Collection, the New York Public Library, Astor, Lenox, and Tilden Foundations.

THE TERRACE AT BELLOSGUARDO, from an engraving.

WALTER SAVAGE LANDOR. Courtesy of the Pierpont Morgan Library, New York, MA 768, f.2.

AUTOMATIC WRITING, produced by Sophie Eckley or Elizabeth Barrett Browning during a private séance. Courtesy of the Henry W. and Albert A. Berg Collection, the New York Public Library, Astor, Lenox, and Tilden Foundations.

EBB WITH "BRO" AND HENRIETTA, oil by William Artaud, ca. 1818. Reproduced by permission of the Provost and Fellows of Eton College; in the school library, Eton College.

HOPE END. Courtesy of the Wellesley College Library.

CAMILLO BENSO DI CAVOUR, from an old engraving.

JOHN RUSKIN, SELF-PORTRAIT. Courtesy of the Wellesley College Library.

ELIZABETH AND PEN BARRETT BROWNING. Courtesy of the Wellesley College Library.

ROBERT BROWNING. Courtesy of the Armstrong Browning Library, Baylor University.

ELIZABETH BARRETT BROWNING, May 27, 1861. Courtesy of the Armstrong Browning Library, Baylor University.

PEN BROWNING on his pony, Stella. Reproduced by permission of the Provost and Fellows of Eton College; in the school library, Eton College.

A Note on the Type

The text of this book is set in Garamond
No. 3. It is not a true copy of any of
the designs of Claude Garamond
(1480–1561), but an adaptation of his
types, which set the European standard
for two centuries. It probably owes as
much to the designs of Jean Jannon, a
Protestant printer working in Sedan in
the early seventeenth century, who had
worked with Garamond's romans earlier,
in Paris, and who was denied their use
because of the Catholic censorship. Jannon's matrices came into the possession
of the Imprimerie Nationale, where they
were thought to be by Garamond himself,
and so described when the Imprimerie
revived the type in 1900. This particular
version is based on an adaptation by
Morris Fuller Benton.

Composed by Dix, Syracuse, New York

Printed and bound by
Quebecor Printing Martinsburg,
Martinsburg, West Virginia

Designed by Iris Weinstein